Autobiography
OF
Rev. W.B. Godbey, A.M.

by

W.B. Godbey

First Fruits Press
Wilmore,
Kentucky
c2018

Autobiography of Rev. W. B. Godbey, A. M.
First Fruits Press, © 2017

ISBN: 9781621717607 (print), 9781621717614 (digital), 9781621717621 (kindle)

Digital version at http://place.asburyseminary.edu/godbey/10/

For all other uses, contact:

First Fruits Press
B.L. Fisher Library
Asbury Theological Seminary
204 N. Lexington Ave.
Wilmore, KY 40390
http://place.asburyseminary.edu/firstfruits

Godbey, W. B. (William Baxter), 1833-1920.
Autobiography of Rev. W. B. Godbey, A. M. – Wilmore, KY : First Fruits Press, ©2018.
510 pages ; cm.
Reprint. Previously published: Cincinnati, O. : God's Revivalist Office, ©1909.
ISBN: 9781621717607 (pbk.)
1. Godbey, W. B. (William Baxter), 1833-1920. 2. Methodist Church--Clergy--Biography. I. Title.

BX8495.G6 A3 2018 287.663

Cover design by Jon Ramsey

asburyseminary.edu
800.2ASBURY
204 North Lexington Avenue
Wilmore, Kentucky 40390

First Fruits Press
The Academic Open Press of Asbury Theological Seminary
204 N. Lexington Ave., Wilmore, KY 40390
859-858-2236
first.fruits@asburyseminary.edu
asbury.to/firstfruits

Dr. Godbey on his 76th Anniversary.

Autobiography

OF

Rev. W. B. Godbey, A. M.

AUTHOR OF

New Testament Commentary, New Testament Translation, Foot-prints of Jesus in the Holy Land, and Many Other Books and Booklets on Holiness.

GOD'S REVIVALIST OFFICE,
"Mount of Blessings,"
Cincinnati, O.

DEDICATION.

Now to the dear Holiness people in all the earth, regardless of nationality, church, race or color, this book, with its forty-seven predecessors, is lovingly, affectionately and prayerfully dedicated by

THE AUTHOR.

Contents.

Preface.

Long have the people clamored for me to write my life. I did not want to do it, but found myself actually incompetent to resist the united appeals of my friends, who girdle the globe. I am intimately acquainted with many of the Lord's dear people from the Atlantic to the Pacific, and from the Gulf to the Lakes, while my travels in Europe, Asia and Africa, in the providence of God, have given me many happy acquaintances in all of these countries.

The Lord has let me live seventy-three years, given me a splendid education, a bright conversion, a glorious sanctification, permitted me to preach fifty-three years and write forty-eight books and booklets. I have no dark chapter in my biography.

Though, as I believe, I was converted at the age of three years, I inadvertently lost it; but was reclaimed at the age of sixteen, when the Lord so revealed Himself to me as to enable me ever since to walk in the light of His kingdom. He kept me through all the precarious and slippery paths of childhood and youth, so fortifying me against the seducing enchantments incident to the juvenile, as to keep me out of their seductive quarrels and to enable me to lead a moral life, without ever contracting the vicious habits which blight the innocency of childhood and blacken the escutcheon of youth in the overwhelming majority of cases. He has so wonderfully kept His healing hand on my body that I have never been a bed-ridden invalid. Though terrible ailments have taken hold on me, He has always healed me so quickly that I lost no time comparatively and was never missed from the battle-field.

While my dear father and mother were utterly unable financially to give me a collegiate education, God, in His signal mercy, not only permitted me to prosecute a thorough classical course, but has permitted me to travel three times in Europe, Asia and Africa, and within recent years to go around the world again, travelling through the great historic countries and the most important missionary fields. God is no respecter of persons. He loves *your* children as dearly as your humble servant. Let them read my biography and see how I began as a penniless boy, but finally prosecuted a thorough collegiate education. I have preached for fifty-three years with the constant blessing of God on my labors, and am still on the battle-field, pressing the war for God and souls, having preached as much by pen as by speech. I have travelled extensively for the glory of God and the establishment of His kingdom in all the earth, so my life's history will be an inspiration to your children to do likewise. There is nothing in it which will not prove a blessing to the reader.

My life has been quite eventful. God sanctified me fifteen years before the Holiness Movement reached the Great South, where I was born and reared, and He used me to preach entire sanctification from the Atlantic Ocean to Mexico in anticipation of the oncoming movement. You will also find in this history a ten years' war with the Campbellites and everything you need on the great baptismal controversy, in which all need light and grace to walk in it.

This book will be about the size and make of my large Commentaries and will sell perhaps for $1.50. You and your children cannot do without it.

God bless you.

W. B. GODBEY.

Exordium.

The Bible is the biography of Christ, excarnate in the Old Testament and incarnate in the New. It also contains the abbreviated biographies of the patriarchs, prophets, apostles and saints. The journey of life is so precarious, perilous and pestilential that we need all possible help by way of information, warning and counsel, especially in youth, in order to qualify us to steer between Scylla on the one hand and Charybdis on the other, as in case of deflection either way, one of the insatiable whirlpools is certain to engulf our foundering bark. The Bible is the most important of all books. Its biographical phrases are pre-eminent in value, especially to the young who are so much better qualified to understand them than its doctrinal teachings, which become so profitable as we advance in years. After the Bible, sainted biographies come next and should be put into the hands of children and young people, accompanied by special encouragement, with time and opportunity to read them. The biographies of criminals, *e. g.*, John A. Murrill, Captain Kidd, Jesse James, Younger Brothers, etc., should be burned to ashes by fathers and mothers as quickly as they can get their hands on them, as every youth who reads them takes a cobra into his bosom. This follows as a logical sequence from the seductive power of sin.

"Vice is a monster of so frightful mien
That, to be hated, needs but to be seen;

> But seen too oft, familiar to her face,
> We first endure, then pity, then embrace."

These poetic lines tell the sad story of millions now in Hell. It is awfully dangerous to hear recitals of atrocious wickedness, and should be avoided whenever possible.

Once when a circuit rider, I happened to be at home chopping wood at the pile in the yard, when a stalwart man that lived in the neighbodhood came along on his horse cursing like a demon. I said nothing, but picked up my hat and started out of the gate. My wife, surmising that I was going to do something with the man, said: "Mr. Godbey, do you let Bill Heddleston alone, for he is worth fifty thousand dollars, and will kill you if you interrupt him." I said nothing, but crossed the street to where I had seen the Campbellite pastor at the window reading, and said to him: "Brother, come with me to the police judge; we must arrest that man." He refused to go, saying: "It is not worth while." I said: "If you do not go with me, I will send an officer for you," as I knew he had heard it all, and would have to witness to it. Then he picked up his hat and went with me. Fortunately, passing a couple of squares, we met the judge. I at once told him about the man passing our house cursing and swearing like a demon eloped from the bottomless pit and that I wanted him prosecuted. Turning on his heel and seeing a policeman at a distance, he roared to him to go into the livery stable, which was directly before him, mount a horse and go after Bill Heddleston with all his might and bring him back to him. So he did. What was the result? He paid his fine of forty-five dollars for cursing in the presence of my wife and children. Afterwards I lived in that house six years, directly on that man's way to and from the county seat, but he ever afterward passed by like a gentleman.

While we should do our utmost to keep our children from hearing bad words and seeing sinful conduct of any kind, let us remember that there is a magic in print, rendering it far more influential than words spoken, which will evanesce much more quickly than seductive iniquities which we read in an elegantly bound book. There are many books in Christian libraries, avowedly good and innocent, which ought to be burned, because they indirectly encourage sin. This point is to be especially guarded in the biographies of the Lord's dear saints, many of whom have been guilty of the darkest iniquities, blackest crimes, vilest debaucheries and grossest sensualities, while they served Satan. Let me warn all such to never write them in their biographies for the youth to read, lest Satan take advantage and the charm of the serpent shall prove too strong for the fluttering bird. The awful whirlpool from which omnipotent grace delivered these souls may catch the reader in the whirl of its suction power, and he may never receive the wonderful grace which delivered the subject of the biography. Truth does not require us to give a catalogue of Satan's awful work in our lives. It is enough to confess it in the aggregate, and drop the curtain over it forever; showing up the brilliant victories of redeeming grace, till they drop it into total eclipse.

I never dreamed of writing my biography, neither had I any predilection in that direction. I am sure I never would have written it had not the dear saints from the Atlantic to the Pacific constrained me to do so. As I, a few years ago, received the call to go around the world in the interest of missions, doing what little I could to conserve the kingdom of God during this fleeting life, I postponed the biography until after that tour, apologizing to my clamorous friends that it would add an important interest to the biography. Therefore I had utterly dismissed it from my mind and had no thought of writing it now, till, on my arrival, they raised the same importunate clamor, insisting that I should postpone it no longer, lest receiving my discharge, I might pass away and they never get it. Therefore I acquiesce, turning over the work to the blessed Holy Spirit that He may utilize it to the glory of God when I am gone.

I am satisfied that the Spirit will make it exceedingly helpful to children and young people, fortifying them against temptation and instructing them in the way of salvation, sanctification, edification, education, and usefulness in their day and generation. My earnest prayer accompanies this biography that the reader may not only do as well as the writer, but excel him in all of these lines of duty, privilege, erudition and achievement. The important feature of biography consists in the preponderance it gives to virtue over vice; sin over ignorance; industry over indolence; frugality over prodigality; holiness over depravity; and victory over defeat. The fact that I have no blank period in my life, practically and effectively given over to Satan, and consequently no black segment in my biography, is calculated to prove eminently inspiring to children and young people to avail themselves of the same economy which fortified me from the cradle. I do not insinuate that I was not a sinner. This I confess with shame. I was born in the City of Destruction like the whole family of father Adam and mother Eve, whose children, like the sands of the sea, have populated the world in all ages.

Quite awhile ago, responsive to a camp-meeting call, I went to North Carolina. At the opening I was introduced to my comrade in labor, Sam Page, a former notorious infidel and drunken saloon-keeper, whose profligacy and wickedness had been proverbial in all the land. Having been wonderfully converted and gloriously sanctified, responsive to his heavenly calling he was then a flaming evangelist, shaking that country with the Pentecostal power, which, in the mercy of God, characterized his ministry. The power descended on us and waves of salvation began to roll over the audience, revealing Him who is mighty to save. Simultaneously with the rolling billows, Sam would leap on a bench and shout aloud, "Look here, all ye drunkards, gamblers, blasphemers, thieves, murderers, and adulterers, and see me. Do you not know that I am Sam Page, the saloon-keeper, drunkard, blasphemer, gambler and infidel? See what God will do for you if you will repent of your sins and seek Him with all your heart as I did. Oh, He will wonderfully save and gloriously sanctify you!" Then I would leap up by his side, throw my arms around him and shout to the people: "Look at me, O ye good Methodists, Baptists, Presbyterians and Campbellites, who keep the moral law and walk irreproachably before the world, but have never been born from above, regenerated by the Holy Ghost, and know not what it is to receive a new heart. I was once where you are and as surely on my way to Hell as Sam Page in his saloon. God loves you as dearly as the drunkards, gamblers, swearers, and debauchees; and if you do not seek and find the Lord, get your sins forgiven and receive intelligent salvation, you are as sure of Hell as the poor reprobates who plunge headlong into the vulgar vices."

As God, in His providence, through a preaching father, a sainted mother and a Christian home, fortified me from the cradle, I have wasted no time in the devil's workshop; but have ever been diligently employed in laudable industries, physical, intellectual and spiritual. Nobody on the face of the earth can rise up and say aught against my life so far as the eye of the world is concerned, yet I was a sinner; but my sins were on the inside, except unhygienical treatment of my body, for which I alone was to suffer. Being a church member from my infancy, and my life irreproachable, so far as the world could discriminate, I was really a practical hypocrite. That word in the Bible means one who plays at religion which he does not possess. I doubt not but that the great majority of church members of this day are in the same dilemma. You see throughout the Bible that the hypocrite abides the common destiny with the liar, the thief, murderer, drunkard, blasphemer, adulterer and fornicator.

We Americans, as a rule, are all of European extraction. Very recently the Asiatics, especially from China and Japan, have been coming to our country. I can only trace my Anglican paternity and my Hibernian maternity but a few generations. My great grandfather was powerfully converted under the preaching of Bishop Asbury, one hundred and fifty years ago. He came home shouting aloud, called up his thirty negro slaves whom he held in bondage under the laws of old Virginia, told them his experience, fell on his knees and prayed for them, got up and thanked them for their good behavior and obedience. and told them they were his slaves no longer, to go and be free; all he asked of them was to meet him in Heaven. So you know he got a genuine case of conversion, because it cost him fifteen thousand dollars, which he cheerfully paid in setting them all free. Though we always lived in slave states, there never was a negro in our family afterward. My grandfather was powerfully converted in a Methodist camp-meeting when my father, his oldest child, was old enough to recognize and remember. He came home at midnight shouting the praises of God, and told grandmother that he was converted. Then he read the Scriptures, sang a song and prayed, and always afterward kept it up, morning and evening. I here give you a few lines of the song he sang that night:

"How happy every child of grace,
Who knows his sins forgiven;
This earth, he cries, is not my place,
I seek a place in Heaven.

"A country far from mortal sight,
E'en now by faith I see;
The land of rest, the saint's delight,
A Heaven prepared for me."

Some time after his conversion he emigrated to Kentucky and settled in the woods. There were many deer and other wild animals in that country. Near their house was a deer lick, whither the animals were in the habit of coming a short time before day. An old hunter in the neighborhood was in the habit of coming before day and hiding in a suitable position to shoot deer when they came to the lick. The Lord gave my grandfather six sons and about the same number of daughters to live to be grown. Five out of these sons became Methodist preachers, and so lived and died. The daughters were as bright and spiritual as the sons; but the old fogy notion that women should not preach embargoed their privileges and kept them out of the ministry. This old hunter relates that the family was in the habit of rising very early and all getting ready to go to their work by sunrise; he, while watching for the deer, would see them going away in different directions in the morning for secret prayer, and when they would meet in the house they generally raised an old-style shout.

The last time I ever saw my grandfather was while I was his presiding elder. I visited him when ninety-six years old, when he had me assist him in making an invoice of his family, which at that time numbered five hundered souls, twenty-five of whom were licensed preachers of the Gospel.

As all names have originated from circumstances, of course our family received its name from the fact of their eminent godliness, the original name being "Godly." Some one at some time writing it happened to replace the "l" by a "b." In England the name is spelled "Godbe;" in France it is generally spelled "Godfrey," *e. g.*, Godfrey of Bouillon, who was the celebrated commander-in-chief of the armies of the Crusaders who captured Jerusalem, A. D. 1099. You will find his tomb, along with that of Baldwin, king of Jerusalem, in the Church of the Holy Sepulchre.

The Godbeys are a very large family, and dispersed throughout the continent. Of course my acquaintance with them is quite extensive. I have never known one of them who was a drunkard, or an infidel, or a blasphemer, or addicted to any of the vulgar vices. Neither have I ever known one of them who had reached majority and was not an orderly member of the church. My own dear father, John Godbey, preached the Gospel in the Methodist Church for sixty-two years and went up to Heaven in a chariot of fire, (*i. e.*, was killed by lightning). He was eighty-three years old, he and mother having passed their golden wedding, living in Smithton, Pettis County, Mo. On Sunday morning he went to the German Methodist Church and worshipped with them, understanding not a word, as the service was all in German, but partaking of the Holy Sacrament with those godly people, which was followed by one of their good old German songs, which they all sang as if Heaven was in view and glory in their souls. Meanwhile he got happy and went around through the congregation shaking hands with them. After adjournment he came home and was standing in the door looking out, contemplating the falling rain and praising God for blessing the thirsty earth, when God dropped down a chariot and gave him a ride to Heaven, without an ache or a pain.

My maternal ancestry migrated from Ireland four or five generations ago. Their name was O'Kelly in the Emerald Isle; when they landed in America, dropping the "O," they simply reported the name Kelly. You will not be surprised when I tell you they were staunch Roman Catholics, claiming the direct succession from St. Patrick. It is said that all of the O'Kellys in Ireland are Catholics. They settled in the wild woods of Kentucky one hundred and fifty years ago, when that was all a howling wilderness, inhabited by wild beasts and savages. They had not been living there long when their baby died, breaking the hearts of the whole family. They were utterly illiterate, and knew nothing about spiritual things, except what the priest had taught them. Therefore, as there was no priest commandable to baptize the baby, they all sank into the deepest grief, believing that without a doubt the sweet and lovely idol of their hearts had actually gone down into the fires of purgatory. Therefore they made inquiry of everybody they could meet, doing their utmost to find a priest to get the soul of their dear baby out of the fires of purgatory; but in their deep distress they were utterly unable to hear of a priest anywhere. The truth of the matter was, no Catholic priest had yet come into that country, and it was utterly impossible to command any sacerdotal service. In this distressing dilemma, they happened to run on a squatter and asked him if he knew anything about a Catholic priest, or where they could possibly find one. He told them just to give up their quest, for they could not possibly find one, as there were none in all that country. But he said to them: "There is a fellow going about over the country, called a circuit rider, and it may be, for aught I know, that he is a priest." Well, they were so ignorant that they did not know what a circuit rider meant, and as the man had suggested that he might be a priest, they thought that perhaps a priest in this new country was called a circuit rider. Therefore they said to him: "Please send that circuit rider to our house as quickly as possible." He said he would watch for him and the first time he saw him, tell him he was wanted at their house. That circuit rider was James Hall, whom Bishop Asbury, when presiding over the Baltimore Conference, had sent to Kentucky, giving him the whole state for his circuit, as there were but few settlements in it at that time. James Hall was the first Methodist preacher whom Bishop Asbury sent to Kentucky. In the providence of God, although he came around only once a month, he happened to be at that time in that part of his round, and the squatter soon met him and told him the news, that he was most urgently needed at Mr. Kelly's. He was surprised, as, since there were so few people living in the country, he had a good chance to get information about every family and he knew that the Kellys were rigid Roman Catholics. He was, therefore, puzzled, soliloquizing in his mind what urgent business they could have with a Methodist preacher. The squatter gave him the needed information, stating to him that their baby had died and they believed its soul was in purgatory, because there was no priest to baptize it, and so were ransacking the whole country, distressed almost to death and hunting a priest to get the baby out of purgatory.

Upon reception of this urgent call, James Hall turned his horse and expeditiously dismounted at the Irish cabin. Going to the door and knocking, the woman of the house responds. He says to her: "I am that circuit rider you sent for. What will you have?" "Oh," she said, "we are so badly needing a priest to get the soul of our precious baby out of purgatory, and we heard of you and did not know but you were a priest, in this country called a circuit rider because you ride around on a horse. Now, please tell me, are you a priest?"

Here you see the absolute necessity of that beautiful gift of the Holy Ghost, denominated wisdom. (1 Cor. 12:8.) Without that gift, do you not see how this broken-hearted Irish mother would have bluffed the circuit rider. But, while James Hall had no collegiate learning, he was wonderfully filled with the Holy Ghost and enriched with His gifts, therefore he was prepared to face the emergency. He responded unhesitatingly in the affirmative: "Yes, madam, I am a priest." In this he did not prevaricate, because every called and sent preacher of the Gospel is a priest after the order of Melchizedek (Heb. 7th chapter). Then the dear woman, determined that no defalcation should supervene, clinched the matter by interrogating him: "But are you a Roman Catholic priest?" Now you see this gift of wisdom again coming to his relief, as he had to be rigidly truthful on all occasions. It would not do for him to answer in the affirmative; meanwhile a negative answer would ruin everything, utterly taking the job out of his hands. Therefore he responds: "Not exactly; but I can do anything a Roman Catholic priest can do." Then she at once settled down in the conclusion that the priests in this new country were in some respects different from those in Ireland; but, "What does that signify if they can do everything that appertains to the office and power of the Roman Catholic priest? If that is so, he can certainly get my dear baby out of purgatory."

After this soliloquy, which instantly passed in her mind, she proceeded at once to inform him that her sweet baby had passed away in the absence of a priest to baptize it, and of course it had gone to purgatory, and he must please proceed at once to get it out. Then he responded: "My sister, your neighbor who gave me your invitation also informed me about the baby. I have had it before God, and am happy to say it is not in purgatory, but in Heaven, and is the happiest, prettiest thing you ever saw, and has never cried nor whimpered since it got there, and the angels all want it in their arms at the same time."

This so pleased the family, that they almost died of joy to think the sweet baby whom they so dearly loved was already in Heaven and the angels so delighted with it. Then he asked them if they had ever been born again, and they answered in the negative, saying that they had never heard of such a thing. Then he told them that, while the baby was already in Heaven, if they wanted to see it again they must be born from above, as the Savior said to Nicodemus. They were so delighted with the glad news which he brought them, and, having all confidence in everything the "priest" told them, they believed it without a doubt, therefore they asked him to come and see them just as often as he could. Here comes in the supernatural spiritual gift of wisdom again. He had no church edifice in all the land, and did all of his preaching in the cabins of the squatters and under the green trees. Therefore the broad invitation they had given him to visit them as their priest was all the open door he wanted to make their house a regular preaching place in his monthly round. So he says to them: "One month from this day look for me to come and see you again, and feel free to invite your friends to be present during my visit." Therefore going around, —for he had an appointment every day in the month,— he published his appointment to preach in the house of the Irish Roman Catholic family.

Sure enough, the day and hour arrived, and the house was crowded with those red-hot, fire-baptized Methodists, for at that time there was no other sort, Satan not as yet having invented the Methodist ice factory, which, in our day, to our deep regret, is doing a lamentably extensive business. Now these Methodists all threw open their alligator mouths and roared like lions, singing the grand full salvation songs which God gave John and Charles Wesley, so loudly that the angels heard them. Falling on their knees, their fire-baptized prayers rose in smoking volumes till it seemed that the clapboards of the roof would all take wings and fly away and lodge among the stars, and the puncheon floors break through under their ponderous leaps and mighty shouts. Meanwhile the bottom of Heaven drops out and swelling floods pour down and inundate the whole congregation. Under the irresistible power the whole family falls prostrate, paralyzed with a nightmare of repentance and seeing themselves forever lost and crying aloud for mercy; while those red-hot Methodists were just in their glory, praying those Roman Catholics through into the kingdom. What is the result? Those indefatigable Methodists never let up till that Irish family was gloriously converted. They joined the Methodist Church and all turned preachers. They, like the Godbeys, are preaching throughout the continent this day. Therefore, you see that my family, on both sides, are preachers; my mother's family by pre-emption Roman Catholics, and my father's family having emanated from the Anglican Church.

Autobiography of Rev. W. B. Godbey, A. M.

Chapter I.

CHILDHOOD.

I was born June 3, 1833, by the waters of Clifty Creek, in Pulaski County, Kentucky. During my infancy my parents migrated six miles east and settled on a farm which they had purchased by the waters of Pitman's Creek, four and one-half miles north of Somerset, the county seat. There, in the providence of God, I lived until I was twenty years old, the family remaining a number of years afterwards. There were ten of us children, five sons and five daughters; one of the former having gone to Heaven in his infancy. The other nine all reached maturity. The four surviving sons all became preachers, but the daughters, by reason of the prevailing dogma against woman's ministry, were unfortunately withheld from the privilege which I am satisfied they would have participated in with great delight. Half of our number—three sisters and two brothers—are now in Glory. My youngest brother, Martin Adams, was very suddenly called to his heavenly home at the early age of twenty-eight. He went around and paid off all of his little debts and settled up everything, telling the family and friends that he was near the end of his life, whereas he was enjoying perfect health and bidding fair to live long. The day was bright and fair, and the family, at that time consisting of father, mother and elder brother Josiah, were all at the house. The latter was leading his horse through the front yard, when Martin walked out after him, and the animal, doubtless mistaking him for a dog or some other animal, kicked him in the breast with all its power, the single stroke with the newly shod hoof proving his instantaneous release from his tenement of clay. His brother darted back and caught him in his arms as he said his last words, "O Lord, I am dead," and breathed no more. He was a very sweet singer, as well as a teacher and preacher, being a collegiate graduate. He was nearly always singing when he was walking about. On that occasion, when he walked out of the house for the last time, he went singing these beautiful words: "Will any one be at the beautiful gate, watching and waiting for me?" This took place in Pettis County, Mo., whither the family migrated after the close of the Confederate War. My two surviving brothers, John K. and Josiah P., are both preaching in Missouri.

I above mentioned the fact of my father purchasing the farm to which we migrated when I was an infant. They lived on that farm twenty-five years, till we children were all old enough to labor and take care of ourselves; my three sisters older than myself having married and gone away. My father, having gone in debt for the farm, never did succeed in fully paying for it. As the years rolled away, with creating new debts to pay old ones, and never getting clear of financial encumbrance, finally the long-dreaded issue came and the farm had to be sold to pay the debts. This was a sad epoch in the history of our family, as we never afterward owned a home. While it was wrapped in darkness at that time, the cloud has long ago drifted away and been superseded by floods of light, victory, honor and glory. When we lost our farm, having no land to cultivate, we all turned preachers, and have been at it ever since. Perhaps, if we had never lost our home, some of us would be there to this day, digging on those poor hills (as it was in a very sterile, rough country), instead of going out with the commission of our Lord to the ends of the earth, preaching the everlasting Gospel.

During my babyhood, my mother went away, leaving me in the care of my three elder sisters. They got hold of some jimson pods and gave them to me for toys in a broken skillet. As I played, some of them broke open and the seeds dropped out. Babylike, I put them into my mouth and swallowed some of them. You know the jimson is a narcotic poison. When mother got home I was in convulsions, cramping as if I would surely die. She sent at once for the doctor, who labored hard to relieve me by emetics. Though I, in the providence of God, survived the immediate effects of the poison, they always believed its after effects lingered with me, stunting my growth, consequently I received notoriety as the dwarf of the family. Frequently when our relatives were about and looked at all of us children in the home, my father said to them in reference to me that he feared I was so stunted that I would never be any account. Though I remained reticent, my ambition arose Napoleonically, soliloquizing, "I will let you and everybody else know about that in due time. Doubtless the poison did stunt my growth, as I have never known one of our family, either paternal or maternal, who is not much larger than myself. I have always been the physical dwarf of the family. This dwarfhood is not much recognized since I reached maturity, but it gave me constant and universal notoriety during my boyhood, as the people in that country were, many of them, physical giants. Therefore I was constantly pronounced the runt, and my parents always referred to the poison of those jimson seeds as the cause. My body continued to grow, however, till I was twenty-five years old, thus much relieving the dwarfhood which rendered me so conspicuous when a child. While I suppose they are correct in reference to the stunt thus received, I have never felt any of the effects of it since I can remember. While perhaps in this way my growth was impeded, I am satisfied it never had any effect on my activity. I have often heard my mother say that when I was eight months old and she was expecting me to begin to crawl over the floor, to her surprise I got up and walked and never did crawl. I was always pronounced the fleetest runner in the entire community, and the most adroit wrestler. Such became my notoriety that they were constantly after me to wrestle, and I was so fond of it that I never refused, unless my competitor was too small. Unless he was considerably larger than myself, I refused to take him. The secret of my success was the quickness of my nerves. When arrangements were made, holds taken, and our eyes fixed on the hat which a boy was holding and whose drop was the signal for us to begin, I was so quick that I always threw my competitor before he made his effort; consequently it did not make much difference how large he was, as his weight, when I had tripped him, would only expedite the velocity and augment the certainty of his fall to the ground.

I have an exceedingly early recollection, and, for the glory of God, I feel it my duty to say it, an extraordinary memory. I could always read a book and tell substantially everything in it by memory. When I was quite a little fellow, I doubt seriously whether I was three years old, my mother took me on her lap and told me wonderful things which electrified me with astonishment and thrilled me with interest, as they were utterly new and I had never heard them before. She told me that the time would come when the dead would all rise from their graves, and the world take fire and burn up. Oh, how this stirred and excited my infantile mind and moved my childish heart. I said: "O mother, where will I be when the world is on fire?" Then she said: "O my child, you will be shouting with the angels in the air." Then I said: "Mother, how do you know?" She responded: "I have given you to the Lord for a preacher; your father is a preacher, and I want all of my sons to preach." If it were now, she would have said all of her daughters, too, for my sisters were all intellectually bright and spiritual, and would have made good preachers. She proceeded to tell me not only that she had given us to the Lord for preachers, but she had the evidence that we would preach. She also told me about my baptism, in which I was dedicated to God forever and became a member of His Church. Consequently I was to be good, preach the Gospel, and go to Heaven when I left the world. Though I do not think I was more than three years old, then and there I received the call to preach, and it rested on me ever afterward. So profound and thrilling was my impression, that I could not wait for the rolling years to bring me into manhood, but told my playfellows that I was a preacher. Then we began to hold meetings, all the children ever afterward recognizing me as a preacher. Those impressions never left me, but strengthened their grip with the lapse of years. Though I am now seventy-three years old, I would rather preach the Gospel to the poor and starve to death, than to be a millionaire and not preach.

I know I received the call to preach through the instrumentality of my dear sainted mother at that time, and I verily believe that I was then converted to God. Of course I had never lost my infantile justification, with which I was born into the world. This brings us to the consideration of a most important Bible truth, *i. e.*, infantile justification and regeneration. When does it take place? We answer: "The moment soul and body constitute personality, which is in the pre-natal state, by the normal economy of grace every human being is born from above." John 3:7. When I was a circuit rider, I made that statement in the presence of my presiding elder, who was a good old man, but not a classical scholar. He at once contradicted me upon the allegation that I had people born again before they were born the first time. The answer to his argument is in the simple fact that "again" in those Scriptures is a wrong translation. Our Savior said *"anoothen,"* whose first meaning is "from above," and this is the true translation. The Bible clearly reveals that every human being is born from above, thus becoming a child of God, justified and regenerated, before the natural birth. If this were not so, all infants dying unborn would be sure of Hell; since, without the supernatural birth, no soul can go to Heaven. Our Savior's treatment of the babies abundantly confirms this conclusion. He everywhere takes them in His arms and certifies *"of such is the kingdom of Heaven."* Therefore, you see in all His ministry that He fully recognizes the infantile membership of His kingdom, positively certifying not only their membership, but holding them up as *bona fide* paragon members, assuring His disciples that they must be converted and become like them. Now if we take these facts and harmonize them with His positive affirmation (John 3:7), *"Ye must be born from above,"* in order to enter the kingdom, the conclusion follows as an irresistible and logical sequence, that all of the infants in all ages and nations have already been born from above, as otherwise they could not be members of His kingdom, as He positively certifies they are. In connection with these Scriptures, let us take Heb. 2:9, *"By the grace of God Christ tasted death for* EVERY ONE," which includes every human being in all ages, whether born or unborn. Now when do you become a human being? We answer: the very moment soul and body are united and constitute a personality you become a human being, and the great and glorious vicarious atonement which our Lord made for the whole human race comes into availability. The Greek word in this passage is *hyper*, which always means "instead of," and is the very word constantly used revelatory of the vicarious atonement. Therefore there is no possible evasion of the conclusion that, by the wonderful redemption of Jesus Christ, we are all justified and regenerated in the pre-natal state, at the moment of the transition out of the fœtal into the personal existence. Unless you accept this conclusion, you consign to the bottomless pit every infant dying before the physical birth. The truth of it is, that the physical birth is not the beginning of the personal existence, by any means. Our Savior's work is perfect, absolutely leaving out none; it is normal economy, but including every son and daughter of Adam's race, so that Satan gets none but those who, having reached responsibility, take the bit in their own teeth and, pursuant to their own free agency, which grace never contravenes, absolutely reject the redemption of Christ. Verily, God's time for every soul to be justified and regenerated is the very moment it enters personal existence, and this actually does take place without a solitary exception.

There are three things which God never made: a devil, a sinner, and a snake. He created angels, with perfect moral freedom to obey or disobey. Some of them unfortunately "kept not their first estate," (Jude 6th verse), fell, and became devils and demons. Isaiah 14:12: "How art thou fallen, O Lucifer, the son of the morning!" God created Adam and Eve upright and holy and perfectly free to obey or disobey. Unfortunately they followed in the track of Satan and lost their first estate, becoming sinners. He created the Nahash, the intermediate link between man and brute, the most intelligent of all the animal kingdom and having the power of speech. Unfortunately for him, Satan subsidized him in the abduction of mother Eve, and, through her, father Adam, thus ruining the human race. In consequence of this Satanic manipulation, God pronounced that awful anathema on him, which resulted in his transformation into the loathsome, venomous, hissing serpent. God is the very essence of everything good, therefore from Him nothing bad can possibly emanate.

A dogma is extensively preached throughout Christendom which certifies, "Once in grace, always in grace," involving the conclusion that if you have ever had salvation you will never go to Hell. When Satan goes into the lying business, he knows how to "do the thing up brown." If you will investigate the facts of the case, you will find the very reverse of the above dogma to be true. Instead of there being no backsliders in Hell, there are none but backsliders in the dismal regions of endless woe. Oh, how the awful reminiscence of their *quandam* happiness in the kingdom of God will haunt them through all eternity, as they wail their hopeless doom. Let us take a momentary invoice of Hell's inmates. We begin with Satan, the fallen archangel, and find him none other than an old backslider. Then we take all of the devils and demons and find them fallen angels, without a single exception, having once been in Heaven, but having failed to keep their probation. Finally we come to the millions of sinners and find, by the positive testimony of Jesus, that, in their innocent babyhood, they were citizens of God's kingdom. Therefore Hell was made for none but backsliders, and never will have any other occupants.

Then you say: "Brother Godbey, since we are all, by the nominal grace of God in Christ, justified and regenerated in the pre-natal state, why do little children need the conversion which you say you received when only three years old?" The Bible is the most beautiful and glorious book in the world. It is its own expositor. If you will give it a chance, it will always explain itself. Psalm 51: 5, *"I was shapen in iniquity, and in sin did my mother conceive me."* This is not condemnatory sin, but the inbred depravity which we all inherit from Adam. A man is poisoned and must die, if that poison is not removed by a stomach pump, or in some other way. You do not blame him because it was in the water he drank, but did not know it till it was too late. An enemy had put it there. Adam is the fountain whence emanated the stream of humanity which has broadened and covered the whole earth. Satan poisoned the fountain, and we all imbibed it. Christ brought us the remedy, which is free for us all to use and get rid of the poison. That remedy is His precious blood, which He shed on Calvary. The first great work of grace realized in human experience, *i. e.*, the beautiful globe denominated conversion, consists of two hemispheres, *i. e.*, *justification,* freeing us from condemnation, and *regeneration,* giving us a new heart and resurrecting the human spirit into the life it lost by sin. This justification and regeneration, which we all receive by the normal grace of Christ in the pre-natal transition out of the fœtal into the personal state, does not remove the depravity transmitted from Adam to every human being, but only conquers it and gives grace to hold it *in statu quo,* in due time to be utterly and forever eliminated in the great work of entire sanctification.

"Now, Brother Godbey, why do these justified and regenerated infants need conversion?" Because this hereditary depravity is still in the heart, and when they reach the age of responsibility it will lead them into sin to an absolute certainty, if not converted. Because, while they are born in the kingdom safe and all right, so that if they were to die they are sure of Heaven, yet they are born with their faces away from God, turned toward carnal desires and appetites. Now, the thing to do is to instruct the little one, turn him around and introduce him to God, so that he will start out in life Godwardly and Heavenwardly; whereas, if he undergoes no change, he is certain to start sinwardly and Hellwardly. If my godly mother and preaching father had understood this great truth, they would have saved me from years of suffering in Satan's kingdom; though, under the blessed teaching and prayers of my dear mother, as above specified, at the age of three years I believe I did get converted, *i. e.,* turned around and was introduced to God; yet I did not know how to abide steadfastly in the kingdom, though I never went into sinful habits. I kept far from profanity; I would not use any bywords or slang of any kind, because I read in my Bible that our conversation should be yea, yea, and nay, nay, and any more than this cometh from the evil one. Though reared in the worst whiskey state in the Union, in my boyhood I joined a Temperance Society, excluding all beverages, and stuck to it. I never tasted beer in my life, and do not know the taste of any intoxicants. Though reared in the greatest tobacco state in the world, I never used it. I do not know the taste of coffee; do not use tea, chocolate, or any nervines whatever. I never knew the number of cards in a deck; never danced a step in my life, nor had anything to do with Satan's fandangoes, frolics, barbecues, circuses, nor theatres. Though my life remained manifestly unimpeachable, yet I lost my hold on God, became a backslider, and so remained till I was sixteen years of age, when the Lord gloriously converted me and gave me grace to ever afterward abide in His kingdom.

We have a vivid illustration of this problem in the lives of John the Baptist and the Apostle Paul. We read in reference to the former that he was filled with the Holy Ghost from his infancy. When Herod was killing the infants in and about Bethlehem, in order to get the one born King of the Jews, lest He might supersede his dynasty on the throne of Israel, though there was no order for this massacre to be extended to Jutta, the home of Zachariah and Elizabeth, a dozen miles distant, yet, through fear that the bloody edict might reach them, they fled away into the wilderness of Judea and returned no more. Among the denominations of the Jewish Church, the Pharisees were orthodox, the Sadducees were heterodox, and the Essenes were the holiness people. The latter, generally too poor to cultivate the rich land, lived in the desert where land was so poor that it was not worth appropriating and they could use all of it they wanted. In this way John the Baptist, in addition to his sanctified father and mother, who "walked in all the commandments and ordinances of the Lord blameless," had the society of all these poor, humble holiness people, fortifying him against all worldliness of every kind. Therefore, instead of backsliding from his infantile justification, he moved directly on into the sanctified experience, and then and there, steadfast, shining and shouting, awaited the happy welcome of his thirtieth year, the Jewish majority, antecedent to which no priest entered upon his office, therefore it was observed both by John and Jesus.

Far otherwise was the sad experience of the Apostle Paul. Rom. 7:9, *"But I was alive at one time without law."* This is a clear allusion to his infantile justification with which he was born and which he retained until he reached the age of responsibility and knew right from wrong. That was the time he needed conversion to introduce him to God and turn away his face from carnal appetites and inclinations, toward God, spiritual and heavenly things. *"But the commandment having come, sin revived and I died, and the commandment which was unto me for life, the same is found to be unto death; for sin having taken occasion through the commandment deceived me and through it slew me."* This inbred sin, which he inherited from Adam and which was born in him, lay apparently dead in his heart like the grain of wheat in the bin. It is said that wheat has been taken from the catacombs of Egypt four thousand years old and sown, has germinated and actually produced a crop. Paul was a very strong character and had a great mind; hereditary depravity in him was great and strong. Until he reached responsbility it remained perfectly still and could not possibly germinate and produce a crop of condemnatory transgression. So that was the time the commandment came, which he unfortunately rejected and antagonized, then and there forefeiting his infantile justification, falling under condemnation and becoming a backslider. Oh, what a vivid contrast between Paul and John the Baptist! The latter lived and died under the Old Dispensation, whose normal plan is justification, but by the wonderful proleptical grace of God he enjoyed the sanctified experience all his life, while the former, his contemporary, having unfortunately forfeited his infantile justification and become a backslider, yielding to the normal trend of an undue emphasis on works in the absence of their concomitant grace, drifted away into the legalism which has been so fatal to the Church in all ages. Inadvertently he substituted intellect and education for the Holy Ghost, being environed by the most ample facilities of literary culture the world could give.

Paul having graduated in the Greek colleges of Tarsus, his native city, and adding to his classical lore all the ecclesiastical culture the Jewish rabbins could give him, while sitting at the feet of Gamaliel, the leading Hebrew theologian of the age, he was promoted step by step till he reached a place in the Sanhedrim, where he was honored by all the dignitaries and magnates, who spontaneously stood in awe, spellbound, as they contemplated his towering intellect enriched with the highest culture, literary, classical, philosophical, theological and ecclesiastical. He was then honored by the high priest with the responsible office of expurgating the Church of all heresies and schisms. Pursuant to the supremacy with which he was thus honored officially, he led off the loyal wing of the Church in what he regarded as the noble work of suppressing the fearful Nazarene heresy, which, in his judgment, threatened the very existence of the Church in which patriarchs and prophets had lived and died and gone to Heaven. Though God, in His mercy, sent him the Holy Ghost to convict him, believing that he was right and that the Nazarene heresy, if not suppressed, would ruin the Church, he resisted Him heroically, as we conclude from our Savior's statement when He shone down upon him as he journeyed to Damascus: "It is hard for thee to kick against the goads." As the ox kicking back against the steel points with which they touch him to expedite his walk, thus wounds his heels till the blood copiously flows, so Paul had been determinedly resisting the Holy Ghost. He never flickered till the glorified Savior appeared to him with a brilliancy eclipsing the meridian sun in his noonday splendor.

The solution of this awful obduracy on the part of great Saul of Tarsus was the fact that, though perfectly honest and sincere, he was not enjoying spiritual salvation, but, with all of his zeal for God, he was a mere legalist. I have no idea that he ever was reclaimed during all of his honored and influential ministerial life in the Jewish Church; not till his wonderful conversion in the house of Judas, under the ministry of Ananias, the normal fruitage of that transcendent conviction which flashed through him like forked lightnings, streaming down from the unutterable splendor of our Savior's glorified person. There are multitudes of preachers at this day, full of learning and zeal for the Church, in the succession of Saul of Tarsus before his gloriious conversion in Damascus, who have substituted dead legalism for the mighty works of the Holy Ghost, which are always new, fresh, and bright.

Oh, the incalculable value of efficient teachers to serve our Sunday-schools as spiritual guides in the experimental realm! If we only had them in every Sunday-school, intelligently instructed in reference to the infantile relation to the Divine economy so that they could lead the little ones of the kindergarten to the Savior before they reach responsibility, and introduce them to Him by prayer, instruction and spiritual songs, and thus get them intelligently converted! This, with Sabbatically instructing and diagnosing their spiritual status, so that, in case they are backslidden during the week, they will get them reclaimed, will be their great work to keep them in the kingdom of God. The great trouble is that our Sunday-schools, like our homes, are radically deficient in spiritual diagnosis of the children and that simple, plain, spiritual instruction necessary to acquaint them with the Savior and qualify them to walk with Him day by day. While I shall always believe that I really found the Lord at the time above mentioned, when I was three years old, my mother, whom the Spirit used to lead me to God and get me converted, for the want of instruction did not know that I was converted, and of course I did not know it myself. If she and my preaching father had understood the beautiful economy of grace in reference to the little ones, I am satisfied that they could have kept me in the kingdom of God. I do believe that my grandchildren, Emma and John Hill, of ten and nine years of age, both got converted before they lost their infantile justification. I have always made them a specialty in my prayers in my almost perpetual absence and in my instruction when with them. I find them ready and able in prayer and testimony, and clearly evincing decisive growth in grace during my absence from them. Little children, even when clearly converted and walking with God, need constant attention to keep them from backsliding, because of the non-development of their intellect which is a powerful fortification against temptation. They are easily and quickly converted and very liable to backslide before we are aware. Consequently acute spiritual diagnosis is necessary on the part of the teachers to detect the lapses and get them reclaimed as quickly as possible. It is the nature of a sheep when it gets out of the pasture to stray off and just keep going farther and farther indefinitely until it is captured by a robber or devoured by a wild beast.

Mother Wesley was wonderfully blessed with spiritual light, diagnosis and an aptitude to teach. She not only taught her large family in the school every day, but took each one aside and interviewed it specially in the interest of its soul.

I date my infantile conversion from this lesson which my mother gave me at the age of three years. This took place before I had reached responsibility and had an opportunity to backslide, as in the case of Paul (Rom. 7:9), where he lost his infantile justification because he had reached the years of accountability and, instead of obeying, disobeyed the Lord's commandment, thus becoming a backslider, which is really the status of every adult sinner in the world, as we see it illustrated in the case of the Prodigal Son, whom we count converted when he got back to his father's house. But you know he was born in that house and never got out till he wandered away from his father's house. A simple analysis of the case will convince you thoroughly that the return of the prodigal was nothing more nor less than his reclamation. "No Scripture is of private interpretation," (2 Pet. 1:20), therefore the case of the Prodigal Son parallels that of every sinner in the world, confirming the conclusion that what we call the conversion of the sinner is the reclamation of the backslider. The true and normal conversion takes place before the infantile justification is forfeited. In this there is neither justification nor regeneration, for these are received in the prenatal state in the moment of the transition from the fœtal to the personal status.

We have in the case of the Prodigal Son's elder brother a beautiful illustration of the gracious possibilities of retaining our infantile justification. You see when his younger brother got home and he returned from the field and heard the rousing jollification and learned from the servant that his father had slain the fatted calf and they were all rejoicing over the returned prodigal, how he refused to go in. He thought there ought to be shouting over him instead of his brother, as he had been so good and his brother so bad. Then, responsive to the pleadings of his father importuning him to come in, he says, "Father, I have never at any time transgressed thy commandment." This shows clearly that he had never disobeyed him, consequently had never forfeited his infantile justification. If the testimony of his innocence of which we here read had been incorrect, his father would have corrected him, but as he left that declaration unchallenged, the normal conclusion is that he was correct, having never actually violated his father's command, which he would have done if he had forfeited his infantile justification. We see clearly that he much needed sanctification to take away the hereditary fret and jealousy out of his heart, which he had inherited from father Adam, and regeneration does not remove, but only gives grace to keep down the depravity, so that it is no longer permitted to rise up and commit actual transgressions. We find this interview of the father with the elder son continues, until the curtain drops, hiding the scene from our vision. I believe the elder son did eventually yield to the importunities of the father, came in, got sanctified, joined the jollification, and, in all probability, before it was over, proved the highest jumper and loudest shouter.

After years had elapsed, when I was a little lad, a group of my neighbor boys came along on Sunday morning, going on a frolicing excursion. Not daring to come to the house, as they knew I was not allowed to desecrate the Sabbath, secretly catching my attention when I was out on the premiscs, they undertook to persuade me to go with them. I positively refused, and proceeded to defend myself by apologetic arguments. I was but one and they were a party, therefore they all turned in on me, pleading most earnestly and persistently, and actually making speeches to convince me that there was no harm in it, and that I ought to go. They argued with me very sympathetically, and told me that I was having no fun; that it was my right and privilege, and that I was making a great mistake in living a life so restricted and scrupulous. Thus they all combined and talked me out of countenance. When they saw no signs of relenting, two of them grabbed me by either arm and carried me away with them. We passed through dense primeval forests, over high hills, and across deep valleys, a route strange to me, till we reached the waters. By the time we got there I was under awful conviction, having yielded to the lashings of a guilty conscience. They saw it, and all spread themselves to cheer me up by telling funny jokes and laughing over them. As I had never gone fishing in my life, of course I had no tackle, but they determined to make a success of their convert, so fitted me out with their best hook and line. Meanwhile the reaction of my conscience got stronger and my conviction went down deeper, and I became so sad that I could not fish, and quit trying. I would have gone home, but was afraid I would get lost in the woods, as we had come through the unbroken forest with not so much as a path. They saw they had a mourner on their hands and did their best to comfort me, but their silly, carnal condolment only added to the burden of my sorrows. I stayed with them till they returned late in the afternoon, when, passing by our house, of course I dropped off. By this time the evening shades were falling fast. I went off behind the garden and oh, how I wept! I confessed my sins, pleading with God to forgive me and promising never to desecrate the Sabbath any more, nor to disobey my parents, nor to violate His commandments. While I was thus pleading, crying, and praying with a broken heart, my mountain burden rolled away and I became light and happy. I do believe that I was there reclaimed from the apostasy into which I had gradually drifted after my conversion at the age of three years.

We lived in a very wild, rough, ignorant community off in the country, where sins and follies ran riot. There was no Methodist Church nearer than three miles and preaching there only once a month, and, as we were poor and had no conveyance, if we went we had to walk. The Baptists had preaching once a month within one mile. We generally attended. The Campbellites preached more in that neighborhood than all other denominations combined. But they ridiculed and condemned Holy Ghost religion with the bitterest denunciations, pronouncing it wild fanaticism, and preaching nothing but their water doctrines all the time without exception. Of course they were spiritually detrimental rather than helpful. I did not claim to be a Christian at all, as for the want of instruction I did not know that the abovementioned blessings were really my conversion and reclamation, as I now verily believe. There was no Sunday-school in all that neighborhood, consequently I never attended any. The Methodists at that time, and I may include the Baptists in that country, though very few in number, the Campbellites having four or five times as many members as all others united, were really humble and spiritual, consequently preaching and talking experimental religion, and doing their best to hold up the banner of the cross and spiritual regeneration against the overmastering tide of Campbellism, which was the popular religion. Meanwhile their preachers in every sermon denounced and ridiculed Holy Ghost religion in all its forms and phases and preached water baptism for the remission of sins. I heard them more than all others, but they did me no good spiritually, and I honestly believe I suffered spiritual detriment by hearing them. I do not think the many preachers I heard of their denomination knew the Lord. I am satisfied they were false prophets, misleading the people. In that great woodland country it was customary for every farmer to have a log rolling, in which the neighbors would all gather and pile his logs, so he could burn them. They also had corn huskings. I was in these gatherings, heard their conversations, and saw them drinking whiskey, and found those Campbellites saying and doing evil things which shocked me, though I did not profess to be a Christian, but only a poor sinner. They claimed to be the only Christians in the world, condemning all others and urging them to come and join them and be Christians, boasting in their exclusive appropriation of the name.

I feel it my duty as a faithful autobiographer here to state that my infant baptism was, in the providence of God, a great blessing to me. My parents often told me about it when I was little, reminding me that I was a church member, having been solemnly dedicated to God in baptism, therefore I must be good and obedient to all of His commandments. I became a good reader when only six years old, reading the Scriptures with great interest. Finding the commandment, *"Children, obey your parents in the Lord,"* I remembered it with the deep and constant realization that, when I disobeyed my father and mother in anything, I was violating the commandment of God. The constant realization that I had been baptized and in this way dedicated to God, rested on me as a potent incentive to obedience, good behavior and rectitude. Baptism should not be given to infants recklessly and improvidently; afterward diregarded, while the children are permitted to go unscrupulously into sin; as in that case it is really taking the name of the Lord in vain, ultimating with the recipients as a hardener of their hearts and wielding a detrimental moral influence over the life. But when it is used by the parents with due reverence for the Holy Trinity and with an appreciation of their privileges as citizens of the kingdom to dedicate their offspring and all their possessions to God, the influence on the parents is exceedingly helpful in tightening up their obligations to bring up the children in the nurture and admonition of the Lord; meanwhile it is to the child a perpetual reminiscence of his relation to God and of the inallienable obligations growing out of that relation. All children need every possible legitimate influence to fortify them against the perpetual temptations to do wrong, arising from hereditary depravity in the heart and all sorts of external allurements in the world. The journey of life is crowded with temptations from the cradle to the grave, our Savior assuring us that "the saved are few," therefore it is our imperative duty to do our utmost from the beginning to build around our children the strongest wall we possibly can in order to fortify them against temptation. In the discharge of this duty we should begin as soon as they are born. We are all the creatures of education. Truly has it been said, "Education forms the common mind; as the twig is bent, so is the tree inclined."

I know I am a miracle of providence and grace; it does not seem to me that I could have dispensed with any of His blessings without serious detriment and jeopardy, therefore I am full of gratitude for the blessings of a Christian home, and among them my dedication to God in infancy. When they told me about it, my bark was already launched and the compass set, steering me Heavenward. Learning those facts, I accepted the situation, and with my earliest susceptibility of recognizing the obligation, realized that the very consciousness that I was already given to God in the ordinance of His own appointment inspired my heart with resignation, reconciliation, joyful acceptance of the situation and sincere and ardent resolution by the help of God to be true. The great mistake of parents is in neglecting their children until Satan gets the lasso around their necks. Solomon says, *"Train up a child in the way he should go, and when he is old he will not depart from it."* It is our imperative duty from the beginning, not only to restrain but to constrain, lest the vicious predilections, hereditary in the heart of every child, get the start of us. Solomon again gives us the benefit of the wisdom which God gave him, when he says, *"If you beat a boy with a rod, you shall save his soul."* I am full of gratitude to God both for the restraint and constraint of the Christian home in which He gave me birth, and feel that when I get to Heaven the first thing I will do will be to hunt my sainted father and mother and thank them for their faithful efforts to bring me up for God, and ask their pardon for all the sorrow I ever gave them by disobedience.

We are living in a dispensation of glorious spiritual freedom, our Savior having broken every yoke of bondage. Some think we would better not baptize the infant, but wait until adultage, so he may choose for himself. The great trouble is that if we do not bring into availability every auxiliary in behalf of virtue and righteousness, Satan may so capture the heart as to forestall the choice on his side. You say, "I am afraid that if I have my baby baptized, when it grows up it will be dissatisfied and want it again." Suppose it does; do not hesitate to encourage a repetition of the ordinance to the satisfaction of the conscience. Baptism was protracted from the day of Moses and repeated whenever they had contracted ceremonial defilement. Many a devout Jew was baptized with water thousands of times. Peter says it should be the answer of a good conscience. Therefore we should feel perfectly free to satisfy our conscience when truly enlightened by the Word and Spirit.

I started to school at the age of five, my three older sisters merely taking me for company. As I had not reached the scholastic age, the teacher gave me no attention and I learned but little. At the age of six I learned very rapidly, and became a good reader of plain English literature. In that school our teacher, Peter McFall, was an elderly man and wore a beard, which I had never seen before, because in that day all of the men shaved off their beards. When I saw him sitting in his chair, his face covered with beard dark and gray, I was affrighted and trembled with awe. In a few days after I entered, seated by a large boy, I saw him put some paper in his mouth and look like he was going to eat it. We lived out in the woody hills, where I never had seen much paper. I was always full of inquiry, disposed to investigate everything with which I came in contact, so in a low whisper I asked him if he was going to eat it, feeling curious to know whether paper was good to eat.

That moment the old teacher roared at me, scaring me awfully, as I was already afraid of him, and ordered me to come to him. He had a long hazel switch with which he whipped the children. He would strike it down on the puncheon floor like a clap of thunder roaring in our ears, thus terrifying us into good behavior and diligent study. As I stood before him faint with terror, he scolded me awfully for whispering to that boy and told me if I misbehaved any more he would take that switch he had in his hand, lap it round me and make the fur fly faster than "old Yates" could make it into hats.

There were no factories then and hats were made in shops, dispersed far and wide over the country. "Old Yates" had his shop in sight of that school-house, and we children went and looked at him with utter amazement, as he would put the skin of a fox, raccoon, rabbit or mink (which abounded in those wild woods), and with his foot on a treadle cause a suspended spring to fly around with great rapidity, jerking all the fur off the skin which filled the space with a cloud till it settled down on the platform, whence he gathered it up and made hats of it. I was so young then that I knew nothing about joking, but believed everything I heard spoken, in its literal sense. I began to soliloquize: If he puts me through such an operation as "old Yates" does those fox skins, I certainly will die meanwhile. Therefore I was awfully alarmed and wondered what was to become of me.

I had in the school a first cousin, John Bishop, two years older than myself, who had incurred the displeasure of the teacher before I entered the school, and, according to his custom, he had chastised him severely with that long rod which he held in his hand all the time as a symbol of his authority. So at the ensuing playtime, my cousin and I had a most serious and sincere consultation with reference to our fate. In this mutual counsel we both gave it as our candid conviction that our lives were in danger. He said that he almost died while the teacher was whipping him, and believed candidly that if he had given him another lick it would have killed him; while I frankly stated to him that I knew, if he did for me what he had said, making the fur fly off of me faster than "old Yates" could make it into hats, I certainly would die under the operation. As our parents had assigned us, and would have to pay if we stopped, the same as if we continued, we knew we would have to go on, but we both said, either to other, that we were willing to suffer any amount of pain if we knew that he would leave life in us, while we mutually, with the deepest sorrow, decided that our lives were in danger. That was an epoch in my life whose effects have continued to this day. I was only six years old and continued to prosecute my education as best I could, then I graduated at the age of twenty-six. But that castigation, in which he never touched me, but scared me almost to death, sufficed amply for the twenty years. I was ever afterward a favorite with my teachers and held up by them as a model student. They often, while pleading with the school to be obedient and studious, called my name and exhorted them all to follow my example, to my embarrassment, as I felt so unworthy.

Chapter II.

STRIPLINGHOOD.

An old Bible agent stopped with us over night, as he was going around supplying the homes with the precious Word. The ensuing morning, father said, "William, take that young horse and go with this man to Clifty and show him the way." With thrilling delight, mounting, I rode before his carriage the five miles designated. When I was about to turn back, he called me to his carriage and spent a few moments giving me the best advice I ever had, which I received with grateful appreciation, in which God actually used him to confirm my call to the ministry, at the same time handing me a Bible as a present. Oh, what an epoch this was in my life! I never had known what it was to own a book. In all my schooling I had used my sister's old books, no new one ever having been purchased for me. Therefore the consciousness of owning a book thrilled me with delight, especially as that book was the Bible. Therefore I carried it home elated with joy and wrote my name in it. Here let me remind you of the importance of giving good books to your children in such a way that they will recognize them as their own personal property. Though my preaching father had plenty of Bibles, which I frequently read with great interest, the presentation of this Bible forever marked a new era in my appreciation of that precious book. From that hour I began at the first of Genesis and perused it, using all of my leisure moments in reading this blessed book. I remember that very soon after this I was lying under an apple tree reading, when a neighbor boy about my age came along and asked me what book I was reading. I told him and he asked me what I was reading about. I began with creation and told him the wonderful things which I had read, my excellent memory retaining it so that I could tell him the thrilling, inspired histories which were so interesting to me. He listened spellbound and expressed the greatest astonishment, saying that he had never heard those things before. As there was no Sunday-school in all that country, and the preaching which was calculated to do me good was only once a month, and a three mile's walk over rugged hills and creeks which were often past fording, I generally spent the Sunday reading the Bible; unless interrupted, as was often the case, by visitors, as all the people in that country availed themselves of the Sabbath to do their visiting, which is all wrong, unless we want to visit the sick, the poor, or the suffering, in the interest of their souls and bodies.

When people died and they buried them about in different places, I was always permitted to go and visit the scene. My father generally officiated in a funeral service at the grave, the coffin's lid being always removed and the people all invited to come and look on the face of the dead for the last time. A near neighbor of ours always made the coffins and would come to the interment, and after people had all looked at the corpse, he would nail the coffin's lid down fast, as they had no screws for them then. The sound of the hammer nailing up the coffin roared in my ears like thunder, and continued to haunt my childish memory night and day. My father would give out that old song, two lines at a time,

"Hark from the tombs a doleful sound,
  My ears attend the cry;
Ye living men, come view the ground,
  Where you must shortly lie.

"Princes, this clay must be your bed,
  In spite of all your towers.
Ye tall, ye wise, ye reverent head
  Must lie as low as ours.

"Great God, is this our certain doom
  And are we yet secure?
Still marching downward to the tomb,
  And yet prepared no more.

"Grant us the power of quickening grace,
  To fit our souls to fly;
Then when we drop this dying flesh,
  We'll rise above the sky."

Funerals were generally attended by all the people in the neighborhood. They always held their service at the grave. As my father would give out this song, and others of a similar character, two lines at a time, the whole multitude would sing them so loudly and with such impressive solemnity as actually to remind us of the judgment trumpet blowing. After this they would let the coffin down into the grave with ropes, whose loud rattling and creaking conduced to the trepidation which always filled my heart on those memorable occasions. The whole crowd remained until the grave was filled up. The falling of the clods on the coffin-lid produced an awful and doleful roar, striking panic to our hearts and causing some to weep aloud.

My father was always sent for to visit the sick and get them ready to die. He preached much at different places and God wonderfully used him in keeping a chronic conviction on me and a perpetual seeking of the Lord. If he and mother had understood the privilege of children to be intelligently converted before they reach responsibility and lose their infantile justification, and, like adult Christians, live in communion and in the enjoyment of justifying peace and soul rest, I shall always believe that they could have kept me in the kingdom of God, but at that time everybody thought that we had to grow up sinners before we could get converted. As above mentioned, I am satisfied that after I learned about God and became a sincere and earnest seeker, I actually met my Savior and enjoyed communion with Him and soul rest, but I knew not how to abide in the kingdom. Drifting away, I was afterwards reclaimed, perhaps several times. As I grew older, and the sphere of my responsibility enlarged, though in my outward life rigidly keeping the moral law, my interior spirit drifted farther and farther from God. Meanwhile I never ceased to pray, really being a chronic mourner all my life, till I was finally and gloriously converted at the age of sixteen, after which I never again drifted out of the kingdom. At that time there was no very decisive change externally marked in my life, as it already had been unimpeachable, so far as the world could discriminate.

In the change of time there has been a great detraction from the efficiency of death-bed scenes and funerals in facilitating conviction and restraint from sinful resources. They were the most potent agencies which constantly co-operated in keeping conviction on me. As I revert to the scenes of my childhood and youth, it seems that I would have been unable to resist the formidable combinations of temptations incident to the juveniles, had it not been for this perpetual series of influences reminding me of my frail mortality, the certainty of death and the irreversible issues of eternity. Now opiates are so administered to the sick, that they are demented and thus deprived of their mental sagacity, pertinent to the apprehension of their real condition. Then there was nothing of this kind; people all died in their senses, either shouting the triumps of faith, or wailing in the depths of despair, both of which are the most potent influences in all the world to arouse conviction and perpetuate them on the unconverted. I then had no Sunday-school training and heard but little true Gospel preaching, though much on the water salvation line, by men who ridiculed the Holy Ghost and His mighty works and really did their best to drown out His convictions by persuading people to join their church and receive water baptism, in order for the remission of sins, and thus content themselves, although utterly destitute of Christian experience. They ridiculed such experience with withering sarcasms. But in spite of all this, these death-bed scenes and funerals, which I was permitted to attend almost every week, kept the momentous realities of death, judgment and eternity constantly moving in vivid panorama before my mental gaze. It seems to me that if I had been withheld from these influences I would certainly have drifted into the seductive whirlpools of vice and immorality which were all around me and from whose voracious powers God, in His signal mercy, so wonderfully kept me. He not only enabled me to pass over the slippery paths of my boyhood, intact and unscathed, but to economize the time in ways profitable to soul and body.

By the blessing of God, enjoying an extraordinary memory, with diligent industry and assiduous application, I was always enabled to stand at the head of the school. These statements, and others of a similar character, will probably disgust squeamish people and provoke charges of egotism. N. B. Not of my own choice, but by the constraint of the people, I am writing my biography, and must be excused for rigid adherence to candor and veracity. As to the charge of egotism which this book may provoke, I have one consolation, and that is, I am dead to egotism and everything else but God and His precious truth. Adam the first, with his egotism, pride and vanity, is already dead, therefore I am invulnerable to all criticisms, however adverse they may be.

In our schools they taught nothing but reading, spelling, writing and arithmetic, and but little of the latter, as the teacher could advance, as a rule, only through compound numbers and often stalled there, leaving us to content ourselves simply with the elementary rules. We made the spelling-book a specialty. I committed it to memory so that I could spell everything in it when given out. We would wind up the week each Friday afternoon by a spelling match, which was always a time of extraordinary interest; besides, we often had these matches at private houses at night. On the closing day of each school session they did nothing but spell by memory in the presence of the great crowds who habitually attended to witness this so-called "cross spelling," which was exceedingly magnetic to the parents of the children, and other visitors. I frequently turned down a whole school and was left standing on the floor without a competitor. It was very common for whole schools to compete either with other in this way on the last day of the session. I remember one occasion of this kind, when the school in a neighboring district had boasted that it was coming to our last day to turn us all down. They had some experts claiming to know the spelling-book by memory. When they arrived and got ready for this competition, our teacher observed to them that he would give them one little boy to represent his whole school on the competition floor. I do not think I weighed more than sixty pounds at that time. So he called out your humble servant and the "cross spelling" began. The teacher of this other school had the book and gave out where he would, beginning with his youngest pupils and taking them all somewhat in the order of their ages to the eldest, thus including his forty scholars. He began with the monosyllables, so as to suit the beginners, and the rule was that whenever the student missed a word, he or she sat down. So he went on through the whole spelling-book, and finally all of his school was turned down except one big stout young man, quite a bragadoccio, who had come making his loud boasts. Therefore when they all had gone down but him, he came to the floor with great pomposity. The teacher was then giving out the last section in the book, where the words are spelled and defined much after the order of the dictionary. He gave out to my big competitor (as we had just reached that point), "dun, to urge for money." He spelled it, "dun." Then he gave out to me, "dun, a brown color," and I spelled it "dun." Then he gave out to him, "done, performed," and he spelled it loudly and pompously, for the great listening crowd to hear, "dun." Then, without waiting for the teacher to give it to me, as I knew he would because my competitor had missed it, I spelled it "done." That wound up the spelling match between the two schools, as I had turned down every one of them; none of the balance of our school having a chance to take part in the competition. Then our teacher made capital of the matter by just telling them that he had lots of scholars like the one he had tried. The old maxim, "It is better to learn a little well, than much imperfectly," is significantly true, and corroborates Romans 8: 28: *"All things work together for good to them that love God with Divine love."*

While my teachers were utterly incompetent to instruct me in anything but rudimentary English branches, God made their incompetency a great blessing to me, by giving me time and opportunity to learn these thoroughly, which are really the basis of an English education. The foundation of a house is by far the most important part. In the prosecution of an English education, the spelling-book ought to be committed to memory, and that followed by the dictionary, with careful and patient study. Rest assured that these fundamentals are by far the most important. Deficiency in reading and writing has its remedy in mastering the spelling-book.

English grammar and geography were not taught in the schools where I was reared. If a man (for there were no women teachers) could take his students through the Single Rule of Three, he was pronounced all right; and if he could teach through the Double Rule of Three, he was regarded extraordinary. When a little fellow, I got into great trouble in the prosecution of my education for the want of competent teachers. My teacher would stall in compound numbers and tell me his head was "wool gathered" and that he had to go off to the woods to be quiet in order to work that sum. Then giving me charge of the school, he would take his hat and go to the woods. Some of the scholars would watch until he got off out of sight and keep watching for his reappearance and during his absence have a jolly time, paying no attention to me, and I, finding that I could not keep them at their books to save my life, just surrendered. After awhile he would come back and tell me that the sum had a wrong answer and I should just skip it. But he stalled so much and pronounced so many of them wrong, that I just found he could not teach me, and I thought I would return home and go to work on the farm.

Our land was not only poor, but covered by dense forests of oak (black, white and red, and hickory and chestnut), while the dogwood, sassafras, black jack, and hazel bushes, brambles and briars literally crowded the earth. Though I was but a little lad, as my growth was so slow, I was wonderfully hardy and active, so that the neighbors confessed that I did more work than the stalwart youths all around me, who were twice my size. While they had much more than the usual amount of physical strength, (for I was reared off in the hills among the giants), I more than made up by rising early and keeping at it all day and losing no time. I wonder now how it was possible for me to chop all day and never get tired. However, I piled all the brush as I went, cleaning up the ground just ready for the fire, (as we burned on the ground all the stuff except the good rail timber which we used in that way). I just lacked the physical ability to maul the rails to fence the ground, wherefore my parents hired a stalwart to do that part, but I did everything else, and when we had the neighbors come in and pile up the logs, I burned off the ground, then plowed and planted it. I used to clear from five to ten acres during a single winter between the seasons of cultivation. As I had three older sisters, and my next younger brother was always sickly, and could not help me, therefore I had all the work to do, as my father was generally out preaching or working at the carpenter's trade, and very frequently too far off to return home at night. In the cropping season he was generally at home. I cleaned up this brushy land, which required so much hard labor, and brought it into cultivation, so that we had a good living at home and everything flourishing around us. I was utterly surprised when, at the age of twenty-one, I came into the blue grass region to prosecute my education, and saw there beautiful, rich, level fields, which are so productive to the hand of industry. It was really fortunate for me, as mother and the children were dependent on me during those years, that I never saw that beautiful country till after those years of toil, during which I had taken for them a productive farm out of the thickets of black jack, dogwood, hazel bushes and saw briars. The land being encumbered with a vast amount of large timber, it was hard to work, and the soil being light, it was soon exhausted and worn out. If I had hitherto only seen the blue grass region, which gives Kentucky the reputation of an earthly paradise, and that richly deserving, I do not see how I could have commanded the patience and perseverance necessary for those arduous toils, in which I acquiesced not only patiently, but delightfully. Oh, how wonderfully God worketh all things well to them who love Him and do His will!

When I was a very small lad, about entering my teens, a debating society sprang up in our neighborhood, discussing freely all subjects of general interest for profitable pastime and erudition. I, of course, went to their meetings and heard them deliver their speeches, alternately discussing either side of the controverted question. As I listened to them, I found myself soliloquizing: "I should like to do that," and I communicated to them my desire to be a participant. There was not a solitary boy in it. The participants were local preachers, civil officers, and other mature men. They readily threw open the door for us boys, and some of us, of whom I was decidedly the smallest and youngest, proceeded to take our places among the speakers. In the schools they never had any exercises of that kind in that country, so this was my first. I was charmed with it, becoming more and more enamored and really carried away by a delightful, growing enthusiasm for the forensic discussion. As the years rolled along, all the old members dropped out, leaving us boys to make what we would of the enterprise. We continued it, holding our meetings every Saturday night, till at twenty I left home to attend a grammar school sixty miles distant. God made this forensic society a most profitable school for me during those years which elapsed after I had learned about all I could in the common schools of that country.

During that time a mathematician came into that community and opened a select school in which nothing was taught but arithmetic. Fortunately he was very thorough, seeming to have it all in his memory, so that with great readiness he was prepared to solve all the problems and elucidate them beautifully. This latter he did on the black board, which had never been used in the common schools there. The name of this adept arithmetician was Obadiah Denham, a most excellent gentleman, whom God made a great blessing to me educationally, under whose instruction I was enabled to master the arithmetic, so that I could teach it from beginning to end. With this progress in the literary course, I conceived the idea of teaching school, not only for my own proficiency and erudition, but especially in order that I might defray my expenses while prosecuting a thorough collegiate education, which was the grand desideratum of my juvenile spirit. I had realized my call to preach the Gospel from my childhood, but, knowing my incompetency, was deeply humiliated at the thought of the undertaking, and therefore I was anxious for every auxiliary aid. For that reason I put out to hunt me a school to teach, but I everywhere met nothing but refusal and rebuff. They said that they knew that I was educationally more competent than any of the teachers who had served them, but that I just possibly could not make the children mind me. In that country teachers were all mature men, and generally old. They thought the management of children the most important consideration and that they would not mind a young person. In my case, although I was twenty years old, I only weighed ninety-tree pounds and had no more beard than a little lassie and my face was rosy like that of a child. Therefore they everywhere rejected me outright. So all the schools about the country had begun and I was left out. Ere long I found an empty schoolhouse, made inquiry for the trustees and waited on them. They responded, like all the balance, that I could not manage the children, because I looked just like a child myself. Then I asked them, as the house was empty, to let me just begin on my own responsibility, relieving them of all obligation to pay or help in any way. To this they consented, therefore gathering up a few poor children I began. So successful was the work that the news went out and students began to come in from all directions, and so continued until I not only had all I could teach, but found it necessary to employ an assistant. When I wound up, the trustees came and employed me to teach their school the ensuing year. After that I never in my life had any more trouble to get a school, but applications crowded on me, more than I knew what to do with. You can appropriate this to yourself, as it clearly illustrates the possibility of your success on the same line. My collegiate education occupied six years and cost me one thousand dollars, every cent of which I made by teaching. As I looked like a little boy those times, my weight not exceeding one hundred pounds, I realized the necessity of paying for my education by mental rather than manual labor, as the latter in that country generally demanded so much more physical strength than I commanded.

Following that educational trend, I have somewhat neglected the spiritual in this biographical narrative. I had been brought into the Church in my infancy by the dedication of baptism, and, as I believe, really converted at the age of about three years, although afterward inadvertently, through childish weakness, lapsing and getting restored a time or two. This restoration was not by any special ministerial effort, as all the preachers and Christians in those days thought children had to wait until adultage before they could be converted to God. Even though I had become a confirmed backslider, though keeping the moral law diligently and living above criticism in a religious sense, yet every stirring sermon, especially those I heard my father and other Methodist and Baptist preachers give, as well as every funeral, powerfully renewed my convictions, keeping me in the attitude of a chronic mourner, day and night praying God to have mercy and save me.

In His good providence, at the age of sixteen, the Saturday night before the fourth Sunday in November, 1849, (if I am not mistaken as to the date), I heard that the

Baptists were having a glorious revival, which was quite a novelty among them, as this was the first that I recollect in that neighborhood. So I hastened away to their meeting. On arrival I found the house packed and even crammed. When I entered the door conviction struck me like a cyclone. It was in every word sung, prayed and preached. The preacher was a very ordinary, unlearned man but the Holy Ghost had him in hand and he preached with all the Pentecostal power and fire which I can conceive of their having on that great and notable day when the Holy Ghost first fell on them at Jerusalem. By the time he wound up, all of my cables were severed, my hold on the willows broken and I was ready for any and every possible Godward move. He threw the altar open and it was quickly crowded, your humble servant going forward. While there were several bright, old-style conversions (and among them my cousin, John Bishop, above mentioned, swept into the kingdom with shouts), yet my burden was a mountain dragging me down to the bottomless pit heavier than ever before. About eleven o'clock, on adjournment, the preacher told his brethren to take all the mourners home with them and keep them through the night and bring them back lest they might be caught by the tempter, fall by the way and never reach the kingdom, which he assured them they were fast nearing.

A good Baptist brother came, put his arms around me and said, "Boy, my house is your home till you get religion." I was a cheap boarder, for I did not eat a bite or sleep a wink, but spent an awful, sleepless night expecting every moment to drop into Hell I never in my life was so glad to see the day dawn as when it came peering in through the clapboard roof of that log-house up in whose garret I was bedded. I arose and dressed, ate nothing, but went to meeting, finding the house packed and jammed with women, and the men all out-of-doors, except a few saints who crowded in the nooks and corners. Therefore in my natural timidity I declined to make an effort to squeeze in. Outside they were talking everywhere, and their silly, foolish jesting, mingled with ribaldry, obscenity and profanity, grieved my soul so terrifically that I was constrained to run away, as I found their society absolutely intolerable. I fled to the woods and wandered on through the primeval forest, that mountain getting heavier incessantly, till I fell beneath my burden, which I could no longer bear. There protrate on the ground, crying to God, soliloquies raced through my mind: "Is it possible that after my baptism in my infancy and my good moral life, which I have lived from the cradle, yet Hell is my doom?" The real trouble with me was self-righteousness; I was unconsciously depending on my good works, church membership, preaching father and sainted mother, and the praying Christians to save me. Here I reached a crisis and a culmination. A panorama passed before me, in which I saw all of those Godly people pass away. The soliloquy came back, my hopes all fled and my doom was sealed. So I reached the point where Calvinistic theology very beautifully says, "Our justification supervenes, *i. e.*, when we utterly surrender all of our own resources and confess judgment against ourselves." Thus my soliloquy proceeded: "O God, I am a wretched, lost sinner, all my works of righteoussnes are filthy rags, loathsome and stenchy in Thy sight; and if Thou dost leave me to drop into Hell, it is all right. I never did deserve anything else." At that moment I reached an epoch which

I never can forget. That mountain burden rolled away and I found myself leaping for joy.

"Hard was my toil to reach the shore,
  Long tossed upon the ocean;
Above me was the thunder's roar,
  Beneath the wave's commotion.

"Panting and fainting as for breath,
  I knew not help was nigh me,
I cried, Oh, save my soul from death,
  Immortal Jesus, saves me!

"Then quick as thought I felt Him mine,
  My Savior stood before me;
I saw His brightness round me shine,
  And shouted Glory! Glory!

"Oh, hallowed spot, oh, sacred hour,
  When love Divine first found me;
Wherever falls my distant lot,
  My soul shall linger round thee.

"And when I rise from the vile world
  Up to my home in Heaven,
Down will I cast mine eyes once more,
  Where I was first forgiven."

That wood was soon afterward cleared up and turned into a corn-field, but my heart, in all my wanderings these fifty-seven years, three times travelling in Europe, Asia, and Africa, and once around the world, has ever turned back to that hallowed spot, dearest to me in all the earth. I verily expect to remember it through all eternity. There the battle of long and weary years between faith and doubt, grace and sin, Christ and Satan, Heaven and Hell, culminated in glorious victory for my poor soul.

I was converted in the Baptist meeting, where nothing was said about sanctification. Indeed, the Methodists at that time were silent on it. My conversion was clearly witnessed to by the blessed Holy Spirit, who gave me power in public prayer to the delight and astonishment of the people, who shouted the praises of God for the blessings which descended on them during my prayers; meanwhile I was faithful in duty and always ready to give a reason for the hope that was within me, with meekness and fear. But I soon found an aching void within which the world could never fill. Painfully realizing that I needed something more to satisfy my longing soul, I talked to preachers and pilgrims, who told me not to be discouraged, because it was the inward conflict which they all had, and that I must endure it during this life.

Reading the old Methodist books, I found much on sanctification as a second work of grace, but in the absence of a teacher or even a witness to it, I did not know how to seek it. Our country was all flooded with water religion, preached by the Campbellites everywhere, who make it a condition of pardon and salvation. As they constantly fought experimental religion, which I knew to be true, because I had it, I had no inclination to fall in with them; but the Baptist brethren, with whom I got converted, practiced immersion, and among all there was so much said about it, that I, being ignorant and deeply solicitous to be right, and knowing I needed something, therefore came to the conclusion that the thing for me to do was to be immersed. Consequently I called on a Methodist preacher to favor me with the ordinance. I found him very unwilling and disposed to argue me out of it. I told him it was not worth while to spend time over it, because I had made up my mind to receive it. My father was a preacher and he was satisfied I would be. Therefore, loathe to give up the Methodist preacher, as he felt sure I would go to the Baptists, he consented to accommodate me, giving me the time and place when he was going to immerse some people, and charging me to tell no one, but to come along and fall in with the candidates and he would wait on me along with the balance. At that time the Methodist preacher had conscientious scruples about rebaptizing people; they are not so particular now. Consequently I came at the time appointed and he immersed me with the others. I received it in good faith, hoping that it would supply the deficiency which I realized in my experience, but in this I was mistaken; I soon found the same aching void within.

Four years from that time I began to preach in the Methodist Church, and have been at it these fifty-three years. I preached fifteen years under a woe, feeling, "Woe is unto me if I preach not the Gospel." Nineteen years after my conversion, in December, 1868, the Lord gloriously sanctified me, giving me that wonderful satisfying portion which I sought in immersion and a thousand other ways, but finally found when I gave up everything else and took Jesus for everything in time and in eternity. I have always been very grateful to Brother William Johns, my neighbor boy about ten years my senior, for immersing me at my request. I have always been glad that under the circumstances I did satisfy my own conscience, doing the best I could. I took it for the full satisfaction of my longing soul, which is but another name for sanctification, but found to my sorrow that it could not do it.

In the preceding paragraph I made allusion to our forensic club, with which I identified myself when a small lad. During the seven years which transpired after I had learned about all I could in the common schools of that country, as above mentioned, God, in His providence, sent that able mathematician into our community, who taught nothing else, making such a specialty that I fell in with him and enjoyed the full benefit of his instructions. I reached a state of proficiency which qualified me to teach the arithmetic through and through, but I had never been to a grammar school, nor to a place where I could study any of the collegiate course. I spent these intervening years cleaning up my father's farm, which had all been worn out (as the soil in that country is so very light, except the woodlands), and getting the family in really comfortable temporal environments.

All this time I was sticking close to my debating society, which we held in school-houses responsive to the people, who were constantly calling for it. When the old members dropped out, soon after I entered it, I am sure that it owed its perpetuity to my humble instrumentality. The retirement of those local preachers and civil officers who launched it, was much in favor of us boys, as it gave us all the time. I was only able to hold three of the boys permanently identified with it. Therefore we four constituted two couplets, as we paired off every Saturday evening on the controversy floor. Two of them, as a rule, spoke but a few minutes, leaving the bulk of the time for the other one and your humble servant, who generally spoke from thirty to fifty minutes, our subjects involving historic research. Therefore we were constantly reading history in order to prepare for those discussions, and of course this was the very thing for our edification. In my youth I was a great night student, competent to get along with much less sleep than now. During those years I worked hard all day and read until midnight, often by firelight, as we were poor, and in that way, improvidently and inadvertently damaged the good eyes which God gave me, which never knew any flicker till I had passed my twentieth year. Having been a good reader from the age of six, during those seven years of my toiling farm life I was a constant reader of history, acquiring the knowledge which I utilized in my weekly speeches in our forensic club. I would study all the week preparing myself to discuss some question which required information, and would therefore superinduce the investigation of history.

In our speeches we constantly utilized the blessed Word of God, as its moral precepts were always pertinent, and when arranging the field of history, we constantly appealed to the Bible whose sacred testimony appertaining to the issues involved was always unimpeachable. Therefore our historic argument included the sacred as well as the secular; consequently our duties in the club kept us incessantly reading the Bible as well as secular history.

This was a most important period in my life; as the manual labor developed my muscles and gave me an iron constitution, which has been infinitely valuable to me during these fifty-three years of constant preaching and teaching. We four regular speakers frequently found our number augmented by others who incidentally came in and were willing to take part in the discussion, a privilege which we always granted. The people gave us splendid crowds during those whole seven years and listened with untiring appreciation. We generally began by six or seven and always held on till eleven or twelve o'clock. To me it was an oratorical school of infinite value, giving me colloquial discipline, which has accompanied me through life, rendering me always ready for extemporaneous speaking. Vast quantities of the information, especially historic, which appears in my writings, I received during those years of hard toil, while following the plow amid roots and rocks all day and reading about half of the ensuing night. Digesting it as I revolved it over and over in my mind the ensuing day, while holding the plow handles or wielding the ax or hoe, I was getting it all into shape so as to spread out before the people an intellectual feast the ensuing Saturday evening.

N. B. *"All things work together for good to them that love God with Divine love."* This includes the failure and feebleness of my eyes. The first flicker of my eyes occurred at twenty-one. Then I had my collegiate education before me, which of course demanded vast ocular labor. During its entire prosecution, for the lack of eye power, I would have to content myself with a single reading of the lesson, looking on the book and taking it into my mind, then looking away, fixing it in my memory and resting the eyes. But when I came into the recitation room, I always knew the lesson, while other young men told me they read it over a dozen times and then failed in the recitation. The failure in my eyes superinduced the necessity of substituting memory for eye power; which is the very thing to develop the memory in largest capacity.

I was so fond of reading, even from my early childhood, that, if my eyes had not failed, I certainly would have become an insatiable bookworm, and have spent my life taking in without giving out. This is a dangerous attitude. The Dead Sea takes in the River Jordan and other waters, but gives out not a drop. If you would not become a Dead Sea, you had better be a faithful dispenser of physical benefaction, intellectual erudition and spiritual pabulum, to all you meet in this probationary pilgrimage. This is my forty-eighth book. These books have gone out to the number of two hundred thousand copies and millions are feeding on them. If my eyes had enabled me to read other people's book *ad libitum*, I do not believe I ever would have been a book writer. The truth of the matter is, I do not write the books of my authorship, could not for the want of eye power. I dictate them all to amanuenses. I have no doubt but that I have actually done vastly more good in the world with these enfeebled eyes than in case they had remained strong and penetrating, like those of the eagle centered upon the noonday sun, whither he wings his upward flight.

Let me exhort you to sink so profoundly into the sweet will of God that you will hail all of His permissive providences as blessings, even though they may be so disguised that uncircumcised eyes will mistake them for curses. I hope your faith is so athletic and doubtless that you actually see God in everything. Rest assured, if you are really lost in His will He will make your darkest adversities your brightest sunbursts. The axiom of Jesus during His ministry was, *"Be it unto you according to your faith;"* therefore when the darkest clouds envelop your sky, remember their upper side in which the sun is shining is white as snow. The truth of the matter is that neither men nor devils can do anything to God's people without permission, and that permission transforms the most terrible calamities into blessings. My life work is in the use of the eye; my greatest physical ailment in my whole life has been this ocular feebleness and failure. Yet when I see how God took me from wearing out my brain reading other people's books to the glorious privilege of dictating all of these books for others to read—an honor and benediction of which I never dreamed—oh, what unspeakable goodness and mercy were thus bestowed on unworthy me!

Chapter III.

YOUTH.

In the preceding chapter you see how God, through my indefatigable perseverance, gave me my first school to teach at the age of twenty, when I only weighed ninety-three pounds and looked like a little boy, so very juvenile, and beardless as a lassie. After the first school, I never had any trouble to get employment whenever I wanted it, and commanded splendid wages. Having taught my first school at the age of twenty, then I wanted to go away to a grammar school and learn English grammar, of which I was utterly ignorant. But as it was universally customary in that country for the boys to work for their parents till they were twenty-one, when they reached majority and received their freedom, I was actually too conscientious to cheat my parents. I was not twenty-one till the third day of the following June, therefore I sold my horse which I had raised on the farm, or rather which my father had given me, for ninety dollars and hired a stout young man to take my place on my father's farm till the day of my majority. This gave me four months to attend the grammar school, where I made grammar my specialty, devoting all of my time to the study of it, and actually mastered it, so that I could teach it and never did recite it any more. Having reached majority and become my own man, according to the civil law, I never again returned to labor on my father's farm, but devoted all of my time to teaching and attending college. God gave me wonderful physical hardihood, and I was an untiring, assiduous student, the teachers in every school certifying that I accomplished more in the time than any other young man they ever knew.

At the age of twenty-one I entered upon the study of Latin and Greek. I carried my books with me everywhere I went and committed them to memory so I could recite them from beginning to end. Though I was then a preacher, I was not sanctified, and had a Napoleonic ambition. One day when we recited our Latin, the teacher assigned us one-half of the conjugation of the active verb "amo" for a lesson, at the same time observing that when he was a student he took a whole verb for a lesson. I spoke out, "I can learn as big a lesson as you or any other man." Then he assigned us the whole conjugation to commit to memory. When the recitation rolled round the next day, I knew every word of it, while all the balance of the class so failed that he reassigned it to them for the next day. We had been studying for about four or five months, when he took me out of the class of beginners and put me in the next highest class, which had studied it one year before I got there. It was not long before I stood at the head of that class. I did not progress so rapidly in Greek, owing to the fact that the teacher, while quite proficient in Latin, was not so thorough in Greek. It was not long until I left that college and went to another, at Georgetown, Ky., which was old and very thorough. I spent six years in the prosecution of my collegiate education, taking the entire regular classical course, finally graduating June 30, 1859, and receiving my Latin diploma. It cost me one thousand dollars, every cent of which, in the providence of God, I made by teaching, as my dear father and mother were not able to give me any financial help.

On our graduating day, when we twenty young men delivered our orations and received our diplomas, six of us were preachers and, sad to say, about six drunkards, and the other eight gentlemen of correct lives. During those six years I saw many young men go out from college, not only without salvation, but on the slippery steeps of dissipation which precipitate their incumbents into the bottomless pit. I have been praising the Lord all my life for a father and mother who were too poor to give me money on which to dissipate. The greatest intellectualist in our class, a younger man than myself, has already gone to a drunkard's grave, leaving the world as he lived, utterly regardless of God. If my parents had been rich, I, like my classmates and college chums, would have been exposed to those awful temptations which plunged them in ruin and, as we fear, eternally. Oh, what a mistake Christian parents make to pile up money for their children when they are so likely to use it to pay their way to Hell! What a glory if they had only given that money to evangelize one thousand millions of poor heathens through the ages sitting in darkness and in the shadow of death. I do believe that I will praise God forever in Heaven for giving me parents who never had one dollar to give me to defray my expenses to Hell. But they did give me a patrimony which outshines all the gold that ever glittered, and all the diamonds that ever sparkled, and all the rubies that ever radiated. That inheritance is God's precious Word and the testimony of His glorious redeeming grace in their own hearts; and an humble Christian home, where God was feared, loved, and obeyed. Well does Solomon say, "Wisdom is better than riches."

I much regret the deprivation of a classical education which has supervened in the last forty years. The proportion of students in colleges now prosecuting the regular classical course is much smaller than it was during the years of my college life. This is in harmony with the general trend of the age to superficialism, which is manifest in every department of practical life at the present day; *e. g.*, in architectural, for while the buildings of all sorts are vastly more fastidious, showy, and ornamental, they are lamentably deficient in solidity, substantiality, and durability. This you will observe in every ramification of the arch. We are constantly constrained to deplore this tendency in the spiritual realm, where we observe it most obvious and significant throughout, *i. e.*, superficial conviction, unsubstantial conversions and unsatisfactory sanctifications; superficial professions all along the line of evangelistic work.

Especially do we observe this superficialism in the educational realm. Learning in all departments has caught the impatient fugitive spirit of the age, dashing through with all possible expedition, rushing to a superficial graduation, reaching the end prematurely and going out into the world professionally ready for business, when the diploma is but a farce and a burlesque. The old style four years' course, Freshman, Sophomore, Junior and Senior classes, which had long prevailed in all the regular colleges, is about given up and superseded by irregular classification, in view of expediting the graduation. It is high time for us to halt and heed the apostle James, *"Let patience have her perfect work."*

We hear them say, "I must finish my education, get out preaching, or off into my missionary field." There is *always* a wide open door for all to preach who will while they are prosecuting their education. Here we have great Cincinnati, with her suburban cities, comprising half a million people, open wide for evangelistic work, and you find it so everywhere; therefore there is no apology for losing time in response to your call to preach. If you ever succeed in this life, you must learn the great problem of harmonizing perpetual study with incessant labor, in the field of disinterested philanthropy to which you are called. The most blessed collegiate education you will ever receive, instead of winding up your student life only begins it, thus qualifying you to dispense with the constant help and guidance of teachers, paddle your own canoe across the stormy river of probationary life and secure a safe landing on the golden shore of a glorious immortality. If you are ever a success in any department of intellectual labor, you must be a student all your life, surviving the migratory abstractions of transitory allurements and reaching that concentration of mentality which will make you an incessant student.

(1) You need a classical education to qualify you to successfully study the blessed Bible. This is obvious from the fact that it was never written in your vernacular nor that of any other person now loving on the earth, but in the Hebrew and Greek, which are now dead languages. God, in His providence, after the Scriptures were written in those beautiful and learned languages, took them out of the world, so that people could not corrupt them, as they do every spoken language. But we have this grand *thesaurus* of God's precious truth revealed for the salvation of a lost world, to which we

can go and drink of the water of life, limpid and pure, as it leaps from the fountain, gushing out beneath the throne of God. You can never drink at these fountains unless you learn those original languages; but you will be dependent on translators. That is all right as far as salvation is concerned. If we drink from the bucket which the translators carried from the fountain, we will never die of thirst, yet, for a thousand reasons I have not space here to mention, we should much prefer to drink at the fountain itself.

(2) We need the Latin and the Greek languages to qualify us to understand the English, four-fifths of which are taken from those languages. In our great, beautiful, versatile and voluminous Anglo-Saxon tongue we have only twenty-three thousand Saxon words, which constitute the nucleus of the great language, comprising the vast vocabulary of a hundred and fifty thousand words, and that vocabulary rapidly increasing. I have no doubt but that the English language which is so rapidly spreading over the whole earth and is now the popular language of the world, so that other nations want their children to learn it, will be the language of the world during the glorious Millennium, whose rising aurora now thrills the hearts of many waiting and longing pilgrims. You never can be very proficient in the great English language without a thorough study of Latin and Greek.

The Alexandrian conquest, B. C. 325, put the Greek language in all the governments under heaven; therefore it was universal in the days of Christ and His apostles. The Roman conquest did the same for the Latin language three hundred years subsequently. Consequently not only the English, but all other languages in present use are so largely taken from those tongues that we need those fundamental languages preparatory to the study of all the modern. A Greek and Latin scholar will learn any of the languages in India much more easily and quickly than the people who have not received a classical education. If you desire thoroughness in any other language, the quickest and surest route is through the meandering halls of classical lore.

(3) We need the Latin and Greek to qualify us for real proficiency in the sciences, all of which we have to study in the nomenclature of these languages. We never can be learned in any sense without studying the sciences, all of which require us constantly to use the dead languages which will be so difficult to learn and retain in the memory in case we have never studied them. For example, zoology, which teaches us all about the animal kingdom, is from *zoon,* an animal, and *logos,* science; therefore it means the science of animals. Astronomy is from *astron,* a star, and *nomos,* law; therefore it means the law of the stars. Whereas the sciences are all expounded in the Greek language, the great bulk of words used in public orations and written dissertations are from the Latin. If you would master languages so as to have command of words and easy fluency of speech, it is really indispensable that you study the Latin and Greek, which constitute the boundless *thesaurus* and illimitable vocabulary of universal language.

(4) We are living in by far the most literary age the world has ever known. During the by-gone ages you could count on your fingers the prominent authors of all nations. Now they are rapidly becoming an innumerable host, flooding the world with literature. It is certainly a glorious privilege to participate in the prevailing aspir-

ation to large usefulness. The study of the Latin and Greek, and actual proficiency in the same, is really indispensable to qualification for efficient authorship.

But you may raise the question of financial inability to acquire these languages. This is really imaginary on your part. That is a circumstance in your favor and not against you. If you had plenty of money it would be difficult for you to resist the temptation to luxuriate and prodigalize; if not to actually fall by dissipation and even debauchery, thus withering and blighting all your hopes of scholarship and usefulness. Read the biographies of the great scholars and you will find they all had to contend with meagre finances, if not actual pauperism, from the beginning of their educational course. I was a student twenty-one years, and a constant witness of these phenomena, *i. e.*, the failure and often the wreckage of the rich students, and the brilliant achievements and college honors conferred upon the poor. So rejoice in your poverty and thank God for thus, in His providence, fortifying you against the temptations which on all sides engulf the rich in ruin both for time and eternity. You cannot go through college without money, but God will attend to it if you will be true. Do not understand me to encourage you to beg your way through. That will never do. If you start on that line, you are ruined before you begin. David says, "I have never seen the righteous forsaken, nor his seed begging bread." You must hold your head up and let all the world know that you are no beggar, but God's millionaire, rich in faith, though not a dollar be in your pocket.

By the help of God, I made and paid every cent of my collegiate expenses by my own exertions. God raised up friends in the strange lands whither I sojourned during those six years, as I was under the necessity of leaving the circle of my consanguinity and acquaintance and going among people who knew neither me nor my ancestors. Among those friends, the most prominent was Adison Parks, of Perryville, Ky., who put his hand on me and took an especial interest in my education, loaning me money, indulging me for clothing and giving me employment as a teacher. This good man did not wait for me to ask him to loan me money, but he would ask me. I remember the year I graduated in college, he handed me a fifty dollar bill, observing, "I expect you will need this before you graduate." I told him I did, but observed: "Brother Parks, I already owe you a lot of money, and do not like to take this, as I am afraid I will die, and then you will never get it, for there is nobody to pay it for me." He responded: "You take it and rest easy about it. If you live, I know you will pay it back; and if you die, please just count it paid, as I would be so glad to help you with the full amount that you owe me." God let me live to pay him and everybody else the five hundred dollars which I owed for my education. When I graduated I was not worth five cents. The churches, Methodist, Presbyterian, and Campbellite, all proposed to educate me gratuitously, but I declined; I knew that in that case they would feel I belonged to them. I was determined to be free and belong to none but God. I shall always praise God for His signal mercy in delivering me in times and ways past my space to enumerate.

When I was toiling hard for an education amid the embarrassments of financial destitution, the Campbellites proposed to send me to their great college at Lexington, Ky., and carry me through the entire curriculum at their own expense. They said: "Then if you will preach for us, we will make you rich." Oh, what a temptation for a penniless boy! It thrilled me with a burning enthusiasm for a thorough collegiate education. It is a wonder I did not get caught in that dangerous lasso. If I had received their education and become their preacher,—how awful to think!—I would have preached my own way to Hell! The preacher's Hell is the hottest and most terrible of all, with the people deceived and ruined by false doctrine, forever anathematizing him as the cause of their hopeless ruin. It grieves me to see some of our dear holiness people assuming a beggarly attitude, which dishonors God, grieves the Holy Spirit, and conduces to their own spiritual leanness, as well as to the delusion of others. God's people are not beggars, but kings and priests. The ink was on the pen to make the title to property in Indiana, said to be worth four thousand dollars. I utterly declined it, and have always been glad of it. The same thing occurred in Texas, which I also declined. It was again repeated in the state of Washington, but, by the grace of God, I was enabled to decline it. Satan is very adroit and ready to use our friends as well as our enemies to tie us up and encumber us, and, if possible, utilize against our full efficiencies for God and souls.

During my collegiate course I alternated the attitude of student and teacher.. In 1857, while in Georgetown College, when the time arrived for me to leave and go to Perryville, I was engaged to teach the public school, which occupied the vacations of the graded schools in the town and precisely suited my convenience, as I wished to lose as little time as possible out of the ensuing college session. I had taught that same school the preceding year at the same time. I just had thirty dollars yet coming to me from my wages the preceding year, and aimed to stay in college only long enough to consume the money I could command. But somehow that time I made a mistake, though I was generally very particular. When I hunted up everything I owed preparatory to settlement before leaving, I found it would take sixty dollars instead of thirty to clear me of debt and carry me to Perryville. I got into serious trouble over it, as I was very unwilling to leave there in debt, as students often did to their deep disgrace. I took it to the Lord in prayer and told Him that I was there, understood as a ministerial student, and had promised them all to pay them before I left, and I feared that my delinquency would damage the interest of His kingdom in that place, as I had been preaching and testifying boldly. I was really in deep trouble and cried to Him with a broken heart. He comforted me, taking all my burdens away, drying up my tears and making my heart glad, yet I could not explain it. I was looking for a letter bringing me the thirty dollars. It came and, to my unutterable surprise, contained sixty dollars. When I opened it and read the bills, I could hardly believe my eyes. Gushing tears of gratitude and surprise flooded my eyes till I could not read the bills. I went around and paid my debts, bidding the people adieu, and mounting the stage, as that was the day before railroads were in that country, I hastened to Perryville. I went at once to see old Dr. Polk, a very venerable local Methodist preacher, who was president of the Board of Trustees. I asked him: "Why did you send me sixty dollars, when you only owed me thirty?" He responded: "When we drew the public money, it amounted to thirty dollars more than we expected, and I felt that we ought to send it all to you, so I went around and asked the patrons what they thought about it. They, without a single exception, responded: 'Of course, send it all to him, for he deserves it; that boy taught us the best school we ever had in town; he labored from sunrise to sunset, as he had so many scholars, in order to give them all due attention.'" The explanation of that is easy and simple. Who ever heard of people overpaying a teacher thirty dollars? God touched the hearts of those stingy Kentuckians to sympathize with the boy, so that they responded unanimously and sent him all the money.

At that time the "woman's rights" problem was only beginning to receive a little attention. I am glad it has subsequently reached a glorious victory. Then, as you see in my case abundantly verified, a boy could prosecute a thorough classical education by simply alternating student and teacher, as he had no trouble to get a place as a teacher, while it was not at all common for girls to teach the public schools. It is very gratifying now to recognize facilities quite as available in behalf of girls as boys, and therefore there is no reason whatever why all the young people who desire a thorough collegiate education may not receive it. The reason why the expenses had better be defrayed by teaching is because it will facilitate the education about as rapidly as if you were enjoying all the opportunities of a student in college. I taught Latin and Greek, and everything else which I was studying in college, whenever I was out in the public schools laboring to defray my educational expenses. I actually graduated as if I had not stopped to teach, because so assiduously did I study while teaching that I never fell behind my classes. N. B. I only taught enough while going through to make five hundred dollars of my expenses, as friends willingly and gladly loaned me the other five hundred; which God enabled me to pay after I had completed my education. The day of my graduation, I was offered a hundred dollars a month for teaching.

During all of my collegiate life I preached also. The colored people, who constituted about half the population, were in slavery and consequently had very little preaching. When I went to Georgetown I soon found the colored Methodists, Baptists and Presbyterians all had separate church buildings. This was really necessary, as they were not encouraged to attend the white churches. As that was a Baptist College, and there was quite a host of preachers attending, but all members of that denomination except your humble servant, when I went with a Baptist preacher to preach for the slaves in the Methodist Church, and he introduced me to them as a Methodist preacher, they were surprised and shouted over it and asked me to preach for them. It soon happened, from the fortuitous circumstances of my being the only Methodist preacher in college, that I had the complete monopoly of the Methodist colored church. This I much enjoyed. They always gave me a packed audience, and we had rousing times. Oh, how the old style shouts invariably roared through the house, when the Spirit fell on the people toward the winding up of the service, reminding me of Gabriel's trumpet. I can never forget their singing. Of course they had no books to bother them, as none could read. It is a conceded fact that the children of Ham excel all of their consanguinity in musical talents. I have never known a negro who could not sing. Though none of their race had learning, there were natural poets among them who made their songs and they all committed them to memory. Oh, how delighted I would be to hear those songs now! In my humble appreciation, the learning which has come to those people since their emancipation has damaged their singing. They can now all read. Therefore they use books like white people and have given up their old songs which were so delectable to my soul. They knew many of these songs and could sing all night. I sometimes was taken to task by their masters for keeping them out so late in the night. We would have the altar crowded and piled with mourners seeking the Lord, and they held on till the small hours of the morning were coming and going, singing and praying and shouting over the mourners to get them through. Of course I could not use authority any more than to pronounce the benediction in due time, then leave them in the hands of God. I give you a little specimen of their songs, of which they had an ample supply so that I never knew them to run out. Of course, in the absence of all learning, they would be characteristic of repetition.

"Joseph had a vision;
The sun and moon and eleven stars
Fell down in obedience to him.

CHORUS:

"Shine, shine, shine like a star
Around the throne of God.

"His brothers' wrath was kindled,
They sold him to the Ishmaelites
And carried him into Egypt.

"They brought him unto Pharaoh
And there was laid the cornerstone
On which to build salvation."

Perhaps you would like another:

"Some say that John was a Baptist,
  And others say he was a Jew;
But the Holy Scriptures teach
  That John was a preacher, too.

CHORUS:

"Let us cheer the weary traveler
Along the heavenly road.

"I took my Gospel trumpet,
  And I began to blow,
And if the Lord will help me
  I'll blow where'er I go."

N. B. If you have a classical education, you can always get employment. So ample will be your resources that, while others are out of work, you will always have more than you can do. My age would now rank me as a superannuated preacher, my work done and without a job, whereas I actually have open doors for a thousand men. My son and son-in-law both beg me hard to quit work and let them take care of me. While I would be much delighted to remain at home and comfort my dear companion, who, like myself, is in life's evening, it seems that I cannot possibly get the time. I am doing more work than the young men. This would not be so significantly true if I had not, amid difficulties, to others insuperable, persevered through my classical course. Therefore I advise all, while you are at it, to lay a good foundation. The difficulties which intimidate you will prove only to be the wheels of the engine that propels you. The apparent adversities are all blessings in disguise. Oh, you plead intellectual deficiency and incompetency of memory. Memory, as well as all the intellectual faculties, is wonderfully susceptible of cultivation. It is certified that Dr. Adam Clarke was pronounced the "gump" of his class and ridiculed for his stupidity, yet he actually became the greatest scholar in the world in his day. It is said that Daniel Webster when he graduated from college and received his diploma had to hear the painful *ipse dixit* of the president, "Here, take it, Dan; but you do not deserve it." This awful public rebuke aroused the gigantic ambition of that hitherto somewhat dormant intellect. Then Dan threw it down on the floor and would not have it, turned on his heel and went back into college, and going through the second time, carried everything before him, putting into eclipse all of his comrades and graduating again with the first honors of his class, and going out to take his place at the front of American statesmanship. It is said that while studying law under a venerable Jewish counsellor, he one day in recitation observed that there were so many lawyers he feared that he could not get a place to practice. His hoary-headed preceptor gravely responded: "Dan, there is plenty of room at the top." He took him at his word and went to the top and found plenty of room. While going through your education, you think the time long; after you get through it will soon get to looking short. I find young people disposed to hurry through their education and hasten away to the heathen field. The great trouble is that when you get there, there is quite a probability that you will be sorry you did not prosecute your education more thoroughly before you came, thus reaching a better state of qualification for your work. Oh, but you say: "The heathen are going to Hell." That is true, but you do not have to go to the dark Orient to find them; they are at your door. If you cannot be useful in saving the heathen of your home city or town, set it down you will also prove a failure in Hong Kong. Mark it down, "Where there is a will, there is a way." Do not forget the old Roman motto: *"Perseverantia omnia vincit."* Perseverance conquers all things.

Chapter IV.

YOUNG MANHOOD.

Our graduating day, June 30, 1859, was a great orationary epoch in my life. An audience of ten thousand, and twenty young men delivering their graduating orations to the spellbound multitude, interspersed with the finest music the country could produce; meanwhile bouquettes rained from the audience at the close of the speeches, congratulatory of the orator.

My wedlock was felicitous in the superlative degree. It has always seemed to me that God, in His mercy, ransacked creation when He selected a helpmeet for unworthy me. When I was a youth attending school at Perryville, a great revival swept through the Methodist Church, converting one hundred and seven souls. I was then a preacher in my humble way; especially doing my utmost to glorify God in the dispensation of the Gospel to the toiling slaves, who were much neglected. While the house was over-crowded and the altar flooded with weeping penitents, the leader called on me to pray. The Lord helped me, and as the converting power descended, a rosy damsel of fifteen bright years arose near me with a radiant face and jubilant shout. I was not personally acquainted with her, although I knew her father, who was a leading member of the church. I saw him rush in and take this rejoicing damsel in his arms. One near me said: "One of Jim Durham's girls has got religion." In the providence of God, five and a-half years subsequently she became my wife. Forty-six years have rolled away. If we both live four years more we will reach our golden wedding. But this is certainly very improbable, as we are both quite out in the evening and she, although six and a-half years my junior, has felt the burden of the conflict more than I, and much indicates physical disability. We have one consolation: if we do not reach our golden wedding in the dear "old Kentucky home," we will have it in the New Jerusalem, where there is plenty of gold, and the nuptial festival will never hear the final benediction.

We entered into our engagement two years before the time appointed for its verification. I still had a year in college. Then I knew I would graduate deeply in debt, and I was not willing to get married until that was all liquidated. Those are two memorable years in my pilgrimage. As I was studying and teaching off at a considerable distance, I visited her but seldom during the time. I invariably found other suitors waiting on her. It kept me in hot water. I thought she ought to dismiss them all, in view of her engagement to me, but was afraid to suggest it, lest she might think I was too particular, and conclude to eliminate me instead of them. Therefore I said nothing about it to her or to anybody else, but kept it before the Lord, wondering if she would finally be true to the engagement she had made with me. Sure enough the happy day rolled around, when we met the crowd at her father's house, with the presiding elder ready to officiate. Those beaux who had given me so much annoyance the preceding two years were also on hand, but they looked blue as indigo and sad as if they were at a funeral. I never saw them afterward. The solemnization of the nuptials eliminated them forever.

Here we see a beautiful lesson illustrated in the gracious economy. Until you get married to the Lord the carnal suitors, arrayed in all the alluring phantasmagoria of the world, will wait on you, to your constant annoyance if you are true to God, as well as your incessant peril, because in an evil hour you may succumb to their bewitching enchantments and enter into wedlock with one of them, which will seal your doom in endless woe.

Immediately after my graduation I became president of a college, and having on hands the entire collegiate course, classical and scientific, through which I had passed as a student of the curriculum, I enjoyed a grand opportunity to review the books and explain them to the classes, thus even making it more profitable than the post-graduate course, which is the frequent resort of collegiate graduates for their establishment before their newly accumulated learning will evanesce. Our school was a booming success; meanwhile the people also seemed delighted and much edified by my preaching.

The great Civil War broke out only one year after our marriage. A terrible battle, the most bloody and magnitudinous in Kentucky during the entire war, was fought at Perryville, and, of course, superinduced the utter abandonment of our college, the dispersion of all the people identified with it, and the occupancy of the building as a Union hospital. Very soon I responded to a call at Russellville, Ind., whither we migrated, transferring Harmonia College. Many of the students followed us thither. There we labored at teaching and preaching till the war was over, and, responsive to the earnest desire of my dear wife, who had become homesick, we returned to Perryville and there re-opened Harmonia College. During the eighteen years of my life as a teacher God signally honored my labors. He permitted me to see much encouraging fruit meanwhile, whereby my heart has been cheered in all of my subsequent pilgrimage. Meeting my students I find many of them efficient preachers of the Gospel, and pillars in the Church of God.

Such was my enthusiasm to do all the good I possibly could that, in addition to the college of two hundred students, I also had a circuit which the Conference had given me to serve as pastor. Rest assured I was a most indefatigable laborer in the vineyard of the Lord. I preached Saturdays and Sundays and frequently at night during the five school days of the week. I had been preaching at Wesley Chapel, one of my churches five miles in the country, every night during the two weeks preceding the Christmas holidays, and after their arrival holding meetings during the day as well as the night. Meanwhile the Lord turned on us a glorious revival, characterized by deep conviction and powerful conversions. However, there was nothing said about sanctification, as no one in attendance (in 1868) had the experience or knew anything about it. We had some splendid local preachers, who were thought to be literally full of religion and overflowing, and it is certain that God signally blessed their labors, but they were utterly ignorant of sanctification. I had read about it in John Wesley's catechism when a little boy, and later in his other books, as, you know every young Methodist preacher is obliged to read them. I had found them full of Christian perfection, but being utterly ignorant of the matter experimentally, I contented myself with my own intellectual exegesis, arriving at the conclusion that uncle

John's head was muddled on regeneration and sanctification, and that he actually mixed them up, using them interchangeably. However, I had been convicted for it all the nineteen years which had elapsed since my conversion, and incessantly seeking it in my blind way, like everybody else, I suppose, by works, thinking I would grow into it in due time.

At one of my churches I had met an old woman, utterly illiterate, who claimed the experience, and I believe had it. As she was incompetent to read the Bible, of course she could not expound it scripturally; yet the testimony of old Sister Baxter, whose house was the preacher's home when on duty in that neighborhood, was so clear and her testimony so positive, corroborated by an unearthly radiance lingering in her face and flashing from her eyes, that it had an effect to convict me. Yet I soliloquized, "Here am I, a collegiate graduate, having read the Bible from my childhood, surely I ought to know more about it than this old sister who does not know her alphabet." During the preceding collegiate vacation, I was travelling in the Louisville Conference and fell into a protracted meeting at Pleasant Run. There I found a glorious revival sweeping along; audience fine, altar well filled, and the meeting running all day, with basket dinner on the ground after the old style. The pastor put me up to preach. In those days I studied hard and made sermons, as I thought, adapted to all occasions. Therefore I selected a revival sermon, as I considered it, and delivered it to the best of my ability, feeling that I was really meeting all demands. I concluded with the usual invitation. The mourners were so convicted that they came as a matter of course till they got satisfied. While the altar service was in progress and the saints were praying for the mourners and exhorting them, a very old woman, a mother in Israel, looking for the fiery chariot, got hold of the pastor's arm, pulled up and, as she was partially deaf, doubtless spoke louder than she thought, for I distinctly heard her sobbing utterances: "Oh, Brother Donaldson, please do not put up that little fop any more, lest you ruin our revival." It was to me a thunderbolt from a cloudless sky. I went away and fell on the ground and wept bitterly, meanwhile soliloquizing: "O Lord, is it possible, after preaching fifteen years and toiling so hard to work my way through college, that after all I am nothing but a 'little fop'! O Lord, do, for Jesus' sake, have mercy on me and give me the needed light and help me to walk in the same." Though nothing was said in that meeting about sanctification, the verdict of the dear mother in Israel, who called me a "little fop," broke my heart and I never survived it. She was like the mother in Israel who threw the stone on the head of Abimelech, when besieging the city with his army, and slew that great military chieftain.

The Holy Spirit used those two mothers in Israel to culminate the conviction which had been lingering in my heart for nineteen years, while I had resorted not only to immersion, but to a thousand other good works, only to be disappointed in my fond aspirations to satisfy my longing soul. Jesus was standing by me all the time, offering me the panacea for all my woes, the elixir for all my griefs, His own precious blood shed on Calvary; but I thought I had to *do* something and did not realize that HE had done it all, and left me nothing to do but believe, shout and obey.

My revival was sweeping on; my local preachers,

licensed exhorters, and bright members working heroically, none of them claiming anything but the regenerated experience and doubtless the most of them believing that is all. I preached on the rich man and Lazarus to a packed audience, with many who could not get into the house. When I opened the altar, it was crowded with seekers for conversion, as I invited no others, having never heard of sanctification, and never did till it reached myself.

After receiving the experience, the Lord wonderfully poured out His Spirit. I had spent hours that afternoon out in the woods crying to God to satisfy my longing soul and give me the full, glorious liberty for which I had been sighing those nineteen years, preaching fifteen of them, little dreaming that there was victory ahead, which would make preaching and everything else a delight instead of a duty. Strong was the cry of my heart for the great desideratum, which had been like the *ignis fatus* flitting before my mental vision all those many years; but like the school boy who ran himself out of breath to find the pot of gold at the rainbow's end, I learned by sad experience the essential difference between pursuit and possession. Such was the longing of my soul as to almost render me oblivious to the dozens and scores who had crowded the altar responsive to my invitation. That was a night I never can forget. God, in His mercy, sent us a landslide from the upper world; a Mississippi River inundated us all, which rapidly broadened into a mighty sea and disembogued into an ocean without bank or bottom. I have been basking in that ocean ever since. Oh, the incommunicable sweetness of perfect love!

"Oh, for this love let rocks and hills,
Their lasting silence break;

And all harmonious human tongues
  Their Savior's praises speak.

"Angels, assist our mighty joys,
  Strike all your harps of gold,
But when you reach your highest notes,
  His love can ne'er be told."

I cannot tell you much about the events of that memorable night. Quite a number of those who came to the altar shouted the victory. About eleven o'clock, I found my own soul flooded and filled beyond all anticipation. My good people, though exceedingly happy in their regenerated experience and heroically pressing the battle for God and souls, as they knew nothing about a higher experience, called everything conversion. Therefore they told me I had gotten conversion. I joyfully accepted the situation, and went on telling everybody I met that God had filled and flooded my soul, beyond all expectation, and I supposed that I had never before been converted all right, and now, in His condescending mercy, He had finished my conversion. Falling in with a very able Methodist theologian, I told him about my wonderful experience, saying that I supposed it was just a completion of my conversion, which hitherto had only been in a progressive attitude. Then he freely took it on himself to correct me, saying: "Godbey, if you had not been converted, none of us have. So do not tell that any more. It is that old Methodist experience of sanctification, or Christian perfection, which, by the grace of God, you have entered." Though he believed in it as taught in our books, he did not enjoy the experience, yet the blessed Holy Spirit made him a great blessing to me in the way of Biblical exegesis, from an experimental standpoint. I also met another very old

Methodist preacher, who assured me it was the great second work of grace, called Christian perfection or sanctification, which the Methodists sought and possessed when he was a boy. Then I proceeded to read the books of Wesley and Fletcher on Christian perfection, as well as my Bible, with new light in a glorious sunburst bespangling the inspired pages. Whereas I had concluded that Wesley was muddled, actually mixing up the two works of grace and referring to them interchangeably, ever after the light fell on me on that memorable occasion, while reading the works of the Methodist fathers, I have seen regeneration and sanctification standing out as conspicuously distinct as the Alleghanies and the Rockies, with the great Mississippi valley rolling between.

Sanctification is a most notable epoch in my experience, marking a radical revolution in my life, and soon taking me out of the school where I had taught eighteen years, and where I thought I was for life. So did my friends, as the signal blessing of God was resting upon my labors and they felt they could not excuse me from the educational work. A notable phenomenon at once supervened in my ministry, and it was thus everywhere I preached; the Holy Ghost fell on the people and a revival broke out in my school. He fell on the students and just about all of them yielded and got converted. When I went to Conference and my name was called and, pursuant to the rules, I left the house, while my character underwent examination, from the lobby I heard the clear, strong voice of my presiding elder, as he told the Conference that a great change had come over me during the year and four hundred people had been converted under my ministry. That was strikingly phenomenal in that Conference, which Campbellism had flooded with an arctic river for a whole generation and about frozen out all of the old Methodist fire that used to make sinners cry and Christians shout. They had so long persistently preached against Holy Ghost religion, ridiculing it unmercifully, denouncing and abusing the mourner's bench, that the Methodist preachers, rank and file, had given up the altar and contented themselves to take in members as seekers of salvation, baptizing them and, after the abolishment of a probation in the Southern Methodist Church, which took place about that time, admitting them to *bona fide* membership, though unsaved, and even promoting them to offices. The result was that the Methodist Church was in an exceedingly low condition; clear and bright conversions, attested by the Holy Spirit and witnessed to in the love feasts, having almost evanesced and become simply a matter of bygone history.

I remained on Perryville circuit two years, preaching all the time I could get compatible with my heavy duties in the college. Then feeling it my duty to devote more time to preaching the Gospel and saving souls, I resigned the presidency and the trustees elected another man. The Conference sent me to Mackville, only ten miles distant. So many of my old students followed me that they constrained me to take a select school of thirty-two pupils, all in the high grades. This was my last year of the eighteen I faithfully served in the educational field. I entered it simply to defray my educational expenses, but after that was done, the people held me with a grip so tight that it seemed I never could break it; at the same time telling me that God was so wonderfully blessing me as an educator that I ought to receive it as an evidence that it was His will for me to continue in that work; no one ever daring to suggest that I should be preaching. Therefore I acquiesced in it and concluded to spend my life in the educational field, as well as preaching the Gospel, thinking that the two move like David and Jonathan in perfect harmony, either with other.

As above specified, sanctification radically revolutionized my whole subsequent life. I had grand air-castles, building big boarding houses and contemplating more. When the fires of the Holy Ghost fell on me in sanctification they burned up all of my air-castles, and I have never seen them since they went down into ashes.

I became a Free Mason at the age of twenty-one. I would have joined sooner, but all have to reach majority before they will admit them into that order. I thought it was all right, because the prominent Methodist preachers, as well as those of other churches, were all in it. They had honored me with the chaplaincy, and I was a regular attendant of the lodge. I had also for similar reasons joined the Odd Fellows and was serving them in the chaplaincy. I also had my life insured, feeling no conscientious scruples about these things. Therefore, when the fires of the Holy Ghost fell on me, filling and flooding my soul and transforming me into a cyclone, those hallowed flames burned up the Free Mason, the Odd Fellow, the collegiate president, the big preacher, and life insurance; thus leaving me quite an ash-pile in that howling wilderness where I had roamed nineteen years, fifteen of which I was preaching the Gospel.

When people have their friends and relatives cremated, they generally carefully urn the ashes and keep them. I was just in too big a hurry to cross the Jordan to urn the ashes of my old friends. Therefore, leaving them in the wilderness, I dashed away at race-horse speed, walked between the clefted waves of Jordan's swelling tide, and soon marched around the walls of Jericho and shouted till they fell. Then, responsive to the bugle call, I marched with Joshua's army into the great interior, stood on the battle-field of Bethhoron, where, responsive to the mandate of Joshua, the sun stood still over Gibeon and the moon over the valley of Aijalon, prolonging the day till he could end his battle in the signal defeat of all the southern armies and the decapitation of thirty-one kings. Then I followed him into the great north, with incessant battles and constant victories, till we confronted the combined power of the northern armies under command of the king of Hazor, on the battle-field of Merom. There they all went down in blood, giving Joshua the land, which he divided among the tribes assembled at Shiloh. While Moses represented the law, and had to die in the wilderness, lest somebody conclude that sanctification is by good works, *i. e.*, keeping the law, Aaron, the high priest, had also to die in the wilderness, lest people should believe that they could be sanctified by baptism, sacrament and church rites. Miriam, the fire-baptized evangelist, must die in the wilderness, too, lest people should look to the sanctified preachers for the blessing. But Joshua is a Hebrew word which means Jesus, whom he gloriously symbolized. Therefore he alone could lead them through the Jordan into the land flowing with milk and honey and abounding in corn and wine. N. B. All I have here imputed to Joshua simply means that Jesus does it.

Sanctification, by the grace of God, is infinitely more to me than I can possibly tell you. When I received the Holy Ghost, He gave me His wonderful freedom. 2 Cor.

5 : 17, *"Where the Spirit of the Lord is, there is freedom."* Sanctified people enjoy the very freedom of God Himself, who is free to do everything good and nothing bad. The sweetness and blessedness of this freedom is heaven on earth. Well do we sing, "Prisons would palaces prove, if Jesus would dwell with me there." I can neither by speech nor pen approximate the absolute, ineffable felicity of this freedom. It puts all transitory things into final and total eclipse. Before I got sanctified I carried, oh, so many crushing burdens. Since that notable hour, I have been light as a bird of Paradise, not encumbered with a solitary burden. Not that I have none, for I have a lost world on my heart, with all the grand and absorbing interest of God's kingdom, but Jesus carries all of my burdens and me, too. He gives me sweet blessedness and perfect rest in His arms, and a glorious balloon ride, soaring above every cloud, through the bright impereon where is the Sun of righteousness, who knows no eclipse; where no storm clouds ever rise to hide my Savior from my eyes.

I am so sorry for my dear brethren in the ministry, crushed with burdens and worn with toils till they are prematurely gray and go into superannuation at the very time they ought to be doing the best preaching of their lives. I just know not what to do for them. If they had any idea what Jesus has for them, they would cut off right hands and pluck out right eyes, gladly and unhesitatingly, to get it.

The Lord, in His great mercy, gave me this experience in 1868, fifteen years before the Holiness Movement crossed the Ohio River. During that time I had very little sympathy appertaining to the experience in my own Conference. The preachers much appreciated the revivals which everywhere attended my ministry, but many of them pronounced me crazy on sanctification.

On one occasion when they opened the love feast on Sunday morning, I was the first to tell my experience, not only of conversion, but of entire sanctification. Our excellent brother, Richard Deering, of Louisville, who, like myself, had the blessed testimony, faithfully witnessed to what God had done for his soul. He was followed by Brother Grinstead, of the Kentucky Conference, who meekly bore witness to this same blessed experience. Then followed Dr. H———, who antagonized our testimony, and suggested that we have no more on that line. He was quickly followed by Dr. K———, who fully corroborated him in his speech, quite condemnatory of our testimony, and said we could have no more of them, as we were drawing a division line among the preachers, as they were not all in possession of that second experience. Then the brethren who did not claim sanctification followed, freely antagonizing the two doctors who had spoken against us, frankly observing that if we had an experience which they had not reached, they wanted us to tell it, so that they might have the benefit of our testimony to help them get the same. So at that time a debate sprang up among the unsanctified brethren, two of them attempting to have the breaks put on the sanctified testimonies, and others urging that we take all we can get, by way of encouragement to those who had not received the experience. Then the leader of the meeting pronounced the controversy out of order, discontinued it and ordered them to begin *de novo*, humbly and freely to tell what God had done for their souls. Then they broke out and sang a good old Methodist song. Meanwhile I went and sat down on the lap of Dr. H——, who was large and stout, and, putting my arms around him said: "Brother Jim, I love you better than ever." Then the tender-hearted man said, "Godbey, I have acted the fool, and I ask your pardon; whenever you can, I want you to come and preach in my church." On that occasion we had a beautiful illustration of the Spirit that characterizes this experience. In the controversy, not one of us said a word nor had any inclination to do so. We all kept perfectly sweet, rejoicing in the Lord and overflowing with love for the brethren who antagonized us. While they were killing our Savior, He was praying for His murderers. Sanctification takes old Adam out of you, and leaves Jesus to reign without a rival in the heart and life. In that case we do as He would do under similar circumstances. I do not insinuate in this that it frees us from the liability of mistakes, because the mind is not made perfect until this mortal puts on immortality. Therefore intellect, memory and judgment will make mistakes. This perfection is simply that of the heart, which, in the superabounding grace of Christ and through the efficacy of His precious blood, is made perfect; while the mind and body are still encumbered with infirmities, which are only eliminated by the great work of the Holy Ghost in glorification, when this mortal puts on immortality.

When I met Brother Donaldson, the pastor of the meeting where the mother in Israel begged him not to let that "little fop" preach any more, lest he ruin the revival, in the Conference, he came to me and threw his arms around me and said, "Are you not W. B. Godbey?" (there are many Godbeys preaching). I responded in the affirmative. Then he said, "I have been reading your revival reports all the year with unutterable astonishment, to see that four hundred people have been converted under your preaching. I got bewildered as I thought the signature was that of the brother who preached for me at Pleasant Run, and how such preaching ever converted so many people I could not understand." Says I, "Brother, the man you heard at Pleasant Run is dead and gone. He lives no more. You now meet a new preacher, who retains the old name, W. B. Godbey." This illustrates the radical revolution which sanctification develops.

The reason why I was sent to Mackville was because when the Conference ascertained the fact that I had a glorious revival everywhere I preached, they at once put their heads together in the Bishop's Cabinet to send me to the hardest field they had; where all revival effort had failed. This was the case at Mackville, where there had been no revival in a dozen years, though combined efforts had been faithfully put forth. Bishop Kavanaugh had dedicated a new church at that place five years before and not a soul had ever been converted in it. They made an especial effort to secure my appointment, owing to the fact that I invariably had revivals.

We had no evangelists then (1870). I am the oldest evangelist in the South, having been put in the field by Bishop McTieyre when he presided over our Conference in 1884. It came about in a peculiar way. As the Conference had no evangelistic appointment, they drifted into the habit of appointing me and another man to a large circuit, or sometimes two thrown together, in order to liberate me for evangelistic work, as my comrade (and sometimes they gave me two helpers), could stay and hold the fort. The brethren in other Conferences got to calling me so urgently that, in 1883, I spent all of my time outside of my own Conference, with wonderful blessings on my labors. When the ensuing Conference convened, the brethren appealed to Bishop McTieyre to confine me to my own Conference, stating that they wanted me to give them all of my time, as they needed all that I could do, helping them in their revival meetings. Consequently, the Bishop sought an interview with me before he opened the Conference, stating the request of the brethren and asking me what I thought of it. I said, "My dear brother, I am here to go where you send me, and am perfectly willing to be restricted to the Kentucky Conference; but you know our work is a unit, and souls in other Conferences are worth as much as in ours. We must also take the 'go' which our Savior put in His commission in its full force. I have been preaching thirty years in this Conference, and have run nearly all over it, and believe I will be more efficient for God on new territory." Then he asked me to read my report, which I had brought to read before the Conference according to the requirement for every preacher. In the providence of God, it had been one of the most fruitful years of my ministry, and all of it outside of my own Conference. While I read it, my tears did flow unbidden. In this I was not alone. The good Bishop well did his part of this joyful and grateful crying. When I got through, wiping his eyes, he said, "Brother Godbey, I am not the man to confine you to this Conference, or any other. I am only sorry that we have no regular evangelistic appointment which I can give you. But I can do this, I can put you in the local ranks, with the distinct understanding between me and you that it is for you to do the work of an evangelist." So then and there he took me out of any Conference and sent me to the whole connection; thus taking the bridle off and turning me loose forever.

For a long time I confined my work to the Southern

Methodist Connection, much to my financial detriment, as, during those times, we had no railroad favors but had to pay full fare, whereas the great North was wide open to me at half-fare. I continued to confine my evangelistic work to the Southern Methodist Connection, simply because my membership was there, till the calls from the Atlantic to the Pacific throughout this great commonwealth bore down on my conscience, and I felt it my duty to discriminate no longer between North, South, East and West, but, like Paul, to be all things to all men, that I might save some. As the years have rolled on, the Lord has continued to broaden my field of labor, three times permitting me to preach in Europe, Asia and Africa. If I could live on, oh, how it would be the glory of my soul to superscribe on my banner, like John Wesley, as you see on his memorial sepulchre in Westminster Abbey, *"The world is my parish."*

Chapter V.

APOLOGY TO MY BRETHREN OF THE CAMPBELLITE CHRISTIAN CHURCH.

Dear Brethren:—

This book is a surprise to me, having been precipitated on me by multitudes of people, who through speech and pen in many different countries have become acquainted with me, and so importuned me to write my autobiography before I pass out of the world, that I actually feel that it is God's will for me to do it. I hereby assure you, as we shall meet at the judgment bar, that I love you with that unspeakable, perfect love which God has given me not only for Himself, but for all the people of His worldwide creation. Therefore you must excuse me not only for the mention I make of your Church, but the phraseology I use. I was born and reared in the midst of your people, constantly associated with them and heard them preach perhaps ten times as much as all other denominations together, as we were poor and I was a hard worker on the farm off in the hills and did not have opportunity to go away from home, and your people did the preaching in that country. I promise you one thing, and that is, to stick close to the facts involved, constantly keeping my eyes on the judgment bar, where I shall soon meet you all. As I am seventy-three years old and have been preaching fifty-three years, with me the battle is over. I would rather drop dead this moment than to misrepresent you, your church, or anything else. The events which I shall have occasion to mention in my biography in connection with your people all transpired.

Your people have undergone a radical change since that time; in fact, they have abandoned the belligerent policy which uniformly characterized them, throughout the circle of my acquaintance, which gradually broadened out till it took in all of the eastern part of the state lying south of Cincinnati, and largely extended over the Louisville Conference in the western portion of the state. I deeply regret my absolute necessity, in a faithful submission of my biography, of freely using the descriptive word, "Campbellite," from the simple fact that you people discard it as a name for your church and even reject it as reproachful. Let me here certify before God and all the people who, in His providence, shall ever read this book, that I do not use it in that sense, but simply as a matter, not of choice, but of necessity. There is no other term in the vast vocabulary of the English language with which I can possibly communicate the facts involved, as you know in the history of my life like this, it will not do to burden it with circumlocutions. This book will be read not only throughout America, but in Europe, Asia, Africa and Oceania, as I have travelled in all these lands and am well known to the Lord's people in all the earth. You know that if I were to use another term except Campbellite they would be utterly confused and not understand the facts of this biography. The truth of it is that you make a mistake in rejecting that adjective, which refers to one of the greatest intellectualists and most profound scholars who ever lived on the earth. Like all others since the Apostles went to Heaven, he did not claim inspiration nor infallibility, and was not free from mistakes, to which we are all liable. I do not think you ought to reflect on me for the free use of words which historic veracity and fidelity force me to utilize in my autobiography. When you read it just remember that I was in the war which swept over the territory of the Kentucky Conference from my earliest recollection, which runs back about seventy years. That war wound up twenty years ago, and you are not in it. I am glad your people have discontinued that belligerent policy, which characterized them for the first fifty years of their history in Kentucky.

I assure you I am not to blame for the eighteen debates in which I was a contestant, because your preachers forced me into them. I was preaching the Word faithfully, as I understood it, and God was wonderfully blessing His precious truth in the salvation of souls, when one of your old debators wrote to me challenge after challenge, to meet him in public discussion and give him a chance with an open Bible to show the people I was wrong. At that time, though some of my Methodist brethren, *e. g.*, Drs. Miller, Fitch and Ditzler, had held debates with your brethren, I had neither attended them nor sympathized with the course they were pursuing. I thought the thing for us to do was to go ahead and faithfully preach the Word of God instead of stopping to hold debates. But this man (Elder William Corn), who had already held a number of debates and had notoriety in that way, after sending me several written challenges, which I had ignored, feeling that was the best way to keep out of the controversy, finally came to my meeting at Barley Chapel in Washington County, in the morning, when a great multitude not only filled the house but crowded around wherever they could hear, and asked me to preach on the conversion of Saul of Tarsus, meanwhile showing the difference between a Campbellite and a Methodist. This I did, giving the spellbound multitude two hours, ten to twelve o'clock A. M., and closing with an invitation for seekers, to which many responded and came to the altar. A number were gloriously saved, testifying to the fact. Among them was one of Brother Corn's members, who in her testimony certified that she had been deceived, thinking she was a Christian when she was not. It was an old style rural "basket meeting," with dinner on the ground and the meeting continuing through the day, therefore we could take our time. When we were about to adjourn for dinner, Brother Corn asked permission to speak, which of course I freely granted. He stated to the audience that I was preaching error and he was prepared to refute me and relieve them of error, if I would give him a chance. He then stated that he had sent me several written challenges which I had never answered. Then he said, fixing his attention on your humble servant, "I here and now repeat all of my challenges which I have sent you, and in the presence of this audience defy you to accept them." I turned to the people and asked them for a word of advice. Then unanimously they spoke out and said, "You must accept his challenge; meeting and giving him a chance to refute you if he can." So we fixed the time and place, to gather under a great beech grove where the Baptists had recently held an association and seated the grounds for a great audience. We made the appointment for about one month from that date. I must confess I was very sorry to have to go into it; but was really left without a choice, there being no alternative but cowardly retreat, which would so easily have damaged the cause of God, as already about four hundred people had been gloriously converted in my meetings in that country and the fire was spreading in all directions.

I prepared for the discussion with great reluctance, feeling that I had better be preaching the Gospel, but you see this dear man would not let me. He forced me to stop and debate with him. About two thousand people convened at the time and place. We proceeded with the discussion, in which he was an old warrior and I but a novice. Rest assured the fire waxed hotter and hotter, heavier and heavier, as we delivered alternate speeches, in which we recognized God's Word as the only authority; freely using other good books as collateral testimony. By the time the debate was over, I was a radically changed man relative to that subject. I went into it being opposed to debates, thinking them unnecessary and fearing that they were productive of evil. When we wound up, I was in favor of debates, believing they did good and were sometimes really necessary to the faithful maintenance of God's truth. I do not believe that the older brethren who lived in those times will censure me for my references to their predecessors on the battle-field. The most of those old warriors have laid the armor down and exchanged the tempest of war for the Mount of Victory. I trow that I will receive a degree of harsh criticism from some of the present generation, who have never smelled gunpowder; having enlisted after the battles were fought and the victories won and silence was prevailing on the field. *"Finally, brethren, farewell, be perfect, be of good comfort, be of the same mind, live in peace, and the God of love and peace shall be with you."* (2 Cor. 12: 11.)

In that debate with Brother Corn, which was my first, I entered with great reluctance, as he was an old war horse and I myself but a beginner; besides, I had always realized conscientious scruples against such proceedings, but I was unutterably surprised at the weakness of his arguments, which I found so easily refuted. As I then underwent a change and concluded that debates are necessary and profitable, I then unhesitatingly accepted all of their challenges, and as the years rolled on I participated in eighteen public discussions; which I know the Lord did wonderfully bless to the good of His cause. When the Bible speaks of debate in a condemnatory way, it means contention and strife in colloquial circles; *i. e.*, a disputatious predilection which mars the peace and harmony of people in families and social groups into which they are thrown by the providence of God. Our Savior and the Apostles, especially Paul, frequently engaged in disputations with the scribes and Pharisees who came around them whithersoever they went, like the lightning on the skirts of a cloud, watching and waiting a pretext for assault. Martin Luther met the Pope and his cardinals in the city of Worms and engaged with them in public debate.

These discussions were conducted in a perfectly orderly way. Each contestant selected his own moderator, who was invariably a prominent preacher in his denomination. Those two moderators selected the umpire, who sat between them, took charge of the audience and kept order, and also gave the deciding vote between the moderators when they differed in any question of interest to which their attention was called. The umpire was not a member of either of the churches represented in the debate and was generally a lawyer, judge, or in some way a very prominent citizen. He called the house to order, called on somebody to pray, and read the proposition for discussion, stating the attitude of the contestants, as to affirmation and negation. The audiences were invariably very large and the interest always intense; the debate occupied four hours each day, from ten to twelve A. M. and from two to four P. M. Meanwhile the preachers of the contesting churches always preached every night alternately either with other. As above mentioned, I was driven into these debates by whip and lash and not of my own choice.

When I was a little child, Alexander Campbell came into that country and preached with great efficiency, capturing some Baptist churches and dividing others, as he had been a Baptist preacher. But he had given up their spiritual doctrines and was preaching water regeneration with all his might. In his "Christian System," a book which I have read very carefully, he says, "Immersion is regeneration." He was a man of great learning and intellect and led the people after him by great multitudes. His people were exceedingly enthusiastic, preaching baptism for the remission of sins, as their great dogma; and at the same time pouring condemnation on all who did not fall in with them. Campbell's name selected for his people was "Disciples," certainly exceedingly appropriate. They afterwards adopted the simple name "Christians," which they used in an exclusive sense, unchristianizing all that did not join them; in fact, usurping the name which is common to the Lord's people in all the earth, and hence when used alone incompetent to designate any especial organization.

As my father was a Methodist preacher, I had a good opportunity to get acquainted with these current events; besides, I was a great meeting-goer myself and a close observer with an extraordinary memory. Therefore you may rest assured that I am not mistaken in what you read in this book. Their attitude was strictly and invariably controversial and belligerent. They always preached on baptism for the remission of sins, utterly denouncing everything but immersion. This one scripture, *"Repent and be baptized for the remission of your sins,"* (Acts 2: 38), they constantly used, construing "for" in the sense of "in order to," and making it the prominent condition of remission of sins. We say a man was hanged for murder and do not mean that he was hanged in order that he might commit murder, because he had already committed it. The correct translation of this passage, as you see in the Revised Version, is "unto the remission of sins;" which water baptism symbolizes, and therefore has reference to.

N. B. Luke wrote the Gospel that bears his name and the Acts of the Apostles, as dictated by Paul. In the former, (24: 47), we have Luke's commission, under which Peter was preaching on the day of Pentecost. "To preach in His name repentance unto the remission of sins to all nations—beginning from Jerusalem." Here we see that the commission under which Peter was preaching offers remission of sins to all nations, on condition of repentance, saying nothing about baptism, which Peter mentions in a hortatory way as a confirmation of their repentance. The very fact that baptism is not mentioned in Luke 24: 47, where we have repentance for the remission of sins to be preached to all nations, forever settles the question that it is not a condition of remission, as the Bible does not contradict itself. Salvation is a pure spirituality and not a temporality. It is immaterial and not material. Therefore when you make anything which is physical and materialistic a condition of salvation, you run the subject into idolatry, and sidetrack the efforts of the soul, however earnest, away from Christ, thus defeating the end in view.

The preaching of the Campbellites from my earliest recollection was constantly belligerent and condemnatory of all who did not join them and take immersion. They denounced all experimental religion, ridiculing and making all manner of fun of it; covering it with burlesque, in order to arouse the prejudice of the people against it. I have attended many a protracted meeting with those people, and certify (for I learned their curriculum till I always knew what was coming), that they invariably began with a labored effort to prove that there is no such thing as experimental religion; at the same time bringing burlesque and sarcasm in all possible availability to conserve the end in view, *i. e.*, to get all the members they could. When they had preached several sermons directly against all spirituality in every form and phase, till they thought they had convinced the sinners that there was no such a thing as finding the Lord and receiving conscious experimental salvation, then they would change their tactics and preach Hell and damnation with all their might, at the same time assuring the people that if they would quit their sins, join the Church and receive baptism for the remission of their sins, the whole matter would then be settled forever and they would then have nothing to do but to keep the moral commandments. When they succeeded in convincing the people that they were correct, then of course they would begin to join, one moving another and the influence spreading till they would sweep in quite a multitude, as they believed that they were liable to drop into Hell before they were immersed for the remission of their sins; therefore they always rushed away to the creek and immersed them. From the simple fact that I know that the whole procedure is untrue and has deceived millions who are now in eternity, I kindly dictate these pages. If you will reflect a moment, you will know that this whole system is radically false. You know that if it were true our Savior would never have come down from Heaven, bled and died on the cross to redeem us from sin, death and Hell. There was as much water in the world to immerse people before He came as since; they had Noah's flood. If the people could be saved by obedience, as these people preach, you know they had the law from the beginning. Therefore you see how they not only minify, but utterly ignore, the work of Christ.

Their whole system consists in a reflection on and vilification of the Holy Ghost, a minification of the atonement and a practical ignoring of our blessed Savior and His mighty works in the salvation of souls. In their preaching, they boldly claimed to be the only Christian Church in the world, following the Bible as their only guide, while other churches followed their creeds. Oh, I have so often seen them hold up the Methodist discipline and denounce it with the bitterest condemnation, drawing the most enviable contrast with the Bible and telling the people they were the only church that had no creed and followed the Bible alone. Of course we have no business with any creed, except the New Testament, which ought to be the creed of Christendom. The Old Testament is all right, true and precious, but we are not living under that dispensation. Therefore, while we duly appreciate it for the wonderful truth it contains, we adopt the New as our only guide, lest we get side-tracked away from the glorious Pentecostal Dispensation, which the New Testament launched and perpetuates.

While these people constantly resorted to those strategic vilifications of discipline, and to boastful contrasts with the Bible, which was utter sophistry, they were the most rigid creedists in the whole country, contending constantly for their little creed, which contained but one item, "Immersion for the remission of sins." Creed is from the Latin word *credo,* to believe, therefore you may have a creed, written or unwritten. All the preaching I heard them do during the twenty years I lived with them was on this belligerent, challenging line; incessantly telling the people that they were ready to meet us face to face and with an open Bible prove the truth of their doctrine and the falsity of ours, and the very fact that we did not meet them was demonstrative truth that we were afraid; because we knew that the Bible was against us. My father was an unlearned Methodist preacher, preaching the true, experimental, Holy Ghost religion with all his might. They were constantly after him, fighting and challenging him and all others who believed in experimental religion to debate with them. He was afraid of them; besides, he had conscientious scruples against debates, which he transmitted to me.

Thirty years ago we had two great men in American Methodism—Bishop Simpson in the North and Bishop Pierce in the South. In the providence of God, the latter came to our Conference. During his abode with us, the brethren told him about the belligerent policy of the Campbellites, fighting us all the time, denouncing experimental religion as false and challenging us to meet them, not only in defense of our Holy Ghost religion, but the doctrine of baptism as we held and practiced it. He asked us why we did not accept the challenge and meet them according to their incessant bantering, in open controversy, assuring us that we ought to be ready at all times *"to contend earnestly for the faith once delivered to the saints."* (Jude 3.) Hitherto the brethren, like my father, had had conscientious scruples against public debates, lest they might stir up strife and grieve the Holy Spirit. But after this deliverance of the Bishop, the brethren somewhat changed their minds and Drs. Miller and Fitch, Hiner and your humble servant, and some others, entered the controversial arena and kept the sword unsheathed until the war was over, and the victory won.

In my case, it was simply a matter of military necessity. From the very hour that the Lord sanctified me in 1868, He turned me into a cyclone of fire, and wherever I preached the Holy Ghost fell on the people, and a glorious revival broke out. There was at that time a vast open field for Holy Ghost revivals in the Methodist Churches, as they had so long been browbeaten and intimidated by the belligerent preaching of the Campbellites, constantly challenging them for debate and ridiculing the mourner's bench, that the people became much prejudiced against it, and the preachers had no courage to invite them to it. Meanwhile it seemed that the Campbellites would get all the people into their Church and we would have none. Therefore Bishop Kavanaugh advised us to invite them to join the Church as seekers, rather than not get them, and take chances afterward to get them saved. Consequently it just seemed that Holy Ghost religion would actually die out of the Methodist Church; therefore the Lord sanctified me and gave me the blessed Holy Ghost and I stood alone in the Conference witnessing to that blessed experience; as it was fifteen years before the Movement reached us, in 1883.

My brethren, far from persecuting me, gladly availed themselves of the good work which the Lord was doing through my humble instrumentality. As I was flooded with the Spirit and the fire, I just could not run revivals on the church-joining line, as my brethren were generally doing. I had to unfurl the banner and beard the lion in his den, preaching Holy Ghost religion like lightning, and, of course, as an inevitable consequence, exposing the silly sophistries of Campbellism, which had so long been preached by those unconverted preachers, showing neither distinction nor mercy, but keeping Hell constantly uncapped and shaking the unconverted over it with Herculean hand. Therefore the Holy Ghost fell on the people in mighty conviction, crowding my altars day and night. Meanwhile souls were constantly passing from death to life. As I incessantly showed up the devil's delusions, hallucinating people with water baptism and church membership as substitutes for clear, radical, know-so, experimental salvation, hosts of church members crowded the altar, and many of the Campbellites came constantly seeking and finding the Lord. After this experience they always left their Church, in which they had fought experimental religion with all their might, and joined the Methodists or the Baptists.

I am happy to say that the Baptists in all of that country, like the Methodists, suffered so terribly at the hands of the Campbellites that they rallied with me without a single exception, fighting heroically, and frequently getting a large share of the converts, whom I had received into their Church right there in my meetings. As the Holy Ghost so powerfully fell upon the people, and honored His precious truth in the salvation of souls, all sorts of religious people who believed in the Holy Ghost rallied with me. Meanwhile the Campbellite Church was losing members all the time, who got converted, crowded our altars, and then joined the church that believed and preached Holy Ghost religion. Amid this state of things, they literally forced me to debate with them. I had to do it in order to protect the cause and establish my converts in experimental religion, which had been denounced and vilified for a whole generation. Therefore we just had to make a new departure on the Holy Ghost line, which utterly upset Campbellism.

There are now four times as many Methodists in Ohio as in Kentucky. Did you know that Bishop Asbury established the Methodist Church in Kentucky, and came from there over to Ohio and established it? Now how do you account for the great difference? It is the simple fact that Campbell's doctrine took better in Kentucky than in any other state in the Union. It is a notorious fact that the Campbellite Church was built up in Kentucky by taking in the children of the Methodists and Baptists, who really had that state before the arrival of Campbell; with the exception of a few Presbyterians. As I preached everywhere in that state during the first thirty years of my ministry, I became conscious of the fact that the Campbellite Church, which predominated in the blue grass region, was constituted of Methodist and Baptist families which they had captured in their sins, by preaching that easy water salvation. Of course it is easy, because they only run down stream. This follows as a logical sequence, because they positively reject experimental religion and fight the Holy Ghost and all His fire; without which they cannot posibly stem the current and run up stream.

In 1873 the Kentucky Conference sent me to preside over my home district in which I was born and reared, and where my father had preached for fifty years, amid a constant war with water regeneration, and with incessant challenges for debate ringing in the air on all sides. Meanwhile the Baptists, who were as interested in Holy Ghost religion as the Methodists, more frequently entered into public discussion with them. Their champions boastingly challenged the whole world to meet them face to face and refute their water theology. As I knew the war had been there, hot and heavy, for more than a generation, and as my preaching would certainly add fuel to the flame, I deemed it pertinent to cut the work short in righteousness. Therefore I advertised in the secular papers circulating throughout my district, my acceptance of all the challenges that had been made or should be made. These debates occupied four to eight days, and great audiences attended and listened spellbound.

My first debate was in Somerset, occupying eight days and afterward at Highland, Lincoln County, with the same man, Elder Joseph Ballew, who not only boldly advocated all of their water doctrines but denied the direct influence of the Holy Spirit on the heart, and in one of his propositions affirmed that a sinner had no right to pray, as that was the prerogative of citizens only and every sinner was an alien until he was immersed for the remission of his sins—that made him a citizen of God's kingdom and conferred on him the right to petition the King, *i. e.*, to pray.

I also had a debate of eight days in Mount Vernon, Rockcastle County, with Elder Kelly, and another in

Estill County, with Elder Harding, and two discussions with Elder Briney. These debates at the different places covered the same ground, they denying and laboring to disprove the work of the Holy Spirit on the heart, the right of a sinner to pray, and experimental religion, and at the same time enforcing all of their water doctrines with every forcible argument. They affirmed that Christian baptism is for the remission of sins. I remember Elder Harding had it written in large, brilliant letters over the pulpit for everybody to see and read, while he felt sure that he could prove it beyond the possibility of a doubt. As he was in the affirmative, of course the *onus proband, i. e.,* burden of proof, devolved upon him. With great force and emphasis he delivered his oration, occupying a solid hour. Then I followed him with an hour in the negative. As the people had listened spellbound to his entire discourse, I began by eulogizing it and stating that it was able and edifying and that I had but one objection to it. Then the people stared their eyes open, thinking that I was just about to get converted to Campbellism, but when I told them what my objection was, that it was this, that "There is no truth in it," their countenances fell. I proceeded at once and had no trouble to make good what I had said and to show clearly that his great and brilliant speech was actually destitute of truth.

Argument 1. I began on his proposition, "Christian baptism for the remission of sins." I proved the proposition false because it is self-contradictory; no one can be a Christian and have any sins to be forgiven, as every unforgiven person is a sinner and not a Christian. To make the proposition logical, you would have to change it so as to read, "Sinner's baptism is for the remission of sins." But the trouble in that case is that there is no sinner's baptism known in the Bible, as baptism is God's mark which He puts on His own sheep and never on Satan's goats. Then I took his arguments in the order in which he had presented them and clearly showed their utter falsity, *e. g.*, "*Repent and be baptized* UNTO *the remission of your sins,*" (Acts 2: 38), and not *in order to,* as he construed it. Then I showed from Luke's commission, under which Peter was preaching, as Luke wrote both his Gospel and the Acts as dictated by Paul, (Luke 24: 47), that repentance unto the remission of sins should be preached to all nations in His name, beginning at Jerusalem. In both of these passages we have *eis aphesin toon amartioon,* unto the remission of your sins. We have this same statement in both passages precisely, while in the commission Luke does not mention baptism, but only repentance as the condition of remission of sins for all the heathen world. In Acts 2: 38, where your English says, "be baptized," you have it in the second person plural, co-ordinate with repent, whereas the Greek is in the third person singular, and agrees with the distributive pronoun *ekastos*. The simple meaning is, "All ye repent unto the remission of your sins." This takes in the whole multitude. Then follows, "And let each one of you be baptized in the name of Jesus Christ." Every pronoun has an antecedent. Here the antecedent *ekastos*—each one—is the subject of *metanoiasate*—repent. All who repented received the remission of their sins according to Luke's commission, (24: 47). Then each one who had repented and received the remission of sins, Peter exhorted to get baptized in the name of Jesus Christ, thus publicly confessing Him.

Argument 2. "*He that believeth and is baptized shall be saved, but he that believeth not shall be damned.*"

(Mark 16: 16.) This was the basis of his second argument in order to prove baptism for the remission of sins. The solution of it is very simple and easy. A school boy will readily understand it. The Bible tells us of a baptism for the soul which our Savior gives, and another for the body which the preacher gives. The pronouns in this sentence must refer to the human soul or body for their antecedent. Let us try them in their application to the body. If that is correct, then the body believes and is baptized and saved. You see that application cannot possibly be the true one, because the body cannot believe anything. It is as destitute of faith as a tree. Therefore we are certain that it does not mean bodily faith. Then let us see about the salvation. Does it mean body salvation? This is impossible, because the body of the Christian dies just as does the sinner's. Therefore it does not mean body salvation. Now, as it does not mean body faith or body salvation, it cannot mean body baptism, from the simple fact that the same thing believes, and is baptized and saved. Now, as you see it cannot mean body baptism, it must mean that of the soul; therefore the solution of the problem becomes easy and simple. The soul believes on Jesus and He saves it and baptizes it; that is all it ever did mean or ever can. This conclusion is abundantly confirmed by the negative clause, *"He that believeth not shall be damned."* If the baptism of the body were necessary to salvation, it would read, "He that believeth not and is not baptized shall be damned." The omission of baptism in the negative clause is a confirmation of the conclusion that it is spiritual; as in that case, it is impossible for a soul to receive the baptism of the Holy Ghost until it believes on Jesus; because He alone can give it, and it is certain He never does give it to an unbeliever.

Argument 3. *"When the longsuffering of God waited in the days of Noah, while the ark was being prepared in which few, that is eight souls, were saved through the water, which antitype baptism doth now save us, not the putting away the filth of the flesh, but the seeking of a good conscience toward God."* (1 Pet. 3:20-21.) You see, a correct reading of it really takes away all of the force which the Campbellites put upon it. They lay great stress on the statement, "Saved by water," when every Bible reader well knows that Noah's temporal salvation, which is here meant, was by keeping out of the water. The most simple and correct translation of *dia hudatos* is "through the water." The floods were beneath the ark in swelling seas, and above in pouring rains, and Noah went up through these waters, above and below and all around him, passing safely through into the post-diluvian world. Where the English Version says, "like figure," the word which Peter used is, "antitype," a pure Greek word, slightly Anglicized from *anitupon*. The rule is to transfer every word which has been adopted into the English language, instead of translating it. This passage, like the others, is plain and simple. Water is one of the types of the Holy Spirit throughout the Bible. Therefore when Peter says the antitype baptism does not save us, it simply means that the baptism of the Holy Ghost, which is the antitype of water baptism, now saves. Then Peter kindly fortifies us against the dangerous delusion of water regeneration, stating that it is not putting away the filth of the flesh, *i. e.*, not water baptism, that does ceremonially purify us from the filth of depravity, which is the word here used. So Peter informs us that it is not the mere outward symbol, but that it is the seeking of a good conscience. The grand desideratum of every true Christian is entire sanctification, which takes away that "filth of depravity" here mentioned and gives us a clean heart, like Adam had before he fell, and makes our conscience good. So long as we have this hereditary depravity, *i. e.*, the filth of the flesh, *i. e.*, the carnal mind, our conscience condemns it, therefore we never do receive this pure conscience, void of offense toward God and man, till we receive this glorious antitype baptism, which Jesus gives in sin-consuming flames, exterminating the "filth of the flesh" and making your "conscience good" in the sight of God.

Argument 4. John 3:5: *"Jesus responded, Truly, truly, I say unto thee, unless any one may be born of water and the Spirit, he is not able to enter into the kingdom of God."* I once read a little book, written by one of their preachers, under the title, "Methodism Not Christianity," in which the author expounded this along with their other favorite passages, using it in the support of their great doctrine of baptismal remission. In his exposition he urged the people to come along and get immersed in the water and give themselves no concern about the spiritual birth, resting assured that God would attend to it, and all they had to do was to see that the water birth was all right. Of course this was calculated to lull the people to sleep in the cradle of carnal security. Satan uses such men to sing lullabies over souls till he can dump them into Hell.

If you will read on, the very next chapter of John's Gospel will explain the statement "born of water." When Jesus was preaching to the Samaritan woman, He said ten times as much about water as he did in the sermon to Nicodemus; she all the time thinking that He meant the water then sparkling in Jacob's well, but He fully relieved her mind by plainly notifying her that He has no allusion to that temporal water, but means the water of life (verse 11). You will certainly let Jesus define His words; consequently you conclude that it means the water of life, which every soul born of the Spirit receives for the first time and continues to drink of forever.

Argument 5. Acts 22:16: *"Having arisen, be baptized and wash away thy sins, calling upon His name."* Here Ananias exhorts Paul to receive baptism in the name of the Lord and wash away his sins, calling on His name. The Greek *epikalesamenos* is the regular word for prayer used throughout the Bible. Romans 10:13: *"Every one who may call on the name of the Lord shall be saved."* Here is the very identical word used in Acts 22:16, and salvation is positively promised to every human being who does it. Therefore Paul's case is no exception to God's universal plan of salvation in answer to prayer. Paul, like every other sinner, got his sins washed away by prayer. Of course baptism is a smybolic washing; the water applied to the body symbolizing the blood applied by the Holy Spirit to the human spirit. The idea that water literally washed away Paul's sins is heathenish in the extreme. I saw the poor heathens in India washing in the holy waters, thinking they could thereby expurgate their sins. No one can read the Pauline Scriptures and believe that his sins were washed away in the water of baptism. Romans 3:28: *"For we conclude that a man is justified by faith without deeds of law."* Baptism is a deed of the ceremonial law of the New Testament dispensation. Paul is the author of the most of the New Testament, and fights legalism, *i. e.*, salvation by works, with all his might from beginning to end.

How strange to see hundreds and thousands of people deluded with the dogma of baptismal regeneration, when there is not a syllable in the Bible which can be construed for its support without a wonderful perversion and making the Bible flatly contradict itself.

During the war period of the Campbellites, they selected their ablest champions to defend their doctrines. I realized during these debates a grand open door to preach the precious spiritual truths of God to multitudes of people, who had been led away by these erronists till they never heard a Gospel sermon. You may rest assured that the legalisms which these people preach are not the Gospel. Romans 1:16: *"The Gospel is the power of God unto salvation to every one that believeth."*

There are two Greek words translated "power." The one is *exousia,* which means power in the sense of authority; but this word which defines Gospel is *dunamis,* which has been adopted into the English language as "dynamite," the greatest mechanical power in the world. When the scientists discovered it, they ransacked the vocabulary of the English language with its one hundred and fifty thousand words in vain to find a term strong enough to reveal their wonderful discovery to the world, but signally failed. Then they went to God's Book to find a word, and though it is hardly probable that they knew the Lord experimentally, yet I doubt not that the Holy Spirit guided them to this very word, which is God's definition of Gospel. Dynamite is peculiar for its paradoxical explosive power. N. B. It does not say that the Gospel is the written Word. This is indispensable; yet it only serves as the vehicle through which the Holy Ghost sends the Gospel to the heart.

In the New Testament we find four distinct phases of the Gospel. That on Sinai, thundering forth the terrors of violated law till transgressors see Hell opened and demoniacal platoons all around them, is the Gospel of conviction, and when faithfully and persistently preached will always produce a conviction which sinners cannot shake off. When you preach to convicted people the Gospel of Calvary, which is the dying love of Jesus, till the Holy Ghost, through the Word, reveals the Savior pouring out His blood to redeem from sin, death and Hell; when you hear Him say with His expiring breath: "It is finished," and you, by faith, realize that He has wrought and finished your salvation on the cross; then your burden rolls away and you receive a new heart. After this comes the Pentecostal Gospel of the glorious baptism which our Savior gives with the Holy Ghost and fire, crucifying and burning old Adam and superseding him by the glorified Savior crowned and sceptred within. Then under the illuminations of the blessed Holy Spirit you are enabled to make an entire consecration and, by simple faith, receive Jesus as your sanctifier. Then another tremendous explosion takes place, blowing the deep, ponderous strata of inbred sin from the profound interior of your spiritual organism, giving you a clean heart and sanctifying you wholly.

The Lord has a Gospel for the sanctified, to keep them on the constant outlook for the return of Jesus with His glorified angels, to take away His Bride. This Gospel keeps your eyes closed to vain and transitory things, calculated to derail and sidetrack you. When you, thus robed and ready, stand watching and waiting the appearing of our glorious Lord, coming in the clouds to consummate the long anticipated rapture of His expectant spouse, then, responsive to the archangel's trump, through the faith by which Enoch was translated that he should not taste death, even so the saints of the latter days will be caught up to meet the Lord in the air, and to thus be forever with Him. This is the glorious transfiguration Gospel, when the same heavenly dynamite that gave us the Sinai conviction when a sinner, a sky blue regeneration when a broken-hearted penitent, a triumphant sanctification when we sought the second great work of grace, will also transfigure these mortal bodies in the twinkling of an eye, eliminating all ponderous matter, till they will not weigh anything, and consequently, spontaneously responsive to the interior impulses of the soul, will rise with shouts of victory to meet the Lord in the air.

N. B. This dynamite (Rom. 1 : 16) is the Gospel. It is God's own definition. Without it you may hear the Word like sounding brass and a tinkling cymbal, but, utterly destitute of the Gospel, you will never be saved. You will see from this Scripture that you receive this Gospel not by works, but by faith alone, as it is the dynamite of God only to those who believe. If you have not received it, mark it down that there is a deficiency in your faith. In all probability the deficiency is in the department of repentance, which is absolutely necessary to put you on believing ground, in order that you may be justified, sanctified, and glorified by faith. Thus alone will you receive these three great and indispensable works of grace.

Oh, what a grand open door did the blessed Lord give me in those debates. Both contestants had equal time, which the umpire diligently kept, securing to each one every minute due him. He had a right to do as he pleased with his time. I had no trouble to answer all of their water doctrines in one-half of my allotted time. Then I had the other half to preach Holy Ghost religion like lightning to the multitude, when God wonderfully used this truth. During a debate of eight days of four hours each, we could pour out on them floods of the precious truth which alone can save a lost world. As the days passed by, conviction descended from God and settled down on unsaved people like a nightmare. There we had multitudes of Campbellites as well as sinners of other churches who so much needed the Gospel, but who, through the manipulations of their preachers, had been kept away from Holy Ghost meetings, which their preachers had denounced and ridiculed, arousing their prejudices against them in order to make sure of holding them.

In the providence of God, I had two debates of eight days each with Elder J. B. Briney, a classical scholar and a great orator.

As uniformly I only needed half of my time to answer their water arguments, I had the other half to preach the power of God unto salvation to every one that believeth. We get this wonderful salvation only through faith. When you resort to other devices, you are sidetracked by Satan every time, and trying to get it by works, which the Scriptures condemn from beginning to end. Rest assured, legalism is Satan's greased plank over which he slides multiplied millions into Hell. Whenever any person is shoving any kind of work as a condition of justification, regeneration, or sanctification on you, you may know he is sidetracking you into legalism, which is the sleekest plank to Hell. You say, "I have the faith, but not the experience." I know you are mistaken. If you had the faith, you would have the experience, because Jesus says: *"As your faith is, so be it unto you."* Matt. 9:29. He makes faith the necessary line of the grace He gives you, and you so find it throughout the Bible, without a solitary exception.

In debating with Elder Briney, I used my extra time to show up the grand spiritual truths of the Bible along the line of experimental salvation, assuring the people that they might take all of those water doctrines and do their best on the line of legal obedience and they would certainly be lost forever. We obey the law because we are saved. If we do it in order to get saved we will be forever lost, because, in so doing, we ignore the perfect work of Christ, which we can only receive by faith. If we resort to our own works, in that way we vitiate the faith which alone can receive and appropriate the salvation of Christ.

While I was exposing that awful Campbellite legalism, he called me to order. The law of forensic discussion, laid down in Hedge's Logic, which we had adopted, permits an opponent to call down a speaker if he gets out of order. Then the umpire had me to sit down and called up Elder Briney to state his point of order. This point was that I was sending his people to Hell and I had no right to do it. Then the umpire called me up to defend myself against the accusation. I simply denied the charge, certifying that I was on the opposite side and doing my utmost to keep them out of Hell, by telling them God's plain way of salvation; while, to my deep sorrow, I knew they were going to Hell if they did not get experimental Holy Ghost regeneration and sanctification, which their false doctrines, which I was doing my best to refute and take out of their way, never could do. Then the umpire and the moderators told me to go on with my speech.

The result was that I used my time perfectly freely, preaching experimental religion to the spellbound audience with all my might till the close of the eight days' debate. The Lord gave me a glorious open door to preach His blessed saving truth to vast multitudes who had never heard it, as the Campbellites had been giving them nothing but a water Gospel for fifty years, which we know, to our sorrow, is "weak as water." All they could ask of me as an honorable contestant in the debate was to answer all their arguments. This I had no trouble to do in half of my allotted time, fully elucidating and expounding to them the precious Word of God, and showing clearly their utter perversion and misapplication by those dear people with whom I was reared, and whom I loved enough to die for them.

The Jews drifted away from the glorious experimental truth which saved the patriarchs and prophets and enabled their fathers and mothers to die shouting and winging their flight to glory. They became worldly, lost their hold on God, idolized the ordinances of the Church, and drifted into dead legalism, depending on their good works to save them, precisely like the Campbellites, as well as millions in other churches, are doing to-day.

After Paul, having long preached this dead legalism, thinking it would save people, and having even defended it by persecuting the spiritual Nazarenes unto blood, got so awfully convicted when Jesus met him on the road near Damascus, and after three days and nights agonizing as a mourner before God, without eating or sleeping, got so wonderfully converted under the ministry of

Ananias; and three years afterward was so powerfully sanctified in Arabia (Gal. 1st chap.; Rom. 7th chap.), and subsequently to the end of his life was flooded with the clear light of full salvation; we do not wonder that he was willing to become crucified, as Christ had been to save the people of his consanguinity. (Rom. 9:1-3.) So during all my debates with the Campbellites I had the perfect love for them which prepared me for martyrdom. If it had been God's will, I would gladly have laid down my life to save them.

Their ancestors had been members of the orthodox churches, brought up in the light of the true spiritual Gospel, that saves people instead of deceiving, coaxing and cheating them out of their souls, which is the normal effect of this awful Campbellite heresy of baptismal regeneration, which they and the Mormons boldly and unequivocally preach and defend with a heroism that certainly deserves a better cause. I give them credit for their honesty, but know they are deceived and deceiving others. I was bound to preach the true Gospel with all the power of the body, soul and spirit which God gave me. In so doing from the time He sanctified me in 1868, the Spirit always fell on the people in mighty conviction, moving them to crowd the altar and seek the Lord till they found Him. Many members of the Campbellite Church, along with unsaved Methodists, Baptists, and outside sinners, crowded the altar, prayed through to God, and got gloriously saved, which forever disqualified them to stay in the Church where they not only could get no soul pabulum, but heard their religion discounted, ridiculed and abused; consequently when they got gloriously converted, they invariably joined the Baptists or Methodists.

This so stirred up the Campbellite preachers that they hounded me night and day with challenges written to me in letters and publicly proclaimed from their pulpits. As I wanted to devote all of my time to preaching and not stop to debate, I retreated from them as long as I could. They hemmed me up and forced me to fight or take down my colors. The latter I could not do, as I had no colors but the blood-stained banner and was preaching nothing but Jesus, omnipotent to save every one that will give Him a chance, and that without a Campbellite preacher or a Mormon prophet to help Him by immersing them in water. I was truly like Nehemiah building the walls of Jerusalem, when he had to carry the trowel in one hand and the sword in the other and have all of his people to do likewise, as Sanballat had stirred up the surrounding nations to fight them and keep them from fortifying Jerusalem by impregnable walls.

The Methodist preachers had yielded to intimidation and given up the altar, contenting themselves to take in members as seekers and risk getting them converted afterwards. This state of things was fast secularizing the Church, as the old ones who had been saved were going to Heaven and leaving the Church in the hands of their successors who knew not the Lord experimentally. I could not preach Bible Holy Ghost religion clearly, forcefully, efficiently and successfully, without constantly exposing the silly, superficial sophistries of Campbellism, which the people had heard so long that many of them believed, and really the popular mind had suffered an awful deterioration appertaining to the orthodox truth of the Bible, which is the actual new creation wrought in the heart by the Holy Ghost, through faith subsequently to a radical and genuine repentance.

Campbell's translation of the New Testament was circulated and read, which gives "reformation" for "repentance," and "immersion" for "baptism," thus really eliminating spirituality out of the Bible. The Greek word for repentance is *metamoria,* which literally means a change of mind. The Campbellite interpretation is simply metaphysical, construing it into a mere change of purpose and consequent reformation. The error lurks deep down on the bottom of Bible theology. The Bible is not a book on mental philosophy, but salvation, and serves as its own expositor. The precious book plainly reveals what the change of mind is; not simply a change of thought and purpose, but the actual removal of the carnal mind, which is hereditary from fallen Adam, and its substitution by the mind of Christ, which is created in the heart by the Holy Ghost in regeneration. In the first great work of grace wrought by the Holy Ghost in justification and regeneration, which constitutes conversion, the old man of sin, *i. e.,* the carnal mind, is conquered and grace given to hold him in subordination so that he does not break out and commit actual transgressions; yet we still have him on hand in the deep interior of the heart and ready to rise in the form of pride, vanity, ambition, lust, passion, temper, envy, jealousy, revenge, ritualism, prejudice, bigotry, egotism, sectarianism, self-will and a diversity of insidious metamorphisms. Consequently every true Christian has the inward conflict till these indwelling enemies, which are the elements of the carnal mind, are all washed away by the cleansing blood in entire sanctification, which is the completion of repentance.

The vast multitudes who came from all the surrounding country to attend those debates had never heard much true, straight, orthodox preaching, as four-fifths of the crowd were either members of the Campbellites or under their influence. My opportunities to preach the Gospel to the people who had really never heard it were almost as if one were in India. Some places where I preached, the people said that they had never heard the Gospel before. Let the Campbellites get the complete monopoly of a country and give the people nothing but their water doctrines, and at the same time abuse and ridicule Holy Ghost religion and tell the people that there is no such thing, and that the people who profess it are fanatics, deceived and deceiving others; in a generation or two the Gospel will go out of that country, and the people become practically heathenized. The doctrine constantly preached by these people, which I heard incessantly during the first twenty years of my life, is literal idolatry. In the house of Noah, whence all the people in the world emanated, they all had a knowledge of the true God; but how quickly they trended away into idolatry. Baal, the sun-god, and Ashteroth, the moon-goddess, led the way in the monopoly of the human heart, as they are the most conspicuous to the eye.

Well has man been denominated by philosophers the "religious animal." Therefore a nation without a religion has never been found. The most simple form of religion which has been found among all nations is spiritism, *i. e.*, the recognition of a spirit at every place, at a fountain, at a river, or a mountain, or a plain. They think that there is a spirit there somewhere having charge of it, and if they do not respect its rights and show it reverence by offering it sacrifice, it will punish them in some way. From this comes fetichism, the religion of charms, *i. e.*, the wearing of something on one's person, like a ring on the finger, to keep away diseases, and fortify you against evils.

You see how exceedingly difficult it was to keep Israel out of idolatry. They would engage in the worship of Jehovah, whom they could not see, but they wanted to see the object of their worship. Baal, the sun-god, was so conspicuous as he rolled his fiery chariot over the skies, flooding the world with his light, that they felt awed into reverence before him and constrained to recognize his majesty by offering him a sacrifice. They believed that he was the god that made them. The American Indians have always worshipped the sun, and do to this day. When they offered Tecumseh, their great chief, a chair, he refused it and sat down on the ground, saying: "The sun is my father, and the earth is my mother and on her bosom will I rest."

The most difficult thing in the world is to get people to be content to walk with an unseen God. In the old dispensation, all the nations on the earth were very religious, but they had their visible and tangible divinities; whereas the Jehovah of Israel no one could see. When He had come among them and wrought great miracles, which they could see and hear, they would be satisfied as long as they lived; but when the generation who had witnessed those miracles was all dead, their successors, who had never seen those mighty works, went into idolatry. The idiosincrasy of the human mind is so constituted that we cannot withhold veneration from everything which is essential to the salvation of our souls; therefore legalism always drifts into idolatry. While the Babylonian captivity forever cured the Jews of paganistic idolatry, so they never afterward went into it, yet they idolized the ordinances of the Church, of which Moses had given them many, and really drifted into idolatry that way.

Hydrolatry is from *hardor*, water, and *latria*, worship. Therefore it means water worship. Rest assured that the view of baptism as a condition of pardon for sins, and essential to it, which is constantly preached by Campbellites and Mormons, is as positive idolatry as any you can find among the heathen nations. I spent three months as busy as I could be night and day dashing over the railroads through India, travelling six thousand miles and preaching constantly through interpreters, and everywhere seeing their idols and witnessing their worship. The worship of water, *i. e.*, this very hydrolatry which is fearfully encroaching on Christianity in America, was the most conspicuous form of their idol worship. They go on long pilgrimages to the holy Ganges and Jumna, for the privilege of plunging in and, as they believe, of washing their sins away. As the poor people in that great country, thirty-three hundred miles long and three thousand miles wide, are many of them too far from these holy rivers to enjoy their benefit, therefore the priests have to meet the emergency by the construction of holy tanks. In the city of Madras, the metropolis of Southern India, the holy tank occupies a whole square. It is conveniently entered by great flights of nicely hewn stone steps, extending all around it, as it fronts the street on three sides. The Pantheon, where all the gods are worshipped, fronts the other side. Thus the crowds can walk down from all sides into those holy waters and wash their sins away. Oh, but you say, "We do not believe the water has power to wash away sins; that is the prerogative of the precious blood alone." But Campbell in his "Christian System" says: "We only preach the blood in the water." But you say: "We do not believe that water can wash away our sins; but we simply depend on obedience to the commandment." Do you not know that salvation by works is downright legalism, which is but another form of idolatry? *"For by grace ye are saved through faith, and that not of yourselves; it is the gift of God, not of works, lest any man should boast."* (Eph. 2:8.) This plain and unmistakable statement of God's infallible Word voices the uniform teaching of the Scriptures. This clear and positive statement, revelatory of salvation by faith alone as the human condition, I can actually centuplicate, *i. e.*, give you a round hundred parallel passages. God has made the way of salvation revealed in the Bible so plain that "wayfaring men, though fools, cannot err therein."

But the Campbellites and Mormons give us James 2:24, *"You see that a man is justified by works and not by faith alone."* They are always using this quotation, thereby showing their ignorance of God's Word. God commands us, 2 Timothy 2:15, *"Study to show thyself approved of God, a workman that needeth not to be ashamed, rightly dividing the Word of Truth."* The Campbellite construction simply makes James flatly contradict Paul in dozens and scores, and I believe hundreds, of passages. If you rightly divide the Word of Truth, you will find no contradiction in the Bible. Paul is speaking of the justification of a sinner in the sense of pardon and salvation, while James is setting the justification of a Christian in the sense of approval, and gives the examples of Abraham and Rahab.

When Abraham offered up Isaac, it was forty-one years after he was justified by faith in the sense of pardon. Perhaps you fail to recognize Rahab as a godly woman, and the English version calls her a harlot. The Hebrew word *zonah* primarily means a woman keeping a public house, with no reference to her moral character. Rahab in this case was keeping a tavern in Jericho which was respectable enough for Joshua's spies to select it for a lodging place. Besides you find her on the faith roll (Hebrews 11th chapter), showing plainly that she was a godly woman. She became the wife of Salmon, the Hebrew, and the mother of Boaz, the godly husband of Ruth and father of Obed, the father of Jesse, the father of David; so you see she was one of the honored mothers of our Lord.

There are four justifications in human life. FIRST, *in infancy we are all justified* without faith or works, but purely by the work of Christ.

SECOND, *the sinner is justified by faith alone*, as he is in the devil's kingdom and if he did any good work the devil would get it. Therefore it is impossible for him to do anything but cast himself on the mercy of God in Christ and trust Jesus for pardon and salvation. The Campbellite policy of having him depend on works is most nonsensical, as he cannot possibly do anything that would not belong to the devil until he gets out of his kingdom, which he can never do till he is freely justified by the work of Christ, which he can only receive and appropriate by faith. Then God freely forgives him all his sins for Christ's sake and the Holy Spirit regenerates him, therefore this awful diabolical priestcraft that sends the weeping penitent to the water instead of Jesus is the cunning device of Satan for his certain damnation. Better that preacher never had been born than to assume this awful responsibility of coming between the lost soul and the Savior, and offering him the vain substitute of church rites instead of the precious blood of Jesus. If this doctrine had been true, the Son of God might have saved His life and stayed in Heaven, for we had the law from the beginning with nothing to do but to obey; we always had plenty of water to immerse people. This horrific, Satanic legalism of salvation by obedience, which those people preached boldly with all their might, (and I doubt not their sincerity, because blind people do not see anything), is shocking and appalling beyond all conception, as it actually treats with contempt the dying love of Jesus, which brought Him from Heaven to redeem us by His blood.

If this doctrine were true, you plainly see the work of Christ was not necessary. Truly, this terrific falsehood hatched in the bottomless pit shoves away Jesus in a corner and gives the Campbellites, the Mormon prophet, and the Roman Catholic priests the field, honored with the investiture of life and salvation. You may take a whole community under this influence and this state of things will normally obtain; the preachers coming to the front and Jesus relegated to the rear. It really becomes a puzzle to know what use they have for Him, as they are just ready to take the candidate's confession, immerse him for the remission of his sins, and thus make him a Christian, after their bogus nomenclature, independent of Christ. Shocking to think! After the poor sinner has been freely justified by the vicarious substitutionary atonement of Christ, received and appropriated by faith, he is then gloriously regenerated by the Holy Ghost.

THIRD, *as bona fide citizens of the kingdom, we must always obey God,* proving our faith by our works, as

James beautifully teaches us, in perfect harmony with Paul's powerful and unmistakable deliverances on the justification of all sinners by faith, "without deeds of law." Baptism is a deed of the ritual law, and therefore, with all other deeds of law, eternally and unequivocally excluded from the realm of justification. It comes in with all other good works, after we are freely justified by the grace of God in Christ, and joyfully regenerated by the Holy Ghost.

FOURTH, *there is also a fourth justification which takes place when we stand before the judgment seat of Christ.* This justification is by works alone. Revelation 22:12: *"Behold, I come quickly, and My reward is with me, to give unto each one as his work is."* You see that while the doctrine of good works has not anything to do with saving us from our sins, which is the work of Christ alone, yet they are the measure of our reward in Heaven. Therefore we should work for the Lord night and day after we get into His kingdom; but beware of Satan's awful lies, telling you that you can get saved by good works. Until you are saved, you are still in the devil's kingdom, therefore, as you are under his influence, he will hallucinate you by the idea that you can be saved by your good works; because in this way he will drive off your convictions, thus making you believe you are a Christian, when he knows you are a sinner. If he can keep you under that delusion, he will soon have you in Hell.

CHAPTER VI.

VARIOUS FORMS OF IDOLATRY.

Churches which do not send people directly to the feet of Jesus to implore the pardoning mercy of God which He purchased on Calvary, are all Hell traps, hallucinating the people with the vain delusion that they are Christians, when they are sinners on the broad road to Hell.

The Campbellite dogma of confession and baptism actually takes away the convictions by rendering the sinner independent of Christ. No one ever does get pardoned till he has given up everything else, finding his own good works all "filthy rags in the sight of God." With this universal surrender he must also give up that dogma of remission by immersion, otherwise he will never be able to reach that utter desperation of all earthly resources which must inevitably antedate his total, unreserved and eternal abandonment at the feet of Jesus, and the final ejectment of his hopeless soul on the mercy of God in Christ; which is absolutely necessary to bring him into a position to receive the free pardon of all his sins. Therefore these false prophets with their legalism actually head off the sinner from Christ and put him on this greased plank of legalism, on which he slides down to Hell.

In my world-wide travels, when seeing the millions of

idolaters, and preaching in the midst of their temples and shrines and amid millions thronging the holy rivers to wash away their sins in those sacred waters, or, a matter of convenience to the people living far away from those holy rivers, washing in the holy tanks, that they might be saved, thus actually worshipping those holy waters; I often thought about the myriads in Christian lands who are wedded to idolatry in different forms and phases. Hydrolatry, *i. e.*, water worship, is very prevalent. Rest assured that every person who believes in baptism in order to the remission of sins, or in any way regards it as a saving ordinance, is a hydrolater, *i. e.*, a water worshipper, which is a form of idolatry exceedingly prominent in heathen lands, and has been developed more or less in the Church in every age.

With the Roman and Greek Catholics, Maryolatry, *i. e.*, the worship of the Virgin Mary, which is none other than a species of idolatry, has actually captured three hundred and fifty millions of people who wear the Christian name.

Eucharolatry, *i. e.*, the worship of the sacramental elements, has not only swept Catholicism in all lands, but the thirty millions of Lutherans throughout the world, I am sorry to say, are by no means free from it. Luther found the Church, just having passed through the Dark Ages (a thousand years, during which not one man in a thousand could read or write), full of idolatry. The Church remained pure till the conversion of the Emperor Constantine, A. D. 321. He did his best to stop pagan worship throughout his world-wide empire, but he could not do it. Under his potent influence millions of heathen were brought into the Church without a knowledge of God in personal experience. Therefore, while they gave up their pagan worship, they soon idolized the sacraments, baptism and the Lord's Supper. They magnified them, as they imputed salvation to them. Soon the triune immersion, in a state of entire nudity and with a lot of ceremonies invented by the priests, universally prevailed. Luther found the Church wrapped in the dismal night of the Dark Ages and had so much to do that he did not get rid of all of the dogmata of priestcraft, which had found their way into the Church.

The Roman Catholics hold the doctrine of transubstantiation, pursuant to which they claim that when the priest consecrates the bread, it is actually turned into the literal body of Christ, which the people eat, and the wine into the literal body of Christ, which they drink. While Luther tried to get rid of that heresy, he hung on a modification of it, which he called consubstantiation. In this he discards the popish dogma that the elements are turned into our Lord's literal body and blood; meanwhile he maintains the real presence of the body and blood. Therefore the people under his reformation still held on to the papistical dogma of sins forgiven in the sacrament.

I remember an illustrative case. A profane, drunken German had married a very bright and spiritual Methodist woman. He was learned and intellectual, but really a wicked man. Though born a Lutheran, when I invited the Christians to the sacraments on the Sunday morning of the quarterly meeting, he came from the rear of the congregation and took his place among the communicants. Afterward some of them asked him why he did it, as he was a notorious sinner. He told them he did it because he wanted his sins forgiven. He was no Christian, but an eucharolater, *i. e.*, an idolater worshipping the Lord's sacrament; just like the man who receives baptism in order for the remission of his sins.

Another form of idolatry common in Christian lands is ecclesiolatry, *i. e.,* church worship. It is very extensive and growing rapidly and is awfully detrimental to spirituality. I have often known a congregation to backslide while building a fine edifice, after the occupancy of which they never more had the Holy Ghost and the old-time power. God was grieved away because they worshipped the fine edifice. Oh, how pertinent for us to constantly pray, like the Apostle John; *"Little children, keep yourselves from idols."*

The retention of pure spirituality is really a delicate matter. This world is so full of sin, and Satan so wise and influential that he is always managing to lasso Christians in some way and get them to worship him instead of God, which is actually done in all cases of idolatry. We are now having a universal fight all along this line, to keep the holiness people in the pure simplicity of their experiences, contented to worship the Lord alone; walking patiently, joyfully and triumphantly with an unseen God; perfectly satisfied with Him, independently of all creatures. Oh, how blessed it is to be lost in Jesus, singing as we go, "You may have all this world, but give me Jesus;" profoundly and jubilantly sunk away into His glorious divinity, and more than satisfied with Him!

Pyrolatry. This word is from *pur,* fire, and *latria,* worship, therefore it means the worship of fire. In all ages of the world there have been fire-worshippers. It is said that an old man called at Abraham's tent ere the sun was going down and asked him for lodging. Of course he granted it, as the Bible makes hospitality exceedingly prominent in religion. In the early ages of the world, when there were so few people in it, a person lodging out alone through the night was in great danger of being devoured by a wild beast. So Abraham took in the old man and gave him his supper. Afterward he asked him to engage with him in the worship of Jehovah. The man asked to be excused, observing that he was a fire-worshipper and never worshipped any other god. Abraham tried in vain to prevail on him to join with him in the worship of his God, but signally failed. Finally he told him that if he could not worship his God, he could not lodge in his tent. Still he persisted in his refusal. Then Abraham led him to the tent door and opened it. When the wayfarer walked out into the howling storm, God spoke to Abraham, and said, "Abraham, I have borne with that old man's idolatry a hundred years; can you not stand him one night?" This knocked over Abraham's objections, so, dashing out into the darkness, he shouted aloud, "Come back and stay with me." Then the old man returned into his tent and said, "What sort of a man are you? You drove me off, and now you call me back." "Oh," says Abraham, "my God spoke to me and said He had borne with your idolatry for a hundred years, and asked if I could not stand you one night." Then the old man said, "If that is the sort of a God you have, please tell me more about Him." Therefore there was no going to bed that night. Abraham proceeded at once to tell him about the great Jehovah, who created the heavens and the earth and everything in them, and the old fellow was so interested and Abraham so delighted with an appreciative auditor, while he preached the unsearchable riches of Christ, for Jehovah was the excarnate Christ, that they mutually sat up all night, and before day the old pyrolater was a genuine convert to the God of the Bible.

While I was in India, I became pretty well acquainted with the Parsees, who worship fire. Zoroaster was a great and good man, who lived in Persia five hundred years B. C., contemporary with Buddha in India and Confucius in China. These three were the lights of the East in their day, and have seven or eight hundred millions of followers now in the great, dark Orient. If they were living they would be Christians this day. Of this I am assured, because they walked in all the light they had. But in the absence of a Bible and living five hundred years before Christ came, they walked in comparatively dim light, doubtless doing the best they could. Their followers are now idolaters, actually worshipping these men, a thing they would utterly have repudiated while living.

Zoroaster was the great founder of the fire worship. It had some votaries before his day, as above mentioned, but he was its greatest exponent, establishing the worship of fire, earth, air and water, which he and his followers to this day denominate the four elements; in which they were entirely mistaken, as none of them are elements. Fire is an incandescent air, for it may be any solid substance. Water is a compound of oxygen and hydrogen. Atmosphere is a mixture of oxygen and nitrogen. The earth consists of sixty-three elements in a vast diversity of proportions.

Satan has a great spite at the holiness people, and is doing his best to tilt them away into idolatry in some of its forms and phases. You can only retain the experience and have the real victory while you are simple-hearted and see Jesus only. When you begin to give attention to other things, spiritual decline supervenes quickly. In sanctification you get married to the Lord, then and there forever discarding all other lovers, *e. g.*, churchisms, ordinances, lodgery, etc. The water god is now making a fearful raid on the holiness people, and they are here and there trending away into hydrolatry, from which no one can steer clear who does not take Jesus for everything and let everything else go. Especially in the South, pyrolatry has prevailed in different localities, and somewhat in the West. I have encountered people who preach a baptism of fire separate and distinct from that of the Holy Ghost. Their principal Scripture is Matthew 3: 11, *"I indeed baptize you with water unto repentance. . . . but He will baptize you with the Holy Ghost and fire."* The English version erroneously says, "He will baptize you with the Holy Ghost and with fire." N. B. The last "with" is not in the original. The true reading is, "He will baptize you with the Holy Ghost and fire." In Ephesians 4: 5, Paul positively tells us that there is but one baptism; that our Savior Himself administers with the Holy Ghost and fire. 1 Cor. 12: 13, *"By one Spirit we are all baptized into one body, . . . and have been all made to drink into one Spirit."* Here you see the charming beauty of the spiritual unity which characterizes the kingdom of God. There is but one body in all the earth, and that body is the Church, as the Word positively says.

The moment a soul is regenerated with the Holy Ghost, "born from above," (John 3: 7) that soul becomes a member of God's universal Church, the body of Christ. Jesus never baptizes the devil's children; the children of God *only* are subjects of His baptism with the Holy Ghost and fire. No one can possibly deny that this one baptism is that which the Savior gives with the Holy Ghost and fire, as Paul here catalogues it in the beautiful chain of salvation, which consists of seven links—one Lord, one faith, one baptism, one body, one hope, one God the Father, one Holy Spirit—constituting an indefragable chain which lifts every faithful soul from earth to glory; and all pure as gold. Surely no one would be so silly as to put a water link in that chain, since you know in that case the chain would be weak as water, as it can be no stronger than its weakest link.

There is no danger of getting too much fire, if it is that of the Holy Ghost which God gives. But remember, Satan is the great counterfeiter who actually counterfeits everything that God does in order to deceive the uncircumcised. Therefore take all the fire you can get, if you are sure it is the fire of the Holy Ghost. How can I know that? Because it will be the fire of perfect Divine love, for God and all mankind; and this can only come into your heart when the Holy Ghost pours it out. Romans 5:5, *"The Divine love of God is poured out,"* not shed abroad, as in the E. V., (which might apply to human love, which has no salvation in it); but this Divine *agapee* is only native in the heart of God, and always exotic in the human heart, in which the *philia,* human love, is indigenous; but it has no salvation in it. You see that the rich man in Hell had the latter; he loved his brothers and wanted to send a missionary to get them saved before they came on his track to that awful place of torment.

Perfect love is the hottest thing you will find in the world. When people profess sanctification, like some identified with the "Burning Bush," and yet mercilessly cartoon the Lord's people, they thus advertise their own spurious profession to the world, as perfect love speaks no ill of its neighbor. This perfect love discriminates between sin and the sinner, loving the latter enough to die for him, but hating the former with an uncompromising indignation, as God cannot look upon sin with the least degree of allowance. When people become unteachable, we know that old Adam is not dead in them, for in that case they would be meek, lowly, humble, and teachable, like little Samuel, whom God called to the prophet's office at the early age of six years, and who said, *"Speak, Lord, for thy servant heareth."* Oh, how unteachable people need the one baptism which Jesus alone can give, to burn up their pride, egotism and vanity, with the fires of the Holy Ghost!

There is no probability that you will ever get too much fire if it is the right kind. N. B. It must be the fire of the Holy Ghost, burning up carnality and making the love which you received in regeneration, perfect. Satan was the great archangel Lucifer, before he fell, towering above the heavenly host in his transcendent intellectual enduement. A great preacher loses his hold on God and backslides, but still to a large extent retains his intellectual power and brilliancy. He still has that copious thesaurus of classical lore and diversified learning, intellectual, metaphysical, ethical, æsthetical and historical, which characterized him while walking with God in the beauty of holiness. After Lucifer in Heaven forfeited his allegiance to God, and was cast out, he still retained, and to this day very largely retains, his wonderful power of diagnosis, interpenetration, stratagem, acumen and shrewdness, which he brings into availability in the abduction of millions from the ways of truths and righteousness. When you go to seeking fire, he is ready, robed as an angel of light, to slip in adroitly and quietly like a weasel and give you wild-fire and fox-fire, to magnetize your longing eyes, bewilder and lead you astray like the will-o'-the-wisp, till you are entangled in the dismal swamps of his wild hallucinations, till he can get you off on some tangent, gradually alienating you from the simplicity which is in Christ. You start out from Union Station on the Grand Trunk line to Chicago. Your train strikes a sidetrack, which runs so parallel with the main trunk that you think surely you are right. But it gradually deflects more and more; night falls and you take a sleep, wake, and ask the conductor, and find that you have gotten entirely turned around and are running back the other way. This illustration would be more applicable in India, where they never tell you when you reach your destination. You have to attend to that yourself, or they will just literally carry you away.

We have no commandment to seek anything but the Lord. Consequently if you lack fire, come to Him for it. The rich young man asked after he had told Jesus that he kept all the commandments from his youth, "What lack I yet?" Jesus told him to consecrate all and follow Him, and he should have treasure in Heaven. When you sink away in the sweet will of God, and take Jesus for everything, rest assured that you will lack nothing. I have found some of our brethren so far sidetracked on the fire line as to become unteachable. When I gave them the positive Word of God, certifying that there is one baptism, (Eph. 4: 5), which John the Baptist, (Matt. 3: 11), says Jesus gives us with the Holy Ghost and fire, they yet contended for a separate baptism of fire after that of the Holy Ghost. Thus they threw wide open the door for Satan to come in and give them wild-fire and fox-fire to run into incorrigible fanaticism in this life, so he can give them Hell fire in the world to come. God help us to beware lest we should become wise above what is written.

You are only safe when in perfect harmony with God's Word. The baptism of fire as separate and distinct from that of the Holy Ghost and fire which Jesus gives is positively contradictory to God's Word and utterly without support. Look out, there is danger in the dark! I have known many of our good holiness people in the last thirty years to go off on a tangent, alien from the precious Word, till their lights went out and left them like Sampson, shorn of their locks. The old prophet says, *"The entrance of Thy Word giveth light."* In the absence of the Word we take the momentous responsibility of judgment and eternity into our own hands. When we refuse to move an inch without a clear, *"Thus saith the Lord,"* then we are on safe ground, God bearing the momentous responsibility. He is able to bear it; we are not. Then let us beware of wild-fire and fanaticism; they have derailed our predecessors, running them into wreckage and endless woe. If you are a child of God, Jesus is ready to give you the one baptism with the Holy Ghost and fire which crucifies old Adam, bears him into the atonement and gives you perfect love and victory forever.

The Lord gave me this experience thirty-eight years ago and to His good providence and His superabounding grace I am indebted more than tongue can tell. If I had not received sanctification, I would now be a superannuated preacher, laid on the shelf in the Kentucky Conference, where I was born and expected to spend my life. When presiding elder thirty years ago, the hardest work I ever had to do was to help superannuated preachers.

We never superannuated a man because he was a hundred years old, but because he had lost his efficiency and we could get no place for him.

I remember once when Bishop Wightman, of precious memory, was in the chair and we had on hand an old man who had a splendid education and had been a hero in his day, but had survived his efficiency, so that we could find no place where the people were willing to receive him. The good Bishop having tried the other six presiding elders, and having signally failed to get a place for him, finally came to me and said, "Brother Godbey, can you not give that dear old man an appointment?" I responded: "Bishop, I am sorry I have no work where they will be willing to receive him. You can appoint him in my district but it will be under my protest." Then he said: "Now, Brother Godbey, I appoint you a committee of one to wait on him and notify him that if he does not ask for a location, we must superannuate him, *nolens volens,* willing or unwilling." He broke down and cried like a child, his gushing tears copiously flowing. My tender heart broke, too, and we mutually wept together, and I said: "I would rather far be beaten with rods like Paul and Silas than to help superannuate another old man." I am now an older man than he was, with more ministerial years behind me, but with open doors enough before me for a thousand men. If I could be a thousand men today, I would have plenty of work for all. Do you not know that sanctification makes us young forever? So my indebtedness to sanctification no tongue can tell.

Satan is wonderfully tricky with the preachers, telling them that if they get sanctified nobody will want to hear them preach; whereas precisely the opposite is true. Before I was sanctified I was scarcely known outside of my own Conference. Now I have not only America throwing before me wide open doors from the Atlantic to the Pacific, but Europe, Asia, Africa and Oceania. I preached for three months in India night and day, nobody recognizing me as a feeble old man. Oh, how delightful it would be for me to go back to India and preach till the angels come for me. You get truly sanctified, lose yourself in Jesus, sinking out of self into the sweet will of God, and you will have more open doors than you know what to do with. Here I am at the end of fifty-three year's ministry, and literally bewildered whither to turn because I have grand open doors, not only in the homeland, but girdling the globe.

Satan tells you that if you get sanctified your Conference will stick you off into a starvation appointment, therefore he terrifies you with the rattle of dry bones and tells you this will be your fate—you will starve to death. Do you know that if you get filled with the sweet, perfect will of God, you will want that very starvation appointment? This perfect love casts out the fear of starvation, unpopularity, persecution, and everything else. When the Lord gave me this experience, I asked my presiding elder to request the Bishop to give me the poorest, hardest, and roughest appointment in the Conference. There were always many petitions in the Bishop's Cabinet, but in the opposite direction, racing after the rich appointments. When the presiding elder presented my request, (as the report reached me), the Bishop said: "Tell me what kind of a brother this is who sends in a request like this, such as I have never heard before." My presiding elder responded: "Bishop, a great change has recently come over this brother and he is now so flooded with love for everybody and so delighted with Jesus that he would gladly go to the North Pole and freeze to death, or to the equatorial deserts and burn to death, or to the swamps and die of malaria, or to the mountains and starve, all for Jesus' sake." A tear came into the old Bishop's eye and he said: "Brethren, here you see you have a preacher on your hands who will not provide for himself; therefore it is incumbent on us to provide for him." What was the result? Why, I can say to the credit of my Conference that they never did give me an appointment that did not give us a great deal more living than we knew what to do with, thus preparing us to help all the poor we met. The preachers are all scared worse than they are hurt. Oh, how fond Satan is of playing the bluff game on them! If they only could see the glorious liberty and unutterable brightness flooding life with constant sunshine; if they would only come over the swelling Jordan to the land where the flowers never fade and the fruit never fails, where corn and wine abound and milk and honey flow, and the sorrows of the past go into glorious eclipse, they would all expedite their flight from the howling wilderness.

I was a member of two honorable lodges in which they complimented me with the office of chaplain. To these I never did return a single time after that memorable epoch when the Lord baptized my soul with the Holy Ghost and fire. Truly I never had time to go back; I was too busy preaching the Gospel. The same fires that cremated the Free Mason, the Odd Fellow, the collegiate president and the big preacher, not only burned up Methodism, but creedism of every form and phase; leaving me nothing but God and His precious Word, which from that day have been my joy and song. The mighty men of the Holiness Movement, Inskip, McDonald, Wood, Keene,

Updegraff, Dodge, Janell, Dunlap, Fillman, Knapp, and others whose names are in the Book of Life, have gone to Glory. I am now one of the oldest men in the Movement. I will soon exchange the battle-field for the Mount of Victory, joining my triumphant predecessors. I am jealous for the cause of God and Holiness; it is everything to me.

Hydrolatry, pyrolatry and ecclesiolatry, and other devices of Satan are now prominent in the formidable batteries which Hell is turning against us. These specious forms of idolatry, along with eucharolatry, augment the formidable columns of ritualism and legalism, which on all sides are shoving out greased planks, with all the plausibility which the sophistry of heretics and fallen preachers can bring to bear, to decoy the eye from contemplating the glorious Sun of righteousness. This is our only security against the refrigerating atmosphere of that dead legalism which, like a ghost from the eternal world, has crept into the churches and breathed on them the pestilential spiritual malaria. It has proven a withering sirocco, blighting every blooming flower, blasting all the fruits and throwing a dark shadow over the once resplendent rainbow spanning the firmament and lighting up the atmosphere with the beauty of holiness. Truly it behooves us to ring the alarm bell and blow the trump of warning all along the embattled line, if we do not want our Sampsons to lose their locks on the laps of the world's Delilahs.

We have holiness churches now in controversy about ordinances. It would be pertinent that they should remember Paul, (Col. 1: 20), *"If you are dead along with Christ from the elements of the world, why are you subject to ordinances as living in the world?"* Entire sanctification nails old Adam to the cross and with him all of the ordinances. These ordinances symbolize the law from which Jesus has made us as free as angels, not only having kept it for us in His life, but paid the penalty for us in His death. Our old man was crucified with Him, (Rom. 6: 6), that the body of sin might be destroyed; therefore old Adam was nailed to the cross and with him the ordinances of the ritual, which symbolizes the law; which our Savior pertinently and eternally satisfies. In reference to these ordinances and churchisms of every kind, we, like Paul, should be all things to all men, that we may save some; remembering that the man of God is not to strive. Therefore you cannot indulge in controversy without disobeying God and grieving the Holy Spirit, consequently suffering experimental detriment.

After circumcision was effete and defunct, Paul took Timothy and circumcised him, on account of the Jews in that country, as they all knew that his father was a Greek. Paul did it simply to render Timothy's ministry more acceptable to the Jews. For the same reason, pursuant to their request, I immersed the "Texas boys" in the river Jordan. While sanctified people are gloriously saved from legalism in all its forms and phases, and rise so far above them that they have really gone into eternal eclipse, yet we are to be careful not to put a stumbling-block in the way of our brother, consequently carefully and prayerfully abstaining from all controversy. We are to recognize the perfect, glorious spiritual freedom of every brother, letting them walk in all the light God gives them, remembering the Pauline rebuke, *"Who art thou that judgest another man's servant? To his own master he standeth or falleth."*

Sanctified people, if true to their experiences, can live

together and in perfect brotherly love labor together for the salvation of souls; though some have the triune immersion of Doweyism, others the single immersion of the Baptists, others the single effusion of the Presbyterians, others the triune effusion of the Lutherans, which I witnessed administered to about one hundred by their native pastor in the greatest leper asylum in the world, after I had preached to them on the baptism which Jesus gives to His people.

Some holiness churches are non-ritualistic, as the Friends, who have never received water baptism in any way nor been convicted for it.

Thus I have mentioned for you a model holiness church, whose members are gloriously saved from ordinances, as all truly sanctified people are. These ordinances we wear as a loose garment, ready to drop them off the moment they conflict with the glory of God and the interest of His kingdom, to which we gladly and cheerfully subordinate them.

During all of my boyhood life, the Campbellites were constantly preaching all over that country immersion in order for the remission of sins, and clamorously mocking all effusion baptisms, pronouncing them farcial and worthless, and boldly preaching everybody to Hell who had not received immersion for remission of sins. At the same time they denied the personality of the Holy Ghost, identifying Him with the Word and preaching that the literal Word is the Spirit, burlesquing and ridiculing the very existence of the Holy Ghost.

One of the greatest leaders they ever had in that section of the country, who stood at the front of their Church for many years and was editor of their paper, "Apostolic Times," on one occasion, when preaching to a great audience at Kirkville, Madison Co., came down out of the pulpit, and stooping down looked under the benches and said, "Please excuse me, I am looking for that little man called the Holy Ghost." Then he followed with one of his powerful sermons against the Holy Ghost, denying His personality altogether. They actually united all their forces in a constant and persistent effort to eliminate from the popular mind the very existence of God in the person of the Holy Ghost.

You cannot conceive of the awful detriment which supervened to the popular mind through that predominant influence perpetrated solidly for a few generations. The normal result is the development of a great crop of infidels, who at the same time boldly claim themselves to be the only Christians in the world, incessantly repudiating the claims of all others even to the use of the name, and arrogating it to themselves in an exclusive sense. They constantly keep the lines distinctly drawn between themselves and all other denominations; contemptuously and condemnatorally denouncing them "sects," in contradistinction to themselves the "Christians," exclusively of all others. At the same time they sedulously, vociferously and incessantly denied that they ever were a denomination, claiming to be the only Christians in the world because they had no creed and took the Bible as their only authority, rejecting all sectarian names, and were consequently *the* Christians. They often said that if the Savior was on the earth He would walk through the towns, passing by every other church edifice but theirs, which He would enter and recognize them for His people, to the exclusion of all others. Their constant and unequivocal preaching, uncompromisingly condemnatory of all the people who claimed Holy Ghost experimental religion, not only denied the personal existence of the Holy Ghost, simply identifying Him with the Word and utterly eliminating Him from the Trinity, but ridiculed His presence and operation on the hearts of the people, so that they developed an awful trend of the popular mind in the direction of the unpardonable sin. (Matt. 12: 30-32.) This our Savior pronounces the "blasphemy of the Spirit." The meaning of blasphemy is contemptuous treatment of God. In this awful blasphemy of the Holy Ghost their preachers led the way, and the people followed them like sheep follow a shepherd.

The normal trend of their work was to drive all real conviction, which the Holy Ghost alone can give, out of the popular mind, and superinduce a species of bold, predominant infidelity on all sides, while at the same time claiming to be the only genuine article of Christianity in all the country, and consigning everything else to Hell. The inevitable result of this pseudo Gospel was to actually eliminate a knowledge of God entirely out of the country. This conclusion follows as a normal sequence from God's Word, which plainly teaches that no one can know the Son of God without the Holy Ghost, as He is His only revelator. (1 Cor. 12: 4.) We read in our Savior's preaching the positive statement that "No one knows the Father but the Son and he to whom the Son reveals Him." Therefore you see that when people reject the Holy Ghost they never can know either the Father or the Son; consequently those who do so actually retrogress into practical heathenism.

Their system of theology is so small and simple that they never lack preachers, because any one who has natural colloquial and oratorical gifts can, in a very little time learn all of their doctrines, which really are condensed in the simple statement, "Immersion for the remission of sins." This is really their only positive doctrine. All the balance is negative, denying not only the personal existence of the Holy Ghost, but all of His mighty works, in illuminations, conviction, conversion, regeneration, witness of the Spirit and sanctification.

The personal Father sits upon the throne of the universe, while millions of worlds wheel in their orbits, responsive to His sovereign mandate. The personal Son now sits at the right hand of the Father and administers the mediatorial kingdom of human redemption, through the personal Holy Ghost whom He sends into the world to shine into every heart, convict every soul, save every penitent, sanctify every believer, and reveal the glorified Savior to every human soul. He gives every faithful pilgrim all needed help, with the eye of Jesus, the infallible Paragon, to travel the King's highway of Holiness, successfully fighting the battles and winning victories, till the probationary war is ended and the *ipse dixit* rings, "It is enough, come up higher."

Since Campbellite theology, significantly *multum in parvo,* "much in little," is all told in the terse phrase, "Immersion for the remission of sins," they can all quickly learn to graduate. They have nothing to do but to deny the whole curriculum of spiritual truth, in which they shrewdly and adroitly bring into availability wit, humor, sarcasm, ridicule, burlesque, and even the awful and horrific blasphemy of the Holy Ghost. Hence our country swarmed with preachers who, to all spiritual people, sadly exposed their experimental ignorance of God; *e. g.*, two of them were holding a revival meeting and doing their best to get joiners all the time. One of them was preaching a powerful sermon against experimental religion and assuring the people that there is no such thing, and proving it by the fact that he did not have it. He said: "Here you see me; I have been through college and read the Bible through, and of course if there was any such thing as experimental religion I would have found it and would have it. But, brethren, I tell you frankly and honestly I have never seen anything of it, and I have not got it." Then turning to his brother preacher, sitting in the pulpit, he said: "Brother Martin, have you got it?" He spoke up: "No, I have not got it." Then he turned to his audience and said: "I prove by us two witnesses that there is no such thing as Holy Ghost religion."

Now recognize and diagnose that meeting for a moment. You see two sinners, utterly unacquainted with God, there pretentiously preaching the Gospel, of which they were utterly ignorant and had no more qualifications to preach than a Hottentot. It is utterly impossible for a man to preach what he does not know. The Gospel is not a speech to be delivered, but *"it is the power* (dynamite) *of God unto salvation, to every one that believeth."* (Rom. 1: 16.) Power is something to be known and felt experimentally. People who have no experience of personal salvation are utterly ignorant of the Gospel.

That whole country was inundated with that awful infidelity, its adherents clamoring vociferously for the isolated legalistic dogma, "Immersion for Remission," and actually fighting with all their might the whole curriculum of Gospel truth, even denying its very existence. So long had they overrun that country with this uncompromising belligerent preaching, denunciatory and condemnatory of the great spiritual experimental truth, which really constitutes Bible theology, and ever warding off opposition by constant bantering and challenging, that they actually captured the ignorant (spiritually) people and took them to the water in platoons. They required nothing in the way of antecedent preparation, except the confession that Jesus Christ is the Son of God; then they immersed them for the remission of their sins and warned them to have nothing to do with experimental religion.

You can see plainly that their work meant recruiting souls for Satan, because this church-joining and baptism, with their actual admonitions against the Holy Ghost, were calculated to harden their hearts and stiffen their necks, "that they might believe a lie and be damned;" thus leaving folks in infinitely worse spiritual plight than when they found them. While "Holy Ghost" and "Holy Spirit" are precisely synonymous, there being but one phrase in the original, *to hagion pneuma;* (it is perfectly optionary with the translator to render it "Holy Ghost" or "Holy Spirit," as he may prefer), in their baptisms they never said "Holy Ghost," but "Holy Spirit," simply meaning the Word, as they utterly denied the person.

The Campbellites boasted over their good confession, (Acts 8: 37), that of the eunuch before Philip baptized him. Alexander Campbell fought all of the human creeds all of his life, and boasted that he took the Bible alone; therefore he adopted this one question as the solitary requirement of people seeking admission into his church. At present no scholar believes the eunuch's confession ever was in the Bible. Erasmus, a noble, godly preacher, contemporary with Martin Luther, while transcribing the New Testament, studying over the baptism of the eunuch, concluded that there ought to be a confession preceding the administration. Therefore, supposing that some careless transcriber had left it out, he composed it according to his own judgment and put it in. Afterwards many old manuuscripts were discovered and as none of them contained it, of course, it became a known fact that it had never been in the Bible. If Campbell had known that, he would not have used it, as he was so stickleristical for the Word, which I confess to his honor.

I also endorse all of his arguments against human creeds. We certainly, as he earnestly contended, need no creed nor authority but the New Testament, which is plain on everything important in the way of doctrine, organization, church government and discipline. While he was a great intellectualist and very learned, his writings constantly show deficiency in spirituality. The dear man actually went into fanaticism on baptism, making it everything in the gracious economy, while the Bible makes it nothing but the outward sign of inward grace which is as real and available without the sign, as with it. A physician has a perfect right to put up his sign; yet he is just as good and efficient in curing the sick without it as with it. Meanwhile the various quacks, who kill instead of cure, can use as brilliant a sign as the best doctor in the world. Hence we see the silly nonsense of attaching saving efficacy to the mere outward sign. It is like hanging the doctor's sign over the sick bed instead of taking the panacea. A fanatic is a person who permits a theory or dogma to lead him away from God's Word. So long as you rigidly follow the precious Word, you will never go into fanaticism.

The Campbellites utterly deny that there is such a thing as our Savior's baptism, which He administers with the Holy Ghost and fire, now on the earth. They unanimously tell us and stoutly contend that it ceased when the apostles all left the world. As a rule they limit it to the day of Pentecost. In this they flatly contradict the Word of God. Therefore we know they are wrong. Acts 2:39, *"For the promise is unto you, and to your children, and to all who are afar off, even as many as the Lord our God shall call."* Peter is here talking about the identical baptism of the Holy Ghost and fire which they had received that very morning; therefore it is absolutely undeniable and inevitable. When people flatly contradict God's Word, always know that they are clearly gone into wild fanaticism. Those people constantly denounce the orthodox Christians of the different denominations who profess experimental religion, as fanatics; at the same time boasting vociferously that *they* are the Bible people. God's true people have always by their enemies been denominated fanatics, and such we are from their standpoint. Whereas they call us fanatics, and do not prove it for the good reason that they cannot, we know we are not fanatics. We believe and preach nothing but the plain Word of God, without twisting or perverting it; meanwhile we know that they are fanatics because they flatly contradict the Word of God.

The above Scripture, enunciated by Peter on the day of Pentecost, irrefutably contradicts the Campbellite dogma which restricts our Savior's baptism which He administers with the Holy Ghost and fire to that day and occasion, because Peter here is so clear and explicit that candor and veracity cannot possibly mistake. Here you see he positively says that this baptism which Jesus had given him that day is for "all that are afar off, even as many as the Lord our God may call." This refers to the Gospel call which is still going on. I have preached in towns where they said they never had heard this call before. In India the whole country has been stirred, especially in the last year, with the literal and actual fulfillment of this glorious promise during the three months of my constant preaching there, this wonderful baptism with the Holy Ghost and fire which constantly attended our ministry. It was not at all uncommon for the Spirit to fall on those people, and they would pray through to God, get saved and sanctified and shout all night. Oh, how gloriously is God this day fulfilling that promise among the benighted pagans, who have awaited the coming of the Gospel herald for thousands of dreary years.

Those Campbellites during my boyhood spent the most of their pulpit time toiling, sweating and vociferating in a desperate effort to drive the Holy Ghost from the people. When they had fought and conquered the Holy Ghost in a community, of course they had things their own way, with nothing to do but to get the people and immerse them in water. Of course the people had to take their word for it and conclude that their sins were forgiven in the act of immersion. As the preachers labored persistently to convince the people that there was no such a thing as a change of heart and a spiritual experience, of course when they got them completely under their influence they did not look for anything of that kind.

After immersion for remission, they only required converts to live a moral life, abstaining from outward, overt participation in the vulgar vices; and to be faithful church-goers, obedient to the active duties incumbent on a church member. The idea of getting to where they did not commit sin daily and hourly they utterly ignored and ridiculed; their preachers confessing that they sinned daily like other people, and preaching to people that nobody could live in this world without sin. They are simply strict and rigid legalists from beginning to end. They preached the law of pardon, confession and immersion for the remission of all their past sins.

They positively deny, and actually in their debates with me affirmed before the vast multitudes that a sinner has no right to pray, and if he does God does not hear him. They constantly falsify the statement of the man who had been born blind and whose eyes our Savior had opened (John 9:31), *"We know that God does not hear sinners, but if any one may be a worshipper of God and doeth His will, He heareth him."* They always used that as a proof that a sinner has no right to pray, and if he does God does not hear him nor answer his prayer. You see in this that they wickedly pervert the Word of God. This man was answering the statement of the Pharisees that Jesus was a sinner because He did not keep the Sabbath. The meaning of the man is that if Jesus was a sinner God would not work miracles through His instrumentality; whereas in the same sentence he says if any man is a worshipper of God He does hear him. Every penitent sinner bows down before God and does worship Him. Therefore you see this, which is the only passage they have for the fact that a sinner has no right to pray, proves the very opposite, that it is his glorious privilege to pray, and when he does, with a broken heart and contrite spirit, God always hears him. That is an illustration of the audaciously wicked perversion to which those dear people expose God's precious Word. Repeatedly, in their debates with me, their champion exponent (as they always selected the best they had) affirmed that the sinner had no right to pray; therefore you see they take the work of salvation entirely out of the hands of God, like the Roman Catholic priest who, when a man joined his church and asked him what he was to do to be saved, said to him, "Give yourself no concern about that; rest easy and I will attend to it. You obey me and I will see to your soul." Their attitude is literally papistical; and though they claim to be the Christians, in an exclusive sense (they did at that time, but think they have given it up), they are in fact anti-Christian.

The Pope is the anti-Christ of prophecy. All of his priests are subordinate anti-Christs. I am sorry I have to give the Campbellite preachers a place in that dark phalanx. Precisely like the Roman Catholic priests, they take the great work of saving the sinner out of the hands of God into their own, telling him to confess and believe, let them immerse him in water and—he is saved. In this their proselytic zeal constantly reminds me of the Pharisees in our Savior's time, who compassed sea and land to make one proselyte, and when done made him twofold more the child of Hell than before. Why? Because he still retained his old sins, and added to it the sin of hypocrisy, thus doubling the condemnation and the certainty of damnation. The meaning of hypocrite is a counterfeit Christian, who has the form and denies the power, and Paul says to turn away from all such. (2 Tim. 3:5.)

Really the normal work of the Campbellites is to make hypocrites, *i. e.*, give them the form and the name, in the utter absence of the reality, which they ignore and do not even claim to have. They claim to be Christians, on the presumption that the form they have passed through makes them such, which is utterly untrue. As Jesus says (Matt. 23:13), they only proselyte him to their church and do not save his soul. Therefore he is twofold more the child of Hell, having added to his old life of sin the new life of hypocrisy, thus doubling the mess for the bottomless pit.

As their system, all the way through, is dead, empty legalism, therefore after they have received their pseudo-conversion and become Christians in their nomenclature, they bring in the law, by which they are to live and retain their place in the kingdom, which of course is farcical, as they are farther from the kingdom of God than ever before. Now that they are citizens of the kingdom, they tell them they are to pray for the pardon of the sins which they have committed since they were immersed, but never ask God to forgive the millions of sins they committed before their immersion. They ridicule the very idea of holiness, rejecting and denying the personal Holy Ghost, claiming that the Word is the Spirit. Here you see again their anti-Christian attitude, *i. e.*, the very opposite of their boasted claim to being the Christian Church to the exclusion of all others. *Anti* means instead of; therefore the Pope is anti-Christ, because he usurps the place of Christ on the earth. The Campbellite preacher does precisely the same thing. He repudiates the Holy Ghost, who is the only Divine personality on the earth; that of the Father, sitting on the throne of the universe, and that of the Son, on the mediatorial throne at His right hand; while both the Father and the Son send down the Holy Ghost to *"convict the world of sin, of righteousness, and of judgment."*

So you see at once the plausibility and feasibility of

their sin against the Holy Ghost, *i. e.,* His blasphemy, which means His contemptuous treatment, by which He is rejected, grieved, and alienated forever, leaving the sinner doomed, even before he evacuates this body and passes out into eternity.

> "There is a time, we know not when;
> A point, we know not where;
> Which marks the destinies of men
> For glory or despair.
>
> "There is a line, by us unseen,
> That crosses every path;
> The hidden boundary between
> God's mercy and His wrath."

Satan is so adroit that he employs millions of false prophets, *i. e.,* counterfeit preachers, to decoy poor souls beyond that enchanted time and across that fatal line, the dismal bourne whence no traveler returns. As anti-Christ means the person who takes the place of Christ in the plan of salvation, there is actually no evasion of the conclusion that the Campbellite preacher is anti-Christ. While God's preacher hides behind the cross, and cries, *"Behold the Lamb of God, which taketh away the sin of the world,"* the Campbellite preacher says, "See, here is water; come, and let me baptize you for the remission of your sins." He really with his church rites gets between the sinner and Christ and substitutes church ordinances for Him who alone can save. He ridicules the idea that you can personally receive Jesus and receive an intelligent know-so salvation, witnessed to by the Holy Ghost.

The true preacher sinks out of sight; having done all he can to lead the soul to the Savior, he then tells him he must go alone and meet Him for himself and receive his own salvation, which he will know better than he knows that he is alive. All this the Campbellite preacher mocks. Why? Because he is really doing the work of anti-Christ. Therefore he does his best by his preaching to convince the sinner that he cannot get to Christ, meet Him and receive his salvation. This is an undeniable fact, since he actually tells him he has no right to pray, whereas prayer is the only possible method of access to the Savior. Hence you see this poor, mistaken man actually heads the sinner off and paralyzes all of his efforts to get to Christ, by telling him that he has no right to pray, and if he does God will not hear him. At the same time he pleads with him with all his might to come and join the church and let him immerse him in water for the remission of his sins, which is farcical and blasphemous. Jesus alone has the power to save a soul (Acts 4: 12). Our work is nothing but to tell the poor lost sinners about Him, and to do our utmost by our prayers and instructions to encourage them in their seeking after Him. This has always been the only way of salvation. God says through His own prophet: *"Let the wicked man forsake his way, and the unrighteous man his thoughts; let him return unto the Lord, who will have mercy on him, and to our God, who will abundantly pardon."* There never from the beginning has been any other way of salvation but for a man to seek and find the Lord for himself and get truly, knowingly, and intelligently saved, which God always attests by His Holy Spirit so that we know it is better than anything else. God is the greatest of all teachers. When men teach us an important truth, we know it; but when God teaches us, we know infinitely better than anything that man can possibly teach us.

When they get people utterly alienated from the influence of the Holy Ghost, there is no longer any probability of their finding Jesus their Savior, as the Holy Ghost alone can reveal Him. Consequently in every protracted meeting they would begin by preaching against the work of the Holy Spirit, tantalizing and mocking frequently in order to stir up the risibles of the people and expedite their utter alienation from the Holy Spirit. After they thought they had convinced them that there was no such thing as Holy Ghost religion, that it was all wild-fire and fanaticsm, then, changing their tactics, they would preach on sin and Hell, not holding up Jesus and His precious blood as the remedy, but obedience and especially church joining, confession and immersion. They would often speak very pathetically of the Savior's dying love, which was much to our edification, but all of that dying love is of no avail to the sinner unless he can find Him and get Him to save him. This he can never do unless the Holy Ghost has revealed Him; on this the Word is clear and explicit. *"No one can say that Jesus is Lord but by the Holy Ghost."* Therefore when they ridicule, and with sarcasm, witticism, burlesque and vociferous speeches have convinced the people that there is no Holy Ghost nor experimental religion, do you not see that they have already effectually headed them off from Jesus, whom none but the Holy Ghost can reveal? Oh, that those preachers could only be converted to God, so they would fly from the office of anti-Christ, as from the mouth of Hell, and take their places where they are so much needed as the preachers of our glorious Savior who is mighty to save.

The human heart spontaneously bows in reverential awe to everything in all the universe on which its salvation from sin, death and Hell depends. I have conversed with many heathen bowing before their idols. They all denied that they were worshipping them; but said that they had them because they reminded them of God. As the holiness people are from all churches, sects and nationalities, therefore we have a constant fight to keep them out of the different initial phases of idolatry, always more or less prevalent in Christian nations. See where Catholicism has gone so deep into idolatry that it is hard to tell whether their condition is any more hopeful than that of the heathen. They actually seem to have lost a personal knowledge of God.

Sanctification gloriously delivers every soul from idolatry in all of its forms and phases. Hezekiah was a great leader of the most prevalent Holiness Movement which had been known in the Jewish Church. He travelled all over the country destroying idols everywhere and doing his best to exterminate idol worship out of the land. Yet his only son, Manasseh, who succeeded him on the throne and reigned fifty-three years, went into idolatry and even had idols put into the holy temple and worshipped there. God permitted the king of Babylon to take him away captive. There he suffered awful horrors, as they made a specialty of punishing him in a most unmerciful manner. But these terrible sufferings brought him to repentance, so that he got down low, humbling himself before God and crying for His mercy till He heard him and delivered him out of his captivity, sent him back to Jerusalem and restored to him his kingdom. After this Manasseh did his best to reform the nation from idolatry, but could not.

The last great Holiness Movement in the Jewish Church was by Josiah. He went down to the bottom of things and did his best to exterminate idolatry out of the nation, travelling extensively and everywhere destroying the idols. The shrine of Moloch had stood in the valley of Hinnom, west of Jerusalem, ever since the days of Solomon. He utterly exterminated it and everything pertaining to idol worship. After all of his faithful efforts to purify the land from idolatry, when he passed away to his heavenly home the people soon began to drift back into the different forms of idol worship.

You have observed all of your life that when people want a revival, they have to take their eyes off of all their ordinances and lay down their churchisms and all of their controversies and get on their faces before God. When they go back to their churchisms they grieve the Spirit, and the revival evanesces. The Holiness Movement is God's revival for the evangelization of the world. He has brought us together from all parts of the world, that we may unite our hearts and hands and, losing sight of the various phases of those churchisms in which we were born, dropping the curtain over the dark, unsatisfactory past and leaving it with all of its wrecks, disappointments, difficulties and failures, march out under the blood-stained banner for the salvation of the world.

While we follow the blood-stained banner, we fight under the flag which means no compromise with sin or error. In that we are utterly free from all partisan alliances, legalisms and creedisms of every form and phase. We have forever closed our eyes to everything but God and His Word. In this exterminating war with sin and Satan we have no fight with churches. God has laid them all on our hearts, and we feel, like Paul, that we are truly indebted to all. We love all of the churches with a perfect love, which prepares us for martyrdom.

This unutterable love constrains us to tell the whole truth, however unsavory it may be to their perverted olfactories. Medical science reveals that the most powerful remedies and most indispensable in therapeutics are invariably the most nauseous to the patient. Palatable medicines are not generally worth administering. Heb. 4:12 tells us, *"The Word of God is a two-edged sword."* If we have the courage heroically to hug the salvation edge, it will quickly cut out of us everything we cannot take to Heaven with us. If we shrink from the salvation edge, we are bound to meet the damnation edge, which will cut out forever all of our hopes of Heaven. If we will not take the precious promises in the Bible, which superabound like a rolling ocean without bank or bottom, we are destined to take the awful judgments pronounced in that volume of infallible truth.

Well has man been denominated by philosophers "the religious animal." When I traveled around the world I saw that the poor heathen were quite as religious as the Christians; but the trouble is there is no Savior from sin in all their religion. Their idols stand between them and God, so that they stop short of Him "who is mighty to save and strong to deliver." In Christian lands, the water god is the most prominent; the same is true in heathen lands. They throng their holy rivers by the millions and plunge beneath the limpid wave to get rid of their sins, in their heathen blindness doing just what myriads are doing amid the glorious light of Christian civilization, showing thereby the universal trend toward idolatry.

Shall we not put away every god but Jesus? When we have Him, we have the heavenly Trinity, Father, Son, and Holy Ghost. Col. 2:9, *"In Him dwelleth all the fullness of the Godhead bodily."* You are complete in Him, who is the head of all government and authority. Therefore you see plainly that when you have Him enthroned, crowned and sceptered, reigning in your heart and life without a rival, then you have the glorious heavenly Trinity, and everything else appertaining to life and godliness. Hence the pertinency of the unceasing battle-cry, "Jesus only." The truth is, the very fact that you are running after other things is *prima facie* evidence that you do not have Him enthroned in your heart. He makes the life a cloudless sunshine, and so satisfies the longings of the immortal soul that you rest in perfect peace, having the full satiety of your hitherto insatiable spirit. If Jesus had been enthroned in my heart, I never would have constrained that Methodist preacher to immerse me in water, because I would have been perfectly satisfied already.

In writing my biography I have already given you quite a history of my debates with the Campbellites, which covered a space of ten years. during the very flower of my young manhood. Some who, in the Providence of God, may read this may conclude that I have a retaliatory spirit; in this I have the consolation that they are mistaken. I know that I love all the people whom I have met on the controversial floor with the perfect love which prepares me to die for them. Of this, God is my judge. If He needs my martyrdom to save others, to establish His truth, and to glorify His great name, I respond with shouts of victory. I am like the Baptist missionary motto, which exhibits an ox standing between the altar and the plow, *"Ready for service or sacrifice."* I have no creed to serve, and no dogma to defend. I have lost sight of everything but God and His precious truth, by which alone sinners can be saved.

Hezekiah, while destroying idols on all sides, exterminated the brazen serpent, because the people would burn incense to it, *i. e.*, worship it. That was idolatry. That brazen serpent was certainly an exceedingly precious memento of a glorious deliverance which had taken place hundreds of years before; and that godly king so realized its consolation as a souvenir of a glorious, merciful intervention, yet when the people would worship it, he utterly destroyed it, grinding it into powder, and throwing it into the brook Kedron.

George Fox, the paragon saint of the Friend's religion, had no objection to the ordinances *per se;* he appreciated them as precious mementoes of redeeming mercy and saving grace, yet he eliminated them altogether and declined to administer them, because he saw the people on all sides looking to them for salvation.

I would a thousand times rather take the place of a dry-land Quaker than a water-log Campbellite. When timber gets water-logged it always sinks to the bottom of the rivers, where it rots and is lost forever. When Christians get water-logged, if they abide in that condition, they will not only forfeit all the saving grace they ever had, but sink to the bottom of Hell. Good Lord, help us to beware of hydrolatry!

I have not yet written anything about the mode of baptism, for all that you have seen is on the design. There is where we meet the tug of war. If you take it like the Campbellites and the Mormons, as an indispensable condition of salvation, you become an idolater and are in awful danger of losing your soul, world without end. This arises from the fact that our Savior is omnipotent and needs no help to save your soul or mine. Therefore when you take in a Campbellite preacher, or Mormon prophet, or a Roman Catholic priest to help Him, you offer Him a downright insult; consequently He leaves the preacher and the water god to serve you. God only saves people when they utterly abandon the water god and every other idol and say to the preachers, "Stand back and let me go and meet the Lord!" Even Mohammed, the Arabian false prophet, in his Koran when he tells about going with the angel Gabriel up to Heaven, to stand before God and receive his commission, said that when they had finally reached the sixth heaven, Gabriel asked to be excused, telling him he could escort him no farther on his way to God; that he would find Him on the throne of the universe in the seventh heaven at quite a distance. Therefore he must go on alone and stand before the effulgent throne of the great God of the universe, hear His message and receive his commission.

I was a chronic mourner all my life, but never got salvation till I was sixteen years old. I was in the midst of a glorious revival among the Baptists, all of the Methodists in that country having united with them in a glorious revival effort. Finally, when I found the Lord and He saved my soul, I was in the woods alone, prostrate on the ground and crying for mercy, my sins like a mountain crushing me down to Hell. When I reached the point of utter desperation and gave up my preaching father, shouting Methodist mother, all the good church members, my own irreproachable moral character, which Satan had manipulated into a mountain of self-righteousness with which he had covered me and was pulling me into Hell, and absolutely realized that none of these could help me and I deserved nothing but a place in Hell, and said: "O Lord, just send me there; I now confess judgment against my own soul," then the darkness which had wrapped me in Satan's midnight sped away and the glorious Sun of righteousness did rise in my soul with healing in His wings. I had been down in a deep valley alone amid the forests, crying from the depths of my hopeless soul. I found myself on the top of the highest hill, leaping for joy. A new world had burst on me and everything looked so beautiful that language is utterly impoverished to this day in an attempt to describe the rapture of my spirit. I could but sing:

"Oh, how happy are they, who their Savior obey;
And have laid up their treasures above.
Tongue cannot express the sweet comfort and peace
Of a soul in its earliest love.

"That sweet comfort was mine, when the favor Divine
I first found in the life-giving blood;
Of my Savior possessed, I was perfectly blessed,
As if filled with the fullness of God.

"My soul mounted higher, in a chariot of fire,
Nor did envy Elijah his seat;
I rode on the sky, freely justified I,
And the moon it was under my feet.

"Jesus all the day long, was my joy and my song;
Oh, that all His salvation might see!
He has saved me, I cried, He has suffered and died,
To redeem a poor sinner like me."

Interview God's faithful pilgrims in every land and clime, and they have one and the same testimony, and tell you with exceptional unanimity, that they never did find the Lord till they had given up all human resources. Our work in leading souls to the Savior does not consist in gathering around them transitory consolations, personal, legalistic, or ritualistic, but in knocking them all away, so as to leave the seeker alone with God. Spiritual people are infinitely valuable in the way of instruction and prayer, but when we have done all in our power, we must leave the soul alone to go to God and settle the matter for eternity. The dogma of baptismal regeneration actually substitutes the preachers and the ordinances for the Savior, which simply means wholesale damnation.

In my deliverances hitherto on the design of baptism and the work of the Holy Spirit and prayer, I have dealt candidly with souls; shown neither distinction nor mercy to the people who incur the awful responsibility in standing between the living and the dead. To extend clerical and ecclesiastical courtesy in a crisis of this kind would simply be not merely homocide, but murder in the first degree. I am glad God gave me grace to declare His whole counsel, *"Cry aloud and spare not,"* when I was in that country where I was born and reared, and where my dear father before me heroically preached the truth which will judge us all in the last day.

As a matter of fidelity and veracity in the run of my biography, I must make a little allusion to the mode of baptism. If you can do so, steer clear of that dangerous heresy, hydrolatry, which is a form of idolatry so subtle and capricious that, like a weasel, it will creep in on you before you are aware. If you are actually lost in Jesus and can stay there, you need not be afraid of the water god, nor any other; but rest assured, hydrolatry will settle on you like a nightmare and you will never know it till the paralysis has carried you beyond recovery. I made a narrow escape from its grab at me; when I took immersion to sanctify me and it utterly failed, I was enabled to pass the water line forever. Then I sought for nineteen years in my blind way without a teacher, and God, in His great mercy, gave me the grand desideratum, for which my soul had so long been sighing and crying. After I had passed the water line, I wandered over mountain and vale, through valley and plain, everywhere crying out for holiness; desiring purity of heart more than anything else in the universe.

Dry land Quakerism is one extreme and triune immersion the other. You are all right in either attitude, or anywhere between, if you have an experience of New Testament salvation which means that you are radically emptied of sin, and copiously filled with the Holy Ghost; lost in Jesus, desiring nothing but God, and daily sinking deeper into His glorious Divinity. In that attitude the triune immersion, Doweyism, ritualistic Quakerism, and the whole procession of intermediate saints, march up the King's highway in perfect harmony. But the moment the water god gets in, he begins to rival Jesus, and proposes to divide the glory with Him; which means confusion, apostasy, and damnation. Our wonderful, omnipotent Jesus needs neither the help of the water god, the Campbellite preacher, Mormon prophet, nor Roman Catholic priest. When Jesus reigns in your heart and life without a rival, you have the everlasting victory over popery, prelacy, priestcraft, doubt, and the devil. While I have no interest whatever in the mode of baptism, I do have the greatest interest in your soul and must warn you against the slightest encroachment of hydrolatry.

God, in His good providence, gave me a classical education. I became a good reader when I was six years old, and never took time to sow wild oats, nor run after the devil. I have been a student all of my life. For the glory of God I have ransacked the vocabulary of all ages and nations for light and information on this controversy which divides the Lord's people. God has permitted me three times to travel in the Holy Land—in 1895, 1899, 1905. With the honesty of a Judgment-bound pilgrim I have examined everything calculated to throw light on this subject, and thus corroborate the precious Word. Therefore I give you the benefit of my life-long study and extensive travel; asking God in His condescending mercy to make me the humble instrument in helping you to study His wonderful revelation. If you are not saved from all prejudice, you had better get down before God and stay on your knees till He gives you a clean heart, as the slightest prejudice will blind your eyes to the truth and may do you incalculable damage. I do believe without a doubt that you will receive my testimony as a candid and truthful witness to what I have seen, and you may go and see for yourself.

As to the Word of the Lord, I shall not give you an opinion. When I was preaching in Philadelphia, a brother came to me and said he wanted my Commentaries on the Scriptures and proceeded to observe that he supposed that they were my opinions, and gave that as a reason why he wanted them, because he desired to know my opinion about the Bible. I said, "Brother, if that is what you want, you need not get them, because they do not contain my opinions, but the Word of the Lord; Scripture explaining Scripture. The Bible is God's dictionary and explains itself." I notify you now that I have neither time nor space in my biography for my opinions, creed, theology, Church rites, etc. Therefore on the mode of baptism, watch me closely and see that I give you the Word of the Lord.

I have used for the last thirty years nothing but the Greek, which our Savior and His apostles spoke and wrote, and which was the learned language of the world during those days. Constrained by the Lord's dear people, you know I have translated it so you can see it for yourself, free from the errors which had inadvertently crept in during the ages of transcription which preceded the art of printing. As this is my last will and testimony, of course I am overly anxious to sacrifice everything for the truth, desiring nothing else.

When God sanctified me, the Holy Ghost fell on the people everywhere I preached, the altar was crowded with seekers and the power was there gloriously manifest in conviction, conversions, and sanctification; of course I had to expose the silly sophistries of baptismal regeneration, in order to convict the people so that they would seek the Lord and get saved. For more than a generation the Campbellites had rolled their belligerent tide over that country, claiming to be the only true Christian people and anathematizing all others and consigning them to Hell if they were not immersed for the remission of their sins; meanwhile it seemed that they would take everybody into their Church. The Methodist preachers had to yield to that perpetual war with constant challenges, so that they had generally given up the altar, and merely took in members as seekers and made no public effort to get them saved. Consequently I found the great majority of Methodists only in the attitude of seekers, never having been converted. When the Lord filled me with the Holy Ghost, making me a cyclone of fire, my preaching stirred everything, raising the multitudes on tiptoe, and filling all houses till standing room was at a premium, and of course stirring Diabolus with his myrmidons till they raced from the bottomless pit to hold their people, whom the Lord, through my humble instrumentality, was taking out of the way. Multitudes of Campbellites were stricken down with conviction and crowded the altars; old and young, great and small, leading members rank and file, and all sorts got gloriously converted. The Lord, as a normal consequence of the blessed work He had done for them, invariably led them out of that Church into the Methodist or the Baptist.

Eternity alone will reveal the good that was done in that ten years' war, the very length of time the Greeks besieged old Troy before she fell a prey into their hands. I was not alone as a contestant with them during those stormy times. Doctors Ditzler, Miller, Hiner and Fitch heroically met them on the gory field, and the results were exceedingly fruitful in the kingdom of God.

During the war we had a glorious opportunity to preach the Gospel to thousands who had never heard anything but that pseudo-water theology which had not a scintilla of salvation in it, and never did bring anybody within a million miles of salvation. An eight day's debate invariably wound up with a great spiritual awakening and revival of Scriptural regeneration and sanctification. As the days rolled by the Spirit would rest on the people in constantly increasing potency, illuminating, convicting, and reviving, till shouts would ring out, reminding me of a camp-meeting. Methodists, Baptists and Presbyterians, and other people who believed in Holy Ghost religion, would get wonderfully revived. The colored people were then in slavery and had no learning, but many of them who had salvation would gather around within hearing distance. These colored people who, as a race, are harder to gull with the devil's sophistry and to satisfy with the dead form without the power than white people, were literally filled and electrified with the Holy Ghost preaching. Meanwhole conviction like a nightmare from the eternal world would settle down on the Campbellites, whose faces looked as long as my arm and blue as indigo, and I know the blessed Holy Spirit gave them an awakening which they never have forgotten. Thus we had glorious consolation of spiritual fruits while the debates were in progress.

After the debates were over it seemed as if we had had a revival in the great community who had thronged to hear them. They served as awakeners of the people, stirring them up to study their Bibles as never before and to read good books and seek a closer walk with God. Many of them took place in my district. When I was presiding elder over twenty counties and during the four years of my eldership, I constantly saw the cheering fruitage of those discussions. They gave me and all others the liberty we needed freely and fearlessly to *"preach the Gospel with the Holy Ghost sent down from Heaven."* 1 Peter 1:12.

If you could go into that country you would see the fruit of those debates among the churches in peace and harmony. Before the war you could not preach straight

Holy Ghost religion, as God requires all whom He has called to do, without an assault by a water-log preacher. Now you can preach Jesus and the Holy Ghost, the blessed Father and the Gospel dynamite, sky-blue regeneration and red hot sanctification, firing on their idols indiscriminately (not sparing the water-god) and go away with your scalp on all right. Before the war you would have been fired on from every point of the compass.

The Lord gave me the experience of entire sanctification in 1868, but I stood much alone in the great Sunny South till the Holiness Movement crossed the Ohio River in 1883, and swept Kentucky like a cyclone. The most of the preachers in that Conference in the grand old state and myriads of members went tiding over into Beulah Land. There you see the grand harvest from the seed heroically sown amid the thunders of battle and the tempests of war.

We have mentioned the universal silence that now rests throughout that memorable battle-ground, as a delectable souvenir of God's blessings in that war. It is a consolatory fact that the Campbellites have buried the hatchet, and of course their antagonists have all done the same, as they are no longer needed to protect the armies while they wage an exterminating war against sin, death and Hell. Kentucky is an Indian word, and means "the dark, bloody ground," because there the tribes so often met, fought, bled and died. But we are glad that the ages of darkness and blood have retreated before the age of Christian civilization. I am glad that the war wound up nearly twenty years ago and that the battlefield is still silent; I hope that it will ever so remain.

Yet we must freely and fearlessly preach the whole

truth. Paul said he was free from the blood of all men because he had not shunned to declare all the counsel of God. On the design of baptism, and the privilege of the sinner to pray, I fought with them for life, because they were vitally useless, involving the problem of salvation, meaning Heaven or Hell for the people. It is a battle along whose moving phalanx fire flashed and blood flowed. N. B. Fidelity and veracity require me to give you a brief historic sketch of that feature of the war which appertains to the mode of baptism, where I never saw a spark of fire or a drop of blood, but they regard it as really a vital issue. This follows as a legitimate conclusion from its non-essentiality for the salvation of souls, which we prove by oceans of Scripture. I simply add one here to the many which have gone before, 1 Cor. 1: 14, *"I thank God that I have baptized none of you except Crispus and Gaius."* These two brethren were the most prominent in the Church, the former the chief ruler in the synagogue and the latter the host of the whole Church, *i. e.*, throwing open wide his doors and entertaining everybody. Now you know positively that if water baptism was a saving ordinance Paul would never have spoken of it in that way, that he thanked God that he had never baptized any of them save those two. You could not get a Campbellite preacher or a Mormon prophet to save your life to say publicly he thanked God that he did not baptize people. Why? Because they believe that water baptism is necessary for the remission of sins.

The very fact that people don't talk like the Bible and do it with a glad and free heart makes it evident that they are not in harmony with it. It seems to me that I am certainly the happiest old man in the world. Why? Because I shout over everything I read in the Bible without a single exception. How do you account for that? Because the blessed Holy Ghost, the third person of the Trinity, who made the Bible, dwells in this tenement of cumbrous clay which I and He will soon evacuate unless Jesus comes to take away His Bride, in which case He will transfigure me in the "twinkling of an eye," 1 Cor. 15:51. I shall then fly away to meet the Lord in the air. If you are going up to live in Heaven, you must have heaven in your heart and in your life. You can never do that till you swallow the whole Bible by faith alone, contented to digest it afterward, like the goose swallowing corn. Praise the Lord, I have done that very thing. I do not know much about it, but, glory to God, I believe it all and the blessed Holy Spirit who made it is teaching me most wonderfully, letting me down deeper into God's glorious Divinity; leading me out into broader latitudes and progressively onward into grander longitudes; permitting me to climb up into loftier altitudes, and quickening my intellect into more capacious apprehensions of God's wonderful, incomprehensible and immunicable attributes. Omniscience and Omnipotence are thus flooding my soul with glory ineffable.

We are past the blood and fire era in our discussion of baptism. The Holy Ghost in His mighty work, and the glorious and the wonderful efficacy of the sinner's prayer for the pardoning mercy of God in Christ, received and appropriated by faith alone, as the poor sinner is still in bondage to the devil till his glorious emancipation by the omnipotent arm of the wonderful Christ, who came from Heaven to redeem him from sin, death and Hell, alone bring salvation. If the sinner does ever so much good work before he gets out of the devil's kingdom in answer to his own prayers, those good works would belong to Satan forever. If you build a golden house like that of the emperor Nero on your neighbor's lot, you cannot hold it to save your life; the laws of every nation under heaven will turn it over to the proprietor of the land. Therefore you see the diabolical "hotch potch" of the salvation by works with which Campbellite preachers gull and deceive poor sinners; positively forbidding them to pray for God's pardoning mercy and telling them that if they do so He will not hear them.

You see all along the lines of spirituality that we wade through blood, amid flames of fire and mountains of the slain. But now as we cross swords on the mere question of mode, you will see neither fire flash nor blood flow, as it is not in any sense a vital issue. There is but one point to guard and that is to fight off all the alien gods. If we can keep them out of the ranks of the holiness people, and settle forever the great problem of Christ crowned within, sceptered and enthroned Lord of all forever, reigning in the heart and life without a rival, the shout of victory will never cease to ring along the embattled line. Col. 2:9, *"In Him dwelleth all the fulness of the Godhead bodily."* Here you see that when you have Jesus crowned within you really have the glorious Trinity, *i. e.*, the Father, Son, and Holy Ghost, as the latter is the executive of the Trinity and the revelator of Christ, whose province it is not only to reveal to the human spirit, but to crown Him in the heart, glorious and eternal Prophet, Priest and King. Therefore if you are not true to the Holy Ghost, you will never so much as get acquainted with Christ, who is everything to the Christian.

"If you are dead along with Christ from the elements of the world, why are you subject to ordinances as living in the world?" Col. 2:20. In the old dispensation we were subject to ordinances, because they were necessary to symbolize Christ and His mighty works. But since Christ has come and has done His work, wrought the great vicarious, substitutionary atonement, and redeemed the whole world from sin, death, and Hell, we are no longer subject to ordinances, as they are in no way essentially identified with the gracious economy. They are mere souvenirs, beautiful in their situations; reminding us of the mighty works already wrought by the great Antitype, at whose coming all the types and shadows, symbols and ordinances, fled away. Therefore the truly sanctified are no longer subject to them, but they are subject to us, as we in Christ have the victory over all of those things which put a yoke on the neck of the Hebrew fathers, *"which they were not able to bear."* They broke down under that burden, symbolizing the failure of the body of Christ after that night of toil and suffering to bear His cross up Mount Calvary. We need a thousand glittering swords constantly unsheathed to fortify our holiness people against the encroachment of alien gods, which have actually captured all of the old ecclesiasticisms. Oh, how they are crowding on all of the Protestant Churches!

A presiding elder, making a speech to raise a princely sum of money to build a church edifice, with a cost twenty times the amount necessary for comfort and convenience, nineteen-twentieths of the money actually being due to the poor heathens who have never heard the name of Jesus, eloquently referred the people to the Temple of King Solomon, which he ornamented with gold, expending uncounted millions. The Queen of Sheba travelled five thousand miles on a camel to hear his wisdom, see his glory and bring him a million dollars worth of gold. Now what was the matter with that presiding elder? Sad to say he had actually gone into idolatry, *i. e.*, church worship. Ecclesiolatry is a specious form of idolatry which is fast capturing the great Protestant Church, which God gave to the world through His noble heroes, Luther, Bunyan, Fox, Knox and Wesley, the immortal leaders of the Holiness Movement in their day and generation. Oh, how fearful are the inroads of these alien gods this day!

Eucharolatry has just about captured the Lutherans, and is making awful inroads into the others.

I am personally acquainted with a great holiness leader, once an evangelist, the flash of whose keen New Jerusalem blade electrified many warriors to redoubled heroism on the battlefield. He is now a pastor and building for himself an institutional church, having accommodations not only for all religious people, but an Atheneum well supplied with reading matter, not only religious but secular, and a billiard room and ten-pin alley for the entertainment of the worldly people. He says this is so they will not have to run after Satan, but so he can have them under his influence with a chance to lead them to God. The last time I heard from him, my informant told me that he saw him walking around bossing the work with a great big Havana cigar in his mouth. So you see he is worshipping at the shrine of two alien gods, ecclesiolatry, the Church god, and tobacco, the filthy god. Therefore, though he yet claims to be a loyal holiness man and sanctified, I need not tell you whither he has drifted, and the end is not yet.

The downward trend in religion never means anything short of damnation, because Satan is manipulating it, and he is making his full calculations upon taking all who tinker with him to Hell. Now while we investigate the mode of baptism, remember I am feeling great concern for the dear holiness people who are the hope of the world. God has raised up this great latter-day Movement, with which He is this day girdling the globe, to preach the everlasting Gospel to all nations and to call out the bride from every kindred and tongue and people; to get her robed and ready for the speedy return of His glorified Son to this world, for Him to put the devil out and reign forever. I am now, in the providence of God, one of the living fathers of this Movement. I am so glad that this great revival of Holy Ghost religion represents all churches and denominations, with their diversified ecclesiastical views and ceremonies.

While in India those memorable three months, in the providence of God, I travelled and preached night and day to multitudes of the dear Indians through interpreters, and to the missionaries and English-speaking people *viva voce*. I did not discriminate by hunting up the Methodists, who, in the good providence of God, have a hundred and fifty thousand members in that country. I went to all, not passing by the German-Lutherans, who are doing noble work. We fellowshipped with them as holiness brethren most cordially, and I never did receive a more fraternal welcome as they made me feel free as Gabriel. I also went and served our feet-washing holiness brethren with great delight. We had the blessed consolation that we enjoy the glorious freedom which forever saves us from a fault-finding spirit, for the fires of the Holy Ghost burned up the critic's cap, and if any of you are still wearing one, I hope the Lord will pour the fire on you and burn it up and that you may never buy another one. Satan has a variety on hand very fantastical and beautiful; he charges you neither silver nor gold if you should desire to purchase one. You can have your choice, as he has but one price and that is your soul.

After God took Hezekiah to Heaven, his own son and successor led the people back into idolatry; after Josiah, the great holiness leader, had gone to Heaven, his son, Jehoiakim, burned the Word of the Lord. God in signal mercy took those loyal kings to Heaven before they saw the evil that was coming. God is still going to have a people on the earth, who will hold up the banner of holiness and give the Gospel trumpet no uncertain sound. After you and I have laid the armor down and gone to our account with God, people of whom we have never heard nor thought will still lead the embattled hosts to victory. The thing for us to do is to wash our own hands from the blood of souls, rising triumphantly above the wild clangor of Satan's musicians celebrating the orgies of alien gods, whether hydrolatry, ecclesiolatry, pyrolatry, eucharolatry, or some other strange god, whose name you have never heard. We have but one God, the great Jehovah, who, accommodatory to the glorious plan of salvation, has revealed Himself to us in the three persons of the Father, the Son, and the Holy Ghost—trinity in unity—and we have this blessed and glorious Trinity all in our wonderful Jesus, *"who is the head of all government and authority,"* Col. 2: 10, and *"you are complete in Him."* Therefore when you get your attention on anything else, rest assured it is going to prove a snare.

When God had so wonderfully used Gideon to break the yoke of the Midianites and liberate all Israel from their hard bondage, they elected him to the kingdom by voluntary acclamation. He said to them, "Neither I nor my son shall ever be your king, but the Lord God of Israel shall be your king forever. But one thing you can do for me, just give me the gold which you took as a prey from your conquered enemies." This they did with jubilant enthusiasm. Then Gideon made a golden image out of it, of course, not dreaming of idolatry, from which God had used him to liberate his country. He only aimed at it as a souvenir of the great and glorious victory which they could never forget. But do you not know it proved a snare to Israel and conduced to alienate them from God, as they had not the stamina to withhold from it that intense admiration which ultimated in the reverence which is due to God alone? We cannot keep our experience beyond the day of our simplicity, and perfect humility at the feet of Jesus.

When we entered upon the Campbellite war, their champion invariably affirmed, "Christian baptism is immersion." Campbell always affirmed it and claimed it was his prerogative to wield the laboring oar, as he had the truth. In debate it devolves on the affirmative to prove his proposition; the negative has nothing to do but to refute the arguments of the affirmative. They had always in their debate affirmed immersion; therefore when they led off, with me in the negative, my only normal work was to refute their arguments, if I could; if not, of course they gained the day. In all of these discussions we obligated ourselves in writing to recognize the Bible as the authority. Of course I had nothing to do but just read the precious, infallible Word and refute all of their arguments from it. The result was that they so weakened on the mode, that after awhile they refused to take the affirmative and wield the laboring oar, but said if I would take the affirmative, they would still debate the subject with me in the negative. To this I acquiesced at once and accepted the situation, granting my opponent the privilege of stating the proposition to suit himself. Then they stated it, "*Christian baptism is affusion*," saying that if I would lead off in that affirmation they would follow in the negative. Of course in their negative arguments, disproving affusion, they would prove immersion. As the years rolled on, the battle still raging, they continued to weaken till they refused to debate at all.

You see from this ten years' war how they fought and lost. As "Immersion for remission" is really their god, they staked everything on it. They had so long had their own way that they were perfectly confident that their doctrines were irrefutable. As the years rolled on and the war waxed hot, the whole country got stirred up with these debates, which we thoroughly advertised long beforehand in the papers of both Church and state, and vast multitudes came from a distance thronging like great camp-meetings. The Campbellites eventually found out that it was not a one-sided affair, as they supposed, but a game at which two could play, and the people far and wide were finding out to their surprise the weakness of their course, and seeing that they had been mistaken. The result was that they got weaker and weaker, till the time came when the tables were all turned around and we became the challenging party; they operating on the negative.

From the days of Campbell they had affirmed immersion. The time came when they refused to affirm it, and said they would be willing to debate if I would affirm affusion. This I did with great delight, knowing that my foundation was sure, the eternal Word of God. The time came when they actually broke down on the negative, as they had on the affirmative, and refused to debate any more. They saw that the weakness of their cause had become a matter of surprise and notoriety. While I, having been brought up under the regime of the good old-style Holy Ghost religion, never had any leaning toward their heresies, yet I supposed that they had stronger arguments than I found when I crossed swords with them. I was overwhelmed with astonishment at the very weakness of their cause. So it was like the controversy of Saul and David, the latter waxed stronger and the former weaker to the end. Consequently, twenty years ago, with our New Jerusalem blades keener and brighter than ever, behold we found the enemies' camp deserted.

Twenty years of conquered peace have rolled away; the beautiful blue grass is growing tall and green on the plains once hardened by the tread of the soldiers and now grown rich by the blood and bone of the warriors there fallen amid the din of conflict. Those of us who passed through the war from beginning to end are full of praises to God for His unspeakable mercies, redeeming that land, the most lovely I have ever seen in my "round the world" tours, from the galling yoke of the cruel old water-god, and elevating it above the inundations of the arctic rivers, which had not only flooded Immanuel's lands and drowned out the crops, but brought down on us a north pole blizzard, which had already strewn the land far and wide with spiritual corpses. This war was, in the providence of God, the glorious antecedent of the Holiness Movement which immediately followed it.

I am so glad God loves everybody with perfect love. I wish all the holiness people would join me in prayer for the whole Campbellite denomination, that they may give up their hydrolatry and give Jesus a chance to save and sanctify them. Here on the "Mount of Blessings," where I dictate these pages, we have constantly in "God's Bible School" two hundred blood-washed and fire-baptized young people. We also have a blessed holiness college at Wilmore, Ky., where many young preachers are preparing to disseminate the blessed saving truths of God. To both of these holiness schools I especially recommend my dear old state, the charming land of old Kentucky, that you make it your special field of labor, and never forget to show your loving kindness to the Campbellites. Do all you can to help them spiritually, as they have spent their lives encompassed with dead legalism and been cultured in the pestilential dogmatisms of anti-Christianity, which Satan, the great deceiver, has been palming off on them for genuine Christianity.

Chapter VII.

ARGUMENTS FOR BAPTISM BY AFFUSION.

"Brother Godbey, please for our edification give us a little sketch of the arguments by which you proved the proposition which they asked you to affirm, *i. e.,* Christian baptism is affusion.

Well, first, "Christian" is an adjective from the noun Christ and means something appertaining to Christ, therefore Christian baptism is really and literally the baptism which Christ gives with the Holy Ghost and fire. You know He never did baptize anybody with water. Now we have nothing to do but to look in the Bible and see how He does it. You well know that He baptized the one hundred and twenty on the day of Pentecost according to the word of John the Baptist, Matthew 3:11, *"I indeed baptize you with water . . . but He will baptize you with the Holy Ghost and with fire."* This prophecy of John the Baptist was literally fulfilled on the day of Pentecost when Jesus did baptize the one hundred and twenty disciples. Now the question of mode is quickly and easily answered. If you will read Peter's sermon on that very occasion you will find he tells us all first thing how the Savior did it, Acts 2:16, *"But this is that which was spoken by the prophet Joel; And it shall come to pass in the last days, saith the Lord, I will pour out my Spirit upon all flesh."*

In many places in the New Testament we are informed that the Spirit and the fire fell on them. So here you have the mode of Christian baptism positively revealed, needing no comment, as I am not writing this to infidels but to Christians who believe the Bible. Therefore you see the question is already forever settled that our Savior baptizes by affusion. That is the only baptism in all the world, the symbolic ordinance with water being the mere outward form of the real baptism which Jesus gives with the Holy Ghost and fire.

The hydrolaters endeavor to relegate the Savior's baptism to that day on which He gave it to His disciples. You know three thousand were converted in the morning service and five thousand in the afternoon. Peter, in that noble sermon doing his best to convince his audience of a hundred thousand people that it was their privilege to have it, that it was not restricted to the apostles, positively certified, in connection with his quotation from Joel which extended it to all flesh, *i. e.*, to every human being of all ages and nations, to them, *"For the promise is to you and to your children, and to all who are afar off, even so many as the Lord our God may call."*

You see, then, from the plain Word of God, that the baptism which the Savior gives with the Holy Ghost and fire is for *all people in every age,* without a solitary exception. Paul tells us in Ephesians 4:4, that this is really the *only* baptism, thus leaving no door open for men and devils to creep in and usurp the Word of Christ. We can only represent it to mortal eyes by the administration of water, which is the symbol of the Holy Ghost. Therefore you see that Jesus, the great Baptizer, who must baptize every human soul that shall ever walk the golden streets, invariably administers it by affusion. On this the Word is so conclusive that nothing but infidelity unambuscaded can deny it. I hope you are already dead to your notions and ideas, which are frequently erroneous because of wrong teaching; what people say is nothing; what God says will judge you and me in the last day.

Second. "Was not Jesus Himself immersed in the river Jordan?" Let Him answer. Matthew, Mark and Luke all tell us about the trouble He got into with the scribes and Pharisees when He came into the holy campus, (E. V., temple), and drove out those animals which they had there to sell to the people for sacrifices, much to the desecration and pollution of that sacred place. Then they demanded of Him His authority for exercising the privileges which belonged only to the high priest. You will find if you will read all of these three records, that He referred them to the baptism of John for His authority, showing plainly that He was thereby inducted into the office of high priest. Now if you know how the high priest was anointed you know how John baptized Jesus. I know you remember this item in the Old Testament, where it says that Moses poured the oil on the head of Aaron. Consequently we know that John poured the water on the head of Jesus. This all of the ancient statuary corroborates, which, without an exception, represents Jesus standing and John pouring the water on His head.

Third. King James' Translation was made by forty-seven scholarly members of the Anglican Church, who had been baptized by triune immersion, which came into use as early as the third century and had not passed out when the translation took place in 1611. Therefore that translation constantly leans to immersion, because it was the mind of the translators, therefore it has given currency to a popular superstition in favor of immersion. Many people think it says our Savior went down into the water. It does say He came up out of the water, which is simply a wrong translation, and if you will look in the Revised or any other translation, you will find it corrected, simply reading, "He came up from the water," only implying that He was at it and not in it.

Fourth. Let us hear the testimony of John himself. He tells us how he baptized Jesus and all the balance. John was the brightest and the best preacher of the Gospel the world had ever seen. Besides, this is not simply the word of the blessed Baptist but the infallible Word of God. Matthew 3:11, *"I indeed baptize you with water unto repentance . . . but He will baptize you with the Holy Ghost and fire."* Here he tells us all how he baptized the people. You know he uses the same word baptize to tell us that he did with water what Jesus was going to do with the Holy Ghost and fire. You know that on the day of Pentecost, when Jesus baptized the disciples in fulfillment of this prophecy of John, He poured on them His Spirit and fire fell on them. If you will let the Lord save you from all your prejudices and superstitions, so you can take John at his word and believe him without a doubt, you will know once and forever that John did to the people with water the very thing that Jesus did with the Holy Ghost and fire. Yes, but, you say, why then did he baptize them in the river? That does not change the question of the action he performed. If they were standing in the river waist deep it is certain that John poured the water on them, because he says so, and we know his word is true. All of that statement "in the river," was simply put down there by King James' translators, who had received the triune immersion and had it in mind. All the statements in the original are merely local, and perfectly correctly translated, "in the river" or "at the Jordan," just as we say Cincinnati is *on* the Ohio River, and not *in* it.

I have been to the Jordan three times and given special attention to the very place where John held his meetings and Israel crossed over. The last time I was there, pursuant to their request, I immersed the three "Texas boys" in the Jordan. We four and our guide and escort hunted in vain for a good place, and of course took the best we could get. It was so muddy, as it always is, that we could not see an inch below the surface, and our guide, Shukrey Hishmeh, born in Jerusalem and educated for a guide, who has been escorting travellers all over that country for the last twenty years, feeling his responsibility in case that some of us should get drowned, did his best to dissuade the young men, telling them that he had seen men drowned right there. But they, fearless of the water, as they are splendid swimmers, somewhat condoled his fears by relieving him of all responsibility, and assuming it themselves, as a guide is responsible for his people, like a railroad company.

Finally we selected the best place we could get, and I waded down in black mud nearly to my knees, and endeavored to find a foothold. Our guide said the river was about fifteen feet deep. As I could not find any bench on the bank, and it was so steep, I had both my guide and our armed escort come in and hold me, lest my feet should slide and I be drowned. The current is so swift and the river has so much fall that a man cannot stand in it; besides it is so deep that it would be over the head of the tallest giant on the globe. So I cheerfully and gladly, pursuant to their desire, immersed my travelling companions in the Jordan; meanwhile those two stalwart, active Arabs held me. But all the facts in the case of John, and especially his testimony, utterly annihilate the idea of immersion.

Fifth. The Word tells us that all Jerusalem and Judæa and the regions about Jordan came out and were baptized of him at the Jordan. Having preached awhile in the desert, where water is so scarce that the people could not get a drink, he moved to the Jordan, which is in full view, just as we always select a well-watered place for a great meeting. The population above mentioned as baptized by John actually reached six millions. John only continued his ministry about six months until Herod shut him up in prison. If he had been an iron man, the physical labor would have worn him out if he had handled all those people immersing them in the river. It was absolutely a physical impossibility; whereas John positively tells us he did not do it. He says, *"I indeed baptize you with water."* In this and many other similar phrases, water is the dative of instrumentality, showing that he handled the water instead of the people. Immersionists try to construe that in water; in that case, however, the grammatical construction would be entirely different, requiring the accusative case, instead of the dative, which we have in all of the passages. There is a rule in the Greek grammar which positively states, "motion to governs the accusative." If he had plunged them down into the water, it would be *eis to hudoa;* whereas it is in some places *en hudati,* and in others just the simple *hudati,* utterly unsusceptible of any other construction, except "with water." When we have to violate Greek grammar and make the inspired writers contradict themselves, you may know we are pulling against wind and tide to establish some human dogma which is alien to the Word of God.

Sixth. John was a Jewish priest, so born. They had been baptizing by sprinkling from the days of Moses; they sprinkled all the people at the tabernacle door, upon the ratification of the Sinai covenant in the wilderness. Heb. 9: 19. But did he baptize them? Most assuredly. Lift your eye up to the tenth verse and read, *"which stood only in meats and drinks and divers baptisms."* The English Version says "divers washings," but baptism is a Greek word which has been transferred to the English language, without translating it, and here we have it in direct reference to the transaction, when Moses actually baptized all the people by sprinkling. Ezek. 36: 25, *"Then will I sprinkle clean water upon you . . . A new heart also will I give you . . . and I will take away the stony heart out of your flesh."* This is a direct prophecy of the Gospel dispensation in which we are now living, in which God gives the new heart in regeneration and takes away the stony heart in sanctification, and you see the sprinkling of clean water on the people as the symbolic concomitant. How sweet, precious and clear do we find God's Bible! Let us take it as it is. I would not change any of it to save my head from the executioner's block.

Ezekiel there in the light of prophecy is looking on the

beautiful and glorious liberty of the Gospel dispensation, when God is converting sinners and sanctifying believers, and symbolizing the glorious work of the Spirit by the beautiful ordinance of Christian baptism, sprinkling the clean water on the people, through the instrumentality of His Gospel heralds.

In the third century the sainted Origen stood at the front of the Church, the greatest scholar and author in it. Writing in his native Greek about the transaction of Elijah with the false prophets on Mount Carmel, when he poured those twelve barrels of water, (Hebrew pitchers), on the sacrifice in order to convince the multitude that there was no concealed fire about, so they would know of a certainty that God sent the fire down from Heaven, uses this word *baptizo*, which is used throughout the New Testament to reveal the ordinance of baptism. You cannot avoid seeing in that case that this Greek word is consistent with the idea of pouring the water on the people. Hence the attitude of the immersionists that it never does mean anything but to plunge into the water is utterly untenable. Here is a great preacher who had spoken Greek from his infancy and written more books than any other man in the Church. You see he uses that word *baptizo* in the sense where it could not possibly have any other meaning except pouring water on that altar.

I have no doubt but that when John baptized Jesus, he took Him alone and poured the water on His head, as Moses poured the anointing oil on Aaron's head. You know he at first refused to baptize Him, feeling unworthy, but when Jesus said, *"It behooves us to fulfill all righteousness,"* then he acquiesced, as the law of Moses required, before Jesus entered upon His official Messiahship into which John was sent to induct Him.

Seventh. People often say that Jesus was baptized to give us an example. In that they are utterly mistaken. You might as well say He was crucified to give us an example. He alone had to be crucified to redeem the world. We are not high priests, but He was, and He had to be anointed before He could enter upon His office. Besides, our baptism is unto the remission of sins, *i. e.,* it symbolizes the remission of sins. That was not so in His case, for He had no sins to be remitted. He received the Holy Ghost immediately after John baptized Him, because His humanity, like yours and mine, needed the Holy Ghost to qualify Him to preach the Gospel and perform His mighty works. But He was not baptized with the Holy Ghost in order to purify Him from sin. He never had any sin, and baptism means a purification, which He did not need. With us the baptism of water symbolizes that of the Holy Ghost, without which we cannot be saved. You must remember that we are all sinners by nature, *"but He knew no sin, neither was guile found in His mouth."* Therefore it is utterly confusing to draw the parallel between us and Him. His life is our example, but this baptism is His induction into the Messiahship, in which He stands alone in the universe. While there is no doubt but that John took Him alone and baptized Him, when he baptized those multitudes there is no doubt but that he took them in groups, as they manifested the fruits of repentance. Like Moses baptizing all Israel at the tabernacle door, on the ratification of the Sinaic covenant, I trow he dipped the hyssop in the water, and swept it over the people as they stood before him. Doubtless John pursued a course of that kind, as we must remember that preaching was his great work; therefore, in his symbolic consecration to a life of repentance and obedience, doubtless he was very expeditious.

"Brother Godbey, give us the definition of baptism." The Bible is God's dictionary and our only lexical authority. In John 3:25 you see baptism clearly defined to be a purification, the Greek word being *catherismos,* the noun from *catherizo,* to purify—it simply means a purification. If you will read the context, you will find it is given in connection with the controversy in reference to the relative importance of the baptism administered by John and that administered by our Lord's diciples.

You will find another clear and unequivocal definition in Luke 11:37-39. When Jesus, having responded to the invitation of a Pharisee to dine with him, coming in sat down at the table without washing His hands, the Pharisee, who was so sticklerlistical about outward purity that he always washed his hands before eating, lest he had come in contact with something unclean, *e. g.,* an animal, camel, donkey, dog, or a Gentile, found fault. Then Jesus responded, "You Pharisees make clean the outside of the cup and plate, but within it is full of iniquity and defilement." Here He uses the prominent word, *catharizo,* whose constant meaning is to purify, and it is here used synonymously with *baptizo,* as applied to the washing of hands. But, you say, in washing the hands we are apt to immerse them. That is so, but not necessarily. This was not a question of washing the Savior's hands, but says He was baptized, *i. e.,* when He just washed His hands, the whole man was baptized.

This is precisely parallel with the ordinary practice of baptism—we put a little water on the head and the whole person is baptized. Why, the sticklerism of some immersionists would actually bring back on us the old yoke of legalism, which the Hebrew fathers were unable to bear. N. B. Jesus has broken every yoke that men and devils ever put on us, then why shall we not be free?

Were not the Pentecostians immersed? I am perfectly assured that they were not. Jerusalem is a mountainous city, above the water line, too high to dig wells. If they were to dig they would not find water. I have been there at the very time of the year when the Pentecostal revival took place, and water was so scarce that if I took a drink I had to buy it. Lemonade was so cheap and delicious that I drank it altogether as a substitute for water. Some will tell you that there was plenty of water at the temple where they had a brazen sea. If they did, no one was allowed to get in it; they drew it out when they wanted to use it. Besides, you must remember that the Christians were discarded by the rulers of the Church and state as wild fanatics and outlaws. The priests who had so recently killed their Leader had charge of the temple and it would have been impossible to get any favors from them. They were all arrayed against the Nazarenes, persecuting the apostles unto stripes and imprisonment, and would have killed them had not the Sanhedrim's great leader, Gamaliel, interposed in their behalf.

I am better acquainted with Jerusalem than with any other city in the world, because it is God's holy city, where the patriarchs and prophets, and Jesus and His apostles, have hallowed the very earth with their tread.

I have been there three times and have spent thirty-two days within its bounds. In Bible times the city was supplied with water from the pools of Solomon, twelve miles distant in the mountains, and conveyed thither by an aqueduct. There was no immersion water nigher than the Jordan, forty miles away, and it is certain that they did not go there, and equally certain that they did not go to the pools of Solomon; if they had they would not have been permitted to immerse in them.

Now take the facts that three thousand were baptized in connection with the forenoon service, and five thousand in the afternoon, and no special time appointed for it. Then consider the fact that they were all Jews who had been baptized by sprinkling from the days of Moses, and the only possible conclusion consistent with the environments is in favor of the simple Jewish affusion, to which they were all accustomed, as baptism is not a Christian institution, but a Jewish, perpetuated into the Christian dispensation.

When Mark, seventh chapter, says that the Pharisees washed every time they returned from the forum, the original says they baptized. Of course it was their simple ceremonial purification, lest they had become polluted by contact with Gentiles, unclean animals, lepers, dead people, sepulchres and many other things by which they might contract ceremonial defilement, and in that case be prohibited from the tabernacle service till the water of purification was sprinkled on them by some ceremonially clean person. They made it a point for some old person or infirm member of the family who needed rest to stay about the house, while all the able-bodied went off and labored through the day, and were nearly certain to come into contact with ceremonial defilement in some way, *i. e.*, the camel and donkey, the most common and useful animals in that country are both unclean and they work with them all the time. Here it is said in the English Version that they washed every time they came in from the market-place where they worked, and my version, which gives it just the way the Lord does, says baptized. The Greek is the very word used for the ordinance of baptism. Now in Leviticus you will find the law of clean and unclean specified; they had to be sprinkled with the blood of the red heifer. This animal had to be blood red without a spot or blemish, thus symbolizing the blood of Christ. The feminine gender represents the wonderful fruitfulness of the atonement, really the mother of all God's children. As it was expensive to slaughter one of these animals for every occasion of ceremonial defilement, the law permitted them to burn the animal utterly into ashes, leaving nothing at all, and then drop just a dust or two of these ashes into water, thus constituting it the water of purification. One animal thus consumed into ashes would suffice a whole community for a long time. Then any ceremonially clean person who had not gone out and incurred the defilement was competent to serve all the balance, dipping the hyssop into the water and sprinkling it upon the subject of ceremonial defilement. This is currently called baptism in the New Testament. In many cases, where in the English Version you have the word wash, in the Greek it is baptize, as you can see in my translation.

There is no doubt but that many a pious Jew was baptized forty thousand times in his life, and perhaps many more, because the Jews had a hundred times as much ceremony in their religion as the Christians do. Those ceremonies symbolize the work of Christ who has already come and His work been fulfilled. As those Jews were baptized frequently every day of their lives, you see the very same people whom John baptized, many of them, when Jesus began to preach, were baptized by His disciples. You remember that when Paul came to Ephesus and found those twelve men who had been converted by the preaching of Apollos who had come from Africa, being a disciple of John the Baptist and a powerful preacher in the Johanic dispensation, but who had not heard of the mighty work of Christ and His crucifixion for the world, (as they had no newspapers then), though they had received the Johanic baptism unto repentance administered by Apollos, yet Paul had them baptized in the name of the Lord Jesus. Hence you see how loosely the Jews held baptism, using it freely to seal their consecrations, in case they made any new departure in the Divine life; *i. e.*, when they received a great and glorious spiritual uplift they symbolized it by water baptism.

In 1 Cor. 15:29, Paul alludes to the baptizing for the dead, *i. e.*, while those flaming Pentecostians were running all over the country preaching from house to house, and telling the people that the Christ for whom they all had been looking all their lives had already come and redeemed the world and gone back to Heaven, and that the thing for them to do was to believe Him and confess Him before the world by baptism, thus passing out of the dispensation of the law and the prophets into that of Christ and the apostles, therefore they proceeded at once to baptize them. Meanwhile they found some of them in deep distress because the father or mother, brother or sister, or other members of the family, had died before the good news of the Messiah reached them, and in their flowing tears they observed, "Oh, that mother had lived to this day! How she would be delighted to receive baptism in the name of our blessed Christ for whom she watched and prayed all her life, but died without the sight. Will you not permit me to receive baptism as her substitute?" Then the evangelist unhesitatingly granted that privilege, and baptized her the second time, as the substitute of her mother who had gone on to paradise. Or a brother begs the evangelist to baptize him in lieu of his dear elder brother, who is now lying in the family sepulchre. To this he cheerfully consents, favoring his pious request. The very fact that it was a common thing for those primitive Christians to receive baptism in lieu of their departed loved ones manifests the broad freedom they enjoyed in reference to the ordinance. Paul merely alludes to it as an argument in favor of the resurrection of the body, which is the subject of that whole chapter, without a word of approval or disapproval. Of course it was an innocent affair, or he certainly would have corrected any disharmony with the will of God. It falls in line with the uniform trend of the Scriptures, recognizing water baptism as a non-essential, in which we all enjoy the very largest liberties. In any form whatever, it is a beautiful souvenir of the one baptism which Jesus gives. Eph. 7: 5.

Was not the eunuch immersed? you may ask. I am satisfied he was not. In the providence of God, I have six times visited the place where we have every reason to believe the event transpired. It is now on the macadamized road due south from Jerusalem about eighteen miles. It is a single water spout, an inch or two in diameter, flowing out from a cliff on the left, as we go south. In that country good water is prized much more than in this, because of its scarcity. Every time I visited Philip's fountain where he baptized the Ethiopian eunuch, I found from a dozen to twenty women with their water-pots, waiting each her turn to put the mouth under the spot and hold it till filled; then setting it up on her head she walked away. There is no mistake about this being the place. Bædeker's guide book, which is the authority for all of that country, as Mr. Bædeker was there thirty years travelling everywhere and investigating everything, says positively that this is the place. Popular sentiment is unanimous in reference to it. It is known far and near as Philip's fountain at which he baptized the Ethiopian eunuch. There is no chance for immersion, unless they would catch the water and keep it a good while; and this would be hard to do because the people depend on it for constant use. It is a splendid article and the only fountain in that neighborhood. Eusebius, the old historian who lived in the fourth century, states that Philip baptized the eunuch at the fountain of Beth-soran, which is the name of that place. The statements, "*went down into the water*" and "*came up out of the water,*" are surely gratuitous, and optionary with the translator, as *eis* means to, just as literally as into, and *ek* means from, just as really as out of. Therefore a perfectly correct translation would read, "went down to the water," and "came up from the water." There is always water standing around the fountain and the people going to it, nearly all barefoot, wade into it, get the water and then come out of it.

When I took my second tour in the Holy Land, in 1899, I was accompanied by Rev. F. M. Hill, my son-in-law, and Rev. J. A. Payne, of California. As I had been at Philip's fountain twice before, when the carriage halted in front of it, I did not get out, but those brethren, anxious to examine it closely, dismounted and I saw them walk down into that waste water, look at the fountain, catch some of the water and drink and bring me a drink. Then they came up out of the water. Both of them had on shoes and I asked them if they got their feet wet, and they answered in the negative. The fact is that "down" is antithetical to the "up," when the eunuch invited Philip to come up into the chariot and sit with him. So when they got to the water, they came "down" out of the chariot. When they came to it, the eunuch said, *"idou,"* behold! He used a note of surprise, saying, "behold water," clearly implying that Philip had not noticed it, which would not have been the case if they were approaching a large stream. The truth of it is there is actually no immersion water on all of that ridge, continuous through the Holy Land and extending from the Great Sea on the west to the Dead Sea and the river Jordan on the east.

I have heard many a sermon preached on the eunuch's baptism to prove immersion. It illustrates the deplorable fanaticism which so frequently takes the place of solid Gospel truth. When I was a boy I do not think I ever heard a Campbellite sermon or exhortation that did not give us water baptism by wholesale, which is no part of the Gospel and never was. If it had been,

Paul could not have said, *"I thank God that I have baptized none of you,"* 1 Cor. 1:14. *"For Christ sent me not to baptize but to preach the Gospel,"* verse 17. It is utterly impossible for you to believe these words of Paul and still say that water baptism is any part of the Gospel. It is merely a symbolic ordinance of the Gospel Church; while the Gospel is not forms and ceremonies, *"but the power of God unto salvation unto everyone that believeth."* Rom. 1:6.

"Power" here is the Greek "dynamite," that wonderfully strong word. The most glorious privilege this side of Heaven is to preach the Gospel and give God a chance to use our humble instrumentality for the salvation of souls. It is bad enough for the poor heathen to go into the Ganges and the Jumna to have their sins washed away. Our hearts break in sympathy as we contemplate them. Then let us not lose sight of the heathen at home, who, amid the clear light of this Gospel land are so manipulated and deluded by Satan through unconverted preachers, who are pursuing that business, as many have frankly confessed to me in debate, for a living, like they would pursue any other employment. It is fearful to contemplate. I have been a preacher in my humble way for fifty-three years. If it would so turn out that I have to go to Hell, I would rather exchange places with the gambler or the drunkard. Rely upon it, the preacher's Hell is the most awful in all the dismal realms of Satan's dark pandemonium. A preacher in Hell, forever tormented by the people whom he had led thither, eternally anathematizing him and lashing him with fire brands, as the instrument of their own damnation, how awful!

Again you may ask, were not the people immersed at the house of Cornelius, when Peter opened wide the door of the Gospel Church to the Gentile world? While he was preaching, you remember the Holy Ghost fell on his congregation and they had a wonderful shouting time. Some were converted and others sanctified, especially the latter, as they received the Holy Ghost. Peter said, Acts 10:47, *"Whether is any one able to forbid the water that these should not be baptized who have received the Holy Ghost as well as me?"* and he commanded that they should be baptized in the name of Jesus Christ. Here we have a clear, notable case in favor of affusion. Why? because Peter speaks of moving the water to the people, instead of moving the people away to the water. In this passage we have *kolusai hudor,* in which *hudor,* water, is the subject and *kolusai* the verb, depending on it for its subject. If it had been immersion, as that was a private house, of course it would have been necessary to go away to the water. That city is on the sea, which would have been very convenient for immersion. But he says nothing about going to the water but does speak of moving the water to them. There is no doubt but that the baptism was administered right there in the house of Cornelius where the Holy Ghost had fallen on the people.

Again, was not Saul of Tarsus immersed? The Scripture certainly favors the conclusion that he received the ordinance by affusion. He had been three days prostrate on the floor, crying to God for mercy. I have twice visited the house of Judas on Straight Street in Damascus. There is no immersion water in the house. It is in the center of that great city. Ananias said to him, "*anastas baptisai.*" Literally translated, it reads, "standing up, be baptized." *Ana* means up; *stas,* standing. Paul had been prostrate on the floor three days and nights crying to God for His mercy. Suddenly the wonderful transition out of darkness into light, out of death into life, out of condemnation into glorious emancipation, supervenes; and meanwhile his blind eyes are miraculously healed and his soul flooded with the Holy Ghost. Then Ananias says, "standing up, be baptized." All the facts and environments involve the conclusion that he rose to his feet and Ananias poured the limpid rill on his head, in the name of the Father, Son, and Holy Ghost.

Were not the people immersed in Enon where there was "much water"? Enon is a Chaldaic word in the plural number and means "springs." *Polahudata* is the Greek which is translated, E. V., "much water." The real meaning of it is, "many waters," as both the noun and the adjective are in the plural number, hence the conclusion is that it was a region well supplied with springs. The argument for immersion breaks down of its own weight because the vast crowds who attended John's meetings needed vastly more water for the people and the animals to drink and for culinary purposes than was required for immersion. John's meetings anywhere would need a good supply of water, if he did not baptize at all.

When Nebuchadnezzar spent those seven years roaming *ad libitum* among the beasts of the field, while his body was "wet with the dew of heaven," Dan. 4:33, in the providence of God, through the Septuagint Version of the Old Testament we have a clear testimony to affusion as a definition of *"bapto,"* which is there translated "wet." The Greek *ebaphee* literally was "baptize with the dews of heaven." We know that he was not immersed in the dews of heaven, but they descended on him.

We frankly admit that triune immersion was the prevailing baptism in the long roll of the Dark Ages, extending from the fourth to the fourteenth century. They not only practiced immersion but gave it to them in a state of utter nudity without a stitch of apparel on their bodies, arguing that there was no authority for baptizing the clothes. They also practiced along with it a lot of superstitious ceremonies. The single immersion is quite modern, beginning in New England when Rodger Williams and Ezekiel Holiman reciprocally immersed each other.

Dr. Dowie believes that the triune immersion runs back to the beginning. The trouble in that case is the utter absence of proof. The historians Moshiem, Neander, Wilson and Orchard tell us that immersion was the primitive mode, ("of course the triune immersion, because the single dip is so recent that we trace it back into the triune"). The trouble with those authors is the fact that they are all modern men living in the eighteenth and nineteenth centuries, and they quote no ancient author, consequently they merely take it for granted and *say* it, while they do not *prove* it. This is the way with Dowie. He knows that triune immersion was the baptism through the long, rolling ages and thinks it runs back to the apostles. In the controversy Dowie has decidedly the advantage in the way of antiquity, but the trouble is that we cannot trace it beyond the third century, when they were running into the ages of darkness and superstition.

The oldest historian who has told us anything about this subject is Lactantius of the third century. He certainly lived near enough to the apostolic age to have a chance to know, as a matter of popular information transmitted through that short space. The apostle John lived down through about thirty years of the second century. Therefore we ought to have reliable information as to the apostolic practice from a man living in the third century. Lactantius wrote in Latin, so we give you his testimony in his own language: "*Iohanes Baptisres tinxit, Petrus tinxit, et Christus apostolos misit ut gentes tingerent.*" I now translate this into English for your benefit, "John the Baptist sprinkled, Peter sprinkled, and Christ sent the apostles that they should sprinkle the nations." The whole controversy of this out of the Latin into the English hangs on that word "tinxit," which is from *tingo.* We have the same word Anglicized in our language, in "tinge," which you see simply results from dropping the terminal "o," and adding "e." You can now take Webster's dictionary and satisfy yourself as to the meaning. Literally, John the Baptist tinged, Peter tinged, and Christ sent His apostles that they should tinge the nations.

I remember that when I was studying Latin in college, I read in Horace about an old Roman who was so rich and luxuriant that he sprinkled his pavement with the best of wine, in order to laden the air with a delicious aroma, and this word "tingo" was there used. You know it could not be construed to mean immersion in that construction.

But after all our researches in history, secular and ecclesiastical, the Bible itself must settle this and all other questions. The hypothesis assumed by some immersionists that *baptizo* has no other meaning, is utterly untenable. Origen, the greatest classical scholar in the Church in the third century, whose father and grandfather had both preached and suffered martyrdom, uses this word *baptizo* to describe the water on Elijah's altar on Mount Carmel, when he refuted the prophets of Baal.

There is no doubt but that *immerse* was perhaps the most prominent pagan meaning of the word. But you must remember that when the great universal language, the most learned ever known, the acme of Grecian learning, was selected by the Holy Ghost to reveal His precious truth, many words at once received a new meaning; *e. g., theos,* "god," in all the writings of the Greek authors, who were an exceedingly religious people, as Paul well said on the Æreopagus, not as the English Version has it, "too superstitious." Therefore the word *theos* was as common in their writing as God is in ours, yet this word never did mean our blessed and true God, who is the subject of the Bible, of whom they were utterly ignorant, but when they wrote *theos* they meant some of their gods, who were really idols. Therefore if we would stick to the pagan meaning of *theos,* we would mean Jupiter, Apollo, Mercury, or some other Grecian divinity who was nothing but an idol.

I could give you many similar illustrations, showing you that the words of this great and learned heathen language, the Greek, received a different meaning, or rather a modified meaning, when they were used to reveal the precious truths of God. We must let the Bible be its own dictionary. Good Lord, save us from a superficial adherence to dictionaries! Do you not know that dictionaries are not the original authority of language, but the classical writings? Luther, Melancthon, Zwingle, and their contemporaries, had no dictionaries. They had not been made. They were a subsequent work, when noble scholars, by diligent study of the classical writings, saw the sense in which the different authors, who were the legitimate exponents of languages, used various words. In this way the Bible dictionaries are made, by a diligent study of the Bible itself, and seeing the signification in which every word is used by the inspired writers. I have often known preachers to get up and read from some dictionary, which only gives the pagan meaning of *baptizo* and *baptisma*, which is not what we want since they were heathens, and though very learned in Greek philosophy and literature, utterly ignorant of the Bible and not acquainted experimentally with the God of the Bible.

We do not need dictionaries to study the Bible, because in its very nature it is a dictionary within itself, and the only one in the world that has any authority in the way of expounding Bible truth. The word "bible" is the Greek "*biblos*," and simply means a book. Thus our Bible, by way of pre-eminence, is named, "the Book," therefore it is its own authority on everything. Of course, subordinate and collateral authorities are valuable and edifying; yet when the Bible speaks, they must all be silent.

As the Roman Empire was the upholder of ancient civilization, when the Barbarians, Goths, Huns, Vandals, and Heruli, after a three hundred years' war, succeeded in her destruction, the Barbarians took the world, bringing in the dismal night of a thousand years known in history as the "Dark Ages," from the fourth to the fourteenth century. Of course the Church went into barbarism, and was literally inundated with superstition and ignorance, *e. g.*, a preacher got up in his pulpit on Sunday morning and began his sermon by crowing like a rooster to wake up all the people to hear him preach.

They then immersed people three times, with a lot of superstitious ceremonies running on for days. When we undertake to plow through the rubbish of the Dark Ages and get back to Bible times, we quickly run into a fog bank, out of which we never escape. Therefore the true plan is to take the blessed Bible and be satisfied with it in everything, always rejoicing in God, and not in Church rites or anything else but our wonderful Savior Himself, who, single-handed and alone, has brought to us this wonderful salvation, so rich and sweet, full and free.

"Brother Godbey, does not Romans sixth teach immersion?" We have the same Scripture by the same author in Colossians second chapter. As these are really the strongholds of immersion, which all of its advocates emphasize constantly as their indefatigable Gibraltar, therefore we should examine these Scriptures very carefully, all the time soliloquizing like little Samuel, *"Speak, Lord, for thy servant heareth."* The great importance of entire sanctification consists in the fact that it is the only experience that can utterly kill out old deep-rooted prejudice, and make us perfectly limber in the hands of the Lord. N. B. Prejudice is so mean, wicked, and Satanic, that we ought to watch and pray lest the smallest vestige of it may linger down in the deep interior of our spiritual organism. The word is from the Latin, *pre,* beforehand, and *judicium,* judgment; therefore it means a judgment delivered before you hear the evidence. I heard of a judge who said he always made up his decision when he heard one side of the evidence, because if he waited to hear the other side he would get so puzzled that he would not know how to decide. The Holy Ghost, with His wonderful Word and penetrating illuminations, is the greatest revolutionist in all the world. Truly He turns the blackest midnight into brightest noonday. Therefore let Him have His way with your mind and spirit and once for all let us briefly examine these Scriptures; meanwhile we are deaf to every other voice.

(1) The Scriptures describing this wonderful transaction are purely spiritual. There is not a mention of, nor even an indirect allusion to, anything physical or material. There is nothing said of water nor of the human body. This wonderful transaction crucifies old Adam and buries him forever into the death of Christ, which is but another name for the great vicarious, substitutionary atonement wrought by our wonderful Savior for the redemption of the whole world, from sin, death, and Hell. The omnipotent agency by which the mighty work is wrought is here denominated baptism. No human being who has not water on the brain, (and remember, hydrocephalus is a most fatal disease), can see one drop of water in this whole translation. God forbid that we should be wise above what is written. In this wonderful transaction, our old man is crucified and buried into His death and left there forever. If he

should from Satan receive the resurrection power, the last state of that poor soul is worse than the first. Therefore it should be our everlasting vigilance and prayer to keep him buried deep into His death, *i. e.*, forever lost in the felicitous oblivion of the great vicarious atonement, where all sin must be buried, otherwise it will be buried in Hell fire, serving as Satan's millstone to drag us down, and eternally sinking us into deeper depths.

(2) The identification of "burial" in these Scriptures with "baptism" can only be the conclusion of a most superficial examination. It says, "we are buried by baptism," (Romans), and "in baptism," (Colossians). These two statements are precisely synonymous. Therefore instead of identifying baptism and the burial, which the immersionists do, *i. e.*, they tell us the baptism is the burial, the Holy Spirit tells us that the baptism is the agent by which we are buried, *i. e.*, the baptism instead of being the burial is the undertaker, who digs the grave and buries the corpse (old Adam), and leaves it there for the grass to grow green over it forever, as the resurrection of old Adam would be certain damnation. There is a resurrection in this wonderful transaction, but it is the new creature, created in the heart by the Holy Ghost in regeneration, and hitherto encumbered with the old body of sin, which having been crucified in burial forever, this new creature is resurrected, to walk in newness of life forever. As we learn in these Scriptures (Colossians) this resurrection is not by physical power, but by the very same omnipotent arm that raised up Christ from the dead. Few men in the world have immersed more people than your humble servant. I always, when putting them down into the liquid grave, sinking them be-

neath the yielding wave, found it necessary to raise them up by the muscular power of my left arm. My last exercise was in the holy Jordan. Now you see the burial is not physical, appertaining to the human body, but spiritual, crucified old Adam being the subject. As the resurrection is not physical by human power, but purely spiritual, as it says, by the power which raised up Christ from the dead, therefore we know that the burial is by that same omnipotent power. Long habituation to hearing a superficial, materialistic pseudo-gospel, has so cultured many people that when they see baptism in the Bible they always think it means the ordinance with water. I have heard preachers confidently quote, "*So many as have been baptized into Christ, have put on Christ,*" enforcing on the people that it indubitably means water baptism, which is utterly untrue; to be baptized is one thing, and to be baptized into Christ is quite another. Baptism has but one meaning and that is a purification, John 3:25; Luke 11:58, 59, and other citations, we could conveniently give. The ordinance of water is a ceremonial purification, but the baptism which Jesus gives with the Holy Ghost and fire is the only actual and real purification. Therefore this is the baptism that puts us in Christ, which water baptism is utterly incompetent to do.

(3) You see in these Scriptures describing this wonderful transaction, (Col.) that baptism is identical with circumcision. If you will examine you will see clearly for yourself that the baptism is in both grammatical and logical apposition with circumcision, and therefore precisely identical. If it were water baptism and physical circumcision, of course they would not be identical.

but in opposition either with the other. How do we know that this is spiritual circumcision? Because Paul says it is the circumcision made without hands. Now since you see beyond the possibility of question the identity of the circumcision and baptism, therefore the baptism is spiritual and not physical. Paul says the circumcision is made without hands, and with the same breath, that the baptism is administered without hands. Jesus is our wonderful Healer. If you have that fatal malady, hydrocephalus, *i. e.,* water on the brain, turn it over to Him that He may heal you now lest you die. Do you not see that the conclusion that this means an immersion in water is taken from the mere jingle of the words, with a luminous analysis of the context?

(4) In the clear light of the blessed Holy Spirit, the author of the precious Word, and especially when corroborated by your own happy experience in your heart, these Scriptures do loom up so beautiful, bright and glorious, that you cannot fail to see the grand harmony of this wonderful transaction in all its phases and ramifications. Then you say, "Brother Godbey, I see clearly that this is all spiritual, without mention or allusion to the human body, water or any other physical entity. But since the spiritual has the burial, should we not bury the people when we baptize them with water? Does it not follow from this that the mode of spiritual baptism is immersion?" We must answer positively in the negative, because God's Word forever settles the mode of spiritual baptism, Acts 2:17, *"I will pour out my Spirit upon all flesh."* Verily you cannot read your Bible at all without knowing that the mode of spiritual baptism is affusion invariably. The Savior pours His Spirit on

the human spirit, thereby purifying that spirit from depravity, which is "old Adam," which this baptism crucifies and destroys, the body of sin. Thus this old dead body is buried into "His death" and, never resurrecting, leaves it there forever; while the resurrection, as you see, brings up the "new man" to walk in newness of life, and is wrought by the same power that raised Christ from the dead.

(5) The burial is simply the normal counterpart of the metaphor, which represents sin as a person, *i. e.,* the old man, and its destruction by baptism, which means a purification, as the crucifixion of that old man and the annihilation of his body. Of course as a logical sequence follows the burial. Oh, what a grand and glorious description of our Lord's mighty work is the expurgation of sin forever out of the heart! Here it is personified by the "old man" who is crucified and sepulchred forever; the burial being the normal counterpart of the death which is superinduced by crucifixion. Immediately preceding this wonderful description of sin's destruction and eternal elimination, we have a clear revelation in that powerful triple compound (Col.) *"apekdusic,"* from *apo,* clear away, *ik,* off, and *dus,* to put on as a coat. Therefore we have its grand meaning in the glorious reality that the old man of sin, that we had long worn as a garment, is not only put off, but thrown utterly away beyond the North Pole, so he can never get back to trouble us any more. This mighty work is wrought by the baptism which our Savior gives with the Holy Ghost and fire.

Paul was a man of greatest intellect and most profound learning, having graduated both in the Greek colleges of Tarsus, and the Hebrew Academies of Jerusalem. Therefore his masterly use of that wonderful Greek language, the strongest in the world, as well as the most vivacious and versatile, as God had purposely prepared it for the propagation of His Word into all the earth, is, in the good providence of God, to all Bible students transcendently edifying and ineffably delightful. It is felicitiously used by the Holy Ghost, its infallible Author, for the illumination of all true hearts who are delighted to sit meekly and lowly at the feet of Jesus, while He teaches them the deep things of God and the wonderful things of the kingdom.

(6) In these Scriptures (Col.) we find this wonderful transaction of entire sanctification, wrought by the baptism which Jesus gives with the Holy Ghost and fire, anteceded by the bold affirmation; *"In Him dwelleth all the fulness of the Godhead bodily; for you are complete in Him, who is the head of all government and authority."* In these bold climacteric affirmations, you see our wonderful Christ, who is sitting on the rgiht hand of the Father, and pleading our cause, really to us verifies the glorious heavenly Trinity in His own personal writing. We are complete in Him alone, and do not need ecclesiastical ordinances, nor ministeral manipulations of any kind to consummate our completeness, as we have it all in Him alone.

In His omniscient, omnipotent and omnipresent intercessions for every son and daughter of Adam's ruined race, pursuant to the wonderful and perfect vicarious, substitutionary atonement which He made with His own blood on the cross of Calvary, He is every moment ready and waiting to settle the awful sin problem in every heart by a radical expurgation. He is this moment ready to pour His Spirit upon you, thus baptizing you with the Holy Ghost and fire. Sin is your own trouble, which here, in the bold imagery of Paul, is personified in the old man (Rom.), whom Jesus crucifies till he is utterly dead and his life is forever exterminated, and then buries into His own death and leaves him there forever.

"There is a fountain filled with blood,
Drawn from Emmanuel's veins,
And sinners plunged beneath that flood,
Lose all their guilty stains.

"The dying thief rejoiced to see
That fountain in his day;
And there may I, though vile as he,
Wash all my sins away.

"Dear dying Lamb, Thy precious blood
Shall never lose its power,
Till all the ransomed Church of God
Is saved to sin no more."

Here our glorified Lord, in whom dwelleth all the fulness of the Godhead bodily, having completely and forever conquered sin death and Hell, is ready freely to dispense the full benefits of His wonderful vicarious atonement to every humble believing soul. Thus He administers a complete expurgation of all iniquity of the heart, crucifying the old man of sin and sepulchering him forever; giving you the victory world without end and leaving us all nothing to do but shout,

"I have found a friend in Jesus;
He's everything to me;
He's the fairest of ten thousand to my soul!
The 'Lily of the Valley,' in Him alone I see,
All I need to cleanse and make me fully whole.
In sorrow He's my comfort, in trouble He's my stay;

He tells me every care on Him to roll;
He's the 'Lily of the Valley,' the bright and morning Star;
He's the fairest of ten thousand to my soul!

'He all my grief has taken, and all my sorrows borne;
In temptation He's my strong and mighty tower;
I've all for Him forsaken, I've all my idols torn
From my heart, and now He keeps me by His power.
Though all the world forsake me, and Satan tempts me sore,
Through Jesus I shall safely reach the goal;
He's the 'Lily of the Valley,' the bright and morning Star;
He's the fairest of ten thousand to my soul!

"He'll never, never leave me, nor yet forsake me here,
While I live by faith and do His blessed will;
A wall of fire about me, I've nothing now to fear;
With His manna He my hungry soul shall fill.
When crowned at last in glory, I'll see His blessed face,
Where rivers of delight shall ever roll,
He's the 'Lily of the Valley,' the bright and morning Star;
He's the fairest of ten thousand to my soul."

"Oh, Brother Godbey, you utterly take immersion out of the Bible." You are entirely mistaken. 2 Cor. 5:17 gives us all the authority we want to immerse all the people in the world, if they get saved and desire it. That Scripture is, *"Where the Spirit of the Lord is, there is liberty."* God has made plenty of water; if He is not stingy with it, we ought not to be. My infant baptism was a great blessing to me, fortifying me against the vices and follies which generally blacken and ruin childhood and youth. I was the only boy in the neighborhood who had received it, but the balance, almost without a single exception, cursed like demons and plunged headlong into wickedness. The Campbellite preachers, the pastors of their parents, were constantly fighting infant baptism. *"By their fruits ye shall know them."* Instead of participating in their wickedness, I faithfully warned them of their impending danger. That baptism was worth more to me than gold and silver, which my father and mother did not possess and could not give me. My patrimony did not consist of a nickel, yet it left me the princely fortune of my dedication to God and the faithful instructions and restraints characteristic of a godly home. When I reached sixteen and God gloriously converted my soul, and I soon got convicted for the victory of full salvation and knew not how to seek it, doing my best, leaving no stone unturned, I constrained the M. E. preacher to give me immersion. I am so glad he did it, because it satisfied me that more water was not what I needed, but more grace. It actually gave me the victory over water, and Church rites of every form and phase, convincing me that God alone could satisfy my longing soul.

In the absence of all human help in the way of preaching and testimony, I sought sanctification for nineteen years; then Jesus gave me what I had sought in the water and over hill and dale, mountain and plain. Glory to His name, I found it all in Him alone! If you say, "Brother Godbey is opposed to immersion," you will treat me unkindly and misrepresent me. God has not restricted us in this matter, but given us glorious and perfect liberty. If you have a conviction for it, do not hesitate to go at once and receive it. I have known multitudes of people immersed by men whom I'm satisfied did not know God. They denounced and mocked experimental religion, which no Christian can do, and exhorted the people to come and receive immersion at their hands for the remission of their sins. If you desire immersion, go at once and receive it at the hands of some man whom God has saved and called to preach the Gospel.

To be candid before God and the world, I have but one objection to immersion, and that I feel it my duty to tell you. In my observation I am convinced that it trends to hydrolatry, which is perhaps the most seductive form of idolatry incidental to the Church of God, *e. g.*, the Campbellites and Mormons, who are downright hydrolaters, positively preach the essentiality of water baptism for the salvation of the soul; they are uncompromising immersionists.

Baptism is not an institution of the Gospel dispensation, as many think, but of the Mosaic, and practiced by Moses himself, when with his own hands he baptized all the people, (three millions) at the tabernacle door, Heb. 9: 10-19. Of course there is a vast difference between the Mosaic and the Christian dispensations. The former was literally inundated with ceremonies, millions of birds and beasts bleeding on their altars, symbolic of the blessed Christ dying on the cross, and multitudinous watery ablutions (baptismos) typifying the mighty works of the Holy Ghost. The latter has nothing but the simple ceremonies of the water baptism and the Eucharist. Millions of Jews were baptized thousands of times during their lives, as they had to receive it every time they contracted ceremonial defilement before they were allowed even to enter the holy campus, much less go into the holy temple. All churches in by-gone ages have gradually grieved the Holy Spirit and drifted away into idolatry in some form or other.

The American Church has not only gone largely into hydrolatry, ecclesiolatry, eucharolatry, pyrolatry, hemerolatry, *i. e.*, day worship, *e. g.*, Seventh-Day Adventism; but some of them have actually gone into pagan idolatry, *i. e.*, Buddhism. I am personally acquainted with a Methodist preacher and his members who have gone into it and are preaching it. At San Diego, Cal., they have built a splendid temple and dedicated it to Buddha, and are preparing to build one in Los Angeles. Our only anchorage competent to prevent this fearful drifting is in Jesus, taking Him for everything, and contenting ourselves with what He gives us. When you lose sight of everything but God alone, and sink away into Him, then He gives you His own liberty, which is freedom to do everything good and nothing bad. I can frankly confess that I can see nothing wrong in receiving water baptism as often as you desire and in the way you prefer.

Of course my Biblical exegesis on this subject, as well as all others, can make no compromise with what God has revealed. While after a long life of constant study, with all the benefits of a classical education, reading the Word in the inspired original with readiness and dispensing with all translations; in the providence of God, visiting the Holy Land three times and investigating everything to my utmost ability; I am perfectly satisfied that the Bible baptisms were all affusions in both dispensations; yet I have no controversy with my immersion brethren. During my entire ministerial life I have faithfully immersed all who made application to me and invariably advised all who had convictions for it to go ahead and receive it. It is certainly perfectly innocent, if any one is stickleristic either for affusion or immersion. Oh, how frequently when I have put them down in the river have I seen the rolling billows pour down upon them.

The only criticism you can offer immersion is simply

that of superfluity; which is certainly an objection. This is the glorious felicity of full salvation. It gives us the wonderful, perfect freedom of God Himself, who is free to do everything good and nothing bad. Besides, it fills us with perfect love so that we love God's dear children who differ from us quite as dearly as those who agree with us.

In this wonderful salvation, while we must make no compromise on essentials, but must heroically contend for the faith once delivered to the saints, sparing nothing where life and salvation are involved; yet in all non-essential ecclesiastical matters we have boundless liberty. This probationary life is a constant battle against sin and Satan, occupying all of our time, so that we have no ammunition to waste on the air. Satan is always manœuvering to get the children of God into a fight with one another simply in order to keep them from fighting him. It is wonderfully sweet to be perfectly free from all ecclesiastical shackels. That does not mean that we become church fighters, we have no time for that. Souls are too valuable, time too short and eternity too long for us to waste an ounce of ammunition shooting to and fro at one another. In this book, as elsewhere, I have not spared Heaven's artillery where life and salvation are involved; but on this problem of the mere manner in which water baptism is administered, it is only a question of revelation in which we desire to know the facts revealed in this blessed and infallible volume of truth, so edifying and precious to me, as a matter of erudition and edification. Therefore we enjoy these explorations through the precious oracles with which God has favored us, that we may have an abundant supply of intellectual and spiritual pabulum.

Let me, in fatherly kindness, make an earnest appeal to all who, in the providence of God, may read these pages that you beware of a critical, fault-finding spirit, which is grievous to God and calculated to alienate His Holy Spirit, without whose guidance, illuminations and revelations in the understanding of His precious Word and providence we cannot successfully fight this probationary battle and run the heavenly race which is set before us. If you have a conviction for immersion, avail yourself of the kind service of one of God's called and sent preachers and fully satisfy your conscience, but do not criticise your brothers and sisters who have not received those convictions, as in so doing you will certainly grieve the Holy Spirit. Never fail to warn them of anything even savoring of evil and to exhort them to the greatest possible diligence and heroism in pursuit of everything which is to the honor and glory of God. Paul said, *"Who art thou that judgest another man's servant? to his own master he standeth or falleth. But he shall stand; for God is able to make him stand."* Be sure you do not discount the godly Quaker who has no convictions for water baptism in any way. You see he is living the life of an humble, devout saint of God. Therefore leave him in the hands of God; neither criticise nor grieve him. Nor dare to burlesque your brother who, under conscientious conviction, has received triune immersion at the hands of some Dowieite. Thousands and millions who have received the same during the long roll of the Middle Ages are now in glory. Do not discount him because of his peculiarities. These little non-essentials, which differentiate the people of God, are to wield no influence whatever in the loving appreciation in which you are to hold one another. If you have a chance to attend an immersion, though you may never have received it, nor now have a conviction for it, ask God to make it a blessing to you, so that you may rejoice with your brothers and sisters. God is so anxious to bless us that He avails Himself of all occasions to reveal His unutterable love and mercy in pouring out His Spirit in showers of blessing on His dear people whom He has redeemed by the blood of His precious and only Son. Do not argue with one another on baptism or anything else. Freely investigate the precious Word together and help one another; *"always esteeming others better than yourselves."* Make no effort to dissuade any of your brothers and sisters from receiving the baptism by immersion. Tell them to walk in the light and govern themselves accordingly; then you pray for them. It is very dangerous to make much of non-essentials. We are to make everything of Jesus, taking Him for everything, and wearing everything else as a loose garment. When you get to criticising your brothers and sisters, remember you need a shower of fire on you to burn up the critic's cap.

As a matter of truth and fidelity in writing my biography, I have freely delivered to you an epitome of what God by His Word, Spirit and providence has delivered to me. If you love me the less for so doing, I can only say I love you the more. If I have administered heavy blows with the sledge hammer of revealed truth, please remember that they are all love-licks. I have given you thus briefly the benefit of my life of hard work and large opportunities in the way of education and travelling. If you can only sink out of self into Christ and continue to sink deeper and deeper into God's glorious Divinity, keep humble, meek and lowly and, like Jesus, go about doing good, you will find platoons of guardian angels from Heaven descended, who will accompany you along the perilous journey of this stormy pilgrimage. They will fortify you against all of Satan's pitfalls and ambushments, and meanwhile, with the splendor of their pinions, will light up your way till you will realize that you are truly walking in Beulah Land where the sun and the moon both shine night and day.

If anybody invites you to preach baptism do as I did the last time they invited me. I was far away in India and preaching in the largest leper asylum in the world, having seven hundred of those unfortunate sufferers who are shut out from the world lest they might transmit that awful plague, before me. The native pastor with sable face and foreign speech through an interpreter asked me to preach on baptism, as he expected to follow my sermon by administering that ordinance to about one hundred of his people. I had no time to preach to them on water baptism, as I knew that had nothing to do with their salvation, but I gladly accepted his invitation and preached to them about the baptism which Jesus gives with the Holy Ghost and fire, and exhorted them to make their full and eternal consecration and trust Jesus to give it to them. Then their pastor poured the limpid rill on their heads, thus beautifully symbolizing the baptism Jesus gives when He pours His Spirit on us. Baptism means a purification. The Holy Ghost is the omnipotent Purifier whom Jesus pours on you when He baptizes you. *"Our God is a consuming fire."* Heb. 12: 18. The Holy Ghost is none other than the eternal God. When Jesus pours the Spirit on you, the living fire goes through you, and how appropriately we sing with the old Methodists,

"Refining fire go through my heart,
Illuminate my soul;
Scatter Thy life through every part,
And sanctify the whole.

"Oh, that He now from Heaven might fall,
And all my sins consume;
Come, Holy Ghost, on Thee I call,
Spirit of burning, come!"

So when they call on you and ask you to preach on baptism, always preach on the baptism which Jesus gives and Paul says is the only one in all the world; the ordinance with water merely being the outward sign. In all these things note that the great salient point is to walk in the foot-prints of Jesus, meek, humble and lowly, and like Him, to go about doing good. Again I entreat you, do not argue. Paul says, *"the man of God shall not strive."* Let your zeal culminate in perfect love for God and His people and all mankind. During the little remnant of my earthly life I will certainly pray that what I have written, pursuant to candor and veracity in the faithful submission of my biography, and responsive to the importunate appeals of my thousands of friends, shall not stir up strife. However, I know that the enemy is always manipulating to clothe the angel, perfect love, with the bear skin so that his Hell-hounds will chase it.

CHAPTER VIII.

THE SEVENTH DAY ADVENTIST CONTROVERSY.

All my eighteen debates were not with the Campbellites. I had one with a Seventh Day Adventist who twenty-five or thirty years ago came from New York and began to preach at a rural village near where I now live. That was before I settled there subsequently to my episcopal appointment to the evangelistic work, which took me out of the Conference and permitted me to settle in a permanent home. His doctrine was perfectly new, having never been heard of in the country. The novelty of the man and his doctrine produced a popular sensation and gave him a splendid hearing by the people. He proved very pugnacious and belligerent; not only heroically preaching his new doctrine, but challenging all of the preachers to meet him in debate. As they had no acquaintance with the teaching of his Church, and were not accustomed to public disputation, they all declined. Meanwhile he began to invite people to join his Church. He was a persuasive, winning, argumentative and hortatory speaker. There was but one church in the village, and that was the union of Methodists and Campbellites, both organizations using the same house and alternating with each other. The people began to join him and quite a revival broke out under his preaching, the fruits of which were only marked by church-joining, and really made no effort to get people spiritually changed, blessed and saved, but made church-joining a great salient point. As he was constantly challenging all the Methodist and Baptist preachers and Campbellites, too, since I had notoriety as a debater, they wrote to me, at that time in a distant part of the Conference, asking me to come and debate with him, and stating that he was producing a great sensation there and getting a heap of members; they could not see that it was for the glory of God. I responded by acceptance. Then we corresponded and appointed the time.

The Seventh Day Adventists, as said above, had hitherto been unknown in all of that country. As I had been born and reared in Kentucky and never preached anywhere else except during the war period when I was over in Indiana, where I did not come in contact with them, therefore I knew very little about them. Consequently I went down to Cincinnati and hunted up their books, of which they had a very few as their denomination had so recently been launched. Having availed myself of their books, I studied up their doctrines and thus prepared to meet the champion who had already spread terror and dismay in that country, so very boldly and eloquently preaching a new doctrine and vociferously challenging all the preachers to refute him. He was constantly proposing to give them half of the time, whenever they would come and avail themselves of the opportunity to refute what they regarded as dangerous error. On arrival I took him aside into the grove and proposed that we draw up propositions, setting his doctrines clearly before the people and at the same time taking positions in the affirmative and the negative, so as to bring the whole matter intelligently and instructively before the people. He was very reluctant to do it, and never consented till I told him I had read his books and knew his doctrines and was going to expose them in the time alloted, whether he would consent to defend them or not. When he found that he really was in a dilemma and had but one way out, and that was to fight his way out, he acquiesced and we drew up propositions occupying the whole week. It so happened that he had divided both the Methodist and Campbellite Churches and had taken in, as best I could learn, the big end of both organizations.

When we proceeded to organize for the debate, I chose an old Methodist preacher to serve as my moderator. Among his accessions from the Methodist Church, he had taken in the class-leader with whom I was well acquainted, because I had once been pastor of that church. The Seventh Day Adventist cause was perfectly new in that country, therefore he had no preacher of his denomination, consequently he selected the class-leader to serve as his moderator; the two moderators selected an umpire, an intelligent and influential gentleman.

Then we proceeded to open the debate and the umpire, having called the house to order and engaged in prayer, as was usual, proceeded to read the first proposition in which your humble servant affirmed the immortality of the human soul and Rev. Skeel denied it. This was quite a surprise and shock to the people. He had been preaching the coming of the Lord, the renewal of the earth, and His reign on it, and other items of a similar character, which were new and striking, and so managed to captivate the ear of the people. As I was in the affirmative, of course I had the first speech in which we were limited to an hour apiece. I spent my time proving from the Bible the soul's immortality, which of course is easily done. In the proposition we used the word spirit, synonomously with soul; simply meaning that invisible entity of humanity which survives the body and lives on through all eternity. Of course all the people believed everything I said, because they all endorsed the soul's immortality. But when Mr. Skeel followed me and spoke an hour in the negative, denying with all his might the soul's immortality, they were much surprised, as he had not hitherto delivered himself on that subject, hence it produced quite a stir and commotion in the mind, all listening spellbound and soliloquizing, "What can this be?" We spent two days arguing on the soul's immortality, myself affirming and he denying.

Our next proposition, which we took up the third day, was the subject of spiritual regeneration. He affirmed that "The new birth, of which Jesus speaks in John 3:5, will take place on the resurrection morn." As the Adventists utterly repudiate the existence of the soul, separate from the body, they therefore ignore all spirituality utterly and unconditionally, until the body is raised from the dead. This resurrection life is man's immortality. This will only be given to those who are in Christ, leaving the wicked for utter cremation and annihilation when the world shall be wrapped in her final crematory fires. This resurrected body my opponent construed to be the new birth, which our Savior preached to Nicodemus. The man repudiated the soul's immortality, and utterly abnegated the great and vital doctrine of regeneration wrought in the heart by the Holy Ghost, a new heart, a new spirit, and a new creation obtainable and realizable in the present life. His doctrine of conversion is much like that of the Campbellites, consisting simply of church-joining and immersion, claiming that in this way we become Christians, and will have a right to the immortality which supervenes with the new birth, which our Savior preached to Nicodemus.

When the people saw that he actually not only denied the soul's immortality, but repudiated regeneration and all spirituality, I just proceeded to show that the man was an infidel. I was well acquainted with infidels, as they had preached all over that country in former years. Therefore the Lord gave me great boldness, so I proceeded to read in the Second Epistle of John, *"If any one comes to you and brings not this doctrine, receive him not in your houses, and do not bid him Godspeed; for he that says to him Godspeed is partaker of his evil deeds."* I made an awful issue of it, saying to them, "This man whom I find to be an infidel, not even believing in the soul's immortality, and utterly repudiating the new birth and all spirituality, has come to you and you have received him into your house, actually joined his church and are bidding him Godspeed; all this notwithstanding the fact that God positively tells you in His Word that if any one comes to you and does not bring this great fundamental doctrine of the soul's immortality and the regeneration of the Holy Spirit you are not to receive him into your house, nor to bid him Godspeed. If you do, you become partakers of his evil deeds." Then I said to them: "God has sent me here to show you the awful thing you have done, receiving an infidel for your preacher, who is worse than the heathen in the fact that they believe in the soul's immortality, but he rejects it altogether, and at the same time repudiates our Savior's great and glorious doctrine of spiritual regeneration, the new birth and the kingdom of God, thus establishing the heart by the Holy Ghost in this life. Therefore God will put me on the witness block in the day of judgment to testify against you, if you do not repent of this awful mistake and ask His pardoning mercy."

About that time the old class-leader, who was serving as Skeel's moderator, just cried out, "Brethren, I have been deceived and I want you to pray for me." Then others around said the same. So we had to turn the debate into a seeker's meeting to get the people reclaimed who had gone off after him. The result was that they all saw what a mistake they had made and dropped him like a hot potato, then resumed their places in the churches. The Campbellite Church discontinued altogether and the Methodists, rebuilding the house, revived and live on to this day. You cannot find a Seventh Day Adventist anywhere about there. I live within seven miles of that place and am satisfied that there is not a single one, though that man had built up a big membership. I know no country anywhere that is clearer from that heresy than Kentucky, and especially all of that region.

Thus you see the importance of open investigation, which we are enabled to give the people in these public discussions. Seventh Day Adventism is an awful infidelity, as the people saw when that man was brought face to face with an opponent and forced either to defend his doctrine, which I had in the books, or reject it publicly. He chose the former and was consequently forced to uncover his unapologizable infidelity to all of the people, and they said outright they had been deceived. Therefore they dropped him, and his church and every vestige of his movement evanesced away, leaving not a trace, nor a track.

This heresy of Seventh Day Adventism is widely spread over the whole country. It is verily a soul poison, destitute of a solitary redeeming truth. It is sugar-coated infidelity. Satan very adroitly sugar-coats all of his pills, so that people will take them; thus imbibing the soul poison which brings certain destruction soon or late. How significantly God says, *"My people perish for lack of knowledge."* That case was peculiar in the fact that this heresy was utterly new and they had enjoyed no available opportunities to study it; therefore this able and captious preacher lassoed them quickly.

Another point peculiar in their case was that they were all acquainted with me and had confidence in my veracity; so that when I lifted the masque and revealed the infidel monstrosity they shrank with horror and gladly retraced the steps but recently taken.

Hemerolatry, i. e., day worship, is the idolatry peculiar to the Seventh Day Adventists. They idolize the Mosaic Sabbath, preaching the holy day instead of a holy heart, without which all are forever lost, day or no day. "Sabbath" is a Hebrew word and means "rest." It is the perfect rest which the sanctified soul receives in Jesus. Therefore with holy people all days are holy. The first Christians were all Jews, and consequently kept both of the Sabbaths, the Mosaic and the Christian, as long as they lived. The Gentile Christians never did keep the Mosaic Sabbath and were not required to do it, Acts 15, but they did keep the first day of the week, Acts 20:7; 1 Cor. 2:16. The Seventh Day Adventists tell us the Pope changed the Sabbath. It is easy to tell it, but they cannot prove it, because there never was a Pope until the seventh century, and the disciples kept the first day of the week without a break from the Lord's resurrection. Confirmation of this we have in Roman history in abundance. Sallust, Seutonius and Pliny, who lived and wrote in the first century of the Christian Era and faithfully chronicled all the notable current events, though pagans themselves, manifested great candor and veracity which I cannot doubt in their narration of the coming and abiding of Christianity in their midst. They pronounced it a strange frenzy which its votaries in some mysterious way had the power to transmit; observing that frequently they communicated it to their executioners, so that they turned Christians and submitted to the same martyrdom Those historians proceed to describe the prosecution of a Christian pending martyrdom, and state that the magistrate always asked; *"Dominicum servasti?"*—"Hast thou kept the Lord's day?" Then he answered, *"Christianus sum, intermittere non possum"* —"I am a Christian, I am not able to omit it."

Then they proceeded to execute them, either burning them or carting them to the wild beasts in the Coliseum. This is positive proof that they were keeping the first day of the week, hallowed by the Lord's resurrection and consequently always called the Lord's Day, Rev. 1:10, whereas Saturday never was so called. If they had been keeping Saturday, as the Seventh Day Adventists tell us, then the judge would have said, "*Sabbaticum servasti?*"—"Hast thou kept the Sabbath day?" But they never did propound that question, which is positive proof that they were not keeping the old day, but the new one.

There is an impracticability in this stickleristical Sabbatic regime of these people. I found it illustrated in my own history when I travelled around the world. As I went from West to East, I had 366 days in the year. Therefore I gained a day, and if I were now keeping the seventh day, it would be Saturday. Should I travel around again, it would make my sabbath Friday. Therefore you see in seven years, I would actually have to adopt every day in the week as my sabbath. Suppose I should go around the other way; then when I got back, my sabbath would be Monday as I would only have 364 days in the year. Should I make another trip, it would be Tuesday, and in seven years travelling around the world from East to West, would again change my sabbath every year if I kept the seventh day. Any way you can arrange it, if the Seventh Day Adventists were right in their hypothesis that you must keep the seventh day or fall under condemnation, one-half the world would be violating the sabbath. When the Old World has Sunday we have Monday. This illustrates the impracticability of keeping some certain number as the day.

At Jerusalem they have six sabbaths every week. They tell me that the Howling Dervishes keep Monday, the Jumping Dervishes Tuesday, and the Dancing Dervishes Thursday, the regular sabbath of the great Mohammedan Church is Friday; the seventy-five thousand Jews in that city keep Saturday, and the Christians, who have their colonies there from all the prominent nations, keep Sunday. [The Dervishes are the holiness people of the Mohammedan Church.]

I am much concerned for the Seventh Day Adventists, lest they may lose their souls, and their hemerolatry, *i. e.*, day worship, instead of being Divine worship, actually drag many of them into Hell. If you will examine Paul's treatment of that subject in Romans and I Corinthians, where he is discussing the subject of eating meats offered to idols, you will come to the same conclusion. He proceeds to state that all those who had reached the clear light which qualified them to see that the "idol is nothing," can eat the meats offered to them with perfect impunity; while those who had not reached the degree of light, so that they still felt that the idol to which the meat had been sacrificed existed, all such should desist from eating the meat offered to them, as their consciences would be polluted with conviction that they were still serving those idols. Then he adds that those who, like himself, had the clear light and saw that the idols were nothing and consequently could eat the meat with perfect impunity so far as their own conscience was concerned, must still abstain for the sake of the consciences of their brethren, who had not reached the clear light which they themselves enjoyed. Paul said, *"If meat cause my brother to stumble, I will never eat any more of it."* The clear and unmistakable conclusion from these deliverances of inspiration is simple and inevasible; the Seventh Day Adventists must either keep the Christian's Sabbath, for the sake of the conscience of Christendom, or fall under condemnation.

The fratricidal Cain told God he was not his brother's

keeper; still God held him to the awful responsibility, and said to him, *"Thy brother's blood crieth unto me from the ground."* Therefore if these people want to go to Heaven they will have to keep two sabbaths every week, Saturday for their own conscience, and Sunday for the conscience of Christendom. They would better solve the problem in a short way, *i. e.,* get sanctified wholly; then they will have an everlasting Sabbath in their hearts wherever they are, and, so far as the day of temporal rest is concerned, they will rejoice to be "all things to all men."

Chapter IX.

THE WHISKEY WAR.

When a little lad the "Sons of Temperance" first organized in our country, and I heard of them eight miles distant. Mounting a horse I hastened to them that I might enjoy the coveted privilege of joining the crusade against King Alcohol. Therefore with great delight I took the pledge of total abstinence, which I have kept intact to this day, having all my life been an uncompromising rum fighter. As a pastor I always made it a rule to run whiskey out of my circuit. In this I always succeeded, though sometimes the Conference would take me away before the victory was complete. But the temperance ball always rolled on, until victory perched on the prohibition banner and they would dispatch to me the glad news.

When the Civil War closed I was in Indiana, where I had spent the period of conflict between the North and the South, as I was a Union man, having migrated away from slave territory, where I remained till after the emancipation and the cessation of hostilities.

Soon after the disorganization of the armies, my principal assistant teacher, who was also a preacher, and twenty years my senior, came to me in the college building bearing the sad news that two soldiers had arrived in town and were making all arrangements immediately to open a saloon. I told him at once that we must not permit it, as it would be a temptation to our students and its very existence would ruin the hitherto unsullied reputation of our amiable town, which had been celebrated for temperance and religion. I suggested to him that we go at once and see the men and do our utmost to dissuade them from their diabolical enterprise. Therefore we got a citizen to give us a polite and favorable introduction to them. Then we proceeded with the utmost kindness and respect, inwardly praying fervently to God for His help, to ask them to be so kind as to desist from their enterprise, as it would be much against our college, at the same time assuring them that we knew that the majority of the better citizens were fairly represented by us in the matter. Though we had taken every possible precaution to avoid giving offence, they pretty soon got angry and notified us that they had a government license paid for, as well as having laid in their stock, and it was too late for them to change their plans. As we continued to plead and insist and even importune, they broke out into angry denunciations and violent threats, looking us in the face with demoniacal oaths, and said, "We have been down South the last four years shooting rebels, and we now have a government license to sell whiskey in this town, therefore, those who oppose us are trespassing on our governmental rights, and we will shoot them as quickly as we shot the rebels."

We, keeping perfectly cool and full of love and kindness, continued to plead with them. Finally we told them, "We are going to hold mass meetings and make speeches to the citizens and arouse public sentiment against your enterprise. Rest assured we are not going to let you sell whiskey in this town. If you undertake it, you will make a failure, loose money, and be sorry for it. Therefore we advise you, as friends, to desist at once."

Though they cursed and threatened us to the last, manifesting the most obdurate determination to go ahead with their Satanic traffic despite the combined efforts of the good people to avert the awful temptation, the ensuing night we gathered a crowded audience into the Methodist Church and harangued them with all our might to unite with us in a persistent effort to prevent the opening of that horrific Hell-hole, to swallow up our students and their children. They entered into the most hearty sympathy with us and unanimously responded to our appeal, resolving that "the institution" should not be conducted in our town; that we would prevent it at any cost. Though the proprietors gave us no encouragement, we continued our mass-meetings and temperance speeches, and they never did open their stock, but went away.

When we moved back to Perryville, Ky., we found it flooded with whiskey, having suffered awful moral deterioration during the war. I first moved the organization of a temperance society, contemplating it as a nucleus around which to rally the prohibition sentiment. In due time we vacated our hall for mass meetings in the Methodist Church. There we had much prayer to God to help us in the awful trouble, and made temperance speeches the great speciality of the occasion. The Lord helped us to arouse popular sentiment against the horrific reign of Satan which had debauched the community during four years.

Though Kentucky is the worst whiskey state in the Union, we have a law investing the citizens with the right of local option, in case that the majority of legal voters can be secured. By the help of the Lord we were enabled to so manipulate popular sentiment as to secure a legislative act including the town and west end of the county, extending eastward to Salt River. As the Legislature was at that time in session, we at once sent away Judges Jones and Armstrong, two of our most prominent citizens, to wait on the Legislature in our behalf. The result was that we secured the passage of the prohibitory law, protecting our town and the west end of the county from the awful nuisance of intoxicating drinks. Having secured the legislative act, the next thing was to enforce it, as they were selling at several different places. In this war Satan raged and stirred earth and Hell against us with all his might. One day they fired on a group of us temperance men from a whiskey tavern across the street. The fire was returned by the temperance men and there was quite a roar of pistols, creating great excitement. One man was killed, and afterward one of our best temperance workers was shot by a whiskey man. They blamed me more than any other and, looking me in the face, as in Indiana, swore they would shoot me if I did not let them alone. I said to them, "If you shoot me, somebody else will shoot you; we will never let you alone till you go out of this business."

Some who persisted in selling without a license were flogged and driven away. Eventually all had closed out but one who was very obstinate, claiming that he had a government license which superseded our local option

During the entire campaign, mass meetings continued to be held in the Methodist Church, prayers were sent up to God and speeches were delivered to the people. Finally a great crowd having spent some time in earnest prayer and a number of speeches having been delivered to the spellbound crowd, they all marched out of the church in a procession. Old Dr. Polk, our venerable patriarch, carrying the open Bible, led the host, followed by the women and then the men, and making quite a demonstration, marched to this saloon. The women aimed to pour out the man's whiskey while the men stood by and saw it well done. Though he looked me in the face and threatened to shoot me, and hitherto proved exceedingly audacious and obstinate, when he saw the great procession he became affrighted, surrendered and begged for time to move his stock away and leave the country, which was granted. This wound up the campaign with a glorious victory.

The saloon element have a clamorous maxim, *"Prohibition does not prohibit."* As a demonstrative proof that that is Satan's falsehood, I refer you to Perryville, Ky., where we drove whiskey out forty years ago and it has never gotten back. For quite awhile they continued their vigorous efforts to revive the saloons, but constantly failed. It has been many years since they have attempted the iniquitous re-enthronement of King Alcohol there. After the expulsion of whiskey, the drunkards became sober and united with the churches. As you know strong drink always shortens life, they have all passed away to the graveyard and, as we hope, to a glorious immortality.

When I was sent to Mackville they had already secured a legislative act protecting the town, but it happened that it only extended one mile out from the corporation limits. Soon after my arrival I was informed that a man was preparing to open a saloon a few paces beyond the mile limitation. I immediately called a mass meeting in the Methodist Church and had prayers and temperance speeches, arousing the people to action in the matter, and appealing to them to solemnly protest against the opening of the saloon at that near proximity. In this the multitudes were concurrent in the negative, protesting most solemnly against the iniquitous institution. I told them all to pray the next morning while I went and talked with the man. I took with me a good Methodist brother to serve as bodyguard. On arrival I invited the man to come out on the pike as we wished to converse with him. Then we proceeded, in brotherly love and kindness, to ask him to please desist, telling him that we had held a mass meeting the preceding night and all the people were very anxious that he should kindly desist, and that we had borne to him their earnest request that he should do them this favor and change his purpose of opening a saloon. Despite all the love and kindness we could possibly show him, he got very angry, saying that he paid for his license, laid in his stock and had the law on his side and it was too late to ask him to desist. When I told him that we had passed unanimous resolutions that he should not carry out his enterprise, he also threatened me with violence saying he would shoot me. When he got into a rage, uttering his violent threats, my attention was so centered on him that for a moment I lost sight of the good brother who was kindly serving me as a bodyguard. Upon looking round I saw him about fifty yards distant and getting away as fast as he possibly could. I simply said to the angry man amid his threats, "If you kill me, somebody else will kill you," meanwhile I told him positively, "Rely upon it, we are not going to let you sell whiskey here." He then accused me of threatening him with the Ku Klux, as that was immediately after the war, when much violence was prevalent in the country and very frequently men were found in the morning hanging by the neck. I showed him that I was his friend and that he would better follow my advice, saying to him, "If you go into this business, you will not succeed. You will lose your money and be sorry for it when it is too late; you will get into trouble which you do not expect, and fortune's wheel will certainly revolve against you." Suffice it to say he gave up his enterprise and went into an honest employment.

When I was presiding elder thirty-three years ago and found illegal distilleries operating extensively in my district, as the government licenses were so costly that they were not able to run a registered distillery, I went to work to rid the country of these nuisances. When I was presiding over the Quarterly Conference in Whitesburg, the county-seat of Letcher Co., and asked the brethren, they told me that there were twenty-three illegal distilleries operating in that county. I said, "Brethren, why do you not notify the government officers so that they will break them all up, as they will certainly do in that case?" They responded, "We dare not do anything of that kind, lest they kill us, for they boldly proclaim that they will shoot any man who informs on them." Then, as presiding elder of that district, I felt it my duty to notify the government officers and appeal to them to rid our county of the awful curse. Consequently I said to the brethren, "I shall certainly report them!" They begged me not to do it for they did believe those men would kill me. At that time there were no railroads in that mountainous country and I did all of my travelling on horse-back. It was very common for men to be shot by concealed assassins as they rode through the mountains. That was so early after the Civil War that those feuds which so long survived in that country were still there. I proceeded at once to write an open letter to the "Mountain Echo," which was published in that country, in which I stated that those twenty-three illegal distilleries were operating, much to the demoralization of the whole country, and that we appealed to the Government to come and take them out. This letter was quoted by the papers throughout the State, producing a general sensation. But the Government nobly responded, sending soldiers and breaking up all those "moonshine distilleries." My friends were much excited for my safety, believing that those men would kill me. They did shoot one of my local preachers in an adjoining county, while I was in the county, by the hand of a concealed assassin. I had signed my name to the letter I wrote appealing to the Government. This was necessary, as an anonymous one would have imperiled innocent parties, involving them in jeopardy. Despite the remonstrances of my friends, I went along without missing a single appointment, solitary and alone, into all of those regions, despite their overt and vociferous threats. Not only were those whiskey nuisances broken up, but we had glorious, sweeping revivals all over my district, actually resulting in doubling my membership during my quadrennium.

My last pastoral charge before the Bishop got me into evangelistic work for life, was at Carlyle, Nicholas Co. The Ministerial Temperance Association in that State appointed me superintendent of the force in that county. I was there three years, meanwhile we organized and pressed the battle in all parts of the county, establishing local option in every district, except the county-seat. There the whiskey men bought the colored vote and beat us for a time. One day I was in a large drygoods store, kept by Brothers Mann & Kennedy, both Methodist preachers, when looking out I saw a fine-looking man riding a splendid horse. Then Brother Mann said to me, "There comes Captain Buckler, the leader of the whiskey party, worth a hundred thousand dollars, which he has made on whiskey. He has now thirty thousand dollars' worth in his warehouse, keeping it till it gets old and will bear a high price." I said, "Please introduce me to him." He very politely returned the introduction. I told him when and where, the Lord willing, I would preach and invited him to come to the meeting, and he promised me that he would. He lived in the country four miles distant, on a splendid blue-grass farm. I had a church in that neighborhood. I found him in my congregation quite regularly, as his wife was a member and he kindly accompanied her. Eventually he invited me to go home with him from a night service. I preached to him faithfully as we rode side by side along the nice turnpike. Next morning I was sitting in the family room before I started to meeting and he came and dropped a five dollar bill in my hand, observing, "I am not in the habit of giving any money to the preachers, but will be obliged if you will take this," which I did with many thanks, then turning away, at once looking back he dropped another five dollar bill into my hand. It was not long till he presented himself as a seeker of salvation and continued in that attitude quite awhile; then during the altar service in the midst of a glorious revival in the town church, he got up and there boldly testified to personal salvation, to the delectation of the large audience who crowded round, joyfully congratulating him. Of course he utterly went out of the whiskey business, not only falling in with the temperance army but prophesying that the Prohibition Movement would continue till it swept alcohol from the nation. God in mercy expedite the fulfillment of this prophecy! This is a cogent argument for entire sanctification, which invariably make all of its votaries radical Prohibitionists.

While there is more whiskey made in Kentucky than in any other state in the Union, which doubtless largely accounts for the large criminal list which makes us all blush for shame, yet God has honored our labors, waging an exterminating war against the manufacture and sale of this awful liquid damnation, and giving us local option extending over large portions of the State, which thus brilliantly contrast with the dark regions dominated by the soul-destroying monster.

Our greatest trouble in the local option elections has been the difficulty of controlling the colored vote. This is, however, much relieved, as those people since the Emancipation have made rapid progress, both educationally and religiously.

Gen. Clay Smith, a Baptist preacher and the first candidate for the Presidency on the Prohibition ticket, has been eminently useful in the movement. When he was pastor of the Baptist Church in Mt. Sterling and T. J. Godbey, a cousin of mine, of the Methodist Church in that city, they had one of the most interesting campaigns I have ever known (as I was there assisting my cousin in a revival meeting). The good people led by their pastors had labored long and hard and reached the point where they knew they had the majority of the white people, consequently the fight was with the sons of Ham. They had made them a specialty and were very hopeful, though they knew the saloon-keepers would buy them if possible. Finally on Sunday night preceding the Monday of the election they had a union rally in the Methodist Colored Church in their special interest; hither the white pastors and leading brethren had assembled. The house was packed and crowds thronged the doors and windows. Gen. Smith proceeded to address them, telling them about how his father owned sixty of them and yet he went into the Union Army and fought to free them. He had been wounded on the battlefield, so, holding up his arm which had been lacerated by a bullet, he proceeded to tell them that he was in great trouble, fighting that awful monster, whiskey, which was sending millions to a drunkard's Hell, and so he much needed help. Thus appealing to them, he said, "When you were all in bondage, and my father owned sixty of you, I went to the battlefield, fought and shed my blood to break your chains, to set you free, and now when I'm in trouble, if you don't help me, I'll be mad." At that moment shouts roared from all parts of the audience, "We are going to help you, boss, that we will, don't be afraid!" Then the pastor turned, stated that their Conference was coming on and they were behind in their finances and needed money, specifying the amount. Then those white brethren walked forward and laid on the table all the deficiency, to the infinite delight of their sable brethren. Next morning all of the pastors were at the polls bright and early, before they opened. Every colored man was interviewed and a ticket given him. On that day the saloons were all giving out free whiskey, but the Christian women had their lunch-stands giving them coffee, pies, cakes and other delicious edibles free. The tide moved up so rapidly in favor of local option that by ten o'clock the saloon men, despairing of victory, ceased to donate the whiskey, but began to sell it, as they knew their race was run and they would get to sell no more after those few days.

CHAPTER X.

FIGHT AGAINST SATAN.

When the Lord sanctified me, baptizing me with the Holy Ghost and fire, in 1868, He actually made me a flaming cyclone. I inherited a wonderfully tenacious physical constitution, the hard work and constant activity through which my boyhood passed making me an athlete and giving me physical hardlihood of a very extraordinary type. From the very hour of my sanctification I was an indefatigable preacher and always ready to blow the silver trumpet, warn the wicked to flee the wrath to come, and cheer the weak believers along the heavenly way. I have often preached six times a day. I was a constant runner from house to house, dashing in, talking to the people about salvation and praying for them.

In time of a snow knee-deep I went to a country church to hold a protracted meeting, finding it very difficult to get my horse across the streams which were all frozen over. A man who was not saved and had no leaning toward the Methodists kindly came out and helped me to get my horse across the creek and said afterward that he thought I was a fool to undertake a protracted meeting in such weather. Though the winter continued like Greenland, before the meeting was over he travelled the five miles to it, continued to go and got gloriously saved. At my first meeting only four persons were present, a backslidden member, a regular hard case, a notorious infidel and a little boy. They all got converted and the infidel turned a preacher on the spot and began to help me with all his might.

The news went out that Tom Camick was converted and preaching with all his might. The people, despite the terrible weather, crowded and packed the house and a great revival broke out that swept like an avalanche over the whole country far and wide. That revival actually trebled the membership in the church, so that they built them a nice new edifice and made a new departure for the land of the blessed. Though that was long before the Holiness Movement ever reached that country, we had some really wonderful manifestations of the sanctifying power. Before the Movement reached the country, it was such an utter novelty that no one would profess it unless he actually got the baptism of the Holy Ghost and fire. The sanctification of Thomas Williams, who stood at the very front of the Church, was miraculous and phenomenal. Though the profession was utterly unknown among the people, he boldly testified to it, till the Lord took him to Heaven. That year between four and five hundred people professed conversion and joined the churches on my circuit.

Meanwhile a very bright, smart infidel came to town and gained a notoriety by cursing our meeting, saying he had heard that "that man Godbey was running a converting machine in that town and that he had come up to get him to turn loose his batteries on him," at the same time challenging him to try it, and boasting that he would find hard material if he did. After we had prayed and testified for an hour by way of introductory to the night meeting, which we generally held from four to five hours and frequently running much longer, I, as a confirmation of the appalling wickedness prevailing in that country, told them what I had heard, and at the same time ejaculated a prayer that God, for Christ's sake, would send His Holy Spirit that moment to open that man's eyes and give him a look into the Hell which was coming to meet him, before he took the awful plunge. As the house was packed to overflowing and the man was a stranger, I had no idea that he was within hearing distance, but he was in the rear of the audience and afterward said that while I was personating him, a lightening bolt struck his heart and he saw Hell open and the devils coming for him. He never ceased to cry to God till he was gloriously saved—became a bright, able preacher of the Gospel.

During those meetings an old Presbyterian brother rode his horse twenty miles to get me to go into his neighborhood and preach. There was no church about there, but he was running a saw-mill and said he would take his own lumber and fix up a comfortable auditorium beneath the green trees and we would hold meetings, pleading with God to save the poor, wicked neighbors. On arrival I found but one business house there and the principal commodity in that whiskey, and soon found that it was a drunken Hell-den. Therefore I preached my first sermon to a large, curious crowd, straight against whiskey, with all my might, portraying it as a hell on earth in which to travel down to the lake of fire and brimstone beneath. I did my best to arouse all the people against it and made an appeal for all who wanted it taken away to rise. Responsive to the appeal as I continued to plead with them, I finally got them all on their feet in the affirmative, except a group of about a dozen. Then I ran to them calling the congregation to their knees and got down and prayed for them with all my might, designating them as Satan's standard-bearers and pleading earnestly that God should have mercy and show them an open Hell before they took the irretrievable plunge. The next morning I received a notice warning me to leave before nightfall or my neck would certainly be stretched, and signed "Ku Klux." At that time immediately following the Civil War, it was very common for men to be hung in the night by unknown bands. I read the notice to my congregation and they pleaded with me to go.

While the excitement was intense, as those whiskey men were doing their best to run me away and there were the fewest number of Christians in the meeting, a woman asked me to go and eat dinner with her. As we passed through the front room I saw a fine looking young man, apparently about twenty, lying on a bed and scorched with a terrible fever. Approaching him I asked about him, and she said that he had been there ten days with the physician giving him constant attention, but he getting worse all the time. I told them Jesus who had rebuked the fever that burnt the body of Peter's mother-in-law is here to-day and could heal this young man if he would have faith. Then kneeling by him I prayed for him, holding my hands on his burning body. The fever left him, he got up and dressed and came to the afternoon meeting; nobody in that neighborhood had ever heard of Divine Healing. At that time it had neither witnesses nor advocates. Therefore when John came and he and his mother witnessed to the mighty work of the Lord in healing his body, saying to the people, "Beware how you treat this man, for he has power to heal the sick," at the same time testifying that he had burnt with typhoid fever ten days and gotten no relief, but was healed while I was praying for him, his mother gladly corroborating his testimony, the result was that conviction fell on the people and we had a glorious revival.

From that circuit the Conference sent me to Burlington, the county-seat of Boone Co., of which Covington, containing about a hundred thousand people, is the metropolis. They gave me that town along with Florence and East Berd, thriving bluegrass villages, containing about fifteen hundred each. At the close of the Conference, Wednesday night, the Bishop read out the appointments. Though the schedule time for the preachers to begin the work of the ensuing year did not arrive till Sunday, I started away on the first train, reaching East Berd Thursday afternoon. Then sending the word all around, we drummed up a good congregation by lamplighting.

Meanwhile the magnates of the Church informed me that they had preaching by just two denominations, *i. e.*, the Methodists and the Universalists, and that they alternated either with the other in perfect harmony, brotherly love and Christian union, and that I must be very careful to say nothing about Hell and damnation, lest they receive offense, which would ruin everything. If they had said nothing to me, I would certainly not have introduced myself by preaching on that subject, but under the circumstances I saw it was "strike then" or my liberties were gone and my year's work a failure.

Therefore, taking for my text, Psalm x: 17, *"The wicked shall be turned into Hell, with all the nations that forget God,"* I uncapped the bottomless pit and shook them over it, exposing the fact that people who do not believe in Hell are unbelievers; that Jesus says, *"He that believeth not shall be damned."* While I exposed the awful doom of the wicked, I held those poor, deluded Universalists over the flaming abyss and the people saw them all dropping in and the devil kicking them for foot-balls around the pandemonium, cursing them for being such fools as to believe his lies and take Hell out of their creed, thus giving him a chance to lead them blind-folded till they dropped down to rise no more.

That one sermon settled my destiny at that place. The news had gone abroad everywhere that I was crazy. They had heard it and then they believed it and were so disgusted with me that they didn't want me for their preacher.

The following morning I hasted away to Florence, a very beautiful town. There we scattered the word all around so that we had a splendid audience at night, the people posting me up, notifying me that they had two denominations preaching in that town, the Methodists and Campbellites, alternating either with the other, and warned me that I should be very careful not to say anything against the water doctrine, such a favorite with the Campbellites, lest they receive offense, observing that they had Christian union and co-operation and were opposed to having anything said calculated to alienation.

I knew I could do no good there if I closed my mouth against the awful, soul-destroying heresies currently preached by those people, deceiving poor souls by thousands and making them believe they are Christians when they are sinners in the broad way that leads to death. Therefore I fearlessly exposed their heresies and labored to show the people the true way of salvation by grace and not by works. Of course that upset them and, as they, too, had heard the report that I was crazy, they concluded they did not want a crazy preacher whom they could not control. Therefore they settled on the conclusion of giving me a free ride to the presiding elder's office in Covington. Therefore Saturday morning I enjoyed this ten mile ride free. The carriage was driven by the leading steward who turned over the crazy preacher to the presiding elder and asked him to supply his place. That was the happiest ride of my life. I shouted all the way and he groaned. I was bright as the vernal rose and he was blue as indigo.

At that time Bishop McTieyre, in charge of the six Southern Methodist Conferences in Texas, which was then truly the Wild West, was calling aloud for a hundred volunteers to supply the deficiencies in the Lone Star State. I made up my mind to respond to his call, saying to him, to put me down *ad libitum* in the Lone Star State. Therefore I ordered my presiding elder to telegraph my name to him, but he positively refused to do it, saying that he would rather transfer any other twenty men out of the Kentucky Conference than W. B. Godbey. He looked me in the face and said, "Brother Godbey, the man that had four hundred people converted last year cannot transfer out of this Conference." Then I said, "What will you do with me? My people have rejected me and hauled me away for a crazy man." "Oh," he said, "that question is easily answered. I will take you from them and give them a dead man, such as they want and of which I have more on my hands than I know what to do with. I will send you where they want you, for our cabinet was crowded with calls for you and I labored hard and got you for my district and sent you where you are most needed, but they have taken the responsibility into their own hands and sent you away, so now they can abide their own destiny." Then he simply exchanged me and another man, sending him to my place and me to his.

When I arrived at my new destination, having no secrets, I frankly informed them of my recent history in transportation, at the same time reminding them that I was ready for another free ride, but they said, "We will not give you any free ride; you are the man we have been wanting and praying for, as we awfully need a revival." Then I went to work in the name of the Lord, who came and converted five hundred people, so enlarging the circuit that we had to divide it in two, lest it be unwieldly, and it has been two ever since.

Of course the older people understand the charge of craziness which was brought against me. All the sanctified people at that time were called "crazy," and candidly, because they were so unlike other people that they actually thought that they were crazy. That was long before the Holiness Movement crossed the Ohio River and rolled its heavenly wave over the beautiful sunny South. The witnesses to sanctification then were so few and so unlike other people that they thought they were crazy. God, in His great mercy, gave me grace to prove true or I would have fallen and lost my experience, as that was a very severe test. Multitudes have fallen under tests of that kind. To have the people believe you are crazy and haul you away, rejecting you as their preacher, is certainly a very trying experience. God made it a great blessing to me, and enabled me to come through it brighter and stronger than ever before.

Cape Gerardo, the city of seven thousand on the banks of the Mississippi River in Missouri, was the first place I ever preached in that great state in 1883. When I arrived, responsive to the call of the Methodist pastor, I found myself preaching to but a sprinkle of a congregation. This originated from the fact that the Methodists happened to be very weak in that city, never having grown like other churches. At that time I was in the vigor of my manhood and early in my sanctified experience, exceedingly athletic and demonstrative. After a few days the pastor took me aside and read to me about two columns in one of the daily papers, written by the editor who had taken it on himself to come to the meeting. He heard me preach and then wrote me up for his paper, describing me in a most hideous way and literally flooding me with burlesque, caricature and ridicule, pronouncing me as the most consummate buffoon he had ever seen, and assuring the people that the finest circus clown in the nation had been unfortunately spoiled in order to make a preacher of your humble servant. Oh, how vividly and ludicrously he described my pantomimic gesticulations; leaping like a kangaroo and howling like a wolf. He never had before seen any person who professed sanctification, therefore, taking me as a sample, he withered and dissected without distinction or mercy, drawing liberally and copiously on his imagination.

The pastor who was so anxious to have a revival and

build up his church, feeling that it was a death-blow to all of our hopes, wept unbidden tears while reading it. Then he said, "Brother Godbey, I'm going around to see the people and straighten this up, telling them that I know you to be a man of good standing in the Kentucky Conference and all this utterly without foundation." I said to him, "Brother, are you not willing for me to have a say-so in this, as I am the one concerned?" This question he answered gushingly in the affirmative. So said I, "Please do not offer one word of apology, but let it alone, just as it is." He was surprised that I was not willing for him to defend me, and asked my reason. "Oh," I said, "when Satan takes the open field against God Almighty, I want you to keep hands off and give God a chance to whip him." The truth of the matter was I knew that writing was the very thing to give me a congregation, which was so indispensable to my usefulness, as the best mechanic can never build a fine edifice without lumber, brick and mortar.

Within forty-eight hours, not only were the seats all filled and crowded in that large house, but twice as many people were in it as could occupy the seats. They were literally crammed and jammed. Wherever a foot could get room, there it was on the floor, every aisle, nook and corner being packed and the multitude actually inundating the house till many had to go away or stay out, and it was mid-winter and very cold. I knew that ludicrous sarcasm, burlesque, wit and ridicule indulged in by the editor was the very thing to attract the people and give me an audience. It had worked literally to a charm. Then God gave me grace to take Mt. Sinai into the pulpit and say to Him, "Now, in mercy, furnish the thunderbolts, lightning-shafts and earthquakes, and I will toss them from the tips of my fingers to the best of my ability." Therefore I lifted the mask from the gapping vortex of yawning Hell and shook the people over it with a strong hand, till conviction settled down on them like a nightmare, revealing judgment, eternity and damnation, in all of their gorgon horrors, till they crowded and filled the altar all around and soon began to pass triumphantly from death to life with jubilant shouts of victory. That old city had never been visited by a glorious Pentecostal revival in the memory of that generation.

Another editor of the daily paper at once turned in on my side, defending me with all his might, and saying to his neighbor, who had criticised me so unsparingly, that he ought to appreciate me for my work's sake. He observed that my predecessors had come hither and standing in the pulpits had preached their studied, eloquent discourses, and I had come in my plain, blunt, rough style, vacating the pulpit, leaping and indulging in what he called pantomimic gesticulations and yet had done more good than all of them he had ever known. Then the other editor came back at him, stating that he was all at random, and did not know what he was talking about. He said he himself had been there and found me without a congregation and knew I could never do any good without people to preach to; his writing had stirred up the people and brought me the crowd; therefore he was the best friend I had. He went on to say that if he had fed me on milk and sugar compliments like editor number two, I never would have done any good, but he had given me the very advertisement I needed to bring me the crowd and give me a chance. So these two papers gave our meeting the best possible advertisement, and all gratuitously.

Professor Henry, of S. E. M. M. College, early in the meeting when I was digging so deep, striking so hard and shooting so straight, took me aside for conversation, begging me to go away, stating that the Methodists had nothing there but a mere hope and I was destroying all that. I asked him why he did not go to the pastor who had called me and ask him to discharge me, as in that case I would certainly go. He said he had done that very thing and the pastor said they had nothing to lose, but everything to gain, by just letting me go my own way; consequently he refused to discharge me. After the power came, this brother was perfectly delighted with the meeting and begged me to go and board with him.

While the glorious revival was sweeping along in Cape Girardo, Pastor Johnson came from Charleston, a beautiful city down the river, opposite Cairo, Ill., in the center of the county. The doctrine and experience of sanctification were a perfect novelty in all that country, having never been preached there before. Therefore it struck the people surprisingly and sensationally. When Brother Johnson reached the meeting at the Cape, the altar was piled and packed with seekers and the power of the Holy Ghost was resting on them, mighty to save and sanctify. Upon entering the room he met the power like a tornado, and having heard that sanctification was preached and sought in that meeting, he shouted aloud as he ran and fell at the altar, "I will have it or die." It proved significantly true; he did both receive it *and* die,

He then engaged us to hold a meeting for him in his large church in Charleston. This was a wonderful meeting; it proved to be a great and glorious revival like the preceding one, crowned with a hundred bright conversions and a number of sanctifications, though the people stood somewhat dazed over the novelty and through curiosity, as it had so long been dropped out of the pulpit that it had actually become strange all over the country. In Charleston the meeting stirred up a great popular sensation, two newspapers again taking hold of it with all their might, the one in the negative, criticizing it, and the other in the affirmative, commending and eulogizing it. The large house in which we met, containing about a thousand people, was densely packed all the time, and the omnipotent Holy Spirit copiously rested on the congregation in mighty conviction and tremendous upheavals during those times.

I always carried with me one or two red hot young Kentuckians, not to do the preaching, for I did all of that, day and night, but to turn them loose like cyclones of fire to run the devil out of the community.

During that meeting the wonderful sensation brought out all sorts of people who are not in the habit of going to meeting at all. That is the great argument in favor of a mighty sweeping revival; it will reach so many people who are utterly inaccessible to the ordinary means of grace. While the fire baptized people were running all over the house during the altar service, one of these flaming Jehus, led by the Spirit, ran on a hard infidel and appealed to him about his soul. He repelled him abruptly, notifying him that he was an infidel and did not believe anything that those people were preaching and professing, and had not been to meeting in fifteen years; but, having heard so many strange things about this meeting, he had come through sheer curiosity which he had already satisfied and therefore would come no more. The young man continued his burning appeal, saying, "The Bible is just as true if you don't believe it as if you do, and you are going to be eternally damned because you don't believe it." Then he poured on him a fresh volley of red-hot Bible shot. The infidel responded, "Go on and find somebody that believes what you say, for I am an infidel and don't believe any of it, and you are losing your time on me." But the young man gave him another tremendous volley, letting loose on him a regular gattling gun. Again he tried to repulse him, saying, "I am an infidel and don't believe anything you are telling me." Then he said, "I have nothing to do with your infidelity; my business is to tell you what God says in this Bible, which is just as true if you don't believe it as if you do. You are going to be eternally damned in Hell because you don't believe it, for the Word says, 'He that believeth not shall be damned.'" Then conviction struck the infidel like lightning, and breaking down he came to the altar and had an awful hard struggle praying to God an hour and a half, when, arising with shouts, he said, "You must excuse me to run home and bring my wife, for she has wanted to get religion a long time and I would not let her." So he went after her and in due time she found the Lord and shouted with him in the kingdom of God. I mention this confirmatory of the conclusion that we are not to be discouraged, but to preach the flaming truth of God whether people hear or forbear, trusting the blessed Holy Spirit to work in them to will and to do of His own good pleasure.

Owensboro is a beautiful city of fifteen thousand (and now, doubtless, doubled, as our meeting was twenty-five years ago). This meeting was in the Methodist Church, seating eight hundred and with a membership of five hundred. The pastor who called me was a noble spiritual man and is now in Heaven. His predecessor, who had been there four years, though a Methodist D. D., was a Unitarian skeptic, ignoring and ridiculing the deep things of God and the mighty works of the Holy Ghost. This city is the greatest whiskey emporium in Kentucky. This pastor had manipulated during his quadrennium to get nearly all of the offices on his board filled by wholesale whiskey merchants. Of course the church was in a deplorable condition; had run away into worldliness, unspirituality and wickedness of all kinds.

During the days of my physical vigor, I always worked by the job and not by the day nor the week, making it a rule to stay till the walls of Jericho fell down flat, let the time be long or short. When I began in this church, of course Satan was terrifically and impregnably fortified in it. The very citadels of damnation confronted me within and without. Of course I had to meet the situation as God, by His Word and Spirit, revealed it to me, night and day having before me the terrible ordeals of the Judgment Day. The contract was heavy and the conflict terrible. I preached night and day and during vacation hours ran everywhere praying for them in their houses and preaching the living Word face to face.

We were moving along in the third week of the meeting; some had been converted and a few sanctified. Among the latter was a prominent church officer who prayed through and received the baptism of the Holy Ghost and fire about two or three o'clock A. M., then put out in those dead hours of the night running over the city shouting, and hunting up his friends and telling them the wonderful news. Really the knock-down power had begun to fall on the people. The rich, worldly members, and especially those whiskey officers, concluded that they could stand it no longer and ordered the pastor to send me away. For some time the pastor had been yielding to their pressure and holding his hand heavy on me, doing his best to moderate me. The crisis arrived, and he notified me that, while he knew I was right and doing what was needed there, he would have to request me to discontinue my work, thus yielding to the heavy pressure of those rich people. Of course, as he had called me, I was subject to his bidding, therefore I acquiesced without a word and proceeded to get ready to go to the next county-seat up the river, where they were calling me urgently. While I was packing my trunk and preparing to leave, this officer who had been so wonderfully sanctified, accompanied by others whose souls had also been blessed with salvation, came to me leading the pastor with them and told me to quit all of my preparations to leave; that they had gotten into the fight and it had to go through, and I could not go until victory for those five hundred members and the many unsaved in their families had come. Then turning to the pastor, in my presence they said to him, "Dear Brother, you cannot send this man off till the war is over and victory won. Hold us responsible for his continuing the meeting."

All this time the good pastor was weeping bitterly, and he said to me that it seemed that he was bound to see a permanent division in his church. There he was between two fires, the irreligious people in his church urging him to send me away, and the godly element protesting positively against my departure and saying unequivocally that I could not leave till the devil was defeated. Such was the burden of the conflict on the heart of the pastor that he went to bed the next night instead of coming to meeting. That suited me precisely, because he kept his hand heavy on me when there. As he was absent I was free as Gabriel. Truly if ever I did my best, it was then, as I knew it was my God-sent opportunity to storm Satan's batteries and break his ranks. That was one of the memorable occasions of my life. I had preached for three weeks and there was awful conviction on the people. It was like a dam holding a great, heavy, pent-up, swelling tide till, no longer competent to bear the pressure, it had to break and let the flood sweep on.

When I made my appeal a hundred mourners came to the altar. Truly the walls of Jericho fell down flat that very night. Then all of the opposition evanesced and we went on for three weeks longer and saw the mighty works of God.

The pastor, having survived his heart sickness, returned to the battle-field, girded for the conflict.

The results of the campaign were really glorious; two to three hundred professing conversion and reclamation and, though sanctification was so new to them, before we got away from that country many were testifying to the experience.

Our next meeting was at Hawesville, the next county-seat up the river. There the Lord gave us one hundred and three bright conversions, a glorious revival of the membership and a goodly number claiming the sanctified experience. It was in every respect a glorious victory for the cause of God. The dear saints of Owensboro chartered a steamboat and faithfully attended the meeting, giving us glorious help.

We also went from there up to Clover Port, the next county-seat on the river bank, where the Lord also gave us a glorious revival with one hundred professions of conversion and a blessed work of sanctification. Those were days of signal victories, marking my pilgrimage with delectable souvenirs of God's mighty works.

That was the last year of my identity with my dear old Conference in which I was born and reared. This year the presiding elder had relieved me, filling my place with another man, who was not a member of the Conference, and consequently received no appointment but desired one. At the close of this year, when the brethren of my Conference requested Bishop McTieyre to confine me to the Kentucky Conference, and he requested me to read my report which I had prepared, when he heard the mighty works which God had been doing through my humble instrumentality, he utterly refused to assume the responsibility to confine me to my own Conference or any other; but heroically pulling the bridle off, turned me loose in the whole connection. Thus the Lord has been enlarging my field of labor. I now realize, as John Wesley so often said, and we see it superscribed over his bust in Westminister Abbey, *"The world is my parish."* I have never been an irregular evangelist, but always in harmony with the appointing power of the Church in which, God by His providence, gave me birth, both physical and spiritual and gloriously sanctified me. Thus in His mercy, He has permitted me already to transcend my three score years and ten.

In the providence of God, in 1884 I was called to Paris, Tenn., where I found an old, aristocratic, proslavery church of four or five hundred members, full of factions, each one wanting the pre-eminence, and the Holy Spirit grieved away, till there had been no revival in a generation. It so happened that the pastor was a transfer from old Virginia, and a noble old-style Wesleyan in doctrine. Though solidly orthodox on sanctification as taught by the Methodist fathers, he did not enjoy the experience, but was of course a nominal lifelong seeker of Christian perfection.

Southern people from time immemorial have been noted for their hospitality. This day there is a decisive contrast in that respect between the North and the South. In the former, I generally board myself, as a matter of choice, because it does not seem convenient as a rule for the people to entertain the preachers. In the latter, as a rule, the members want the preacher to board with them and I have to adopt the style of the old-time school teachers, who always boarded among the scholars. In this case I was impressed with the exceptional phenomenon, as no one invited me to enjoy the hospitality so characteristic of Southern people, but the pastor boarded me and my two stalwart, red-hot Kentuckians.

God has wonderfully blessed me with that gift of the Holy Ghost denominated "discernment of spirits." 1 Cor. 12:8-11. As my coming had been thoroughly advertised, the people gave me a splendid curiosity congregation to begin with. I always made it a rule to preach for conviction with all my might, praying incessantly that God would send it before the curiosity had evanesced. If I could possibly couple conviction on to curiosity, I would hold my congregation. In my general diagnosis of the large crowd that first looked me in the face, I found but the smallest number of people who seemed to be walking in the light of God's countenance. Of course, many of them had been saved in former years, but the Spirit had been grieved away and the darkness of condemnation had again supervened. Satan, as he always does, had captured them with his favorite lassoes of dead legalism, cold ritualism, lifeless formality and hollow hypocrisy.

As upon this early diagnosis, I found about nine-tenths of the people under condemnation, with but a few enjoying the experience of full salvation, therefore the Spirit told me to take Mount Sinai for my pulpit, and He would furnish the thunderbolts, lightning-shafts, earthquakes, cyclones and typhoons. Consequently I stood before that crowded assembly, tossing Heaven's flaming artillery from the tips of my fingers, preaching for conviction with all my might, and keeping in mind the homely maxim of Sam Jones, "Never try to scald hogs till you get the water hot," as in that case you will set the hair, so you cannot get it off. I was making no altar calls, as I did not feel led to wear myself out on nominal seekers, insufficiently convicted for a really genuine conversion. I was constantly shaking over Hell all the people in the churches or out of them indiscriminately, who had not the clear witness of the Spirit to a *bona fide* Scriptural regeneration, actually knowing their salvation as consciously as their very existence. My clear, straight and constant exegesis of real matter-of-fact, know-so, personal salvation, was too high for many of the church members to appropriate, therefore they, along with the outsiders, had to take their place under the black banner of condemnation, exposed to wrath and Hell, world without end.

As the days went by, the audiences kept up splendidly, crowding the house and listening spellbound. At the end of the week the pastor came to me with flowing tears and informed me that he would have to send me off, as his official board had notified him that he could not retain me any longer. They had really gone back on me almost from the beginning, and he knew it, but was so anxious for a revival that he had held on, hoping it would come and relieve him. All of this time I had made no altar calls, but was preaching with all my might for conviction; meanwhile I had a great deal of prayer, diligently testing my congregation and giving all who had grace enough to exercise it in public an opportunity to glorify God in oral prayer. I also had testimony; giving all an opportunity meekly to tell what God had done for their souls. When the pastor gave me my discharge, I acquiesced without a word, pronouncing my blessing upon them, and proceeding at once to get ready for the morning train, as they had but two a day going in the direction of my next appointment. It so happened that my young men could not get their washing in time for the morning train, therefore we had to postpone till four o'clock P. M. Meanwhile I was packing my trunk and fixing up to leave, when the pastor returned to my room, accompanied by a fine looking gentleman in the prime of life, whom he introduced to me as his presiding elder. He said, "Quit packing that trunk; if you get away from here in a month, it is as early as I expect." I responded, "The pastor who called me has already discharged me, and consequently I am preparing to go." Then he said, "As presiding elder of this district, I have rights as well as the pastor, and I am not willing to let you leave. I want you to stay here a month yet, and then I have many places in my district where I want you to hold meetings." I asked him why he differed so widely from the pastor in reference to the continuance of my labors. He responded, "When I drove into the city this morning, the members of our church, as fast as they saw me, ran out of their business houses and halted me in my buggy and said, 'We are so glad you have come, we have been wishing you would.' 'Why, what do you want?' 'Oh, we are in a heap of trouble; and so much need a revival. Our pastor called a man to help us in a revival meeting, and he has actually ruined us all, he has preached away what little religion we had; instead of encouraging us, he has blued us to death, flooding us with discouragement till we are about to doubt whether we ever had any religion, and he puts the standard so high that we cannot claim it now if we ever did have it. He is preaching justification, which he says is the lowest standard of religion which can possibly give people a place in the kingdom of God; so high, that people do not commit sin; besides he tells us that justified people, living an unsinning life, must be sanctified wholly before they can go to Heaven. Besides, he is so plain and rough, preaching Hell and damnation all the time so awfully that he actually scares everybody.' I hear a general complaint, the people saying they cannot sleep at night. When they go to sleep, they are awakened with frightful dreams, in which they see Hell opened and black devils around them, and are awakened by awful nightmares. When I asked about the congregations, they say they are splendid; our big house is crowded; but they are the hoodlums and the low class of people, and other denominations, and all sorts of people." Then he said to me, "The truth of the matter is, this whole town is stirred as I never knew it and I have been intimately acquainted with it thirty years. During that time it has never had a revival and we have made efforts every year and they have all proved signal failures. We never have succeeded in getting a man here that would hold a congregation. We have tried all of our bishops; they have come and preached themselves out of a congregation in less than a week. They tell me you have been here a week, and the house is crowded all the time. But they say, 'While all that is true, the whole thing is against our church. He is so awfully rough; digs us up so terrifically that outsiders are tickled to death to see us all get blistered and peeled so unmercifully. He is so terribly hard on the churches, constantly saying that all church members who commit sin are on a bee-line to Hell. Therefore he is actually sending, not the other denominations, to Hell, but even us Methodists because we all commit some sins, of course. He puts the standard of justification so high that he brings us all under condemnation and consigns us to Hell; and then he is all the time roaring on the sanctification, which we did not know we had to have. He not only proved it with the Bible, but seems to find the Methodist doctrines full of it. The truth of it is, he has thrown a black cloud over all the churches in the city, and put religion back so far that we are afraid we will never get over it. We saw in a day or two that our pastor had made the fatal mistake of calling the wrong man. We have been trying several days to get our pastor to close the meeting, thus sending him off, but he is very unwilling to do it but says that the man, though in a rough, plain way, is telling us all the very truth we have always needed, and that he certainly has the Bible and the Methodist doctrines on his side, in everything. Therefore he tells us we ought to bear with the terribly rough and plain manner in which he presents it, as it is all for our good. But we are so glad you have come, and of course you will send him away, for we are so sorry he ever came because he has discouraged us so instead of reviving us, as we expected; he has just about convinced us that if we ever had any religion, it is all gone, and, as he often says, we are on a bee-line to Hell. He has so much to say about empty ritualism, lifeless legalism, dead formalism, and hollow hypocrisy. The fact of the matter is, his talk is so awful, and actually insulting, that we resolved to never hear him any more; but somehow, though we feel so bad, and his preaching makes us feel worse and worse, yet we cannot stay away. We have been thinking that surely his congregation would leave him, but we are astonished at the way they all hold on; some of them say that he has withered them so awfully that they have a curiosity to hear what he is going to say next time.' "

Then the presiding elder added, "As I have never known the old, dead town so stirred in the last thirty years, mark it down, you cannot leave. Write to the people to whom you are going and postpone your appointment another month, for something wonderful is going to come out of this thing; and as to our church, it has been dead ever since I have known it and all revival efforts have signally failed. The truth of it is, it is divided up into factions, each wanting the pre-eminence and all at war with each other. So you go ahead and I am going to stay with you awhile; and though the people say you are awfully hot and rough, please neither cool it off, nor soften it; but if you have anything hotter and rougher, let us have it." So I acquiesced in the verdict of the presiding elder and went on with the meeting.

I had preached for a week straight, constantly on Hell and holiness, proving clearly that they all had to have one or the other. Without a clear and unmistakable experience of justification, there was an impassible mountain and unbridgeable river between them and the attitude in which it was possible to seek sanctification. Pursuant to the perfect freedom which the presiding elder gave me, I continued to take Mount Sinai for my pulpit, pleading with God to furnish all the ammunition He wanted me to use, and promising faithfully to "cry aloud and spare not, showing Israel their sins and His people their transgressions." Therefore, responsive to the prayers of the presiding elder, God gave me a regular gattling gun, loaded to the muzzle with red-hot shot and shell. This I used for four days with all my might, God wonderfully helping me. The arrival of the presiding elder and his presence in the meetings seemed to help the congregation, and seemed to augment the conviction which had already settled upon the people like a nightmare. Still I made no altar calls, but conducted the meeting with preaching, much prayer for conviction on the people, and free testimony for everybody who had grace enough to give it.

At the expiration of four days, and eleven days from the beginning, God, in His mercy, descended, raining fire from Heaven on the whole congregation till there was a general break-down; many people actually falling from their seats. Then for the first time I opened the altar, and it took half of that large auditorium to accommodate the seekers for pardon, reclamation and sanctification. Then I changed my tactics altogether; vacating Sinai I went at once to Calvary. Hitherto I had said almost nothing about love and mercy, so utterly engrossed was I in preaching the terrors of violated law; holding all transgressors with a strong hand over the burning pit, and warning the wicked to flee from the wrath to come. Now it seemed that the conviction had actually come and taken possession of the whole congregation, till everybody was crying to God for mercy. Therefore it was an auspicious time to preach the Calvary Gospel, the dying love of Jesus, pointing all the broken-hearted penitents to the "Lamb of God that taketh away the sin of the world."

"I saw One hanging on the tree,
In agonies and blood,
Who fixed His languid eyes on me,
As near the cross I stood.
Sure, never to my latest breath
Can I forget that look;
He seemed to charge me with His death,
Though not a word He spoke.

"My conscience felt and owned the guilt,
And plunged me in despair;
I saw my sins His blood had spilt,
And helped to nail Him there.
A second look He gave which said,
I freely all forgive,
My blood is for thy ransom paid;
I died that you might live."

I preached no more on Hell and damnation, as I felt so sorry for the people writhing under conviction, which had settled down on them like a nightmare from the eternal world. They looked pale as corpses and in spirit were as blue as indigo. Despair was hovering over them on raven pinions and claiming them for her victims. Now my theme became the wonderful and glorious vicarious atonement wrought on Calvary by the dying agonies of God's humiliated Son, who vacated the throne of His glory, and descended to this dark, lost world, spontaneously to die for the Hell-deserving millions of this Satan-dominated earth; and all because He loved us so.

"Oh, for this love let rocks and hills,
Their lasting silence break;
And all harmonious human tongues
Their Savior's praises speak.

"Angels, assist our mighty joys,
Strike all your harps of gold,
But when you reach your highest notes,
His love can ne'er be told."

The people could hardly believe that I was the same man who had so ferociously exposed all their sins, sparing nobody and nothing, but so ferreting out their black iniquity, which they thought nobody knew, that many were puzzled and bewildered to know who had told me all about their black and crooked lives. Soon their faith began to apprehend and appropriate the omnipotent grace of redeeming mercy, and the light of the bright upper world began to fall on them like the effulgent gleams of the rosy-fingered Aurora, the daughter of the dawn, peering above the Oriental horizon; she the herald proclaiming the delectable rising of the gorgeous king of day, climbing the skies in his flaming chariot, drawn by steeds of fire, thus chasing away the dismal darkness of the long, dreary night. Thus the Sun of righteousness in His unutterable glory arose on those broken-hearted penitents with healing in His wings, chasing away their dreary midnight.

Until this time, I, with my two young men, had lost no time in visiting the people, going everywhere, preaching on the street, from house to house, and doing everything in our power to bring the people to God. Now since the light had come and souls were passing out of darkness into light, out of death into life, out of despair into hope, the glorious Sun of righteousness was climbing the beautiful Orient with healing in His wings, flooding dozens, scores and hundreds of weeping penitents, backsliders and hungry Christians with His glorious effulgence, and wonderful reactions and revolutions began to develop on all sides. People rose up spontaneously and after the good old style, characteristic of Southern hospitality, took us all to their homes and strove with each other for the privilege, as they wanted us everywhere. Meanwhile, to my surprise, many publicly confessed to me their unkind criticisms, and begged my forgiveness; at the same time making confessions to me and others and mutually asking pardon. Oh, how delightful to see those old factions united in peace! They who had filled the church with strife, animosites, bickerings, calumniations, talebearings, emulations, controversies, jealousies, envy, prejudice, bigotry, selfishness, self-love, ambition, avarice, egotism, and many other things which reflected much discredit on Christian character, fellowship, philanthropy, generosity, hospitality, liberality, and all the beautiful and amiable graces which constitute the brilliant constellation which shines so brightly in every true Christian character.

The meeting ran on, all told, four weeks. One hundred and forty-three were gloriously converted and a large number sanctified; while the church got wonderfully revived. While I was preaching the Sinai Gospel, it seemed that we had no friends there at all and many regarded me as an enemy. But the reaction was so radical and complete that everybody became my friend, all classes, even the slaves. The presiding elder threw open his whole district to me and begged me hard to traverse it and hold other meetings. This I did to the extent of my opportunity, as I was flooded with calls.

Soon after our meeting at Paris, we went to Brownsville, Tenn., which is said to have the largest Methodist Church in the Memphis Conference. There of course, as usual, I began preaching the Sinai Gospel in order to secure conviction on the people, without which we can neither have conversions, reclamations nor sanctifications. Conviction is the corner-stone of any true revival. A revival is the best thing in the world and a fuss with the devil the next best. Rely upon it, we will have the revival or the fuss with the devil, and the bigger of either the better. We frequently had the latter, winding up without the revival. You see it would have gone that way at Paris if the presiding elder had not come, but his hand was on me and held me. It was always a question whether the preacher would have the grit and grace to hold me while I preached the Sinai Gospel, which was indispensable to conviction, as the people dread it as a child does the extraction of a tooth. If I had begun on the Calvary Gospel, preaching nothing but the dying love of Jesus, I might have had a church-joining, but no revival. That is the reason why so many revivals are superficial, and evanescent, because they have no bottom. As a rule, almost any preacher would let you preach Sinai if his people would, but when it comes to blowing them up and tearing them all to pieces with dynamite, they flicker. I never knew a case where they received the Sinai Gospel and did not get convicted. The plan of salvation is perfect. The reason why the world is full of sinners is because they are not convicted; if they were truly convicted, like Saul of Tarsus, they would refuse to eat or sleep till they get saved. The province of the Sinai Gospel is to reveal Hell in all its gorgon horrors, and shake people over it till they conclude they are dropping into it; then, in every case, you will see thunderbolt conviction, followed by radical repentance and glorious conversion.

The reason why genuine revivals in the churches are not at all common is because the Sinai Gospel has gone out of the pulpit; the reason of this is because there are so many unsaved people in the churches that, in many instances, they have the control of them, and actually rule out the Sinai Gospel of Hell and damnation, from the simple fact that it renders them so uncomfortable. They require their preacher to comfort them and make them feel good, which is actually helping the devil to ease them down to Hell. But God commands us rightly to divide the Word of truth, 2 Tim. 2: 15. That means to preach the Sinai Gospel to sinners and backsliders all the time until you get such a conviction on them that they will cry to God night and day till He comes down and delivers them. It means that we should preach the Calvary Gospel to penitents, till they are enabled by faith to receive and appropriate the dying love of Jesus, in which case they invariably get gloriously converted. It also means, as Wesley commands his preachers, to preach to Christians perfection; constantly, urgently, and explicitly. Then it means that we should preach to sanctified people the Transfiguration Gospel, *i. e.*, the glorious appearing of our blessed Lord, when this mortal shall put on immortality and this corruption shall put on incorruption; and death shall be swallowed up in victory.

We live in an age of shocking delinquencies, which are everywhere characterizing the popular pulpit. The Sinai and Transfiguration Gospels are even dead letters in the vocabulary of the popular preacher. When he crowds into his little sermonette some part of the Gospel, it is generally Calvary and sometimes a little of Pentecost. In his thirty minutes he has so much to tell the people about worldly interests, history, the strikes, and the political phenomena, that he has not much time for the Gospel. Any person who will candidly, heroically, and persistently preach the Sinai Gospel will bring conviction on the people, which always superinduces not only a willingness but an anxiety to be saved, and a readiness to avail themselves of every open door, that they may fly to the Savior, and get a real, matter-of-fact, personal experience of salvation. The Sinai Gospel always stirs Hell and raises the devil, who is ready to fight everything that attempts to take any of his people out of his hands. Satan is neither a fool nor a coward; he knows that the persistent preaching of his Hell, with its appalling horrors, will foster conviction in the people so that they will be no longer satisfied with citizenship in his kingdom, which simply means the constant liability to drop into the bottomless pit.

I have no idea how often, responsive to the call of a Methodist pastor, I have gone and begun preaching in a church, when his members, finding the fire too hot, have forced him to close the meeting on me; which was simply an indirect method of running me off. In my own Conference I never would retreat; that is the reason why I got that free ride. They could not run me, therefore they hauled me. Outside of my own Conference, I was always exceedingly deferential to the pastor's authority, therefore when he wanted me to leave, I always did it, frequently, however, God raised up somebody else to hold me, as in the case at Paris, Tenn. Frequently the members would turn the bread question on the pastor, telling him if he did not send me off they would send him, and that meant for him not only to forfeit his place but his living.

In at least a large majority of the calls to which, as an evangelist, I responded, where they broke down under the Sinai Gospel, and drove me away, *i. e.*, peremptorily closed the meeting, which meant for me to leave, if they had only borne with me till I got through the Sinai Gospel, the trouble would all have been over. But I had to stand on Mount Sinai and hurl thunderbolts and lightning-shafts till conviction did its work; otherwise we could have no real salvation. We might have held a meeting in which people would join the church and they would count it a revival, but it would only have been nominal and superficial, resulting in little or no permanent good.

In case of no revival, we simply wound up with a fuss with the devil, which I always considered the next best thing, because Satan is not fool enough to waste his ammunition on the wind, but always shoots at something. When you stir the devil, if you do no more, and see no souls saved, you ought always to thank God and take courage, feeling assured that your labor is not in vain; you have cast your bread upon the waters, and it "shall be gathered not many days hence."

John Wesley, when presiding over his Conference and hearing the reports of the preachers, always made it a rule, in case they reported nobody converted or sanctified and nobody made mad, to say, "Well, brother, you have mistaken your calling, consequently I will excuse you from another appointment, and that procedure is corroborated by good, solid wisdom. We are working for results; therefore if nobody gets blessed or edified under our labors, and no one is offended, it is *prima facie* evidence that we are not really called of God. Satan gives us no soul without a battle, therefore if your preaching converts nobody, offends nobody, sanctifies nonobody, edifies nobody, set it down you have mistaken your calling, because the Gospel is the most positive and available thing in the universe; it always strikes fire. If it does not bring Heaven's fire down, it is sure to bring Hell fire up; but as a rule they come simultaneously. When God sends down the heavenly fire, Satan knows it means detriment to his cause. Therefore he stirs Hell and brings into availability his heavy artillery; giving up no soul, save at the point of the bayonet."

After I had been preaching a few days at Brownsville in that great, aristocratic Methodist Church, the dear brother pastor as usual began to put the brakes on me, endeavoring to tone me down, lest I might give offense. Of course, that is an exceedingly unwise procedure. If you send for a man to fight your battle, of course you want him to win your victory. Consequently you make a great mistake when you put manacles on him, and do not let him fight his best. You not only ought to be willing to let him do his best, but be ready to help him in the fight yourself with all of your forces. Rest assured when you go into the war with the world, the flesh and the devil, it is indispensable that you bring into availability all your ransomed powers, because you may rest assured that Satan lays under contribution all his forces, stygian and terrestrial, and is sure to fight his best, because man's extremity is God's opportunity; you need not expect God to come to your relief till you actually bring into availability all of your own resources. It is so in seeking pardon and sanctification, as well as in the work of the Lord indiscriminately for the salvation of others.

I know what it is to stand alone on the battlefield, day after day, with no person to whom I could speak sympathetically or judiciously. Oh, those days of conflict which I have endured bombarding Hell's batteries with all my might, while, instead of helping me, the preacher and his people were on my back, and I had to carry them and, at the same time, make the best of it I could, with the combined powers of men and devils. The most glorious experiences in my life have been amid those very environments; encompassed by the panoplied armies of his Satanic majesty, not only including the peers of pandemonium, but the magnates of earth, while the dear old pastor had his hand on me like a mountain, trying to hold me down. One day I was feeling the conflict most obviously, and returning from the afternoon meeting as usual by way of the post-office, the pastor, having arrived a few minutes earlier and received his mail, was reading a letter when I got there. I observed his tears were flowing copiously. Having finished, he handed it to me, at the same time laying his hand on me, with these words, "Now do as you please, you are free, I put no more brakes on you." He let me keep the letter which I read with interest. It was from Brother Brookes of Paris, with whom the Lord had so wonderfully blessed my labor in the best revival which had visited them in fifty years, and where God had sent in the presiding elder to liberate me from the embargoes put on me by the people through their pastor, which were about to culminate in my dismissal from the work.

The letter went on to say, "I take it for granted

Brother Godbey is with you and your meeting is in progress. I do not expect to hear of any victory from you, as it is too soon. You may expect the thermometer to fall and the mercury to sink lower and lower till you will all come to the conclusion that you have made a mistake and called the wrong man. I want to tell you beforehand that if you come to that conclusion you are wrong; we did it here, unanimously thinking that we had made a mistake and called the wrong man. But now we all know that the mistake was ours, and that we had the right man all the time, and the work that made us blue was just as important as the work that made us bright. Therefore when you see the mercury falling do not be jostled; it will rise again, and rise higher than you ever thought it could get, till we all to glory go."

When the pastor read that from his brother, who had just passed through the same ordeal, he then took all the brakes off and made me feel free as Gabriel. Then we moved on; God wonderfully used the hard, flinty, Sinai Gospel with its keen New Jerusalem blade. In due time the altar was crowded with seekers. The Holy Ghost descended on the people in unstinted measure, and the glorious revival rolled over the church, attended by hundreds converted, reclaimed or sanctified.

We give you one more case in dear old Tennessee, the twin sister of beloved Kentucky, whose "Old Kentucky Home" I hear the people sing about in every country under Heaven, as well as on ships plowing every ocean.

I was called to preach in a camp-meeting in East Tennessee, about eighty miles from Knoxville. I arrived Saturday afternoon and was happy to find one of our noble holiness evangelists had preceded me on the field of battle. He was preaching sanctification all the time and it had been his constant theme, so I was informed, from his arrival. A few people were seeking holiness. The first service after my arrival was Saturday evening. The crowd was very large and attentive; the brother preached on sanctification, and winding up asked me if I had anything to say. I got up on a bench and surveyed the multitude seated beneath the canvas, while many who seemed to have been crowded out were standing around in the beautiful silvery light of the moon outside.

When I surveyed the audience, the Holy Spirit that moment flashed on me His extraordinary gift of discernment of spirits, 1 Cor. 12:8-11, in whose clear illumination I was enabled to read the people like I read Greek and Latin. I saw that we were in a hornet's nest, though no one had posted me on the fact that there were no sanctified people in that country. The camp had been pitched by the Holiness Band in Knoxville, about a dozen of whom had come out to lead the campaign against Satan and his myrmidons. I soon learned that the people in the community had unfortunately become prejudiced against sanctification and the holiness people. For this unhappy state of things, the preachers were principally in fault, who were violently opposed to our mode and had done their utmost to arouse the people and fortify them against the influence which they contemplated during the encampment. This was abundantly evidenced by a letter I soon received from a Methodist pastor forbidding me to take part in the meeting and threatening me with prosecution and decapitation if I did not desist at once and leave the grounds. Of course, I did not comply with the letter, but simply responded in a kind and loving invitation to him to attend the meeting, and let us have a glorious refreshing from the presence of the Lord, mutually helping each other, as we travelled along the King's highway to the land of the blessed, where sorrow never treads and pleasure never dies. I heard no more from him, and know not whether he ever came to any of our meetings or not.

As my brother evangelist already had the night meetings, I encouraged him to keep them and let me preach in the day time. This he did till the following Tuesday, when he left for another field of labor; of course, turning over the meeting exclusively to me. I continued to teach the blessed Scriptures to the dear saints during the day, but preached at night to the vast audience, and of course the Sinai Gospel was my constant theme. I kept Hell uncovered, as flamiferous and horrific as I could paint it in the bold phraseology of God's precious Word. I preached from such texts as, *"The wicked shall be turned into Hell with all the nations that forget God,"* Psalm 9: 17, and our Savior's frequent and unmistakable utterances on the lake of fire and brimstone that burneth forever and ever, "where the worm dieth not and the fire is not quenched."

We had a few seekers, but the crowds were proud, stubborn, haughty, rebellious, and even defiant. So we moved on through the week; the schedule time impending expiration the ensuing Sunday night. On the Sabbath the crowds were immense. Morning and afternoon I preached mainly to the Lord's people on sanctification, however at the same time showing up a clear Bible

As the evening service, which uniformly opened at sunset, drew nigh, I felt we were approaching the crisis; yea, all day I felt impressed that a cyclone had left Heaven and was travelling that way; when it would strike, I could not decisively opine. Having opened with the setting sun and spent a solid hour in prayer and testimony, I took my stand to preach the Word, aiming still to give them Sinai, as God in mercy might condescend to help "a feeble worm thrash a mountain." I do not think I had enunciated my text, till suddenly that cyclone struck the multitude; the people all around me leaped to their feet and not a few fell on the ground. As yet my altar invitation, which had hitherto received so meager a response, had not been given, but the people unhesitatingly rushed to the altar from all parts of the auditorium, quickly filling it to overflowing, then falling in the aisles and filling them up, and all crying aloud for mercy.

At that time the blessed Holy Spirit was most copiously poured out on the entire assembly in His convicting, converting, and sanctifying power, and abundantly rested upon the sanctified Knoxville band, inspiring them with those wonderful extraordinary gifts, (nine in all), 1 Cor. 12:8-11, pursuant to these supernatural enduements. They all went to preaching with all their might to the people nearest them; thus actually developing a regular Pentecostal scene. I tried to conduct the meeting but signally failed; and certainly all right, because the Holy Ghost was in charge, managing it in His own infallible way. He gave every one the message He wanted him to deliver, as well as the utterance pertinent to that delivery.

My attention was arrested by a stalwart man making for the altar with all his might. He fell prostrate in the middle of the aisle and roared out an importunate prayer with stentorian voice, pleading with God to have mercy on his lost soul. I felt anxious to speak to him and try to help him, but all of my efforts to command his attention signally failed. His eyes seemed set on something far away beyond everything about him, as if looking into the ethereal regions with all the power of sight and diagnosis. I somehow felt constrained to linger about him and make him a subject of special prayer; meanwhile souls were passing triumphantly into life and sweeping victoriously into Beulah Land every few minutes, bright as a meridian sunburst and with tremendous shouts of victory.

The scene, pre-eminently Pentecostal, swept on the even tenor of its way, without the slightest intermission, for two solid hours before we could even have a song. Meanwhile there were many centres of the work round about and all moving independently of each other; *e. g.*, while some were up shouting, others were down praying with seekers and others preaching to sinners with all their might and exhorting the weak believers to plunge beneath the crimson flood that washes whiter than the snow, and then to

"Rise to walk in Heaven's own light
Above the world of sin;
With heart made pure and garments white;
And Christ enthroned within."

After this stalwart man had prayed importunately for about fifty minutes, I saw an amber haze begin to gather on his countenance; it continued to increase, growing brighter and brighter till his whole physiognomy was literally illuminated with preternatural splendor and his eyes flashed with an unearthly brilliancy. Then, springing to his feet, he clapped his hands like roaring thunder. I was impressed that he must have been a blacksmith, his hands were so heavy and brawny and his entire physique so muscular. Oh, how his roaring shouts made the welkin ring! About this time he caught sight of me, having hitherto labored in vain to get his attention. Then he leaped and snatched me up, tossing me as if I had been a baby, alarming me seriously, lest he let me fall and hurt me. While tossing me, he shouted out, "I am the man who cursed you last Sunday, calling you the stumbling-block of this meeting, and saying if you had stayed away, we might have had a respectable camp; that your coming had disturbed everything and made the people mad. It is true you were the stumbling-block, and I stumbled over you on my way to Hell. Now I have gotten turned around and am running at race horse speed the other way, and expect to never let up till I leap through the pearly gates and shout the victory."

Though the camp-meeting was scheduled to close that night, there was no chance, for it would run by its own momentum. I had to leave the ensuing morning for another engagement, but the work moved on. Afterward I heard of many souls saved and sanctified.

Reader, it is your privilege to enjoy all of those nine gifts of the Holy Ghost, which you see catalogued in 1 Cor. 12:8-11. They are all indispensable in their place. In this important emergency, the gift of spiritual discernment was especially utilized.

In 1883, the pastor of my old church, where I held my

membership when a little boy, and where my father had been reared, saved, and called to preach, and his five brothers had also entered the ministry, called me repeatedly to come and help him in his work. Pressure of engagements detained me a long time. This pastor, J. H. Williams, was a Gospel son of mine and always peculiar for his low estimation of his own ability and consequently inclined to despondency. As the church was in a somewhat backslidden state, his faithful efforts to stir them up had produced reaction against him and conduced somewhat to his depreciation among them. My long postponement and the great difficulties which confronted him in his work, and which his diffidence conduced to magnify, had all conspired to a degree of discouragement which had collapsed his energies. Therefore, somewhat yielding to the tempter, he had concluded to give up the work, quit the ministry forever and return to his father's farm. When I arrived, he met me and told me he had no appointment for me, that I had waited so long that he had concluded to give up the work, quit the ministry forever and go home. I remonstrated against the unhappy verdict he had given, as I felt it to be for his own detriment for time and eternity. Then I asked him to let me preach anyhow; to this he responded that of course he would not prevent me, but if I did, it would be entirely upon my own responsibility, as he had made up his mind not only to leave this work but to abandon it forever. However, I constrained him to go with me to the place and attend the meetings in which I would do all the preaching as well as conducting them. As we had no announcement beforehand, the audiences at the beginning were quite small, but gradually increased until they became really splendid, eventually crowding the house and filling all the environments. That meeting proved phenomenal in the extreme. Such was the wonderful power of the Spirit in conviction that the people fell and lost the power to stand on their feet, lying prostrate, and unable to rise and walk, till the Holy Spirit administered to them the resurrection power. People would fall under the power during the morning service, and lie there till the afternoon or until night. Sometimes during the night meetings, which generally occupied about six hours, this knock down power would come on the people, disqualifying them to stand or to walk, and they would have to stay all night. As it was in the country, and the people came from a distance, as well as near by, many were unable to get away except as carried by friends in vehicles, which was very seldom done, because the land was rough and had no turnpikes, and the people nearly all came on horses or walking.

After this wonderful Pentecostal power descended, the meeting became like Heaven, in the fact that there "*congregations ne'er break up, and Sabbaths have no end.*" The workers had to divide up the time among themselves, and some of them stayed there with the seekers who had lost the power of locomotion. It was really a marvelous return of the old-time power, which not only characterized the apostolic age but early Methodism. The old Methodists called it "having the power," *i. e.*, the power of God to such an extent as utterly to supersede human power.

I may observe, with reference to the discouraged young pastor, that before the revival was over, it seemed as though his members would pull him all to pieces, for the pure love of God which had fallen in showers and filled their souls. Though, by the intervention of the enemy, they had gotten out of harmony so that the desire to separate was mutual, under the wonderful baptism of the Holy Ghost and fire, they all received such a copious Benjamin's mess of sweet, perfect love, that he changed his mind, not only remaining with them till the close of the year, but, pursuant to their request, was returned and stayed with them the full pastoral limit of four years, and would have remained longer if the Lord had permitted. As that was my native church, Soule Chapel, Pulaski County, Ky., I can never forget that meeting which gave me a precious souvenir of the old-time power, which my ancestors had enjoyed at that place, when first thither they came, felled the trees, built their cabins and erected an altar to the God of their fathers, whom they had worshipped beyond the Atlantic.

In my ministry I have often seen that knock down power. In this meeting while preaching to the house packed and jammed, doors and windows full, and many who could not reach any position of convenient audience taking chances out in the yard, while thus preaching, I have seen them fall under the power of the convicting Spirit till they blockaded the aisles, and actually this wonderful, supernatural, slaying power was so prevalent as to knock those standing in the doors, so paralyzing them that they could not get away, thus blockading the doors and the aisles. People were found out of doors, prostrate on the ground and utterly unable to stand on their feet, so wonderful was the slaying power of the Holy Ghost in the atmosphere of the holy place.

The Lord has used my humble instrumentality to

preach sanctification from the Atlantic Ocean to the Mexican border. I saw these extraordinary phenomena in all parts of Texas, and especially at Waco Camp-meeting. There, in the early years of its history, so many would lose the power of locomotion that we found it necessary so to organize the workers as to keep some on the ground all the time. I found it necessary to have my lodging at least half a mile from the tabernacle, as at all hours of the night the vociferous shouts of new-born souls was likely to awaken me. During the three months He let me preach in dear India, I frequently saw this same wonderful slaying power among the natives. On winding up a meeting, it was no surprise to see some of our seekers utterly incompetent to go away. In Sister Ramabai's great work, where she has eighteen hundred people identified with her educational institutions, nearly all the time I was there I could hear them praying and shouting all night after I had preached to them. At the same time there were many among them prostrate under the power, and unable to stand or to walk.

You readily see the Divinity and the utility of these phenomena; in order that God may demonstrate before the popular eye the infinite superiority of His power to that of man. It is exceedingly gratifying thus to witness God's signal mercy to the poor heathen, thus gloriously contra-distinguishing Himself from the pagan gods, who, to an ocular and an auricular demonstration, are utterly powerless. The present year (1906), will be forever remembered in great heathen India for the outpouring of the Holy Spirit. It is really epochal as India's Pentecost. This ought to prove a grand inspiration to all friends of the missionaries, who enjoy the glorious privilege of living in delightful America and using the money which God gives them, by proxy, to preach to the poor heathens. No one can travel among them and witness the power and presence of God working so mightily and mercifully in their hearts and not realize in the profoundest depths of his soul the consolatory fact of God's superabounding love to these poor children of pagan darkness.

In 1800 and 1801 the camp-meetings at Caneridge, Ky., were wonderfully characterized by these physical phenomena. They began with an ordinary bush arbor, as was customary in that day. The power descended on them, knocking them down on all sides, and causing them to jerk in a really phenomenal manner. The long hair of the women amid these jerks would become disheveled, and crack like whip lashes. At that time the pioneers were very sparsely dispersed throughout these western states, but the phenomena of this camp-meeting were so extraordinary as to attract the people from far and near, in order to witness scenes hitherto unknown and unheard of in the memory of the existing generation.

James Finley, living up in Ohio at that time, aspired to be the champion athlete. As the news of this wonderful camp-meeting spread through that country, that every one going got knocked down, many of the pioneers, wicked and unbelieving, went through curiosity, actually defying the power of that meeting to knock them down. But it became a paradoxical fact that all going thither had to fall under the power. Though the meeting was pitched for a few days, according to custom, it went on two or three months, actually continuing till the oncoming winter broke it up.

Eventually, as so many people had told this young man, James Finley, that he would get knocked down if he went to that meeting, he therefore made his boast that there was one young man they could not knock down. So, mounting his fine horse, he rode away to the camp, a hundred or more miles. On arrival, hitching his horse, he went to the scene. When looking around he saw twenty preachers here and there on stumps, logs, rocks, wagons, and mounds of earth, preaching with all their might, manifesting physical demonstrations such as he had never seen before, and meanwhile the people falling all around them and crying for mercy, rising with shouts, and jerking as if convulsed by epileptic fits; while gazing around upon the scene, such as he had never before beheld, a strange weakness began to creep over him, worse and worse, till he found himself in the very act of falling, when catching himself he ran away from the scene to where he had hitched his horse. There he endeaverod to recover his equilibrium as best he could and bolted himself up on his boasted championship, reviving his energies and recuperating his prowess, fostering afresh his boasted claims to the championship of the world. So, having taken a rest, he went back, determined to stem the tide, as he had boasted to all his neighbors that they could not knock him down. Again having reached the situation and looking around, he saw that the tide had gone up and the power was sweeping everything before it. Despite all he could do, bolstering up his prowess, he found that same strange weakness coming on him and rapidly increasing and permeating his whole body. His knees knocked together like Belshazzar's and he found himself actually falling, and so hurried away, with great difficulty making his escape.

This time he made a special effort to enlist Satan more efficiently in his behalf; riding away about a mile to a tavern where he bought some brandy and drank it, thinking it would settle his nerves; then returning to the scene of conflict the third time and looking around he saw that the tide was much higher, having decisively gone up since he left. His attention was especially directed to a crowd of about five hundred who had just arrived on the scene, therefore he soliloquized, "I will look at them and see how they get along; probably I will learn from them how to stand it better." While making them the especial object of his attention, he saw the whole crowd fall simultaneously on the ground, as suddenly as if a battery of a thousand cannons had been turned on them. As he saw them rolling, floundering, and jerking, and heard their loud wails and shrieks and ejaculatory prayers, he almost fell to the ground. Taking fright, he made his escape with great difficulty and, though the most active young man in the world, competent to actually leap over his horse like a kangaroo, he found himself just too weak to mount him and with great difficulty got on him from a stump, and had to hold to the saddle-horn to keep from falling off.

Riding away he was surprised and disappointed when that strange weakness still stayed with him. Having with great difficulty ridden for ten miles, he fell off his horse, finding himself utterly unable to walk; thus he realized that the very thing they had all told him about, in reference to the knock down power which would come on him, had already been verified.

Meanwhile the awful conviction of his lost estate settled down on him like a nightmare, and he saw Hell open and the devil after him. I have often seen the spot where his physical powers so utterly failed that he could hold on his horse no longer, and tumbled down in the middle of the road. The people gathered around him, gazing on him from a distance, afraid to go near lest he might have some awful contagious disease which they would contract. But it so happened that an old Dutchman was living in the village, who had been to the meetings and got knocked down and wonderfully saved, so when he came he told the people not to be afraid, that the man had no contagious disease, but he had been to that camp-meeting and it was the power of God on him to save his soul. They were to, rest easy, for in due time he would be all right.

Then the Dutchman asked them to help him carry the young fellow into his house (for he was large and heavy). Though the old fellow's speech was so indistinct that it was hard to understand him, he spent the whole night with him in prayer and exhortation. With the dawn of the ensuing morning, the glorious heavenly daybreak peered into his soul. Therefore with tremendous shouts of victory, mounting his horse he went on his way rejoicing, confirming the testimony of his predecessors that nobody could go to that camp-meeting and not get knocked down by the power of the Holy Ghost. He became one of the greatest Methodist preachers that ever blew the Gospel trumpet. You would all do well to purchase the "Life of Rev. Jas. B. Finley," and read it appreciatively. I assure you it will prove an exceedingly profitable inspiration.

God is not going to let Satan's people capture this world and run away with it, without so revealing His supernatural power to the elect that the lost millions will be left without excuse. The reason why He so miraculously interfered at Caneridge, Ky., was because the people were pouring into this great, rich, and beautiful valley of the Ohio and Mississippi by millions, and without the means of grace requisite to resist the awful tide of infidelity which was threatening to inundate and really capture this country, through the current circulation of that dangerous book, Payne's *"Age of Reason,"* which was everywhere scattered through the settlements of this new country. The French infidels had captured that empire but a short time previously, when, during the French Revolution, they got the political power into their hands, banished the Bible, closed all the churches and turned them into lecture halls, abolished the Sabbath, appointing every tenth day for recreation and rest, and sending agents throughout the whole country to superscribe on every graveyard, "Death is an eternal sleep." Payne, Voltaire and Reausseau had filled the whole country with their infidel writings, which had been carried into this new country and circulated extensively, before the people had time to organize churches. God wanted this delightful land to become the grand citadel of His kingdom, as we now rejoice to recognize that it is, that it might send millions of missionaries to light the dark regions of the antipodial world. Therefore He came among them with His miraculous power, which put to shame the votaries of Satan's Hell-hatched lies.

During my late tour around the world, as I paused and gazed on the statue of Voltaire on the public square in

Paris, I thought about his prophecies, that one hundred years would take the Bible out of the world forever. It is a significant fact that in less than a hundred years, his own office, in which he wrote that awful prophecy, became a Bible Depository, and is still used in that way. Well did Dr. Talmage say that the age of miracles is not passed, but we are sad to admit that with many the age of faith is past.

For reasons I know not, this extraordinary power was principally manifested in the South. I surmised that it was a manifestation of God's presence rebuking the sin of slavery and emancipating those people who had toiled in hard bondage for two hundred years. I am so glad you may see this extraordinary manifestation of His power among the heathens and especially in India to-day.

In 1884, the Lord gave us a wonderful revival at Piedmont, Mo., doing mighty works. In that meeting I observed an extraordinary phenomenon among the railroad men. That is a great railroad center where they have extensive shops and all change engines. A leading railroad man received conversion, reminding me of Saul of Tarsus in the brilliancy which characterized it. He at once turned evangelist among his comrades, like a cyclone of fire. Many of them were unable to reach the meetings till nine o'clock P. M., so we at once accommodated ourselves to their conveniences with great delight, not only holding the meetings at other hours accommodatory to the citizens, but continuing on till midnight, and after, in the especial interest of the railroad people, male and female, who came pouring in about nine; and it seemed, so far as I could tell, that the revival reached everybody.

Our newly saved and sanctified railroad evangelist organized a meeting in a running car, for the benefit of the train men who had no chance to attend church. Those fire-baptized railroad men thus prayed and preached their lost comrades through into the kingdom, while the train was speeding over the track at forty miles an hour. While the work was glorious in the local churches and among the citizens, this railroad phase of the revival far excelled all I ever knew. I mention it by way of special encouragement in the interest of our railroad people.

N. B. Our noble brother, E. A. Fergerson, my Gospel son, continued to run his engine a number of years after God had made him a flaming evangelist.

While preaching in Augusta, Ga., amid a glorious revival in Wesley Chapel, a noted railroad conductor was working most efficiently in the after meetings, leading souls to the Savior. Several years subsequently, when I was preaching in Columbia, S. C., I found him in the pastorate of the Gospel Tabernacle, built by our sainted Brother Oliver, and the signal blessings of God upon his work. He told me that when I was with him in that Georgia meeting, I looked him in the face and said, "Brother, do you not know that God wants you to conduct a Gospel train?" He said God spoke to him at that time, answering my question in the affirmative. Consequently he resigned his conductorship and turned preacher.

Let these cursory references remind every reader to make our millions of railroad people in all the earth a special subject of prayer; that they who carry us on our pergrinations to preach the everlasting Gospel may themselves receive the message, board the Gospel train constantly running from the City of Destruction up the royal railway to the New Jerusalem, and live with us in the land of the blessed when this stormy life is forever hushed, amid the immutable realities of eternity. I make it a rule every time I buy a ticket to get in a word of straight Gospel truth to the agent, and on every occasion when delivering it to the conductor, despite all the expedition, to dispense to him the message of life. The dear saints are mistaken in the prevalent impression that these hurried and worried railroad men would not appreciate our words of Gospel grace, crowded in amid the pressing expedition of their official business. I have long followed the habit of speaking to all the people with whom I come in contact in the interest of their souls. I can testify that in forty-nine cases out of fifty, these railroad officers receive my words of Gospel grace and love appreciatively and, generally, respectfully thank me for my interest in their souls and assure me of their gratitude for my prayers in their behalf. Always keep your heart in touch with God when you approach people in the interest of their souls, and you will be surprised at the grateful appreciation they will manifest to you.

While a circuit rider, overtaking a man walking along the turnpike with some lightning conductors on his shoulder, I constrained him to hand them to me and let my horse carry his burden. The end I had in view was an opportunity to preach the Gospel to him. Of course he would stay with me while I carried his goods. Therefore as he walked by my side, I preached to him the living Word with all my heart, exhorting him to flee the wrath to come. Several months subsequently, he met me in another part of the country, full of joy and gratitude; and reminded me of my former kindness in carrying his burden and preaching to him the Gospel meanwhile, (as I had forgotten him), testifying that my little message brought him down on his knees before God, where he prayed night and day, till the glorious, heavenly Dayspring flooded his soul. He had joined the Presbyterian Church and was happy in God, working for Him and pressing on toward the bright upper world.

Reader, do reckon yourself henceforth simply God's mouthpiece, always administering the message of life to souls you meet in your pilgrimage. Oh, that you may, by the blessed enduement of the Holy Ghost, be able to say like the Hebrew prophet, *"God hath made my mouth a sharp sword."* The Word of the Lord is the sharpest sword that has ever flashed beneath the skies, Heb. 4: 12. When all the swords that have ever glittered on earthly battlefields have failed, the Gospel sword with the bright New Jerusalem blade, sharper than the lightning, has no trouble to cut its way through. Then, oh, Christian soldier, be sure that you never go out without it, lest the enemy slay you.

At Farmington, Mo., immediately after the glorious revival at Piedmont, the Lord gave us a most extraordinary victory, one hundred and sixty-six bright conversions, eighty-one sanctifications, and all of the orthodox churches in the city gloriously revived, with hundreds happily reclaimed from a backslidden state. The meeting was in midwinter, and the snow was knee deep, and though it lasted more than three weeks, there was no moderation of the weather. We opened with very few as the people dreaded the cold, but after the power descended from Heaven, it seemed that they utterly lost sight of the wintry storms, which swept in blizzards. They said that the whole country throughout a radius of twenty miles was drawn into the revival. I made it a rule to stand out in the middle of the house, so that my voice would be clearly audible and the more forcible to all of the crowd. I am satisfied that twice as many people as the seats could accommodate squeezed into the house; even standing room was at a high premium. In the awful jam and cram, all courtesies were forgotten, and each one felt exceedingly fortunate if he could only get inside, as without no one could endure the cold. Ladies stood four solid hours without moving. Meanwhile the power of the Almighty so inundated the multitude that situation, environments and all temporalities sank into oblivion.

I was under the necessity of securing the service of two stalwart brethren, one on either side, to actually take charge of my person, in order to get standing room. Could you not have gotten it in the pulpit? No, I had to vacate that for the babies, as there was no other place where they would have been at all secure, and the interest was so intense that nobody was willing to stay at home with them. My ushers had all they could do to keep the crowd from pressing me out of all the standing room in the house. With great difficulty we managed to get the seekers together so we might pray with them; the major part of the altar work, however, took place after the crowd had been somewhat relieved by the retiring of some of the people after the benediction, which was given soon after the sermon, in view of possibly relieving the immense pressure of the multitude.

Not only the Methodist Church, with which we held the meeting, received an accession of more than a hundred members, but the Baptist received about fifty When a great Baptist D. D. in St. Louis heard of the big sanctification in Farmington, fearing the "heresy" might affect his church in that place, he came to preach a series of sermons in which he proposed to refute the "fanatics." When he arrived and started off on that line, the brethren unhesitatingly put the brake on him, notifying him that the "sanctification" meeting had done them more good than their own preacher had done in twenty years. Therefore, while they gladly welcomed his ministry if he would content himself to preach the Gospel, if his purpose was to refute the doctrine which they had heard in the revival, they said they would respectfully excuse him, because they had received an accession of fifty members out of that revival and could not afford, under any circumstances, to permit anything that would discourage them. Therefore the great D. D. returned to St. Louis, where he wielded a more potent influence than he was about to get at Farmington. When I heard it I praised the Lord for giving those Baptists good, solid sense, as well as religion. When the same man wrote me up in his paper of which he was editor, epitheting me a "modern sanctifier," he stated that he must admit that along with my "heresy" I managed to crowd in more of the real Gospel than my comrades.

The pastor at Frederickstown, Mo., from the time he heard of me in the state, had been so persistently calling me, that I knew he must be in a serious dilemma some way. At that time sanctification was an utter novelty in that country, and very alarming to the churches, as the reports of wild fire and fanaticism had gone everywhere. A general trepidation was prevailing, lest the infection might get into the church. When I got to Frederickstown, and called at the parsonage, the preacher's wife said to me that I was too late; that when God sanctified her husband a short time previously his members pronounced him crazy, and held a meeting in view of discarding him from the pastorate. Though in this they did not quite have the necessary majority of the official board, their effort so discouraged him that he had concluded to resign his pastoral charge and was then gone to St. Louis to negotiate for some business by which he could make a living; meanwhile he would do his preaching to the neglected poor in the slums. I had her telegraph to him to come home at once. On his arrival I said to him, "Now, brother, I am here to help you in a protracted meeting, as you called me, and though you have made up your mind to resign the pastorate, while you have it in hand God is opening the door for you to glorify Him in the salvation of the people to whom your Conference sent you to preach the living Word." Thus I persuaded him to let me proceed with a protracted meeting, though the difficulties had so discouraged him that he had given it up altogether. I told him that the only available remedy for the trouble in the Church was the grace of God; which is as free as the air we breathe and there is no reason why we should not have it.

So we proceeded at once. The Lord came in wonderful, Pentecostal power, giving us about one hundred bright conversions, a glorious sanctification work and a general revival in the city, resulting in an accession of about four score to the membership. Though the people had made an effort to turn out their pastor for insanity, because he got sanctified, when they got the same kind of dementation, it would have done you good to see them hug him. It actually seemed like they would pull the dear man to pieces.

Satan says sanctification divides churches. We found this church divided, but sanctification united it. They not only kept their pastor, but when his time was up they petitioned for his return.

Between these great revivals at Farmington and Frederickstown, responsive to an urgent call, I went to a town in that part of the country which was honored with a Methodist college. They were intensely anxious for a great and glorious revival, such as God had given us at Farmington; but, like many others who ever and anon called me, they just would not let me preach the Sinai Gospel, which is the only power to convict people, without which a revival would be an empty farce. Therefore I had to go away and leave them resting in their carnal security. The students and the people would have taken the truth, but the president of the college flickered under the fire, his teachers following him and a carnal pastor helping them to magnify Satan in the defeat of the revival which was so much needed, especially to save the students. I must confess that I left with much reluctance, for this was one of the most inviting fields I ever knew; but I just could not reap the harvest without a sharp sickle, which they absolutely would not tolerate. I went from there to Frederickstown, where God did that glorious work which was so much needed, especially in the Methodist Church, where the footprints of Bishop Marvin, of precious memory, who long lived there, were still delectably visible.

The Lord gave us a glorious revival in Jefferson City, the state capital, in which he wrought mighty works, bringing salvation and sanctification to many hungry souls. There He profoundly impressed me with the lesson of His boundless free grace as never before. At that time witnesses to sanctification were few and rare. When we entered upon the work and began to marshal the forces for the oncoming battle with sin and Satan, I found about three or four people in the city clear in the experience of sanctification.

Among them was an old Mormon, whose testimony was beautiful; he was inundated with the Holy Spirit and flooded with the sweet, perfect love of God, indubitably manifested by the words dripping with honey and all of his inspiring utterances electrified with flowing tears, really surprising me as I felt that I was in the presence of a weeping prophet. I never, of course, held any sectarian meeting, but always threw them wide open for the Lord's people of every name, order, nationality, race, and color. But as I had never before come in contact with Mormons in my meetings, I felt a little staggered. The pastor, Brother Cobb, a leading man in the Methodist connection, perceiving my perplexity, unhesitatingly relieved me with the assurance that the Christian character of this Mormon brother was accepted throughout the city without impeachment, and that all had unshaken confidence in his piety, and said for me to give him perfect liberty in the meetings and use him with the utmost freedom. His prayer was flooded with the unction and power of the Holy Ghost, as well as his testimonies and exhortations. Through his influence the members of his Church attended the meetings, got saved and sanctified and took an active part along with the Methodists and other denominations. I may observe that there are two branches of the Mormon Church in the West —the polygamous and the anti-polygamous. Those people were identified with the latter, having but one wife. I then became more than ever convinced that God is no respecter of persons and always ready to bless the humble and meek, lowly and faithful, with the unstinted bounty of His superabounding grace.

We had a glorious, old-style, Holy Ghost revival, with people praying through to victory and shouting. Glory to God! Methodists, Mormons, and others all mixed up, making them feel like singing:

> "My brethren, can you say
> That you are on your way?
> I care not for your name,
> Religion is the same.
> Perhaps you think me wild,
> Or simple as a child;
> I am a child of glory
> Just born from above,
> My soul is full of love;
> Come hear me tell my story.
> My soul doth long to go
> Where I shall fully know
> The glories of my Savior;
> Then as I pass along,
> I'll sing a Christian song;
> I hope to live forever."

We should never condemn people for a mere cognomen. God saves truly humble, penitent, believing souls, in spite of the devil and doctrinal error.

The Mormons, like the Campbellites, preach baptism in order to the remission of sins, which is a very danger ous error. Yet we find some clear, bright witnesses to experimental salvation among those people, whose testimony is not to be discounted for their doctrinal errors. God is so anxious to save people that He never misses a chance. He is infinitely more merciful than we are. Certain sins if committed blacken the name of the poor victim with eternal infamy, and people never do forgive them. Yet it is not so with God, who gladly forgives the vilest sins, when He sees the real and genuine fruits of repentance. King Manasseh succeeded his sanctified father Hezekiah, the great leader of the holiness movement in his day, and, closing his eyes to the light of his father's example, not only led the Jews back into idolatry, but even polluted the temple with idols and worshipped them there. Yet, when a captive in Babylon, amid awful tortures, he repented in sackcloth and ashes, with a true and genuine repentance; God heard him, delivered him from the captivity and restored him to his kingdom in Jerusalem, where he spent the remnant of his life, faithfully proving to the whole world the genuineness of his repentance.

There is but one problem in the salvation of every soul, and that is the really genuine work of repentance, wrought in the heart by the Holy Ghost, so changing the subject that if he had a thousand opportunities to commit the same sins again, he would have his head cut off rather than yield. That is all God wants, *i. e.*, the real, radical change of heart, which means a change of life forever. Without this real and genuine change of heart, the soul going to Heaven would commit sin there and have to be cast out like Lucifer and his followers. (Revelation twelfth chapter.)

In 1884, when Bishop McTieyre took the bridle off and turned me loose to go to the ends of the earth and preach the unsearchable riches of Christ, I immediately darted away to Texas, the great Lone Star state, and began in Texarkana on the Arkansas line, as the name implies. When I began in the Methodist Church, I found but few people, as religion over the city was at a very low ebb, and the churches deserted.

Looking round over the city, going from house to house and praying with people, I of course looked at the different church edifices, as they were pointed out and designated by name. Near the Episcopal Church, on the same lawn, I recognized a very large building, and upon inqniry was informed that it was the dancing and skating hall, where the people thronged and participated in those recreations; that it was the property of that Church, and the frolickers paid their money for those amusements, which money was used for the support of the Church. The Presbyterians had also been renting it, and conducting similar amusements in the financial interest of their Church.

I found for the above reason that the Episcopal Church was the leader of the city, to which the young people *en masse* rallied and there held their membership. I found that Satanic institution had actually built their Church, till numerically it stood at the front, the leader in popularity and influence. God laid it on my heart to attack Satan in his citadel without mercy. Therefore I waited till Sunday night, as I was satisfied that novelty and curiosity would at that time give me a large congregation; having antecedently preached to naked walls and empty seats. Sure enough the house was packed on Sunday night to hear the new preacher. God blessedly saved me from all modesty, so that I positively specified the very thing I was striking at and preached my sermon on Satan's church, by which I designated that dancing and skating rink, which was owned by the Episcopal Church, and used to popularize and support it financially. I literally dissected the matter before the crowded assembly, and unhesitatingly consigned all the people identified with it to the devil, to whom they belonged, preachers, officers and members, and showed them plainly by the Word of God that they were all on their way to Hell as fast as they could go; thus showing up the appalling state of wickedness in their city; recognizing Satan's church in the lead. No wonder the outside world was so desperately wicked, which was a notorious fact to all the people. I availed myself of the opportunity to give them a horrific sermon on Hell, showing up those churches in the awful responsibility of actually leading the people to the extent of their ability right down to Hell; thus cunningly and audaciously attracting them to the devil's church, in which they were encouraged to dance and skate their way down to Hell. I showed it up as Satan's literal Hell-trap, in which he was so adroitly using the preachers and leading members to capture the young people and put them on that greased plank and shoot them on the downward road. The Lord wonderfully helped me to warn them of their awful danger and, responsive to my invitation, gave us an altar crowded with seekers; thus opening a glorious revival.

My rough and terrible assault proved an awful awakening to the people, the Holy Ghost wonderfully using it in conviction. The Presbyterians at once sent me word please to spare them, as they were all repenting in sack cloth over the wretched mistake they had made, and to rest assured that they would never be guilty of it again. Meanwhile, the Episcopalians who owned the institution, received such an awakening that they sold it out to Satan's people and undertook to wash the blood of souls from their hands.

My treatment of that crying iniquity was so summary and decisive that it produced an awful excitement in the city. Two daily papers immediately took it up, the one against me and the other on my side, and went into the war hot and heavy. On Tuesday morning following, an anomalous circular was found distributed throughout the city, ordering me to leave at once or meet Judge Lynch face to face. The next morning another circular was found throughout the city, exhorting me to take courage and hold on, assuring me that I had plenty of friends in that place, and need not be afraid. Of course these sensational papers gave me the best possible advertisement, so that I had to stand in the door, with the house full of women and a multitude of men without, and preach them the glorious Gospel. Meanwhile the revival swept on, penitents crowding the altar, seeking and finding the Lord. Brother Lively, who has since been presiding elder many years, came seventy miles to attend the meeting, and you do not wonder that he got sanctified.

That was the beginning of my work in Texas. The Lord gave us a glorious victory. He let me preach this wonderful salvation Gospel from Arkansas to Louisiana, to the Mexican border, and from the Gulf to the Pan Handle.

While I was moving along holding meetings, pursuant to the invitation of the pastor I held two revivals at Arlington, a beautiful town midway between Dallas and Fort Worth. The good people were anxious to settle me there, proposing to donate me a splendid home, which I gratefully, lovingly, and respectfully declined to accept. The same was done at Russellville, Ind., and likewise declined. I never, never wanted gifts, but always preferred to pay for everything I received. My collegiate education cost me a thousand dollars, whereas I might have received it gratuitously. I feel that it is a great mistake for any of us ever to accept a price which our friends set upon our heads, lest in so doing we might make the awful mistake of Judas when he sold Jesus. When we have taken *Him* for our everlasting portion, we have passed the temptation of bribes.

At Alvarado, the Lord gave us a four weeks' revival, which continued to run on after we left, resulting in two hundred and fifty conversions and sanctifications. The whole country was stirred for twenty miles in all directions. As a rule the meetings would hold till eleven or twelve o'clock at night, the people lingering spellbound to the end, knowing that it would take them the balance of the night to drive home. Bud Robinson came twenty miles in a jolt wagon to attend the meeting. There he heard his first sermon on sanctification and got convicted for it, being at that time a preacher. He says he never survived that conviction till he entered into the experience.

From Alvarado, we went to Maxahatchie, where the

Lord gave us another glorious victory, about one hundred souls thronging the altar and praying through to a clear, bright testimony to the power of Jesus to save even to the uttermost.

We found in that country deep and inveterate hostility to sanctification, resulting mainly from a fatal fanaticism which had visited the land in preceding years, preaching a counterfeit sanctification, which required husband and wife to separate. Satan is the great counterfeit and never fails to counterfeit everything that God does. In that case the people come in contact with his counterfeit and find it a rattle-snake *sub rosa,* get bitten and ever afterward ignorantly fight the genuine. This high-handed scheme of counterfeiting the blessed work of God has always been Satan's great gun. The rationale, when sounded to the bottom, would really beat Diabolus at his own game; because the counterfeit of anything is a proof of the genuine, as *it is impossible to counterfeit a nonentity.*

The Lord was continually giving us a great revival. All of the churches in the beautiful little city of Hillsboro, county-seat of Hill County, in the midst of the great, black, rich prairie land five hundred miles long and one hundred and fifty miles wide, of which the Methodist was the strongest numerically and influentially, had entered into a union against sanctification, determined to keep it out. But the bright young pastor of the Methodist Church was so filled with curiosity that he came away twenty-five miles to our meeting to see for himself. Lightning was in the air, therefore on arrival he soliloquized, "Surely God is in this place." Conviction settled on him so that he became a seeker of sanctification and, in due time, triumphantly entered Beulah Land.

When he received the experience, he said to me, "Brother Godbey, I cannot go back to my work alone; the opposition there is so awful, you must go with me." Such was his importunity that I postponed my engagements and went along; himself having preceded our arrival by a few days, giving publicity to the impending protracted meeting. Therefore on arrival we found a congregation assembled in the Methodist Church awaiting us. The ruling spirits of the church were so enraged when they heard that a holiness meeting had already opened that they proceeded at once to assemble the official board in order to turn us out and lock the doors against us. Therefore the first day, after I had gone from the morning meeting, when I crossed the square to dine, the young pastor came to me weeping, and notifying me that the official board had met and were then preparing to close us out of the house. I said to him, "Brother Fields, I am an old presiding elder and know the law on this subject. You go and tell them that Brother Godbey has no meeting here, but it is yours, and he is merely an humble helper. The law gives the pastor the control of the house during his time as appointed by the Conference. Therefore, say to them, If you close this house, you shut out your own pastor, and I will bring charges against you at the next Annual Conference." Then they at once conceived the idea of telegraphing the presiding elder, who was a notorious holiness fighter.

In the providence of God, I had just received the first shipment of my "Christian Perfection," sent from the publishing house to me at Hillsboro. On arrival, I had opened the box and mailed a number of them to my friends, and among them had sent one to Brother Stockton, presiding elder of the district in which I was preaching. On reception of the book he began to read it, and found it so full of dynamite that he had to quit reading and go to praying for sanctification. So he and his wife were on their knees in their home praying for sanctification when the telegram reached them. Responsive to the call, he at once arose, boarded the train and finished reading the book as he ran along.

When he arrived at eleven o'clock, our morning meeting had just reached the altar service. I had made the call and the people were rushing to the altar from all directions. When I saw the familiar face of the presiding elder enter the door, I read his countenance like a book, and saw that God had complete possession of him. He came trotting down the aisle and fell at the altar. We all went to God in prayer; about half an hour had elapsed when He turned on us a heavenly landslide. Meanwhile quite a number tided over Jordan into Beulah Land, with loud shouts of victory, and among them the presiding elder. Rest assured we had a hallelujah time.

Three o'clock was the hour appointed by the board to hold their session, in view of closing the meeting. When the time was at hand, the presiding elder and pastor, arm in arm, both fresh and bright in the Beulah Land experience, crossed the square with shouts of praise ringing from their lips. When they entered the office room, the presiding elder saluted them in Christian affection and notified them, "Brethren, you have sent for the wrong man if you want that holiness meeting closed. By the grace of God I am one of them and for running that meeting right along, till Gabriel blows his trumpet." So they found themselves utterly defeated, as both the pastor and the presiding elder had entered the experience which they had combined to fight out of the church. Then the revival moved on without obstruction, as there was no chance to stop it.

But the Presbyterian pastor, Brother Jacobs, started a competitive meeting in his church, which the disaffected Methodists and other anti-holiness people attended. Among his great sermons against sanctification, he preached one about Job, which he and the people who heard him regarded as absolutely unanswerable. In view of its sterling value, they had it published in one of the city papers, which was handed to me. My people became interested about it and asked me publicly to answer it, to which I readily consented, at the same time respectfully inviting its author to be present and see that I did not misrepresent him. As it was pre-announced, they gave me a tremendous crowd that night, eager to hear me answer the powerful argument which they had read in the paper. Brother Jacobs sat in a chair directly in front of me, as, holding the paper in my hand, and touching the salient points, I proceeded to answer his arguments.

So I began, "The Bible tells us about a debate which God had with the devil in reference to Job. In this debate, if you will read the book of Job, you will see that God told the devil that Job was a perfect man, and asked if he had considered him, how there was none like him in the land. History repeats itself, over and over, as the ages roll on and disembogue into eternity, so, in the providence of God, we have this same debate now about Job. It was not my pleasure to meet him as I did not live on the earth in his day. Therefore I personally know nothing about him, but simply give you what God tells me, and assure you that I verily believe it. I see in the Bible, and so do you, that God says Job was a perfect man, and told the devil so. Consequently I believe it without a doubt. If Job was perfect, since grace is free and God is no respecter of persons, others can be perfect, too. And I read in the Bible that Hezekiah, Asa, and others, were perfect in their generation.

"While God said Job was a perfect man, Satan denied it, and charged him with much imperfection. We have this same debate now going on between Brother Jacobs and myself in reference to Job. He takes the position that Job was not a perfect man, but very imperfect, and in that he precisely agrees with Satan. I tell you, Job was a perfect man, for the simple reason that God said he was, and I believe everything God says, because I know He cannot be mistaken. I am glad that in this debate with my brother, your pastor, I am on God's side, and am sorry that he has made the awful mistake of taking the devil's side, and advise him now to recognize that mistake and change his attitude, bidding adieu to Satan and coming over on God's side."

At that time, Brother Jacobs, taking his hat, walked out of the door, and I never saw him afterward. Every preacher who undertakes to argue against perfection, or sanctification, which is the same thing, will get into the same trouble and find himself pulling the devil's end of the rope, and actually helping the prince of the bottomless pit to propagate his falsehoods.

Perfection is from the Latin, *facio,* to make, and *per,* complete; therefore, it means to make complete. Sanctification is from the same Latin word, *facio* to make, and *sanctus,* holy; therefore it simply means the work by which we are made holy. Here you see sanctification and perfection are precisely synonymous.

As the meeting moved on, we had some of that knock down power, which you saw expounded in an earlier part of this chapter. Among those thus smitten down was a stalwart man in his vigor and prime. I stayed with the seekers till eleven P. M., then went away to take my needed rest, leaving some of the saints to watch with those who could not get away. About two o'clock in the morning, some of his friends procured a wagon and carried him home and sent for the doctor, who on arrival diagnosed him thoroughly and decided that he was in perfect health and nothing at all wrong with his body. Then they asked him why he could not walk. The doctor responded, "I cannot tell you; I only know that he has no disease, and is all right physically. As to why he cannot walk, you will have to ask somebody else." So he left him, but when the Great Physician came to his relief, he had more life and activity than his comforters.

When I went to the camp-meeting in the country, the following summer, I found quite a gifted layman, full of faith and the Holy Ghost, leading the embattled host. Upon investigation, I found he was the leading steward who tried so hard to close the doors against our holiness meeting, and still held out, after the sanctification of the presiding elder kept them wide open. The air was full of conviction, therefore God's lightning reached him and gloriously sanctified him, so that when I arrived I found him the leader in the fight against sin. Fortunately for him, he was an honest man, like Saul of Tarsus, and open to conviction. All such are very apt to get into the light sooner or later.

Though I had many calls to the West Texas Conference, bordering on the Gulf and Old Mexico, about two years elapsed after I began my work in that great dominion of the Southwest, before I was able to reach that distant land. With ample calls to keep me all winter, I ran through the state, passing multitudes of pressing calls, in order to serve the brethren in the West Conference. My first appointment was at Blanco, a county seat, forty miles north of San Marcus, where we disembarked from the Sunset Railroad. Having with my junior co-laborer stopped at a hotel, the Methodist pastor, characteristic of Southern hospitality, sent for us to come and stay at the parsonage. Therefore, responsive to his kind invitation, we gladly availed ourselves of his generosity. Sanctification puts us where we have no secrets, therefore I not only told him all of my calls by his brethren, but presented him my books on sanctification, of which at that early day I had only written three.

The next morning embarking on the hack, we went away twenty-five miles to our appointment. There the Lord gave us a glorious revival. When we returned to San Marcus to leave on the railroad, calling at the parsonage whither our mail was ordered, and reading it, I found every door closed except one, and that was Uvalde, a county seat, far out on the Mexican border. The reason why they all closed against me was because the pastor at San Marcus, to whom I had communicated my entire program and presented my books, had written to every one of them, sounding the alarm trumpet, notifying them of their awful impending danger in having made the mistake of calling a wild, fanatical holiness crank, who would certainly ruin their church if he ever got into it, and exhorting them to close at once and write me at that office, rescinding their calls, and he would see that I got it.

The only reason why Uvalde was not closed, was because the pastor was a Gospel son of mine, having preached in my district three years, when I was presiding elder. Therefore he did not heed the warning given, but kept the door wide open, only hoping that I would come. Therefore we went away two hundred miles over the Sunset Route, arriving on Wednesday. The town of five thousand was the emporium of a great cowboy region, where the people made their living by their herds and flocks out on the ranches. About half of the population were Mexicans. I found it significantly the "Wild West," the rendezvous of ruffians, thieves, gamblers and murderers, who, having committed crimes in the States, had fled from justice.

When we began the meetings in the Methodist Church, which was the largest in the city, I found just a few old people who cheered me with a clear testimony to their justification. They had a grand choir, consisting of about forty, who sang melodiously and vociferously, but I hardly think any of them knew the Lord. Though there was a large membership, in the clear light of the Spirit and facilitated by His beautiful gift denominated, "discernment of the spirits," 1 Cor. 12:8-11, I quickly saw that it was not worth while for me to spend time preaching sanctification to the very few justified people in my audience, but the work incumbent upon me, by the help of the Lord, was to preach conviction on the multitudes of lost souls who encouraged me with a splendid curiosity congregation. Therefore I took Mount Sinai for my pulpit and proceeded as God gave me His thunderbolts, lightning-shafts, earthquakes, cyclones and typhoons, to hurl them on the Hellward-bound multitude with all my might, as God constantly gave me a vivid panorama of a bottomless Hell, with those people in solid columns rushing toward it at race horse speed. I saw most demonstratively that the devil had them by the throat, and was dragging them into Hell. I had moved along on this awful Hell and damnation line and did not know that I was making them terribly mad. I was doing my best to alarm their guilty fears before it was eternally too late. Therefore with the long Gospel mattock, I dug up their sins, exposing them without distinction or mercy. Of course, nearly all of my audience were guilty of dark iniquities, bloody atrocities, terrible crimes and diabolical transgressions of various sorts. Amid all of my arduous efforts to portray the dismal doom of the damned, the unutterable horrors of the bottomless pit, and the revolting contemplations clustering around an eternity of woe, I was simply doing my best to snatch them as brands from the eternal burning.

I was preaching for conviction, having called no seekers, but patiently waiting amid an assiduous tide while the Holy Spirit was doing His work, fastening conviction on them which they would not be able to cast off.

Sunset was the schedule time for the night meetings to begin with song and prayer, for I was sedulously availing myself of all the help I could get in public prayer for the conviction of the lost people. My shot proved too hot for that magnificent worldly choir, in which, as I was reliably informed, saloon clerks, gamblers, blasphemers, libertines, and drinking men were participants. Therefore my terrific preaching on the doom of the wicked soon skedaddled that splendid choir; leaving the singing for the few people who were blessed with the knowledge and fear of God.

One evening when I was standing on the veranda and ringing the bell for half an hour by the sun, good old Brother Walker, a superannuated Methodist preacher, who was living there with his sons, came to me and said, "Quit ringing that bell, and go with me to our house, where we aim to guard you till the two o'clock eastbound train, and send you away before they kill you; for they have gotten so mad at your plain, straight, rough preaching, so boldly exposing all of their sins, that they have taken gross offense and are going to mob you to-night."

I knew it was coming, as it was almost a daily occurrence to kill men there. The last night I was at Blanco, a woman with tears in her eyes, warned me not to go to Uvalde because her dear brother had been killed there. When I arrived in Uvalde an old Methodist preacher met me and told me that he brought four promising sons to that place and they had all been killed. I had gone out and walked through the graveyard and seen superscriptions on the tombstones stating that the inmates were murdered. I saw a double grave superscribed, "These men were both murdered," giving the date. I suppose all the men there went armed. But I did not heed the old preacher but continued to ring the bell. He still tried to get me to quit, assuring me that I would have no congregation, because they had been cursing me all over town and arrangements were made to mob and kill me that night. But he said that the good people had made arrangements to guard me at his house till the first east bound train at two o'clock and put me on it, thus sending me away and saving my life. Then I said, "Brother Walker, we will turn the proposition round; you stay here with me and I will protect you, for I see that you are afraid, and I am not." So I continued to ring the bell, and, as I expected, a large audience assembled and filled the house, which was quite capacious.

We went on with the introductory songs and prayers beginning at sunset and the people gathering till I supposed they had nearly all arrived, then I proceeded to take for my text, Psa. 9: 17, *"The wicked shall be turned into Hell and all the nations that forget God."* As I looked them in the face and dispensed to them the awful truth of their coming doom, I concluded that old Brother Walker was correct in regard to their purposes. I saw the lurid glare of Hell in their faces and the very fire of the pit flashing from their eyes, and could hear them grit their teeth, and could see clearly that Satan had them and that they were full of demons; I realized that the very powers of Hell were present. Rely upon it, I preached my best, and God wonderfully helped me.

My sermon was lengthy and all of it on the horrible doom of the lost, describing the unutterable horrors of Hell, and doing my utmost to portray an eternity of woe, telling them that God sent me there to warn them of their impending danger, and He would put me on the witness block in the day of judgment to testify against them, because I had faithfully delivered God's solemn warning, and they had hardened their hearts and stiffened their necks. But I would be clear of their blood in that great day when we would all stand before the flaming judgment bar.

As I went on I could see changes in their countenances, paleness superseding the redness of wrath and indignation. As I continued to portray the awful doom of the judgment, and to paint an eternity in the flames of Hell, I began to hear groans, sighs and sobs. These increased more and more and became louder and more acute; then they began to fall from their seats and to scream, actually by their moans, groans, shrieks and cries, drowning my voice. Then for the first time during the meeting, I threw the altar open for the people who wanted their sins forgiven and their souls saved before it was eternally too late. Behold; one hundred people made for the mercy-seat, falling at the altar and crying.

Oh, what a revival followed! Twenty-three days I there remained, witnessing the mighty works of God. The conversions were bright as a sunburst, and all, so fast as they got saved, went to work heroically at the altar with the seekers, and in the congregation with the sinners.

Conviction so rested on the town that it was said they closed all the saloons, and they were many, and they had good reason to close them because all of their clerks were at the mourner's bench. The town was notorious as a gambling hell. They closed all of the gambling houses.

The drummers coming, stood on the streets bewildered and saying, "What in the world is the matter with Uvalde?" It seemed that a heavenly cyclone had dropped down and seized the whole town in its whorls, as if the archangel of doom had already descended and was blowing his mighty trumpet, for a solemn awe had taken possession of all the people. Debauched men, drunkards, gamblers, libertines and murderers were coming to me in vacant hours and saying, "Preacher, are you praying for me? Do you not know that I am the worst man in the world?" It seemed that everybody you could find was either crying over sin or talking for Jesus or shouting the praises of God.

The second Saturday and Sunday of our revival was the regular time of the quarterly meeting. When Dr. Harris, the presiding elder of San Antonio District, came along, I met him with congratulations of rejoicing and praising God for his arrival, saying to him, "My dear brother, I am an old presiding elder and know the duties of your office. Of course you are in charge during your appointed time and I am only an auditor and your humble helper at your option." Then he said, "No, brother, please excuse me from preaching, as I shall not take your place in any of the evening services." When I insisted that he should feel free to fill his regular appointment, he said, "I have read in the Bible of a man by the name of Uzzah, who dropped dead because he took hold of God's ark. I shall certanily profit by his sad fate, for I have never, (and he was on old man) seen a meeting like this in all of my life. The power of God here manifest throughout this whole town actually excels anything I have ever known. Therefore I am not willing to do anything, lest I might grieve the Holy Ghost, who is working here as I never saw in all my life. Truly the people old and young, great and small, saints and sinners, all manifest to me that they are wrought upon by the Holy Ghost as I never saw before. And I do realize that it is most unmistakably the presence and power of God." Such was the verdict of the presiding elder on his arrival Saturday morning to hold his quarterly meeting. He utterly refusing to take the meeting it devolved on me to do the preaching; therefore I preached to them on sanctification, closing with an invitation for seekers. Among others, he took his place at the altar; the Lord sent the power and souls tided over.

After dismissal he took me aside and said, "I have a confession to make to you. Whereas the preachers in my district had called you to come and hold revival meetings for them, since your arrival they have again written to you, rescinding all of those engagements and closing their churches against you." I responded, "Please, brother, give yourself no trouble about that; it is all right; God will open doors enough." Then he proceeded, "But, brother, hold on and let me make my confession. You must not blame those pastors for rescinding their calls and closing you out. *I* am to blame for that, because I ordered them to do so, pursuant to a letter received from the pastor at San Marcus, stating that he had entertained you in his own house, and gotten acquainted with you and found you to be a wild fanatic, crazy on holiness, and if I did not want all the churches ruined, the thing to do was to keep you out. Therefore I wrote to all of my preachers, as he sent me the list of your calls, (as you had given it to him), ordering them to write you at San Marcus, in care of that pastor, rescinding their calls. I also wrote to Brother Shaw at this place to rescind and close you out, but I am very glad he did not obey my order, which I assure you I gave in the integrity of my heart. As to all the balance, I see now I was led astray by the San Marcus pastor, who (as I hope, innocently) misrepresented you as a wild fanatic. I find you nothing but an old-style Methodist preacher on the Wesleyan line and preaching (as we all ought to) with the Holy Ghost sent down from Heaven. I have thoroughly investigated to my own satisfaction, since I came to this town, and find it is truly the work of God and is as free from fanaticism as anything I ever saw, and just what I want throughout San Antonio District. I will now write at once to all these brethren, confessing my mistake and telling them to renew their calls at once."

The preachers thereafter no longer waited on the slow run of the mails, but poured telegrams on me from all directions, urging me to come at once. The result was that I found the whole Conference open to me and stayed there six months, going from city to city, and witnessing the mighty work of God.

The time of the quarterly meeting was really opportune, coming as it did twelve days after my arrival, because I found Satan so impregnably fortified that if the quarterly meeting had come off a week sooner, it would have been too early for the coming power. Consequently the presiding elder would have skedaddled me out; but the twelve days' run by the blessing of God had brought us over the crisis. Then the walls of Jericho had fallen down flat and God had descended, so putting His subduing hand on the whole community that all of the people coming, recognized His presence, halted in their tracks, trembled and soliloquized, "Surely God is in this place, and this is none other than the house of God and the gate to Heaven."

In this we have a brilliant illustration of what God will do if you are true to Him. That place was so awfully wicked, and the Church so captured by Satan, that the terrific Gospel, which was absolutely indispensable to their conviction, actually provoked that mob, who aimed to kill me. But God is always more than a match for the devil and all his myrmidons. He came to my relief, and put down His omnipotent hand on all the people in a conviction which suddenly and unexpectedly paralyzed all their Satanic devices and put the importunate cry in the deep interior of every heart, "What shall I do to be saved?" Even the presiding elder, who, with all his culture, (for he was both an A. M. and a D. D.) had been deluded by Satan and manipulated to run me out of the whole country, in one short hour after his arrival radically revolutionized, confessed, and rescinded all of his actions against me, and became my right hand helper, throwing every door open and writing to all the preachers notifying them that it was a God-sent opportunity to have such a revival in their churches which they badly needed but never dreamed of.

My own heart was never disturbed by all of those machinations of the enemy, but I rested perfectly in Jesus, fully assured that He would manage His part if I would be true. Though I was fifteen hundred miles from home, having come that distance to answer the calls of the preachers. still God took care of me and gave me victory. Never be discouraged at the most formidable combinations against you; great things are as easy for Omnipotence as the smallest.

From Uvalde, we went to Florisville, another county-seat. There, with an audience of fifteen hundred, the Lord gave us another glorious revival, hundreds getting converted, reclaimed or sanctified. While I was moving ahead, preaching the Sinai Gospel with all my might, utilizing the engineery of prayer and testimony, co-operatively with my Sinaic thunder, lightning, earthquakes, cyclones and typhoons, the Baptist pastor who had already been sanctified and was taking an active part in the meeting, got up and spoke about two minutes, then threw the altar open for sinners who wanted salvation to come and seek. About eighty of those wild cowboys crowded to the altar. I had already been inviting seekers for sanctification, but had given no invitation to sinners because I did not think the conviction was sufficient.

In those days I never held little short meetings, as I do now, for the especial edification of the Lord's people and the conversion of sinners who are ripe enough, but at that time I made it a rule to stay till Satan was defeated and the glorious victory came.

This premature call for sinners really damaged the work, because we found it difficult for them to reach a satisfactory conversion, because their conviction was not deep enough. As a rule, our holiness people are too expeditious in their revival work. They call for penitents prematurely and find them difficult to lead into a bright and glorious experience. Without a genuine Holy Ghost conviction, all sinners are gum logs, neither splitable into rails, nor rivable into boards, but the real and potent illumination and conviction of the Holy Ghost turns all of these old gum trees into chestnut and white oak, so that they split like a top and rive like lightning.

While I was always flooded with calls, I made it a rule never unduly to expedite the work, thus going ahead of the Holy Ghost. Consequently other calls had to wait till I could reach them. I made it a rule to preach Sinai till conviction settled on the people like a nightmare. Then it was easy to get them brightly and triumphantly converted. I have closed many a meeting without an altar call, when I knew that they would crowd it if I gave them an invitation, but I wanted the Spirit to have time to do His work. I have frequently gone on till the sinners would come to me, trembling like Belshazzar, and say, "Preacher, are you never going to have a mourner's bench? I feel that I will be dead and in Hell before the sun goes down, if you do not give me a chance to seek the Lord." Then of course I would open the altar.

Premature calls not only give unworkable material, on which to wear ourselves out, but conduce to superficial professions, which are worse than none. Evangelists often think that a long meeting will not receive proportional financial support. I always found it the very opposite. The most liberal financial remuneration I ever received was for meetings running for six weeks. Paul's first protracted meeting at Corinth lasted eighteen months. An eleven months' protracted meeting constitutes a bright oasis in my pilgrimage.

Seguin, Texas, a flourishing county seat of eight thousand, was also the scene of a great battle and a glorious victory. On arrival, the cultured pastor, a collegiate graduate and a member of the General Conference, responsive to my interrogations in reference to Christian union and co-operation, answered me very encouragingly, "Yes, brother, that is all right. Our eight churches in this city are in perfect harmony, and we all work together in our revival meetings. Therefore you can perfectly rely on their sympathy and co-operation."

However, to my sorrow, I soon found that the union was in the dance, at the card table, and in the whiskey bottle. Looking out of my window I saw two men drinking alternately out of the same bottle, and asked a citizen who they were. "Oh, that man with the gray clothes is a Methodist steward, and the gentleman in blue is a Baptist deacon." I found my pastor in perfect harmony with all, and so appreciative with the Roman Catholics that I actually wondered why he did not join them. He tried in vain to get me to join him in the celebration of some of their days.

Having reconnoitered the situation thoroughly, I found that nothing but straight, red-hot Gospel dynamite would amount to anything in the prosecution of the contemplated siege. Therefore I opened fire on the enemy's works all along the line, sparing nothing, but bombarding every citadel which Diabolus had fortified for the protection of his people, not only throughout "Vanity Fair," but in all the churches as well. The Lord wonderfully helped me to do my best. I fought like a dog in a yellow jacket's nest, wielding my gattling gun without distinction or mercy. The Holy Spirit signally used His Word.

After several days of bombardment, I opened the altar, which was crowded and filled with seekers. I immediately found myself lassoed by Satan through the instrumentality of a cultured, high toned pastor, who seemed to be utterly destitute of spiritual illumination. Electrified with the splendid audience, and thrilled with encouragement when he saw them crowd the altar, he, thinking, "Now is the time for me to augment the membership of my church," availing himself of his pastoral prerogative, as soon as I got the altar filled with penitents, instead of working to get them saved, proceeded at once to exhort them all to join the Church, and gave them an urgent invitation.

The result was that he broke up the altar service, and got no joiners, because convicted people do not feel like joining the Church, on the contrary they realize their utter unworthiness to take that step. He persisted however in his church-joining enterprise, though receiving no encouragement in the way of response.

Thus I was actually caught in Satan's trap, and manacled by the irresistible authority of the pastor. Of course, I could do nothing but turn the trouble over to God, who sent in the presiding elder of the district to cut the gordian knot and set the meeting free. I found him at the opposite pole of the battery, the very reverse of the pastor; exceedingly humble, good, sensible, and in full sympathy with the Wesleyan doctrine of sanctification, he was earnestly seeking the blessing but was not clear in the experience.

In a private interview, having posted him in reference to the dilemma, he told me to go ahead, preach, and throw the altar open and make my full calculation upon having my own way—he would attend to the pastor. Sure enough, when they crowded the altar, the pastor got up to give his invitation again, taking it for granted that all who came to the altar ought to join the Church, holding the exceedingly superficial view of the Spirit's work which led him to conclude that the very fact of their coming to the altar was ample evidence that they were in good fix to join the Church, whereas the awful Sinai preaching that I was giving them brought such a conviction that they would never join the Church until they got converted, which is certainly the normal economy of Gospel grace.

When the pastor was about to open the doors of his church, the presiding elder walked up, put his hand on his shoulder and said, "My dear brother, as presiding elder of this district, I feel that I have some official rights, among which I claim the privilege of controlling this meeting." Then the pastor very politely responded, "All right, brother, I turn it all over to you and shall have nothing more to do with the management of it; it is now in your hands." Then, in the presence of the pastor, the presiding elder said to me; "Now, Brother Godbey, the control of the meeting is in my hands. Therefore I turn it all over to you, now you are monarch of all you survey. Your rights there are none to dispute." Then of course the brakes were forever gone, and we had a wonderful soul-saving time. There were people of all denominations and outsiders crowding the altar, praying through to God and rising to witness to His mighty power to save. Before the meeting was over, we saw the glorious Christian union about which I had spoken to the pastor. Whereas before it had been Satan's union in his kingdom, we saw that union now wonderfully verified in the kingdom of God.

After waiting long, the Lord opened the way for me, responsive to the pastor's call, to go to Whitesburg, Texas. There we met some noble C— P— holiness people, who gathered from the surrounding country from far and near, delighted with the prospect of a holiness meeting. With that heroic working band, we could have had a wonderful revival, which the pastor so much desired. But after about a week of hard work, laying the foundation for a great Pentecostal blessing on the people, the carnal element of the Methodist Church unfortunately having the pre-eminence and hating good, humble, spiritual people, complained that they had come in and taken the meeting out of their hands, which was not true. God had sent these good people, as that town imperatively needed a working force to defeat the devil and pray down a revival and lead the people to the Lord. But the enemy forced the pastor peremptorily to close the meeting; thus signally defeating the revival which was so much needed.

I knew that he grieved the Holy Spirit in obeying his carnal members instead of God. When shortly after that I heard that he had died, I was deeply impressed that God took him out of the world for that signal act of maladministration, by which he made Hell rejoice and Heaven weep.

A similar case once occurred in Kentucky, where I went to hold a holiness meeting in the Methodist Church, by invitation. The pastor of another church, an able and highly educated man, having heard of my appointment, published that he would preach in his church the first Sunday morning of our meeting, aiming to forestall and defeat our meeting by proving to the people the falsity of our position; utterly refuting and annihilating the doctrine and experience of entire sanctification. Sure enough there was a great meeting in his church that very Sunday morning, but it was to attend his funeral, as he had suddenly and unexpectedly to all dropped dead in his tracks, the preceding Thursday. As he was a leading Free Mason, they had postponed his funeral till Sunday, so as to give ample advertisement and enjoy the leisure day for the grand convocation of the fraternity.

We had a similar corroboration in case of one of the greatest theologians ever in America, who, early in the Holiness Movement, prepared a series of able lectures in which he claimed to utterly refute the doctrine and experience. After Inskip, MacDonald, and a few others who were then preaching it, had visited the city and, with the blessing of God, had led some of the people into the experience, the anti-holiness people sent for Dr. H—— to come and dig it out by the roots.

In a New Jersey city, where God had sanctified a band of people, Dr. H—— had an appointment to deliver his lecture and demolish the "fanaticism"—meanwhile the holiness people wrote to all of the leading preachers in the Movement (few in number at that time), to unite with them in prayer to God to defeat the contemplated assault against His work, and to protect it for His own sake.

Dr. H—— came and had delivered one lecture, which was introductory, getting the people ready for that important work of demolishing their fanaticism; then he took sick and met the audience no more, but soon died, and was carried away in his coffin.

I also had a parallel case in a Colorado city, whither I was called for a revival. I found a splendid church edifice, a large, wealthy membership and a vigorous, able preacher; everything encouraging except the spiritual interest, which was constantly at a very low ebb. However, about a dozen good holiness people gathered in to enjoy the Feast of the Tabernacles and lend a helping hand to push forward the salvation wagon. I quickly saw that my deep digging with the sanctification mattock was going awfully hard with the pastor. I began on Monday and went on till Friday, when he just seemed to be in agony. Therefore, taking me aside, with flowing tears, he said, "Brother Godbey, as I called you here, I am very sorry to have to send you away, but I cannot help it. Your preaching is actually killing us all; my wife is one of the best women in the world, and you have got her so awfully upset that she has not slept in three nights. I thought I could stand it better but I have not slept in two nights; and, to tell you the truth, my leading members are walking the streets like crazy men, actually incapable of attending to their business. If I do not send you away, we will all die. I have a good church here of noble Christians, but you are tearing it all to pieces. I called you that we might have a revival and get the sinners converted, but instead of that your awful preaching is actually upsetting and smashing all my members and making them, and me, too, feel like we have no religion."

I said, "All right, brother, I bid you a loving adieu." I never saw him afterward. He weighed one hundred and eighty, and was in the vigor of his manhood, but he died that year. He said to people who told me, "I will die before I will take what that man is preaching." When I heard of his death so soon afterward, I felt deeply impressed that God took him at his word and let him die.

When they closed me out at Whitesburg, Texas, and I had to leave, it so happened that my next appointment was five hundred miles distant, and, as usual, I had two red-hot young men, whom I carried as helpers in the work. At that time no evangelists in the South received any railroad favor. Therefore we needed forty-five dollars to buy tickets to the next appointment in northwest Missouri. From the day the Lord sanctified me, in 1868, I have always lived by faith, never charged anything for my work, nor even insinuated for a contribution. As these people had rejected us and closed us out, of course, I would not dishonor the Lord by asking them for travelling expenses.

At that time, we lived at Carlysle, Ky. All my life I always made it a rule never to let my wife get out of money, even if I borrowed it. In my travels in all of the early years of my ministry, before I had written books and carried them with me to donate and sell to people, to help them experimentally, I frequently found it necessary to borrow money to make my next run, invariably sending back the first I got, even if it necessitated my borrowing again. So at this time I had no money anywhere on the earth, but when I reached this dilemma and the time came for us to travel, minus the necessary finances, I got on my knees before God, and turned over to Him Farmers' Bank of Carlysle, Ky. I stayed on my knees till I heard from Heaven and realized that God had His hand on that bank; then, taking the pastor to identify me, I went to the bank in Whitesburg, and presented a draft on the Farmers' Bank of Carlysle, Kentucky, and drew out all the money we needed to purchase the three full fare tickets. Independently we went to the depot with shouts of victory ringing from our lips, bought our tickets and went on our way rejoicing. Long before we completed our tour and returned to Kentucky, the Lord gave me the money and I sent it to the bank.

On reaching home I went at once from the depot to the bank to face the officers with a personal apology for drawing on them when I had not a cent of money on deposit, which is very irregular, from a financial standpoint. Looking over the counter as I went in, I said to the cashier, "I have come to apologize for drawing on you when I had no money on deposit." He looked me in the face and said, as a tear came to his eye, "Preacher, when I received that draft, as it put me in an awkward position, knowing that you had no money here, I turned it over to the Board for them to decide before I paid it off. This done, then I read it to them and told them that you had no money on deposit and asked them what to do. After a silent minute the oldest man among them said, 'I like that preacher; he is an honest fellow, and I expect he is in a tight place; I move that we pay it.' The motion carried unanimously. So, preacher, if you get in a tight place again, call on us and we will help you out."

Pastor Avarill had gathered up the people, built a big bush arbor and pitched a camp-meeting in a thickly settled region of Cartright Prairie, Texas, and called your humble servant to preach. The people had grown rich and prosperous, cultivating that wonderful soil, black as a crow and about one dozen feet deep. They had been much neglected by the Gospel heralds and had grown desperately wicked. Of course I just had to go down into the cesspools of iniquity, unearth the vices and expose their follies, without distinction or mercy. We had an awful battle with the powers of darkness of earth and Hell combined against us.

As the days went by the battle waxed hotter and hotter. My plain, rough preaching made them awfully mad. They beat me twice with prairie dirt because they could not find rocks, as there were none about, but those clods felt on my body hard as rocks. They also poured the eggs on me in unstinted profusion. I remember well the physique of the hoodlum who led the ruffian rabble in egging me. I could see old Diabolus in him, big as a rhinoceros. Of course I never expected to hear from him again, but several years afterward when I was preaching for the Free Methodists in St. Louis, they told me about the evangelist who had conducted the camp-meeting, calling my name, and telling the circumstance of pelting me with the eggs, saying that when he threw an egg with all the power of his stalwart arm, hit me between the eyes, deluging my face and knocking my spectacles off, and I took it so sweetly and lovingly, manifesting not the slightest resentment, then conviction struck him like lightning. Of course he thought nothing of it, expecting it to evanesce very quickly, but in this he was mistaken. On the contrary it held on like a leech and went down deeper and deeper till he felt he would die, broke down, sought and found the Lord. Then getting convicted for sanctification, he at once set out to get it. Toiling on day after day and trying to make his consecration, he reached the point when he had actually run up against great old China, where they kill the missionaries but can get no farther. Then he said, "All right, Lord, give me China, that will be to me a heaven contrastively with Hell, so let me have it." There God wonderfully sanctified him, giving him the glorious baptism of the Holy Ghost and fire. He was at that time on his way to China.

When I was in China during the present year I was anxious to hunt him up, but found two formidable impediments in the way of evangelistic work in that country. The greatest difficulty is the problem of conveyance, as they are not at all supplied with railroads. In India I travelled six thousand miles preaching night and day for three months, but in China this is not possible. Another difficulty in travelling through China is the awful state of hostility to foreigners which, when I was there, really disqualified us for evangelistic work in that country. I was anxious to meet my hoodlum who had pelted me with the eggs. Oh, how I wanted to see him and give him an old-style hug.

Despite the rough treatment they gave me at that camp-meeting, the Lord did a wonderful work, which abides to this day. Those wicked people got converted and sanctified and established a permanent holiness camp-meeting, which is still continued. They have often called me to come back and preach for them, saying they would rather see me than any other man in the world.

My Gospel son, Brother Fred Adams, called me to his camp-meeting far out in the wild west of the North-western Texas Conference. As it was eight miles from the railroad at Jacksonville, the county-seat, and the distance I had to come so far, they could have no very correct idea as to the time of my arrival. Therefore all the people on the camp-ground, the meetings already having begun, had a mutual understanding that everybody going to town should watch the train, make inquiry and catch me when I landed. It so happened that a clever German brother was the first one to pick me up the moment I stepped off the car, mount me on his jolt wagon and carry me to the camp-ground. Of course I at once began to preach to him, asking him if he had ever been born again. He was utterly bewildered to give me an answer and said he had never heard of such a thing before. Verily I caught him in surprise, like Jesus did Nicodemus.

So I proceeded to explain it to him and assure him that he must receive the supernatural birth from God out of Heaven, wrought in the heart by the Holy Ghost, whom God would send to him in answer to prayer. I told him the Spirit would execute that mighty work which would make him a new man, and bring him into a new world, putting a new spirit within him, giving him a new heart, and superinducing a new life which will shine and shout through this world and brighter eternally in the world to come, not only making this life all glorious sunshine, but giving him Heaven forever when the storms and sorrows of this probationary pilgrimage shall have passed away.

While I was thus preaching to him with all my might, he suddenly broke silence to notify me that it was not worth while for me to do all of that good preaching to him, because he was a born Roman Catholic. When he was about to start to America he said the priest came to see him and bade him farewell, saying to them, "You are now about to sail for America, that far off land, and if you ever live to cross the great Atlantic Ocean, which of course is uncertain, as you may rest assured the storms will howl and the tempests rage, seeking to wrap you in watery winding sheets, you say you are going to Texas which is far away on the borders of Old Mexico. When you reach that howling wilderness in the wild west, you will not be apt to ever see another Catholic priest. Therefore the thing for you to do is to settle the matter once for all, that you will stick to the Catholic Church, come what may, or go what may. I assure you that it is your only safety. If you stick to the Catholic Church, though you may have to go through the fires of purgatory, you are as sure of Heaven as if you were in it. It is only a question of time; rest assured you will get there in the blessed finale safe and sound. Therefore all of you (his wife and sister) come and kneel down before me and take a solemn oath that you will live and die in the Holy Catholic Church."

He then informed me that they took that oath, and consequently never could think about leaving the Catholic Church; so, as I was a Methodist preacher, though my preaching was really good, he never could join the Methodist Church. I then informed him that he was utterly mistaken; that I did not want him to leave the Catholic Church, but certainly expected him to live and die in it. But I told him that if he did not get born from above, as the Savior told Nicodemus to do, the devil was certain to take him to Hell when he died. The thing for every good Catholic and everybody else to do is to be sure that they are born from above. When I succeeded in convincing him that I had no purpose whatever to take him out of the Catholic Church, but was perfectly willing for him to stay in it, he again became silent and very attentive, actually listening spellbound, as he did not well understand English.

Now, while the wagon ran those eight miles I had nothing to do but preach to him. Rest assured I did my best. Before we reached the camp, I saw that the lightning had struck him. Before we dismounted I asked him if he would attend all of the meetings. He responded in the affirmative. I found him all the time sitting directly in front of me and giving the most profound attention.

Arriving on Thursday I spent all of my time until Sunday night preaching on sanctification, especially in view of getting our forces armed and equipped for the oncoming campaign, as I was satisfied that a great multitude were coming from all parts of that vast wild west. By Sunday we had many tenters on the ground and a vast multitude of people not only filling the great auditorium but overflowing it. On Sunday night I preached directly to the unconverted, using as the text, Psa. 9: 17, *"The wicked shall be turned into Hell with all the nations that forget God."* The immense audience listened as if the archangel of the final judgment morn had descended and was sounding his mighty trumpet and calling the nations to the flaming Tribunal of the omniscient Judge of the quick and the dead.

As that was my first message that I had directed to the unconverted, I took plenty of time, knowing that the great majority of those people had become exceedingly wicked in that wild country. While dispensing the living Word, I warned them to flee the wrath to come, at the same time revealing the appalling horrors of a bottomless Hell, amid penal fires unquenchable. The blessed Spirit wonderfully helped me to portray the eternity of woe most certainly awaiting the unconverted.

As the moments fled away and conviction settled down on that lost multitude like a nightmare from the eternal world, groans, sighs, heaves and sobs became distinctly audible. The tide of conviction rising higher and higher, they began to weep aloud in different places through that great auditorium. The scene intensifies as conviction comes like an incorrigible paralysis on the people and they begin to fall from their seats, losing the physical power of locomotion. The moans increase on all sides till they rise like the roar of many waters, so drowning my voice that I am constrained to open the altar. Quickly a multitude rush to it and crowd it to overflowing. Looking round I see an altar out in the auditorium where the people have fallen and seem unable to get away. I look in the other direction and see another altar and the dear saints pressing the battle. In still a third direction I see another altar, and oh, how the Christians are toiling to lead the penitents to the Lamb of God that taketh away the sin of the world! They are actually peregrinating the crowd like the resurrection angels, when the Lord shall descend to catch away His waiting Bride.

The first one to rush to the altar when I gave the invitation was that German who had carried me to the camp. Oh, how he prayed to God, for Christ's sake, to forgive his sins and give him a new heart. About ten o'clock he came through bright as a meridian sunburst and shouting all over the tabernacle. Forgetting that he was in an English-speaking audience, he fell to exhorting in German and singing songs.

Wonderful was the work of the Lord that memorable Sunday night, when many passed out of darkness into light, while others were fording the Jordan and entering Beulah Land.

At eleven o'clock I proceeded to dismiss the congregation although I knew many would linger until they found the Lord. When I was about to pronounce the benediction, this joyful, newly-born German begged me most importunately not to dismiss, saying, "You see I have got it, but here are my wife and sister at the altar and I want you to hold on till they get it." I told him to rest easy for God would surely give it to them, and so He did in His own good time. The meeting proved a glorious victory; before it was over this German had not only been converted, but sanctified. At the conclusion of the encampment, when Brother Adams invited people to join the Church, this German, accompanied by his wife and sister, was among the first, they having forgotten all about the oath sworn in Germany at the knee of the priest, solemnly obligating themselves to stick to the Catholic Church and die in it.

This illustrates the great mistake there is in fighting churches. That is not our business. We have all we can do to fill our regular contract to fight the devil and sin. Holiness people make two mistakes—they fight churches instead of devils, and doctors instead of diseases. Let us take warning and make these mistakes no more. I had to convince that German that I had no fight with his Church, but only wanted his soul saved. A fight with his Church would simply have aroused his carnality in its defense. A similar mistake is made in fighting lodgery. The thing for us to do is to preach Jesus and tell people how to get saved. You have nothing to do but get them saved to the uttermost, *i. e.*, sanctified wholly, and lodgery, along with sectarianism, dies a natural death. If you want to kill, always shoot at the heart. Otherwise you may inflict flesh wounds and make a great show with flowing blood, and yet your enemy convalesce and soon meet you again in battle array.

CHAPTER XI.

MATURITY.

In the Mosaic dispensation thirty was the majority and fifty maturity. In writing up my biography I have dated my young manhood from my sanctification in 1868, as it took that experience to bring into availability the gifts which God had conferred in creation but which still remained latent in my constitution, myself ignorant of their existence. Man is a trinity consisting of body, soul and spirit. In this probationary existence the physical first predominates. It was so in my life as well as yours. It took the new birth to supersede the body in the pre-eminence of the soul. While, in the good providence of God, and through the hallowed experience of a godly home, a preaching father and a Christian mother, God fortified me against the seductive vices and bewitching follies universally incident to childhood and youth, so that I never went into them, and by His providence and grace I retained from the cradle an unimpeachable moral character, my principal transgressions being selfward through sheer ignorance of hygenical laws; yet during my juvenile life, antecedently to my conversion at the age of sixteen, while the physical predominated over the intellectual and spiritual, I delighted in and excelled all of my comrades in the innocent recreations of foot racing, wrestling, ball playing and everything else which did not conflict with a good conscience, illuminated by the Word and Spirit of God. My conversion forever superseded all of these physical sports, yea, they at once went into total eclipse and I left them forever. Not that I was convicted that they were sinful, but I had received something so much better that I no longer had any appreciation of them. Thus in my pilgrimage I travelled on another long stadium in advance of them, leaving them utterly out of sight.

The glorious experience of regeneration thus having brought the physical into a total eclipse, at the same time it brought the intellectual into indisputable and irreversible pre-eminence. Then I moved out with all my might into the prosecution of my collegiate education, not only pursuing but preferring the hardest studies and actually delighting in the most arduous intellectual labour, *i. e.*, the Latin and Greek languages, the higher mathematics and the natural sciences. In the providence of God, nineteen years elapsed during my regenerated experience, and during all of that time I was a most assiduous student.

Graduating from college at the expiration of the tenth year of that period, I at once became president of a college in which, with my assistant teacher, I taught the whole classical curriculum. Thus I was given the most athletic intellectual gymnasium possible.

When the Lord sanctified me at the age of thirty-five, He brought the spiritual into decisive pre-eminence, thus enthroning the spirit, dominant in my being, and throwing the intellectual as well as the physical into eclipse. Then I became like John Wesley, *homo unius libri*, a man of one book, and of course that Book was the Bible.

During the preceding nineteen years I had ransacked all the world for books and gathered up a library at the cost of a thousand dollars. After I passed this great and decisive epoch in my experience, I immediately began to give away my library, because I no longer had time to utilize those great volumes which I had hitherto so highly esteemed. Therefore during the last thirty-eight years my time has been occupied in the spiritual realm, studying the deep things of God, profoundly realizing that I know nothing but what God has revealed to me in the realm of His providence, Word, and Spirit. I am infinitely delighted sitting like a little child at the feet of Jesus. Meanwhile the blessed Holy Spirit, the Author of the precious Word, is revealing to my spirit the deep things of God and the wonderful things of His kingdom, while the constant cry of my heart goes up, "Nearer, my God, to thee."

"To Thee and Thee alone
The angels owe their bliss;
They circle round the blazing throne,
And dwell where Jesus is.

"Thou art the sea of love,
Where all my pleasures roll;
The circle where my passions move,
And center of my soul.

"Not all the harps above
Can make a heavenly place,
If God His residence remove,
Or but conceal His face.

"To Thee my spirits fly
With infinite desire,
And yet how far from Thee I lie!
O Jesus, raise me higher!"

SECTION ONE.

The Commentaries.

I must mention two whom God decisively used to develop a new epoch in my life. The one is Rev. M. W. Knapp, and the other Brother J. L. Hunton, a preaching layman of Hillsboro, Texas, and now at Orange, California. I must ever glorify God for using Brother Knapp to launch me into authorship and Brother Hunton to cut me loose from my native land and give to me the Old World in addition to the New for my field of labor. I do owe a debt of gratitude to these brethren as God's humble instruments in the development of this great and interesting epoch in my life, which I can never pay.

I had read the writings of Brother Knapp and he had read mine and we had corresponded, but never met till he migrated to Cincinnati in 1892, then of course we had him come over into Kentucky to preach for us in our Holiness Convention, when I, for the first time, looked into his inspiring face. I was a little surprised to find him twenty years my junior, as his trenchant pen had impressed me with his seniority.

I had written my *"Baptism," "Sanctification," "Christian Perfection," "Victory"* and *"Holiness or Hell,"* all of which had received a wonderful circulation and appreciation, infinitely beyond my anticipation, and God had used them as pioneers of the Movement, especially throughout the great South, whither its coming was a score of years more tardy than in the vast North. Those books are all distinguished for their brevity, perspicuity, vivacity and Biblical orthodoxy; meanwhile the didactic phase of them is of infinite value to the Biblical student, at they teach the great truths of regeneration and entire sanctification, so tersely, clearly, experimentally and demonstratively that the blessed Holy Spirit has used them in leading multitudes into the happy experience of full salvation. Besides, they are all pre-eminently characteristic of *multum in parvo,* much in little, and consequently are well adapted to the busy millions of Christians who are hungry for this delectable full salvation and, like myself, are seeking it blindly, as I did for nineteen years because I did not know how to get it. If either of the above books had reached me I would have entered Beulah Land in my blooming youth, instead of waiting till life's meridian. Brother Knapp had read and circulated all of those books. I simply wrote them in order that they might help me preach this great salvation and reach multitudes whom I would never have the opportunity to meet face to face and dispense the living Word.

I also wrote them especially to leave with the people to whom God, in His providence, had permitted me to preach the Gospel, in order to establish them in the faith, so that their experiences would not evanesce through the chicanery of the intriguing foe. I have seen wonderful fruitfulness which, in the good providence of God, has supervened through the media of these straight, clear, scriptural and irrefutable presentations of God's blessed, saving truth, revelatory of the glorious privileges and invaluable inheritance which He hath bequeathed to His humble, faithful and teachable children.

The holiness people had been exceedingly clamorous a full dozen years for me to write commentaries expository of the New Testament. This conception had originated from my constant habit of teaching the Scriptures during my evangelistic meetings, utilizing the day time in the instruction of the Lord's people and preaching in connection with my evangelistic meetings at night. For the last thirty years I have been constantly using the inspired Greek in my ministry, reading and expounding it freely in the Bible School department of the meetings which God has permitted me to hold in my extensive peregrinations. This clamor for the Commentaries on the part of the holiness people had become general and was growing more and more importunate. Through shrinking from the weighty responsibility, I continued to postpone the arduous work, yet I dared not refuse lest I grieve the Holy Ghost, as I had quite a credulity for the trite maxim, "*Vox populi, vox Dei,*" the voice of the people is the voice of God. This maxim is reliable as a rule, when they are God's people, but of course utterly unreliable in case of Satan's people.

While others had done their best to shove me into the work of writing commentaries, somehow they had never succeeded. Though Brother Knapp in his wonderful *suaviter in modo,* sweetness in manner, reminded me of an angel instead of a man, yet he had a power over the human will which was absolutely indescribable and apparently irresistible. When he undertook to put me out in this great work, I realized that I had come in contact with an irresistible force. Consequently I acquiesced without a murmur, promising him to begin the work so soon as I could make a tour in the Holy Land, recognizing the ostensible fact that the Land and the Book are so intimately associated that no one is prepared to write up the latter without a personal acquaintance with the former. Therefore I was at a standstill, committed to begin the Commentaries so soon as I could make that tour.

While thus hesitating to enter upon the work, for the above reasons, I was delivering a Bible reading to an audience of about five hundred at 8 A. M. during Waco, Texas, Camp-meeting, when a man roared out from the audience, "Why do you not write those Commentaries? I am afraid you will die and we will never get them." I responded, "I am waiting to make a tour through the Holy Land, after which I am under promise to begin at once." Then he said, "Why don't you go?" My answer was simple and easy—"I have not the money." Resuming the Greek lesson, I proceeded, thinking no more about it.

When the hour closed and we adjourned for the next service, Brother J. S. Hunton came to me and said, "Brother Godbey, I have fifteen hundred dollars lying in the bank which I do not especially need, and the Lord tells me to send you to the Holy Land." Of course you see God, in His providence, raised up that noble saint to cut the gordian knot and send me to that far off land, which I had all my life longed to see, and to put my unworthy feet down on the very ground hallowed by the tread of my condescending Lord, who came all the way from Heaven and sojourned there thirty-three years, that He might bleed and die for me. Therefore God used Brother Hunton in the enlargement of my field of labor, which hitherto had been confined to this continent.

Thus cut loose from beloved America, He has permitted me to prosecute the third tour in the Old World, preaching the Gospel in Europe, Asia, Africa, and

Oceania. While I never can repay Brother Hunton the debt of gratitude I owe him for thus enlarging my evangelistic field, and giving me the Old in addition to the New World, my one regret is that this notable epoch in my history did not supervene twenty years sooner, as in that case I might have preached so much in the great heathen fields which girdle the globe. With the acquaintance I have now in the other grand divisions of the earth, if I were young enough I would continue my peregrinations in these heathen lands so long as I had the physical ability. But as I am now seventy-three (1906), with deep regret that I did not get an earlier start, I have to accept the situation and content myself to encourage the work of pagan evangelization by my prayers, speech and pen and my limited financial ability, during the little time I shall abide in this tabernacle.

Having, through the generosity of Brother Hunton, visited the Holy Land, I at once entered upon the great and arduous work of writing the Commentaries. I never became a literary recluse, in order to do any of my writing. You who read them will certify me that they all smell of gunpowder, having been born amid the tempest of war and the thunder of battle. They have been written in all parts of the United States, whithersoever He has led me in my toiling peregrinations. I constantly made it a rule to dictate to an amanuensis in the morning, teach the Bible in the afternoon, and preach in the evangelistic meetings at night. I am so thankful to God that He has let me do so much work for Him, which certainly is the highest privilege this side of Heaven. The Commentaries written by your humble servant differ widely from all their predecessors in the following respects.

(1.) They are rigidly exegetical, *i. e.*, they explain the precious Word so plainly that the reader understands it so clearly that he can explain it to others.

(2.) They are lucidly experimental, *i. e.*, bearing constantly on Christian experience, which is so pre-eminently important. If you would pass through the pearly gates, the Bible must go through your heart and shine out in your life. Our preaching should be constantly, earnestly and explicitly experimental, as otherwise it is intangible, impracticable and of no substantial availability. The whole Bible is rigidly experimental and our preaching must be its veritable fac-simile. These Commentaries are the very thing to feed your own soul and make you the efficient dispenser of soul pabulum to others.

(3.) They are also strictly practical, bringing the precious and infallible Word into constant availability so we can utilize its heavenly wisdom in our daily living. The Bible is really every man's guide-book, the infallible director of the pilgrim prosecuting his toiling march along the King's highway of holiness in this world of sin and sorrow, to the glorious and eternal rest which awaits the faithful probationer beyond the range of tempest and sorrow "where the wicked cease from troubling, and the weary are at rest."

"Oh! 'tis sweet to think, hereafter
When the spirit leaves this sphere,
Love with deathless wings shall waft her,
To those she long hath mourned for here.

"Hearts from which 'twas death to sever,
Eyes this world can ne'er restore,
There as warm, as bright as ever,
Shall greet us and be lost no more."

(4.) They are not critical. I have kept close company with all of the prominent critics of Christendom from the Apostolic Fathers down to the present, who day and night, like my predecessors, have written critically, but the Lord did not so lead me. He used some of my scholarly holiness brethren to advise me to leave out the critical phase, which is the most prominent in all of the older commentaries. They start out and tell you what this critic says, what another says, etc. The reader goes ahead and reads the expositions of the different critics, gets bewildered, and actually reaches nothing tangible and utilizable. These Commentaries, instead of perplexing you with criticisms, explain the Word in a plain style so that you can feed on it in your own soul and dispense it to the hungry around you.

(5.) They are non-sectarian. I do not believe any really candid person can read them and locate the author with any of the sects or denominations. Where does the non-sectarian and undenominational part come in? From the simple fact that the Bible is positively free from sectarianism and denominationality. Of course we have all come into the world and grown up under some sectarian influences, but it is a conceded fact that real sanctification saves us from carnality in all its forms and phases, and that includes sectarianism.

(6.) They are pre-eminently adapted to all who feel called of God directly or indirectly to dispense the glorious Gospel of His once humiliated but now glorified Son. That Son is now enthroned at His right hand, coronated, sceptred and interceding for a lost world, which He, in His wonderful condescending mercy, by His vicarious substitutionary atonement redeemed forever from sin, death and Hell, having so triumphantly conquered all of our enemies as to eternally preclude the faintest apology for the damnation of a solitary soul. Most transcendently important, interesting and delightful is the glorious privilege of dispensing this message of life and salvation to the lost millions now thronging the broad and frequented road down to a devil's Hell. They are manipulated, deluded, hoaxed and bamboozled by millions of excarnate demons thronging the air and incarnate devils, in the form of counterfeit preachers and false prophets, literally inundating every land and clime in these latter days of the Pentecostal dispensation. This world is now flooded with a population of sixteen hundred millions of immortal souls, one thousand millions of whom are sitting in heathen darkness, and enveloped in the thralldom of death. Human longevity has been cut down from a thousand years in the antediluvian ages and a hundred years in the postdiluvian, to the fleeting span of only twenty-four in India and but little more in other heathen lands. Thus we have now a thousand incentives playing on every intelligently and victoriously saved soul to rally to the rescue of his perishing comrades, who by millions on all sides are precipitating themselves into Hell at race horse speed. Since the glorious Gospel, with which the blessed Bible is flooded from Alpha to Omega, is God's predestinated medium of rescue for every fallen son and daughter of Adam's ruined race, we are no longer excusable for folding our arms and sitting in the easy chair of carnal security, while we sing, "I am bound for the Promised Land." It is high time that we all arise, take our Gospel trumpet and begin to blow the shrill bugle blasts which hush the seraphim and cherubim to listen to the sweetest music that ever thrilled immortal ears, while contemplative angels bending over the heavenly battlements stoop to listen to the welcome notes of Gospel grace (1 Peter 1: 12). And here on earth the old, the young, the great, the small, the rich and the poor, the cultured and the rustic, stand and tell the lost multitudes about the dying Saviour and the beautiful home in Heaven He has purchased for the homeless millions. Oh, how they will bless you through all eternity, while they tell the angels that God used you as an humble instrument to "pluck them as brands from the eternal burning."

In this greatest soul harvest the ages have ever known, is it possible you are going to lie supine? Arise, arise, oh, sluggard, shake off thy slumbers and awake to an opportunity to which the angels would gladly speed their flight, vacating Heaven and leaving their golden harps, ethereal pæans and celestial trumpets, to take your place in the slums and preach this delectable Gospel and rescue the perishing multitudes, whom Jesus has redeemed with His own precious blood. Will you not hasten to the rescue, and lend a helping hand lest some Oriental coolie in the Judgment Day shall take your crown?

(7.) Those Commentaries are alone in the fact that they have been written exegetically, experimentally and practically, whereas their predecessors are all written critically, *e. g.*, Clark, the prince of commentators, starts off on an exegesis basis, instead of telling you what it means in direct, plain terms, so you will understand it and can intelligently dispense it to others. He proceeds to tell you what the critics say about it, quoting the exposition of this one, that one and the other, till he gets you bewildered among the critics and there leaves you incompetent to settle on any clear exegesis of the passage. You really have no time to spend in learning criticism, which I could have given you, but I did not feel that the Lord wanted me to perplex your mind in that way. I felt led by the blessed Holy Spirit, the infallible Author of this precious message of life and godliness, in a plain, simple way to give you the explanation which you need to feed your own soul and dispense truth to the perishing millions who throng your pathway through this world of sin, sorrow, wretchedness, disappointment and wreckage of human hopes and aspirations.

All the commentaries by my predecessors were written for the learned clergy. The Lord told me to write mine for the rank and file of His dear people, who had never enjoyed the opportunity of a collegiate education, but who have much to do in winning souls, in view of the illimitable extent of the harvest enveloping the globe with its crowded fields white for the sickle. There is a paucity of reapers, inadequate to the glorious work of garnering the golden grain which is wasting by wholesale, the antipodian pagans having but one missionary to every million souls or more. Therefore it is actually homocidal longer to depend on the collegiate clergy to evangelize the world. We just *have* to use aides from the people, bless them in their labours of love and go off and leave them.

John Wesley's great holiness movement solved the problem of saving the world not through the classical clergy, but the uncultured laity. For this grand achievement, *i. e.*, the evangelization of the world by the rank and file of God's faithful people, I wrote those Commentaries which any men and women who have never seen the inside of a college, but who have an ordinary English education, can read, and thus qualify themselves to preach the Gospel to the illiterate millions who crowd this Babel world. These lay preachers do better work and we find their humble labors more fruitful of souls than that of the theologians, from the ostensible fact that their language is more easily understood by the ignorant denizens of slumdom, whom the learned preachers habitually overshoot, *i. e.*, make the sad mistake of putting the fodder too high for the sheep, so that they starve to death with an abundance of food in full view,—a torture intolerable to contemplate. God is wonderfully using these books. They are going to the ends of the earth, already being in current use in all of the great mission fields which envelop the dark Orient.

(8.) Not only do the dear people need plain and intelligent explanations of the precious Word, so that they can instruct others, but they need fortification against a thousand innocent mistakes, into which they will certainly drift if they undertake to preach the Gospel without a simple, lucid explanation which they will be enabled to understand experimentally and practically. This is necessary so that they may realize in their own minds the mastery of the situation which is indispensably essential to that independence of thought and utterance which is the concomitant of the glorious spiritual freedom everywhere necessary to the successful enforcement of the message enunciated.

Our Savior inaugurated His Gospel with a three years' course in a Bible School, which was indispensable to qualify His disciples for the great and responsible work of launching the Gospel Church. For this reason He had to prolong His ministry three whole years, meanwhile He was a constant fugitive for His life, incessantly flying from His enemies, who were thirsting for His blood and plotting to kill Him, or from His friends who were enthusiastic to crown Him King, in which case the Romans would have killed Him as a rival of Cæsar. When Jesus wanted preachers He chose "unlearned and ignorant men," (Acts 4: 12). They were stalwart men, though, hardened by the rough and tumble life of Galilean fishermen, accustomed to toil all night as the better time to catch fish and take chances to snatch up a little sleep on the sand during the day at intervals of domestic labor, and then be ready for the ensuing night of sleepless toil. He has never changed His economy. He is still calling the illiterate millions to go and tell their lost contemporaries the glad tidings of salvation, rich, sweet, full and free.

When He wanted a teacher, He put His hand on Paul, the greatest scholar in the world and the most competent exegete of the glorious plan of salvation. Though His greatest enemy, He had no trouble to put him just where He wanted him and use him to reveal the major part of the New Testament, at the same time so ably and lucidly expounding the deep things of God as to make him a glorious sunburst on the precious, revealed Word, lighting it up to all coming generations.

This grand army of evangelists, whom God is raising up in every nation under Heaven, has no time to perplex their minds with scholastic theologies. They want the simple nonsectarian explanation of the Bible so that they can preach it to others. The theologians have even muddled the very word "preach," leading the popular mind to the conclusion that it means to study hard, manufacture a sermon mechanically and roar it out to the people with certain rhetorical intonations, inflections and nicely rounded cadences. The word *enaggells*, from *en*, good, and *oggells,* to proclaim, simply means to tell the good news in the plainest and most simple phraseology, so that people will be sure to understand it, because it is verily to them the message of life and salvation. In these Commentaries you not only have the truth explained just as you would want to preach it to the people, but you are constantly fortified against the dangerous errors which undermine the glorious plan of salvation, actually vitiating and even ignoring the vicarious substitutionary atonement which our Lord made for the redemption of the whole world, which is to be received and appropriated by simple faith. These pestilential heresies, which are freighted with Hell's heaviest artillery, are directed against the very vital truth of the Gospel, *i. e.*, the glorious redemption wrought by the Son of God with His own dying agonies and flowing blood, crimsoning the cruel cross of Calvary, and the great and mighty works of the Holy Ghost in conviction, regeneration, sanctification and glorification. These heresies are not only boldly proclaimed from pulpits, but are advocated in great volumes of learned books, actually undermining the stupendous work of the Son and Spirit and bringing back the paganistic idea of God in nature, in contradistinction to the stupendous revealed truths of God in grace, the climactic glory of Biblical revelation in all of its transcendent beauties and resplendent victories, flashing over the inspired pages from the *Alpha* of Genesis to the *Omega* of Revelation. This great double heresy against the Son and Spirit, so ably and extensively propagated by Unitarians in the East and Campbellites in the West, has infected the American atmosphere with a fatal soul-poison which we find clandestinely creeping in on all sides, like the vampire at midnight gently fanning his victim with his wings, thus lulling him into still profounder slumber while he sucks the life blood away. These myriads of lay preachers must have straight, clear, orthodox teaching in order to qualify them to understand the Word in its simplicity, beauty, force and victory, at the same time heroically fortifying them against Satan's heresies, which are sweeping over every land like the withering sirocco over Lybia's burning marl, blighting and blasting every green herb and blooming flower. These Commentaries are a God-send to the millions who have no facilities of classical education, and whom nevertheless God is calling and ready to honor their ministry with blood-bought souls, already caught in Satan's Hell-traps and on the brink of irretrievable woe, lingering and waiting for "the beautiful feet" swiftly running with the evangelistic message of life eternal and salvation non-forfeitable.

SECTION TWO.

New Testament Translation.

When the Commentaries began to circulate throughout the country, and the people reading them found the original Scriptures, which I always read and use in all my expositions, so much plainer and more easily understood than King James' translation, which not only contains two thousand errors in the New Testament alone, but, as it is nearly three hundred years old and the English language has undergone much change in that time, much of the phraseology has become antiquated, so that it no longer reveals the blessed truth so clearly and vividly to the mind of the student as does the verbage now in current use.

Therefore people began to plead with me to translate the New Testament out of the critical original into plain, current English. The reason why we have the two thousand errors in the English Version is because they had crept into the Greek during the long roll of the Dark Ages, which intervened between ancient and modern civilization, when barbarism actually captured the world, hovering over all nations like a nightmare. As the Roman Empire was the upholder of ancient civilization, when she fell under the invasion of the Goths, Huns, Vandals and Heruli, the barbaric ancestors of great Russia, after a three hundred years' war, in 476 A. D., ancient civilization passed away, followed by that dreary period of a thousand years, historically epitheted the "Dark Ages," during which not one man in a thousand could read or write. Of course the perpetuation of the Bible by transcriptions would necessarily involve the introduction of much error, both by the omissions, as many beautiful passages rich in saving truth slipped through the fingers of the transcribers, and by the additions, as still more were added, first in the form of bracketed explanations, which eventually found their way into the body of the text, as transcribers overlooked or inadvertently neglected to perpetuate the parenthetical clauses. The predilection in favor of addition transcended the subtraction. Antecedently to the art of printing, A. D. 1551, the only possible chance to procure a Bible was to have it written off by hand, a work of immense labor and incalculable responsibility. During those fifteen centuries of course a vast amount of error incidentally found its way into the blessed Scripture. The printing of the Bible by Stephanus, in London, in 1551, was a sunburst on the English speaking world, as it forever did away with the necessity of transcribing, which was not only so immense a labor but was constantly fraught more or less with deterioration from the precious truth, thereby transmitted from age to age.

One hundred and twenty-five years ago an institution denominated "Biblical Criticism" sprang up in Christendom, having for its object the recovery of the Scriptures precisely as the Holy Ghost gave them, thus restoring to the Bible all of the lost passages as fast as they could find them, and eliminating all of the interpolations which, along the rolling centuries, had found their way into the inspired volume. The result has been that a number of Greek Testaments have been printed, exhibiting the achievements of the critics, *e. g.*, Scholtz, Lachmann, Griesbach, Tischendorf, and Westcott and Horb. At present Wescott and Horb is the standard, as it is the youngest and consequently contains the benefit of all antecedent researches. It is, however, identical with Tischendorf, as they continued to publish his Testament after his death, giving their own names to it. Tischendorf's Testament, which I have used ever since it was published, has for its basis the Sinaitic manuscript, so-called because Tischendorf discovered it in the convent of St. Catherine on Mt. Sinai, in 1859, the very year I graduated in college. Hearing the wonderful news of the greatest discovery of modern times, in the providence of God I procured from Germany a copy of the first book which was made from the parchment roll.

This great scholar and critic, Tischendorf, spent his whole life in constant toil, for forty years in Palestine and all of the Bible lands hunting everything that would throw light on the living Word. Meanwhile noble and generous King William of Germany paid all of his expenses, a princely fortune, as he often had fifty to one hundred men laboring excavating the ruins of cities, that he might find everything that could possibly throw a ray of light on the vital fact of just what constitutes the inspired volume. Finally, while searching in that venerable monastery which was built in the second century to commemorate the giving of the law, he got his eye on an old parchment roll, externally indubitably demonstrative of its great antiquity, and the blessed Holy Spirit revealed to him that it was His Word. Then he at once proposed to the monks in charge of the monastery to buy it from them; soon, by his persistent effort, finding it necessary to tempt their cupidity with a really extravagant sum, as they are jealous of relics, and generally hold them with a tight grip which filthy lucre alone can relax. Having paid them for it with the money so generously furnished by his king, throwing his arms around it with a bounding heart, he returned to Germany, after an absence of forty years, in which he had patiently and faithfully toiled hunting it.

On arrival he submitted it to those shrewd chemists standing at the front of the scientific world. Chemistry, though the greatest of the sciences, is the youngest. Out of chemistry has originated all the machinery that now sends the world rushing into eternity at electrical speed. Then those chemists submitted the manuscript to their powerful alkaline solutions whose normal effect was to limber up the great roll of sheep-skins, till they could pick them off one by one with perfect security and spread them out like a great book. Another effect of the chemicals was to bring out the old writings of which hitherto no mortal eye could see a letter, such was the great antiquity of the writings. They looked, and behold it was all legible, and what was it? A complete copy of the New Testament, and dating back into the very blaze of the Apostolic Age. The venerable man of God who had spent his life hunting it took a big shout and went to Heaven, actually too happy to tarry longer in this tenement of clay. He was like good old Simeon who had spent his life looking for his Lord to appear, and died with the infant Savior in his arms.

The Christian world knows not its indebtedness to the King of Germany who alone, at his own expense, kept Tischendorf and his laboring men in the Bible lands for forty years hunting everything that could throw light on the infallible Word, and finally culminating in the glorious discovery of this manuscript, where God had, in His signal mercy, preserved it ever since the Apostolic Age, thus bridging the broad chasm of the Dark Ages and bringing the Christian world back into the resplendent glory of the Apostolic Age, when holy men of God actually spoke as the omniscient Spirit gave them utterance.

"Brother Godbey, how do you know that this Sinaitic

manuscript, which you have been reading these long years and have recently translated, was actually written in the Apostolic Age?" I take pleasure in answering your question. There is no date in the manuscript, but it is written throughout in the old Uncial capitals, which were used by the Apostles, but superseded by the Cursives, which came into use in the third and fourth centuries. The Apostle John lived about thirty years of the second century. Hence the chirography of this manuscript incontestably identifies it with the Apostolic Age.

N. B. Matthew wrote his Gospel in Judæa for the Jews fifteen years after our Lord's ascension; Luke wrote his for the Greeks in Corinth as dictated by Paul, twenty-five years after the Lord's ascension; Mark wrote his in Rome for the Romans as dictated by Peter, thirty years after the Lord's ascension; John did all of his writings for the Christians in Ephesus, sixty-five years after the Lord's ascension. Each book in the Bible was written separately from all the balance, the compilement having taken place some time afterward.

As this manuscript was written in the old Uncial, it must have been at least as early as the third century that they were compiled into a volume. All the facts involved really confirm the conclusion that this was the first compilement of the New Testament. We have these words in reference to it! "*Codex Sinaiticus, omninum antiquissimus et solus integer.*" "The Sinaitic manuscript, the most ancient of all and the only one entire." Of all the old manuscripts which have been discovered, this is the only one that contains the whole of the New Testament and the ablest critics pronounce it the most ancient of all. Of others, the Vatican manuscript is the largest aside from the Sinaitic. The most of the manuscripts which, by vast and persevering researches, have been discovered, consisted only of a single book, *e. g.*, the Gospel of Matthew, or the Epistle to the Romans, etc.

We have a wonderful providence in the preservation of this manuscript through the long roll of the Dark Ages, while ignorance and superstition enveloped the whole earth in the sable mantle of an intellectual and spiritual night.

You see the revelation of God's precious truth which survived in primitive purity in this manuscript. It had to await two great and wonderful inventions in order to be revealed to the world, *i. e.*, the art of printing and the science of chemistry. Without the latter it would have been utterly impossible ever to have deciphered it, as it was so very ancient that it had utterly faded out into solid raven blackness. Without the former it would have been corrupted after its discovery, because it would have been subject to transcriptions in order to its perpetuity as through all the centuries antedating the art of printing. We see God's wonderful providence in preserving it during those 1500 years in that old monastery, which was built there to commemorate the giving of the law. Thus He offsets the two thousand errors which crept into the New Testament alone, and many more in the Old, as it is so much larger. We now may rest assured that we have the full revelation which God made in its pristine purity, and can feel that neither interpolations nor omissions can ever again contaminate this limped stream of living water flowing out from beneath the throne of God "clear as crystal," since the art of printing has forever precluded the necessity of transcribing it any more.

As the publication of my Commentaries, expounding the Scriptures in the pure, original Greek, evoked a universal clamor for a translation in which the people would have the New Testament in the charming beauty and simplicity in which they had found it elucidated in the Commentaries, therefore, the clamor becoming not only universal but importunate, Brother Knapp, as the spokesman of the Holiness people, the last time I ever looked in his inspiring face, bidding him adieu for a midnight train at the close of his last camp-meeting in this world, continued importunately to plead with me to translate the New Testament, at the same time offering me a thousand dollars for that arduous work. When I bade him adieu, he still held my hand observing; "I am never going to let go your hand till you promise me to translate the New Testament." Then I acquiesced, went at it and was in the midst of the work when the telegram arrived calling me to his funeral. As he was twenty years my junior, I expected him to preach my funeral. Thus you see, in the case of the Commentaries, God used that paragon saint to bring into the world the literal translation of the manuscript through my humble instrumentality. It has received a wonderful circulation in a short time, actually girdling the globe. Since my arrival from my last tour, in one mail I sent away ninety-two copies to India.

There are two reasons why none of the people who do not read Greek like English (and but one in a million does) cannot afford to do without this translation. The first is, because it is the only translation in the world in which you get just what the Lord says, all He says, and no more, and that is what you all so imperatively need and cannot afford to do without. The other reason is because it harmonizes the Gospels in such a manner that at a single look you see everything the Lord said and did. Besides it gives you the Lord's entire ministry, arranged in topics as they transpired in consecutive order. Some things none but Matthew wrote, others Mark alone reveals, in others we must depend on Luke alone for the blessed revelation, and meanwhile John much of the time stands alone. Some things two of them give, others three, and still others the entire four. In the harmony, you have everything whether by one, two, three or four, all exhibited before the eye at a single look, everything the Lord said and did. And at the same time the topics are so arranged in consecutive order that you will all the time know where you are and at what date in the Lord's ministry. Therefore the harmony is absolutely indispensable to enable you with full intelligibility and efficiency to study His wonderful ministry.

Robert Ingersol, the great infidel, was truly an intellectual giant, towering among his peers, *primus inter pares*, "first among his comrades," while he utterly discarded the Bible, believing not a word of it, and consequently freely and even recklessly criticised Moses, the prophets and Apostles. He broke down in his attempt to criticize Jesus, calling Him, "The youngest Jew," (certainly He was the youngest Author in the Bible, only thirty-three when they killed Him. At that age I had never dreamed of writing a book.) Bob said so significantly, "That young Jew just beats them all."

The longer I live the more profoundly I appreciate all

the works of Jesus which have come down to me in the blessed Volume of Truth. Paul is deep, but Jesus still deeper. Peter is fire, but Jesus is dynamite. Take the Harmony in which you see all His utterances on every subject, arranged in parallel columns, and ask the Holy Spirit to help you to apprehend the deep truths He communicated. As for instance when the Pharisees, who were the orthodox wing of the anti-administration party and most inveterately opposed to Roman rule, united with the Herodians, who were the Roman party, in order to lasso Jesus and get Him into trouble. Approaching Him together they asked Him the insidious question, "Tell us, Shall we pay tribute to Cæsar, or no?" If he had said "Yes," they, the Pharisees, were just ready to have Him arrested and arraigned before the Sanhedrim for disloyalty to the theocracy. If He had said "No," then the Herodians were ready to have Him arrested and brought before Pilate for disloyalty to Cæsar. Therefore, they felt perfectly sure that they would gore Him with one or the other horn of the dilemma. But you see He simply asked them to hand Him the coin which they used to pay tribute, the denarius, the most common in circulation at that time, and bearing the image of Cæsar. When they handed it to Him and He looked at it, He said, "Whose is this image and superscription?" and they responded "Cæsar's." Then handing it back He merely observed, "Render unto Cæsar the things that are Cæsar's, and unto God the things that are God's." To this neither party could possibly take any exception, but both were utterly dumbfounded; and without another word they went away. For three years all the great, scholarly men of the Sanhedrim put their heads together to lasso and down Him, but utterly failed.

When the holiness people constrained me to translate the New Testament, they did not ask me to give them the harmony of the Gospels, but I knew not one of them in a thousand had any harmony, and that all the harmonies that had been made so abounded in error that it was a pity for people to use them. Therefore I felt it my duty to give them the harmony of the Gospels in a correct translation, so they could all intelligently and successfully study the Lord's ministry with all the possible facilities to master the situation.

Even since they discovered the Sinaitic manuscript, I have made it a rule to carry with me the inspired Greek everywhere I go. As I travelled around the world last year, (1906), I actually, by snatching up the fugitive moments now and then as I might happen to have a little leisure, read it through five times. The whole Bible is too heavy to carry constantly, under all circumstances of manual labour and business peregrinations, but not so with the New Testament. It is small enough to carry in your pocket everywhere you go and riding on the car or waiting for the train, you can read so much of it and treasure it up in your memory, besides constantly using it as your sword both of defense and offense. Let me insist that you now adopt the rule of constantly carrying a New Testament. You will soon get so used to it that you will feel lost without it. Rest assured that the longer you pursue that habit the more you will be delighted with the precious Word of the Lord and the sweeter and richer it will become. It will develop in you the habit of studying the Word each revolving day. It will also be a constant inspiration to you to minister this blessed saving truth to the people with whom, in the providence of God, you come in contact. So my life-long habit has become the carrying of the Greek Testament, feasting on it night and day. I'll advise you to carry the translation of your humble servant, as in it you have the Word of the Lord faithfully translated out of the pure original, without addition or subtraction, so that you can rest assured that everything you read is just what the Lord has revealed. Besides, it is the only one that harmonizes the Gospels so that at a single look you can see everything the Lord said and did and study His ministry in its regular historic order. You can find other harmonies, but they do not contain anything but the Gospels, and besides, they are much encumbered with errors. You want the entire New Testament in a single volume, convenient for you to stick in your pocket and carry everywhere you go, and that volume ought to contain the Gospel harmony, to prepare you for the clear, topical study of the Lord's ministry in consecutive order. All of this you have nowhere in the world, except in the above translation. In the other current translations, whereas the most of the errors are corrected, some of the large interpolations are retained to the detriment of the student who does not want to encumber his memory with anything but the real and literal Word which the Holy Ghost has revealed. Besides, these translations do not give you the harmony of the Gospels.

SECTION THREE.

"Footprints of Jesus."

My "Footprints of Jesus" has been wonderfully blessed

in its circulation among the people, and also very extensive. The most intellectual and cultured people in this commonwealth, whose names I could give you, have told me that it was the most interesting book they had ever read. In a mysterious way it is exceedingly magnetic to people. A sanctified woman in a New England city, who was in the habit of reading all of my writings, said to me, "Brother Godbey, I do wish you had a book which my infidel husband would read. He is a scientist and a great reader, but never reads the Bible nor any religious book." I said, I have a book here that he will read if he gets his hand on it. She bought it unhesitatingly, carried it home and handed it to him. He read it night and day and in forty-eight hours was in the meetings and asking everybody to pray for him. He is now the best reader I have, reading everything I write with the greatest appreciation, and always making me stay with him when I go thither to preach. He is a very humble, beautiful Christian character. This book has an especial charm for children, who read it over and over with delightful edification. Sinners read it like a novel and get their souls blessed. It should certainly be in every home.

SECTION FOUR.

"Life of Jesus and His Apostles."

My "Life of Jesus and His Apostles," containing nearly five hundred pages, elegantly bound in cloth, should be read and studied by every lover of the Savior. In it you will find a lucid exposition of His wonderful life, inimitable ministry, mighty works, tragical death, triumphant resurrection and glorious ascension. His life is really the only model in all the world to which we can look without the shade of possible cavil or criticism. Oh, the inestimable value of that life! We have but to read it and see how to live and die. In the old world a thousand millions of people are looking upon Buddha, Confucius and Zoroaster, whose bright light did shine out in India, China and Persia about 500 B. C. There can be no doubt but that they were great intellectually, morally, educationally and philanthropically, as the people to this day are looking to them for examples. They were not at all satisfied with their own lives, and died longing after a perfect example. Oh, if they had only lived in the Gospel dispensation, received the Bible and learned about the Son of God living and dying upon the earth, not only to redeem us all from sin, death and Hell, but to give us a perfect model of human life! He is really the only Man that ever came into this world perfect and left it in the same glorious plight. Adam began alright and how long he enjoyed his original perfection in Eden we know not. But to our sorrow we know that Satan slew him, and for that reason Satan is called, "A murderer from the beginning." Jesus Christ is the only son of Adam and Eve who ever retained His perfection to the end of life, therefore He is the paragon for every human being to emulate. Can we receive the perfection of His humanity? We can by the wonderful plan of salvation, which He died to propagate upon the earth, with the exception of the infirmities which cling to us as the effects of the fall. Of course He never had any infirmities, neither would we have if we had not fallen. These infirmities will inhere in our spiritual organism, there to abide till illuminated by the third great work of the Holy Ghost in glorification.

In regeneration we receive a new heart, *i. e.*, new life into the fallen human spirit. That life is antagonized by the depravity hereditary is the heart till illuminated by the expurgation of the cleansing blood dispensed by the Holy Ghost in the human soul, thus conferring a perfect work of grace, which consists with the infirmities, engendered by the fall, which always encumber the saved soul till this mortal puts on immortality. In the wonderful economy of grace, justification takes away the condemnation supervenient upon our own transgressions, and sanctification expurgates our depravity by the wonderful elixir of the cleansing blood, while it is the province of the Holy Ghost in glorification to eliminate mortality, thus forever removing our infirmities. The glorious work of God in Christ, wrought by the Holy Ghost, puts us where we cannot only enjoy that experience of perfection in the heart, but actually live it before the world, however still encumbered with infirmities, and longing for the glorious redemption which will transfigure both the soul and the body, forever sweeping away all the dark debris of the fall. Therefore our wonderful Savior leaves us without excuse.

Jesus has done a double work, perfectly redeeming us from the condemnation of the violated law by His vicarious, substitutionary atonement, clearing every conceivable difficulty forever out of the way, and perfectly and eternally satisfying the law, so there is no conceivable apology for the damnation of a solitary soul. Besides, He sends His omnipotent Spirit to awaken, illuminate, convict, regenerate, adopt, witness, sanctify and fill every soul, thus actually by His own omnipotent energies restoring to humanity the image and likeness of God, and effecting perfect reconcilement and reinstatement in the kingdom, which we forfeited by the fall and, though encumbered by the infirmities incident to mortality and consequent upon the fall, yet these infirmities do not vitiate the beautiful experience of Christian perfection which He has given us.

This is not a perfection of works, *i. e.*, legal obedience, which would be vitiated by our infirmities, but it is a perfection of love, in which He takes the will for the deed. We "love the Lord with all the heart, soul, mind and strength, and love our neighbor as ourself," actually "esteeming others better than ourselves." This perfect love our Lord sees in our heart and life, and is delighted with it, neither does He discount it in consequence of the pecadilloes incident to our frail mortality, which will all eternally evanesce before the transfiguration glory.

This unutterably wonderful Savior has not only satisfied the law passively by paying our penalty, by which He has redeemed us forever, but He has actually lived our life for us on the earth, actively keeping the law on earth for us, and thus procuring a double satisfaction. Meanwhile He has exemplified the very identical life we are to live, leaving us without excuse, because He has taken all the difficulties out of the way, graciously, by His omnipotent Spirit, conferring on us the life and giving us all needed help to live it day by day, thus utterly and eternally sweeping away every apology for sin, either actual or original, whereas the infirmities normal to our fallen state really have no power to vitiate the perfect spiritual life in our hearts for the obedience of perfect love, which we live. These infirmities in the Bible are denominated sins of ignorance, and, though incompatible with the heavenly state, have no power to either condemn or pollute in the present life, as they are abundantly provided for in Christ. This we see beautifully and powerfully illustrated in the cities of refuge, which were three in number on either side of the Jordan, so that the involuntary homocide could surely reach one of them, unobstructed by Jordan's flood. If the avenger of blood overtook him he would certainly kill him, but there was no reason why he should overtake him, as he always got the start of him and as there was no real obstruction in his way. He had nothing to do but to run with all his might and fall headlong through the gate of the city and in that way was perfectly safe. If the avenger of blood should then slay him, his nearest relative would certainly kill the avenger. These cities of refuge beautifully symbolize our wonderful Christ, who has actually provided for everything. These infirmities are accidental violations of the divine law, illustrated in the Bible by a man chopping down a tree and the axe flying off the handle and killing a man who happened to come up behind and the chopper did not see him; hence they rank as mere accidents in which we do wrong while aiming to do right.

While the Christian perfection we enjoy in this life is not vitiated by these sins of ignorance, the angelic perfection, which we receive in glorification and enjoy in Heaven, would be utterly marred and ruined by accidental transgressions of the Divine law. Therefore the angels are forever kept even from sins of ignorance.

But our blessed Christ has so wonderfully redeemed us that He has provided for the elimination of all these infirmities which conduce to sins of ignorance.

While biography is doubtless the most profitable line of reading, it is of course a universally conceded fact that every biography in all the ages is incident to infirmities, except that of our glorious Lord. Therefore while we may derive vast help by acquainting ourselves with the lives of the Lord's people, yet they are to be taken more or less at discount in every case, leaving a large margin for infirmities. We all in this life need a perfect examplar. My teachers used to tell me always to aim high, as I was very likely to drop down below the mark of my aspiration. As our glorious Lord has taken it on Himself to come to this world, and has given us a perfect example showing us how to live and die, therefore the value of His biography is absolutely inestimable to us. Oh, what a world we would have if every human being in it would acquaint himself with the life of Jesus and walk in His footprints! No human being can do it without the prevenient concomitant grace which He freely gives through the blessed intervention of His Holy Spirit. But we are so happy to say that He leaves us without excuse. When He so frequently rings out the proclamation, "Follow me," rest assured He is not mocking us, because He freely gives us all the help we need to obey that and every other commandment. N. B. Obedience legitimately appertains to citizens of His kingdom. No sinner can possibly keep our Lord's commandments, because he is a citizen of Satan's kingdom who is too strong for him and assuredly will not let him obey the Lord. But if he will cry to God He will send him His Holy Spirit anywhere this side of Hell, to defeat the devil, break his chains and set him free. In regeneration he is born into the family of God and becomes a *bona fide* citizen of His kingdom. Then by His sustaining grace and sanctifying power he can walk in the footprints of Jesus, to his infinite benefit prompted by the Lord's infallible example, both in life and in death. This "Life of Jesus and His Apostles," you will find infinitely valuable as an expositor of His wonderful preaching, by far the best preaching the world ever heard or ever will till He comes in His glory.

It so happens that the Bible does not follow any of the Apostles to the end of their lives, except poor Judas, who died first of all by awful suicide, and James, the elder brother of John and son of Zebedee, whom Herod Agrippa beheaded with the sword. The destiny of the other Apostles we have to find in history. After those awful, exterminating wars by the Romans, began to gather the formidable tempests threatening the very existence of the Jewish nation, whose nationality they did obliterate. All of the Apostles, pursuant to our Lord's commission, (Matt. 28: 19), then divided up the great heathen world and separated, never to meet again this side the pearly gates, each one going to his respective field of labor.

MATTHEW received Ethiopia as his appointment, whither faithfully going, he preached heroically till bloody martyrdom gave him his discharge for a kingdom and a crown by the side of his martyred Predecessor, in the bright upper world.

MATTHIAS, who was elected to take the place of fallen Judas, also received his appointment in Africa, being sent to Abyssinia, where he also faithfully preached till his enemies cruelly murdered him and he exchanged Eastern Africa for the New Jerusalem.

THOMAS, the famour doubter, whose doubts were all consumed in the Pentecostal fires, received India, the largest country in the known world at that time, as his field of labor. When I was there a few months ago, I travelled in the region of his ministry and near the place of his martyrdom, as they informed me. Thousands of people are there to-day, known as the Christians of St. Thomas and claiming to be his followers.

JUDE received Tartary, a great and powerful nation at that time, bordering on China, which would have been included in his field of labor if they had let him alone. But as the Brahman priests led the cruel mob that perforated the body of Thomas with an iron bar, and hung him up between two trees, so the cruel pagan priests, in the case of Jude, instigated the barbaric reprobates to tie him to a tree and enjoy a shooting match at his expense, gambling with each other who could shoot an arrow in his right eye, etc., thus literally plugging his body full of arrows.

ANDREW received Armenia as his field of labor, whither faithfully going he preached heroically till they crucified him on the X cross, which to this day is known among Roman Catholics as St. Andrew's cross.

BARTHOLOMEW, who is Nathanael, a native of Cana in Galilee, received Phrygia, a very barbaric country in Northern Asia, whither he faithfully went and zealously preached the living Word with the Holy Ghost sent down from Heaven. Meanwhile, the seal of God settled down on his ministry and he saw a great harvest ripe for the sickle; so, pressing the battle with redoubtable energy for God and souls, Hell was stirred and Satan raised an awful hubbub. The civil commotion was intense and the excitement wild and furious, so that the king concluded that the available remedy was to drive off the preacher. Consequently he ordered him to leave his country and never return, as he blamed him for making the awful trouble which threatened the very stability of his government. Then when he did not obey the royal mandate, the king got so awfully mad at him that he had him skinned alive as an effectual terror to evil doers, since he concluded that he was an awfully bad man as he had raised such a terrible hubbub among the people.

PHILIP received Syria as his field of labor, which contains Baalbek, the universal metropolis of Asiatic idolatry, whither all nations from the days of Cain had resorted bringing their sumptuous offerings to Baal the sun god. Therefore of course it devolved on Philip to actually beard the lion in his den. This he did most heroically, going right into Baalbek, preaching Christ and thundering against idolatry like a messenger from Heaven. They did not stand him very long till they reciprocated his great doctrine, "Jesus crucified," by crucifying him.

SIMON Zelotes, as history informs us, received for his appointment insular Europe, *i. e.*, England, Ireland, Scotland and Wales, the land of our American ancestry, and the cradle of the great Anglo-Saxon race. Those countries not only abounded in the popular religions of Greece and Rome, but in the native Drüidism. Thus you see this fiery apostle, named "Zelot" because the dynamite predominated in his character, was the apostle of our ancestors. He, too, while preaching the Gospel all over those countries was permitted to go to Heaven with a martyr's crown.

LUKE, the faithful and indefatigable amanuensis of Paul, honored to write the most of the New Testament when his senior preached, was arrested at Nicapolis, Greece, and carried away to Rome the second time, for prosecution, under charge of burning the city, not personally, but because it was imputed to the Christians and he was their prominent leader. He was finally hanged on an olive tree in Greece.

MARK, the faithful amanuensis of Peter, who is said to have dictated the Gospel that bears his name, received Egypt, the oldest nation in the world. Faithful to his appointment and off to the land of the Pharaohs, he went like a hero to the battle-field, peregrinated the country, and everywhere contended for *"the faith once delivered to the saints,"* till an awful persecution in Alexandria culminated in a cruel mob, who dragged him through the streets by the feet till the angels descended and took him out of their hands. When you go to Egypt do not forget to visit his tomb as well as that of Alexander the Great.

PETER is said to have received Rome, the world's metropolis, with all of Italy, the dominant country of the globe, for his field of labor. His Epistles located him at Babylon, which was then a heap of ruins and uninhabited and with no historic corroboration of any apostle ever travelling in that region. Babylon is not only the current name of Rome in the prophecies, but is said to have been in common use at that time. After they had beheaded Paul, the saints importuned Peter to leave the city lest they might be deprived of his ministry and leadership, as well as that of his noble compeer, who had already sealed his faith with his blood. Therefore, acquiescing in their earnest appeal, going out along the Appian Way beneath the twinkling stars, he suddenly met Jesus going rapidly into the city. Turning his face on Him he says, *"Domine, quo vadis?"* ("Whither goest thou, Lord?") Then Jesus answered, "Peter, I am going to Rome to be crucified again," and suddenly vanished out of his sight. Peter understood the lesson, turned around, went back to Rome and told them that he was to be crucified there, and so he was, on the Campus Martius, where the cathedral of St. Peter now stands, the most celebrated building in the world, whose erection occupied two hundred years and cost two hundred million dollars. If you ever go to Rome and travel out the Appian Way due south, you will come to a nice stone church on your left, superscribed, *"Domine, quo vadis?"* marking the spot where Jesus met Peter, as history certifies.

PAUL being the great apostle of the Gentiles, it seems that they mutually recognized in him a practical episcopacy, including the whole Christian world and especially Asia and Europe, extending from Jerusalem to Rome. He was brought to Rome the second time, in A. D. 68. His first imprisonment there had taken place in A. D. 61 and occupied about three years, when having stood his trial and been acquitted for the want of evidence, he was permitted to travel and preach till arrested at Nicapolis and carried again to Rome. This second time, he was incarcerated in the Mamertine prison (which you will visit if you ever go thither) till Nero got ready to sit in judgment aganst him. You will also be interested in visiting the old Judgment Hall on the Palatine mountain in the ruins of Cæsar's palace, where Paul was tried for his life and condemned to die, under the implication of the general charge against the Christians for burning Rome. As he was a Roman citizen, they could not crucify him, therefore, they led him out through the west gate, which this day bears his name, and decapitated him with a sword.

Among all of the different books written on the life of our Lord, mine is the only one that gives a chapter on His descension into Hades, His triumph over Satan and his myrmidons and the abolishment of the intermediate Paradise, the emancipation of the Old Testament saints and their ascension with Him into Heaven. As the No-Hellites, Millennial Dawners, and Seventh Day Adventists, as well as the Universalists, are now preaching that He abolished Hell when He descended thither, while His body hung on the cross and lay in the sepulchre, it is very important that you have this book in order to refute them, because it clearly shows up their cunning falsifications. You will see that there is not a word of truth in their hypothesis of His abolishment of Hell, which He certainly did not; but He did abolish the intermediate Paradise, leading up with Him the Old Testament saints. (Eph. 4:8-10.) He left Hell there in Hades with all of its inmates, where they will remain until the final Judgment, when they will all be called up to stand before the great white throne and receive their awful adjudication, (Rev. 20:14), antecedently to their final and eternal ejectment into the lake of fire, located in outer darkness (v. 15).

These No-Hellites are so very adroit and cunning, pressing in everything that can possibly give the slightest plausibility to their Hell-hatched falsification, that you need all the help you can get to panoply you against their insidious sophistries with which they are now hallucinating millions of superficial Bible readers into the diabolical delusion that Hell has already been abolished. This book, "The Life of Jesus Christ and His Apostles," you should not only carefully read but study, and so commit it to memory that you can readily appropriate in your Biblical thesaurus the priceless truths appertaining to the wonderful life and ministry of our Lord and His Apostles.

SECTION FIVE.

"Glorification."

This is the only book in circulation on this subject, which is the third great work of the Holy Ghost in the reconstruction of fallen humanity back into the complete similitude in which God created humanity, in His own "image and likeness." As the Gospel constitutes the heavenly enginery by which this stupendous work is executed, therefore we should all have an intelligent apprehension of this mighty mechanism in all its forms and phases.

(1.) THE SINAI GOSPEL of Hell and damnation for all who contemptuously reject the redeeming grace of God in Christ, which is received and appropriated by simple faith, subsequently to radical repentance and perfect submission, and confirmed by a life of unfaltering obedience, is fundamental in the scheme of redemption and constitutes God's stupendous enginery of conviction through the medial of thunders, lightnings, earthquakes, cyclones and typhoons, characteristic of the awful scenes which filled Mt. Sinai with terrors so the people all trembled and quaked and dared not touch the mountain, and if a wild beast happened to run into it he fell dead. And even Moses, the mediator of the old covenant, did exceedingly fear and quake while he stood between the panic-stricken multitude and the appalling manifestations of insulted, aggravated and outraged Justice. It is impossible to have a real scriptural revival till you bring down conviction from Heaven, interpenetrating the hearts of the people and resting on them like a nightmare, and stalking before them like an avenging spectre. This is utterly impossible without the Sinai Gospel which is God's provision for that solid, real, radical, substantial conviction which reveals Hell and the devil and superinduces unequivocal self-condemnation and hearty approval of the Divine administration, condemnatory of the wicked to eternal damnation.

(2.) The Sinai Gospel is normally followed by the CALVARY GOSPEL, preaching the dying love of Jesus, manifested in the great vicarious substitutionary atonement which the Son of God, with His own precious blood, made for the whole human race, so perfect, full and complete as to eternally preclude the slightest apology for the damnation of a solitary soul. The Calvary Gospel never fails in the justification and regeneration of every soul whom a genuine Sinai conviction has brought into a position for available reception and appropriation of the perfect and triumphant efficacy of the vicarious substitutionary atonement, nor does it fail in the glorious transition of the soul out of darkness into light, out of

Satan's slavery into God's glorious freedom, out of spiritual death into the glorious liberty of God's dear children.

(3.) When people are truly justified and radically regenerated by the Holy Ghost, His speedy illuminations will invariably superinduce the profound realization of the second work of grace for the eradication of the hereditary depravity which primarily dropped Satan's black lasso around the neck of the soul and dragged it away into his filthy drudgery, polluting it with the very slime of Hell. The absence of conviction for sanctification is *prima facie* proof that the regeneration is radically deficient and that the soul is indulging a counterfeit hope, manipulated by Satan and fostered by a *sub rosa* compromise with sin. This second great work of grace is secured invariably by faithfully preaching the PENTECOST GOSPEL, which never fails in the desired results, unless there is deficiency on the part of its predecessors, *i. e.*, the Sinai and Calvary Gospels.

(4.) From the days of Adam and Eve the antediluvian saints were constantly looking for the coming of the world's Redeemer in mortal flesh. For this grand desideratum patriarchs, prophets and saints both before and after the flood were in constant and prayerful anticipation through the long run of the four thousand years down to the happy day when Zachariah and Elizabeth, Joseph and Mary, Simeon and Anna, joined the angels in their song of triumph over the manger of Bethlehem. Since our Lord bade the world adieu and ascended up to Heaven from Mt. Olivet, the same longing anticipation which had characterized the saints of all ages again settled down upon the apostles, New Testament prophets, disciples, martyrs and pilgrims, constantly and longingly looking for His glorious return to the earth, to dethrone Satan, deliver His Bride and reign forever. Heterodoxy on the coming of the Lord is the sad concomitant of a false hope in Christ. Therefore the TRANSFIGURATION GOSPEL, which keeps the saints constantly on tiptoe watching and waiting for the Lord to return and transfigure them, is the grand bulwark against all diabolical intrigues to chill the ardor, curtail the hopes and superinduce a retrogressive trend on the part of sanctified people, which would soon vitiate the experience, entrench upon regeneration without delay, undermine justification and settle the poor victim of Satanic delusion in confirmed apostasy, the certain antecedent of damnation.

(5.) Man is a trinity consisting of spirit, soul and body, *i. e., pneuma, psuchee* and *sooma.* The pneumatical and psychical glorification take place when the soul evacuates the body and this mortal puts on immortality. The soomatical glorification takes place when this mortal body is transfigured into the similitude of our Savior's glorified body. When He was transfigured on the mountain, Moses and Elijah both appeared with Him invested in their transfigured bodies, the latter representative of all the living saints who shall be on the earth when our Lord comes to take up His Bride and who will be transfigured through the translation, whereas the former represented all of the buried saints who will be transfigured by the resurrection.

(6.) Our wonderful, omnipotent Savior, in His glorious vicarious atonement, has not only provided for the glorification of humanity, spirit, soul and body, but has also included this earth, which is to be sanctified by the crematory fires, (2 Peter 3) and gloriously renovated by special Divine creative intervention (Rev. 21). Thus Peter and John each tell us about the grand restitution which, in glorious mercy, awaits this earth when the purgatorial fires will sanctify out of her all the pollutions with which sin has affected land, sea and air, thus eternally expurgating every atom of impurity and defilement and superinducing the Edenic purity which antedated the fall. Then omnipotent intervention taking this whole world, terrestrial and aerial, in hand will recreate it into primitive heavenly similitude, restoring it back to its original place in the plain of the ecliptic, where, resuming its own orbit, whence Satan arrested it in view of augmenting the dominions of Hell, deflecting it away from comradeship with kindred celestial spheres, he has utilized it these six thousand years as a preparatory for the pandemonium in the glorious finale. This wonderful Savior, pursuant to His infallible promise, *"The meek shall inherit the earth,"* Matt. 5:5, will confer this beautiful, sanctified, renovated, celestialized world as a soldier's bounty, and the faithful pilgrims who, through the long roll of the ages, have heroically confronted Satan and his stygian hosts on the battle-field, and proven true amid all the temptations superinduced by Diabolus and his myrmidons, will receive it.

This book, "Glorification," is cheap, brief, focalized, consolidated, and expository of these great fundamental truths appertaining to the work of Christ, which should be so familiar to every witness for Jesus as to enable us always to have them at our tongue's end.

SECTION SIX.

"Incarnation of the Holy Ghost."

This book is just the size of the preceding, "Glorification," and contains precious truths exceedingly vital in the gracious economy and transcendently important, not only to every Biblical student, but especially to every soul who would enjoy a clear, bright, satisfactory experience, which is the only certain guarantee of a home in Heaven. During this probation the great interest of every soul is, in the first place, real, actual, and unmistakable salvation, so confirmed by the witness of the Spirit as eternally to put to flight all doubt and fear, giving victory brilliant as a sunburst and so incontestably witnessed by the Spirit as to leave no room for Satan in his cunning caprices to inject doubts. In the second place it is of the greatest conceivable importance to us that we shall never forfeit our inheritance by apostasy.

How can we secure these grand achievements? We answer, there is but possibly one way and that is conservatism to the Holy Ghost, who is the Executive of the Trinity. The exegesis of our Savior's statement in reference to the admissibility of the sin against the Holy Ghost, (Matt. 12:31-32) arises as a logical sequence from the adjustment of the Trinity to the redemptive scheme. The Father, in His infinite mercy, grants that redemption of the human race, the Son volunteers to procure the redemption by His vicarious death and sufferings, while the Holy Ghost becomes the omnipotent Executive. The Person of the Father sits upon the throne of the universe, while worlds in countless millions move responsive to His *ipse dixit.* The Son sits coronated, enthroned at His right hand. The Holy Ghost is the Spirit of the Father, (Acts 5:3, 4) whom He sends freely into this world, omnipotently executive of the glorious plan of human redemption. The Holy Ghost is also the Spirit of the Son, (Acts 16:6-8) whom He freely pours out on every human soul who, duly and humbly appreciative of His blessed privileges in the plan of salvation, enters into a receptive attitude, for conviction, regeneration, sanctification, infilling and anointing. Hence the unpardonableness of the sin aganist the Holy Ghost you see follows as a logical sequence from their judgment of the redemption scheme, between the Persons of the blessed Trinity; as the Holy Ghost is the only Divine Personality on the earth to whom probationary souls can have access, contemptuous rejection of Him settles forever the problem of that soul's perdition. As Jesus said, "All sins against the Father and the Son can be forgiven, but the blasphemy of the Spirit, (*i. e.*, the contempt of the Holy Ghost), can never be forgiven in this age or in that which is to come."

N. B. Beware of the tritheistic heresy, *i. e.*, the recognition of three distinct Divinities in the Persons of the Father, Son and Holy Ghost. There is but one God and three Persons in the Godhead, the Father, the Son and the Holy Ghost, accommodatory to the plan of salvation. The pagans have the heresy of polytheism, this is many gods, also pantheism, which imputes divinity to everything. Tritheism would simply fall in line with these paganistic dogmata, whereas Bible truth settles the doctrine of monotheism, *i. e.*, one God, beyond the possibility of controversy, at the same time revealing and elucidating the three distinct personalities of that isolated, omnipotent Divinity beyond the possibility of cavil.

The man that rejects the Holy Ghost can never be anything but a practical atheist, *i. e.*, a man without any god. This arises from the fact that the Holy Ghost is the only revelator of the Son (Cor. 12:1-4) and, as Jesus repeatedly says, the Son alone knows the Father and no human being can know the Father unless the Son reveals Him. Therefore you see clearly that the man rejecting the Holy Ghost never can know either the Son or the Father. Therefore you see how everything appertaining to the soul's salvation depends on conservatism to the Holy Ghost. If the worst sinner will heed His normal illuminations, He will give him such a conviction as to put him in a position where he can repent of his sins and by His help receive God's pardoning mercy in Christ, which at once brings the sinner into the kingdom, where the Spirit gloriously regenerates him, giving him a new heart and a new spirit, and actually transforms him from a spiritual corpse into a living soul. Then, if the man is true to the Holy Ghost, the Spirit will reveal the old man of sin, still hiding in the deep interior of his heart, though awfully stunned and subjugated in regeneration. With the humble and submissive appreciation of the light thus given, by which he is enabled fully to consecrate and appropriate by simple faith the crucifixion of the old man, and the expurgation of his hereditary depravity by the cleansing blood of Jesus and the glorious baptism of fire of the Holy Ghost and the triumphant Conqueror on Mt. Calvary, thus really and truly he will become the happy recipient of entire sanctification. In that case the Holy Ghost migrates into the holy temple which He has purified by the application of the precious, cleansing blood. The soul thus sitting at the feet of Jesus joyfully receives His best and greatest gift, the Holy Ghost, (Acts 2: 38) who comes into the heart to honor Jesus, forever crowning Him Lord of all in the heart and life, to reign eternally without a rival.

We constantly recognize the fact that the Son of God incarnate came into the world when born in Bethlehem. Do you not remember how, in the human body, He came to see Abraham when living on the plain of Mamre and actually abode in His tent and ate dinner with him, announcing to Sarah the conception of Isaac and to Abraham the destruction of Sodom and Gomorrah the ensuing night? Christ was as real to the Old Testament saints, in their blessed Jehovah, though excarnate, as He is this day to the New Testament disciples in the glorified Person of the Lord Jesus. After the similitude in which the Son of God was incarnated at Bethlehem, the Spirit of God was incarnated in the disciples on the day of Pentecost. Hitherto having operated on the people extrinsically, though frequently exceedingly powerfully, *e. g.*, picking up Elijah and Ezekiel and other prophets and carrying them away and dropping them down on some lonely mountain or in a dreary valley filled with dead men's bones, He now, in the Pentecostal dispensation, comes into the heart and abides, operating powerfully and delectably, though intrinsically, *i. e.*, from within, in contradistinction to His normal operations from without, antecedently to Pentecost. Peter tells us positively (Acts 2: 38) *"Repent, and each one of you,* (*i. e.*, each one who has repented) *be baptized in the name of Jesus Christ, and you shall receive the Holy*

Ghost." His office is to baptize His people with the Holy Ghost and fire, (Matt. 3: 11). Paul said to the Ephesian disciples: *"Have you received the Holy Ghost having believed?"* showing that it is the privilege of all believers to receive the Holy Ghost. When they answered in the negative, he called them all to the altar, and put his hands on them and prayed until the Holy Ghost came on them and they were enabled to testify.

As the Holy Ghost will not dwell in an unclean heart, therefore entire sanctification is the normal standard of the Church. *"Be ye holy, for I am holy."* If we ever go to live with God in Heaven, we must be holy, because He is holy. Entire sanctification, *i. e.*, the expurgation of all inbred corruption under the cleansing blood, applied by the blessed Holy Spirit, is God's standard of Bible salvation. This sweeps all the barriers out of the way preparatory to God's return to His temple, whence He has been alienated by sin. Therefore when Jesus gives you the Holy Ghost, He always cleanses the heart from all unrighteousness, and then comes in to abide forever.

As God's work is perfect in human redemption, therefore He makes no provision for sin. As Satan, an irreconcilable enemy, is infinitely stronger than we, when God gives us this wonderful uttermost salvation, He always heads off the devil effectually by committing His temple, (the sanctified heart) to the Holy Ghost, who takes up His abode in it forever. Then you are as sure of Heaven as if you were in it, if you remain true and loyal to the indwelling Holy Ghost. This follows as a legitimate sequence, from the simple fact that the blessed Holy Spirit is more than a match for the combined powers of earth and Hell; Satan and all his hosts assault in vain, while the blessed Comforter dwells within. The thing we want is to settle matters for Heaven and keep them settled forever. The way to do that is to secure the constant indwelling of the Holy Ghost, *i. e.,* have Him come and incarnate Himself in your heart. This He is anxious to do, thus to give you perfect rest and constant victory forever; from the simple fact that He assuredly conquered Satan and all his myrmidons excarnate and incarnate, world without end. Therefore this book, "The Incarnation of the Holy Ghost," will prove infinitely valuable to you, not only in the acquisition of a *bona fide* and triumphant Christian experience, but in the retention of the same to all eternity.

SECTION SEVEN.

"Church—Bride—Kingdom."

This is a book I wrote by special request of our sainted Brother Knapp. It not only expounds all of these blessed institutions of God's transcendent and redeeming ways, but contrasts them either with the other and fortifies the reader against the confusion which so extensively prevails, not only in the laity, but the clergy as well, relative to their entity, institutionality, prerogative and availability.

Church and Kingdom are substantially identical, except the fact that the former consists only of the souls who, responsive to the call of the Holy Ghost, have come out from the world and identified themselves with God, therefore, it has an objective signification; whereas the latter comprises simply the souls, terrestrial and celestial, who sustained their relation of loyal obedience and conservatism to the Divine sovereignty. Therefore you perceive that the subjective signification of the word includes the constituant membership of our heavenly King in all worlds. Our Savior (in John 3:5) clearly and forever settles the question that the spiritual birth is absolutely necessary for membership in the Lord's kingdom.

The same is equally true of the Church *i. e.*, the *ecclesia,* from *ek,* out, and *kleoo,* to call—hence, the called out people. All these have left Satan's kingdom and crossed the line into the heavenly. Therefore the testimony of our Savior settles the question that they are born from above.

The world is flooded with false doctrines in reference to both the Church and the Kingdom; multitudinous claimants on all sides roaring themselves hoarse with the vociferous appeals, "Come unto us and let us immerse you in water, for this is the door into the Church," whereas our blessed Christ says in John 10: *"I am the door,"* therefore neither baptism nor church rites of any kind constitute the door, but Christ Himself. Neither is any preacher the porter; only the Holy Ghost, the sole Revelator of Christ, can show you the door and lead you in it. It is said that there are now six thousand sects and denominations in Christendom, each one claiming to be the true Church, thus bewildering the poor Hellward-bound millions almost as confusedly as the Brahman priests of India do their devotees, telling them that there are three hundred and thirty millions of gods. Neither the Church nor the Kingdom is any sect, denomination or ecclesiasticism, but the body of Christ, (Eph.

1:23). Christ is God, and consequently a pure spirituality. A spiritual head with a material body would be a monstrosity. Therefore the Church is a pure spirituality like her Divine head. While in this world these human spirits all dwell in bodies which are conventionally identified with the Church antecedently to the transfiguration glory, which will eternally eliminate mortality and confer spirituality, the work homogeneous with the transformation of our spirits, wrought by the Holy Ghost in regeneration and sanctification. Therefore, antecedently to the glorious transfiguration, the human body is neither a member of the Church nor a citizen of the Kingdom, except in a modified, conventional sense. Therefore it will never really be known who does constitute the mystical spiritual body of Christ till the sons of God are made manifest in His glory, (Col. 3:3).

The supernatural birth makes you a member of God's Church and a citizen of His Kingdom, just as the infants in the United States are counted in the census and signify as much in the citizenship as the adults, although they have nothing whatever to do with the government till they reach majority. In a similar manner regeneration makes you a citizen of the Kingdom, but during your minority you have no voice in the government, (Gal. 4:4), *"But I say unto you so long time as the heir is an infant he differs from a slave as to nothing, even though being lord of all, but is under tutors and guardians until the time appointed by the father . . . ."* And verse 7, *"So thou art no longer a slave but a son, and if a son indeed, an heir through God."* Here we have a contrast between infancy and adultage in the Kingdom. The minority is the servile period and the majority the filial. Now this is the same person all the way through, the difference simply consisting in his relation to the Divine government, before sanctification being a servant and afterward a son, both characters existing contemporaneously throughout, but during minority the servile predominating and after majority the filial.

We have the same facts set forth in Heb. 13:14, "*For every one partaking of milk is unskillful in the word of righteousness, because he is a babe, for solid food is for the perfect who have their senses exercised by use unto the discernment both of the good and of the evil.*" Here we see the same two classes again contrasted by the phrases *nelpios,* an infant, and *teleios,* an adult, *i. e.,* a perfect man. The Apostle here says the infant is unskillful in the word of righteousness, *i. e.,* he does not well understand how to apply it to himself or to others, while the adult, or the perfect man, as the Greek says, has his spiritual and intellectual senses developed by use so that he can discriminate between the good and the evil.

We have the same contrast developed in the parable of the virgins who represent the kingdom of Heaven on the earth. You remember how they all alike set out with lighted lamps to meet the Bridegroom, but afterward five of them concluded that security demanded that they should lay in a supply of oil for coming emergencies, the other five thinking that it was not necessary, as the lamps were burning very nicely and they were getting along real well. Eventually the Bridegroom came and they all started to meet Him. Now while the five who had laid in the supply of oil had no trouble whatever, you remember that the five who were delinquent in this respect utterly forfeited their place in the Bridehood. There is no intimation that they lost their place in the Kingdom. The English Version statement, "Our lamps are gone out," led all of the old commentators astray on the subject, relegating them as apostates. The true reading, "Our lamps are going out," indicates a low state of grace, normal to the unsanctified, but it is utterly incompatible with the conclusion that their state was graceless. They were still citizens of the Kingdom, but never had been members of the Bridehood.

I have heard preachers contend stoutly for the identity of the Church and the Bride. This is a mistake which you will all readily see. Regeneration makes you a citizen of the Kingdom, (John 3:3) identifies you with the body of Christ, and makes you a member of the Church, (Eph. 1:23), but assuredly does not make you a member of the Bridehood, whose pre-eminent signification is the idea of wedlock. All brides are married and always imply the existence of the groom, the cognomenal counterpart, somewhere, either present or absent. It is one experience to be born into the Kingdom and an infinitely different one to get married to the Son of the King. The latter positively implies adultage, as infants are not marriageable. Our Lord is coming back to this world for His Bride only. He is certain duly to care for the infants, both spiritual and physical, but they are not members of His Bridehood. Those who enjoy the study of the sweet, precious Word and are delighted with the erudition of the Holy Ghost, the Author and Revelator of the deep things of God, would be much edified studying this book, "Church--Bride—Kingdom."

SECTION EIGHT.

The Booklets.

These are twenty-seven in number, all directly expository of the great and absorbing theme, "Holiness to the Lord," which floods the Bible from the Alpha of Genesis to the Omega of Revelation. These booklets contain about fifty to one hundred pages each and are all bound in paper and sell for only one dime per copy. Therefore you see you can actually command a splendid library with the small sum of two dollars and a half. When I graduated from college, having been a student twenty-one years (from five to twenty-six years of age), I proceeded at once to ransack all of the world for books and gathered up a library at the cost of one thousand dollars, much of it consisting of costly works sent from Germany and England. The Lord, in His mercy, has let me write forty-eight books and booklets. I honestly believe that if these had been put into my hands instead of the one thousand dollar library, they would have done me more good than that wagon load of books. While many of my books are large, containing three to six hundred pages and substantially bound in cloth, the twenty-seven booklets, about which we now give you a word of information, cost but a dime per copy and therefore amount in total cost to but very little; the whole sum necessary to secure the entire library would probably be in the neighborhood of $15.00. God, in His mercy, blessed me with splendid educational facilities, so that I read English fluently at the age of six, and after years of toil actually used the New Testament scriptures in thirteen languages and dialects and the Old Testament in all of the important classical languages. I have been an assiduous student all my life and lost comparatively no time sowing wild oats in the realms of Diabolus, like most people, and having spent fifty-three years preaching the Gospel and teaching not only the Bible, but the entire collegiate course, I am certainly very anxious to give the rising generation the full benefit of my seventy-three years on the earth and all the additional remnant which God, in His infallible providence and superabounding mercy, shall add to my preceding years, which already begin to render me somewhat an example of human longevity.

The booklets are

(1.) "SPIRITUAL GIFTS AND GRACES." When first written this produced a general and wide-spread sensation among the scholars of Christendom, who had aquiesced in the conclusion that all of these gifts had left the world when the Apostles went to Heaven. Consequently this book was really a sunburst on the spiritual people of the different denominations who seized it with universal avidity and devoured it with insatiable voracity, seeing clearly and confessedly its pure Biblical orthodoxy, and at the same time recognizing the glorious feasability of receiving and appropriating these gifts and graces like the people of the apostolic age. We all must have the nine graces, love, joy, peace, longsuffering, gentleness, goodness, meekness, faith and holiness, (Gal. 5:22) in order that we ourselves may be saved. Therefore you see that the nine graces are an absolute *sine qua non,* which none of us under any circumstances can afford to forfeit as we must get to Heaven whether other people do or not.

Meanwhile the nine gifts of the Holy Ghost, wisdom, knowledge, faith, gifts of healing, the workings of dynamite, discernment of spirits, prophecy, languages and interpretations, constitute the Christian's panoply by which we conquer Satan's host and rescue the lost millions from sin, death and endless woe. You see, then, if we have not the graces we will lose our souls, while if we do not utilize the gifts, though with the graces we get to Heaven, we will have no stars to shine in our crown for the angels to admire through the ages of eternity and, as some say, will have to go bare-headed.

(2.) "VICTORY." This book has received a wonderful circulation and God has everywhere set His seal upon the truth. Bound in cloth, it only costs twenty-five cents, but in paper it ranks as a dime book along with the twenty-six dime booklets in paper. It means just what it says, "Victory over the world, the flesh and the devil." It tells you the Lord's secret of getting it and keeping it. Its circulation has gone up to forty or fifty thousand, and it is still going to the ends of the earth. It was published early in the Holiness Movement. I have known many preachers to attribute their sanctification to reading it. Like all of these small books it is characteristic of *multum in parvo,* "much in little," and evidently adapted to laboring people.

(3.) "HOLY LAND." This book is the size and price of the two preceding, twenty-five cents, bound in cloth, and in paper one dime. It gives you an account of my first journey to the Holy Land. It has received quite an extensive circulation and been read by myriads with great delight. Children and young people are especially carried away with it.

(4.) "DIVINE HEALING," gives this precious truth a clear, terse, brief, scriptural exegesis, such as the people need to push them in reference to their blessed privileges in our wonderful Christ, who is the Savior of the body as well as of the soul, having commissioned the twelve and also the seventy whom He sent out not only to preach the Gospel and cast out the demons, but to heal the sick.

(5.) "DEEPER THINGS." This booklet is devoted especially and pre-eminently to the elucidation of the deep things of God, after which all truly saved and sanctified people do sigh and long, importunately pleading, "Lord, let me down into the deeper depths of Thine own blessed and unsearchable Divinity; broaden me out in grander and progressive longitudes in the Divine life; and let me climb into loftier altitudes, that I may rise so high above transitory things that all of Satan's mountains which he can rear to obstruct my race for glory shall dwindle into mole hills, so that I may actually overstep them without an effort."

(6.) "THE VICTORY OF CHRIST." This booklet describes our Lord's wonderful descension into Hades, Eph. 4:8-10, 1 Peter 3:19:20, Luke 23:43, Matt. 12:40 and other corroborative scriptures with some important Old Testament references, setting forth the fact that when Jesus expired on the cross instead of going up to His Father, He went down into Hades, the unexpected herald of His own victory achieved on the cross which He proclaimed to all the inmates of the pandemonium, signally triumphing over them. Then crossing the chasm impassable to finite beings, Luke 16:26, He entered that intermediate Paradise, denominated "Abraham's Bosom," v. 24, met the thief and all of the Old Testament saints there awaiting Him, spent the Sabbath with them, and with the incoming week evacuating that Paradise, led them up to Jerusalem, received His body out of the sepulchre, and after forty days ascended into Heaven, accompanied by the mighty host of Old Testament saints who tarried with Him during the forty days, invisible because disembodied.

(7.) "GOD'S NAZARITE." In this valuable booklet you will find the beautiful character of the Old Testament holiness people lucidly expounded, much to your edification. We need all the helps we can get from both Testaments to edify us in the deep things of God, to qualify us to travel the King's highway of holiness, and to fortify us against the multitudinous temptations incident to all pilgrims who undertake to tread the narrow way.

(8.) "DEMONOLOGY" gives you the history of Satan, fallen Lucifer, and the origin of all his mrymidons, the devils and demons. It also fortifies you against their insidious metamorphisms, playing the angel and even playing the Holy Ghost, and thus deceiving multitudes of people and leading away mighty men and women whom God has blessed and made to shine in the front ranks of the holiness people. None are too great and strong to be caught by the fugitive lassoes of these minions of the pit. Therefore we cannot overestimate the value of everything calculated to awaken and fortify us against these subtle intrigues of Satan, devils and demons. To our sorrow we see their fatal work whithersoever we turn our gaze and are constrained to exclaim in deepest grief, "How have the mighty fallen!" How we bewail the sad contemplation of master spirits in the Movement, sidetracked, derailed and ditched through the chicanery of the evil spirits which throng the air, so cunning and adroit in playing the Holy Ghost and the angel on the unwary saints. See the myriads of Spiritualists all thus led away by evil spirits playing brother, sister, father, mother, friend, etc.

(9.) "WORK OF THE HOLY SPIRIT." This is the companion volume of "Demonology," which you observe immediately preceding, and important by way of fortification against the demons which are after all the people in the world without a solitary exception, and doing their utmost to deceive them and lead them to ruin. Astronomy has developed the existence of one billion, one hundred and seventy millions of worlds, constituting the celestial universe. Revelation twelve tells us that when the Dragon was driven out of Heaven, his tail drew one-third of the stars, *i. e.*, in the revolt of Lucifer the archangel, one-third of all the mighty hosts of celestial intelligence followed in that sad and awful revolt, having forfeited their probation. You are astonished at this conclusion. Why not be astonished at what you see in this world where, according to the testimony of Jesus, the proportion who fail to sustain their probation and make their way to Heaven is greater. Matt. 7:13, 14.

With this alarming testimony of Jesus in reference to the paucity of the saved, we should all take the utmost heed and be constantly on our watch-towers. You must remember that God never created devils, demons nor sinners, but all of the fallen angels now verify the unhappy character and abide the awful doom of the former; whereas, the wicked millions of earth and Hell are but the evolution of Adam and Eve, whom He created perfect and upright. Among these twenty-seven booklets, which you get for one dime per copy, these two *i. e.,* "Demonology" and "The Work of the Holy Spirit," which have always been circulated in pairs, as they represent the opposite sides of the battle-field which envelopes the whole earth, are of transcendent importance.

(10.) "WHY WILL YE DIE?" Ezek. 33:11. This booklet is an appeal to the unconverted and exceedingly appropriate for extensive promiscuous distribution by way of warning the wicked to flee from the wrath to come. In this respect it stands isolated in the entire catalogue of my writings, as all the balance are more directly to Christians in the interest of sanctification and subsequent holy living and especially the great enterprise of universal evangelization, which, in the economy of God's Kingdom, becomes the glorious privilege of all who have the honored privilege of a place in the sacramental host marching under the blood-stained banner of the conquest of the world for Christ.

(11.) "THE SABBATH." You need this book especially to qualify you to meet the Seventh Day Adventists, who are dispersed throughout this continent very widely and are a very enterprising people in the interest of their sect, whose constant battle-cry is "The Mosaic Sabbath." They befog the consciences of multitudes who are sincerely seeking after light and truth and, in the integrity of their hearts, are endeavoring to keep the commandments of God and do His will on earth as the angels do it in Heaven. They tell them boldly and unhesitatingly that Saturday is the only true Sabbath and that our Sunday in the Pope's counterfeit, assuring the people that he made the change. The innocent rank and file of Christendom look upon the papacy as running far back near the beginning of the Christian age, which is quite a mistake, as there never was a pope till A. D. 606, when Procas, the king of Italy, crowned Boniface III, Bishop of Rome, Supreme Pontificate of all the churches, and he was the first Pope. You will see in this booklet, clearly proved by Scripture and history, that the disciples kept the first day of the week without a break from the resurrection of the Lord and that the Gentiles never did keep the Mosaic Sabbath and were not required to do it, the Jewish wing of the Church having kept both days till they evanesced and the Church became all Gentile.

The trouble with the influence of these Seventh Day Adventists is not simply their fight against the Christian Sabbath, but their infidelity. It is not generally known that they are actually downright infidels of the materialistic order, actually repudiating all spirituality, even the immortality of the soul. They are called "Soul-Sleepers," but it is a mistake. They do not believe you have any soul to sleep. The only immortality which they allow is that of the body of believers in the resurrection, whereas the wicked are forever annihilated. These people use the day question to lasso your conscience and draw you in with them. Then, at their leisure, they lead you away into infidelity and freeze you to death. This booklet should be circulated to the ends of the earth to fortify honest people against that pestilential influence.

(12.) "SATAN'S SIDE-TRACKS." This booklet proceeds to show up ten prominent side-tracks which Satan, through his false prophets and counterfeit preachers, is now currently bringing into availability. He is so cunning and adroit that, slipping in like the vampire at midnight, he manages to lay down a side-track which is so parallel with the main track that unanointed eyes will not identify it. Then he has us run on the same direction a considerable time and deflects so gradually that the travelers do not detect it but think they are still on the King's highway, till eventually it gets completely turned around and runs directly back in the opposite direction. Still Satan is on board dressed in railroad uniform and with great care and adroitness playing the Holy Ghost, while his myrmidons so cunningly play the angel that you think all is well and the trainmen are all in their places. Meanwhile you are looking for the "New Jerusalem" and expecting to see your glorified relatives and friends on the platform to greet you, when your train runs into the union depot. But finally, when it is eternally too late, you wake up to the fact that you are on the wrong train and in the company of devils and have actually reached Hell.

(13.) "NO-HELLISM." This booklet shows up the Bible doctrine of a real Hell of fire and brimstone clearly and beyond the possibility of doubt, and gives you overwhelming scriptural refutations of the boasted theories manipulated by the No-Hellites, *i. e.*, Millennial Dawners, Seventh Day Adventists and Universalists. When we consider the lamentable fact that the Sinai Gospel of Hell and damnation for the finally impenitent has actually gone out of the pulpit, it is high time that we all rally to the rescue of this great fundamental Bible truth. Where the Sinai Gospel is not preached conviction evaneces from the community and wickedness in every form and phase comes in like a flood. I have heard a great holiness evangelist, preaching in the largest camp-meeting in the world, say that he read several books on future punishment which cost him $1.00 apiece, and afterwards got more light and help on the subject by reading this dime booklet than all of them. Oh, how we need millions to scatter throughout all Christendom to wake up the people before they awaken in Hell! So wicked is the human heart that all need the Hell-scare to bring them to a real, genuine repentance, which is the only antecedent of that experimental salvation and radical holiness which is the only guarantee against damnation.

(14.) "MATRIMONY." This is the only institution which survived the fall and came down to brighten this dark, fallen world with a perpetual souvenir of the lost Paradise. Where this institution is not held sacred and appreciated in the fear of God, Christian civilization topples and falls. There is so much reckless deportment in connection with the matrimonial relation, and horrific, diabolical abuse of this sacred institution, that it is transcendently important that we give special attention to this fundamental Bible truth. Whereas Judaism was infantile Christianity, Moses provided for divorcements in case of irreconcilable uncongeniality and incompatibility, which disqualified them to live together in peace and harmony. But our Savior swept all of that away and restricted divorcement to the sin of adultery alone, which, in its very nature, destroys the matrimonial unity, which is the fundamental truth of the institution. In that case the divorcement is only for the protection of the innocent party. The wicked usurpation of this privilege is awfully condemnatory in the sight of God and all good people. Yet the wicked have the audacity recklessly to avail themselves of the divorcement privilege for the perpetration of the vilest sins. The signification of divorcement has been wofully misunderstood, arising from the erroneous translation of Matt. 5:31, 32, *"But it has been said whosoever may put away his wife let him give to her a divorcement. But I say unto you that every man putting away his wife, except for the cause of fornication, makes her commit adultery, and whosoever may marry the cast off woman commits adultery."* In the English Version, the Greek word *apolelumenen,* which means "the cast off woman," is erroneously rendered the "divorced woman," which is positively untrue. Great confusion and domestic mal-administration have supervened from this incorrect reading. The Savior did not say that the man who marries a divorced woman committed adultery; but you see at once the clearness of the case, when he marries her who had been driven away by her husband and is still his wedded wife. They had a quarrel and perhaps he whipped her and drove her from home, but she had not yet been divorced, therefore, of course, the man marrying her is guilty of adultery in its most literal sense. Whereas in case the woman had been divorced a man would have a perfect right to marry her and would not be guilty of adultery, because the end for which the divorcement is given is to liberate the innocent party for another marriage, *ad libitum.* God believed in matrimony. It is His own institution and prevents more sin than anything else. Divorcement (for sin of adulterv) is also God's institution. It is right and proper in its place, and not to be wickedly usurped, but only used at the option of the innocent party. N. B. God's work is not shoddy like man's. When He grants a divorcement, it utterly ratifies the preceding nullification of the matrimonial covenant, which covenant unified the parties till destroyed by the sin of adultery.

Our Savior's word for "divorcement" is *apostasion, i. e.,* apostasy, now a plain English word, whose meaning is well known. A backslider is one who has lost ground and depreciated spiritually, but has not necessarily forfeited his justification. When this takes place, he has crossed the line and has gotten back in Satan's kingdom where he was before his conversion and is now an apostate and will have to get converted again, justified and regenerated, or drop into the Hell of the apostate along with Judas Iscariot. Of course the divorcements given by the courts are of no value unless there is a scriptural guaranty. A second marriage without a scriptural divorcement is utterly null and void, leaving the parties living in adultery. In that case they should separate and repent, but of course will never be free to marry another unless the truly wedded consort should be removed by death. It is of the greatest and most vital importance that all people should understand the true signification of Christian wedlock and also that of the scriptural divorcement, which invariably returns the innocent party back to celibacy where matrimony found him or her. We should all encourage matrimony in its right place as it is a most effectual breakwater against sin. Celibacy through life is only justifiable when utilized in the interest of God's kingdom, (Matt. 19: 12).

(15.) "SIGNS OF HIS COMING." This booklet, containing about fifty or sixty pages, is a valuable compendium of prophetic data which you will find exceedingly convenient for reference, and to use when you desire to impart information on this great and mighty truth of our Savior's return to this world, which is certainly very nigh. All the chronologies concur in the conclusion that we are certainly living in the time of the end of the Gentile age, and great and wonderful events are going to transpire whose adumbrations are strikingly ominous in all lands.

According to the Lunar Chronology, which measures time by the revolutions of the moon around the earth, the Gentile times have already expired and are fifteen years over. According to the Calendar Chronology, which measures time by the revolution of the planets around the sun, the Gentile times only lack twenty-seven years. According to the Solar Chronology, which measures time by the revolution of the earth around the sun, there are only sixty-two years yet remaining to complete the period of the Gentile times, when we are assured that our Lord will appear (Luke 21:24) on the throne of His millennial glory, dethrone Satan and all of his subordinates, and establish His kingdom from the rising of the sun to the going down of the same.

> "For He shall have dominion over river, sea and shore,
> As far as eagle's pinion or dove's light wing can soar."

Now, let us remember that Daniel, the twelfth chapter, gives us forty-five years as the Tribulation Period, during which the Ancient of Days (Dan. 7:9) will shake down every potentate, political and ecclesiastical, thus clearing the way for the glorious reign of His Son. N. B. Just before the tribulation shall set in, our Lord will descend and take away His Bride (Dan. 12) to the Marriage Supper of the Lamb, (Matt. 25) which will continue contemperaneously with the Tribulation on the earth and at its expiration our Lord will return on the throne of His millennial glory, (Rev. 20) arrest Satan and take him out of the world, establishing His glorious reign in all the earth.

Now you see above that the Lunar Chronology has already expired the Gentile times plus fifteen years, the Calendar Chronology will expire then in twenty-seven years, and the Solar Chronology in sixty-two years, but as the Tribulation belongs to the Gentile times, therefore the Rapture will take place forty-five years before its expiration, which gives us, according to the Lunar Chronology, the Rapture over-due forty-five plus fifteen equaling sixty years; Calendar Chronology, forty-five minus twenty-seven, equaling eighteen years Rapture over-due; and Solar Chronology, sixty-two minus forty-five, equals seventeen years until the Rapture of the saints is due. Therefore you see that the Lunar makes the glorious Rapture of the saints due sixty years ago, the Calendar eighteen years ago, and the Solar seventeen years from this date, *i. e.*, in 1923.

The Mohammedans and Jews use the Lunar Chronology, the European nations the Calendar, and the Americans the Solar.

These facts ought to keep all enlightened Christians on the constant outlook for the appearing of our blessed, glorified Savior to transfigure and take us up to the Marriage Supper of the Lamb. Are you robed, ready, watching and waiting? If not, settle it quickly. Radically and eternally plunge beneath the crimson flood that washes whiter than snow, and then rise to walk in Heaven's own light above the world and sin, with heart made pure, garments white and Christ enthroned within.

(16.) "MILLENNIUM." This is one of these dime booklets which tells you briefly all about the glorious reign of our blessed and wonderful Savior on the earth in His personal, transfigured majesty, following His descension from the Marriage Supper of the Lamb accompanied by the transfigured saints of His Bridehood, who, during the tribulation on the earth while the Father was hackling out of all nations the incorrigibles whose character is utterly incompatible and unharmonizable with the glorious reign of perfect justice, purity, righteousness and love in all the earth, passed through an adjudication in Heaven, by which they received their respective places in the Divine government according to their personal idiosincrasies and adaptation to conserve the glorious millennial reign, as the faithful and loving subordinates of the King of kings and Lord of lords, (Rev. 20:4-6).

Our great and pressing expedition at the present day is to get the Bride ready in every nation under Heaven, since our glorious Lord will need charter members for His millennial kingdom in every nation. He informs us (Matt. 19: 28) that the Apostles will be the first rulers in His glorious coming kingdom. He also repeats the same at the last supper (Luke 22:28). There are just about twelve great nationalities now upon the earth, which will be given, according to His promise, to the twelve Apostles, as His chief subordinates, all the members of the Bridehood having their places in perfect harmony and symmetry, with infinite delight serving our glorified King of kings, as He rules all nations in righteousness and love, *i. e.*, with a rod of iron, (Rev. 19: 15). While the millennial reign will be in righteousness and love, yet we see here the rod of iron, which will preclude all overt sin. The people will be free and still on probation, so that they can commit sin, but in the absence of Satan and all of his myrmidons to tempt them it is not at all probable that they will. Yet, in the event that any do rebel against the authority of the King, such will be suddenly cut off and dropped into Hell.

As all the Apostles went to their respective fields of labor and suffered martyrdom, there is at least a probability that each one will receive his original evangelistic field in the glorious coming kingdom. In the prophecies, America is included with Europe, as we are all Europeans. Oh, what incalculable inspirations pass over the inspired pages, filling every Christian heart with the glowing enthusiasm for a place in the Bridehood and a participation in the glorious millennial reign as the subordinates of our blessed Christ!

(17.) "THE CHRISTHOOD AND THE ANTI-CHRISTHOOD." This booklet expounds the wonderful Christhood in its infinitesimal official ramifications through His numberless ministers after the order of Melchizedec, filling the whole earth and continuing forever, uninterrupted by death, as in the case of the Aaronic ministry, but abiding eternally and, in the wonderful gracious economy, lighting the world with the glory of God manifested through the vicarious substitutionary atonement, wrought by His Son, our glorious Christ, on the cruel cross of Calvary. Through the diversified media of His called and sent ministry, this wonderful Christ reaches and saves all the lost souls who will appreciatively reciprocate His mercy. God out of Christ is a consuming fire, (Heb. 12:18). God in Christ, divine and omnipotent, is the only hope of lost souls.

Anti is a Greek word which means "instead of," as Jesus says, "Who of you is a father, and if his son ask bread, will give him a stone, or if he ask a fish will, instead of a fish, give him a serpent?" There our Savior uses the preposition *anti* before fish, meaning that the cruel father in that case gives his son the serpent as a substitute for the fish. Satan rules this world (2 Cor. 4:4), doing his best to pass himself with the people for God, and in most cases, especially in heathen lands, is eminently succeeding.

The Pope is the antichrist of prophecy, generally, especially in Revelation, denominated the beast. The Greek word is *theerion,* which means a wild beast, bloodthirsty, *e. g.*, the lion, the tiger, etc. This beast mentioned in the Bible and applied to antichrist is the symbol of carnality which has always predominated in the leadership of the fallen Church. The Pope boldly claims to be the vicar of Christ and the vicegerent of God, thus actually usurping the place of Christ and robbing Him of His sovereign prerogative. He is also, in this antichristian attitude, co-operated by a million of priests, dispersed throughout the whole world. We find people who are not Roman Catholics who actually make this awful antichristian claim, *e. g.*, Campbellites and Mormons, who, instead of sending all the people to the blessed Christ, King of kings and Lord of lords, *"the only name given under Heaven among men by which it is possible to be saved,"* say, "Come and join our Church and we will immerse you in water for the remission of your sins, and thus make you a full-fledged Christian."

Satan in all ages has been doing his best through false prophets and counterfeit preachers to actually usurp the throne of Christ, whereas the Lord's preachers do nothing but hide behind the cross and cry, *"Behold the Lamb of God that taketh away the sin of the world,"* thus serving as humble heralds, and telling all the people about the wonderful Christ who alone can save. The ministers of antichrist say to all the world, "Come to us and we will take you in hand and you may rest easy about your souls, as you have only to do what we tell you." There is an irrepressible conflict in all the world between Christ, His called and sent preachers, and the antichrists with their vast panoplied hosts who are not acquainted with God, and consequently do not claim that He has called and sent them. The Pope and all antichristian preachers claim that God has turned over the salvation of the world to them, thus clearly evincing to all clearly illuminated people that they are actually manipulated by Satan and led captive at his will.

(18.) "APPEAL TO POST-MILLENNIALISTS." This is another of the twenty-seven dime booklets. In this I, in the honesty of my heart and the fear of God, with the open Bible and facing the great white throne, appeal to my dear post-millennial brethren, feeling that they have not really the light relative to this matter, which God, in His mercy, has given to me. Therefore in perfect love I appeal to them to halt and look the facts squarely in the face and govern themselves accordingly. The post-millennialists tell me that we must make a millennium on the earth and after it runs a thousand years the Lord will come and take the world; *i. e.*, we are to make the Millennium and give it to Him, whereas the Bible clearly reveals that He is to bring the Millennium and give it to us. It is a significant fact that Jesus commands us all to be constantly looking for Him. This was true of the Apostles and the primitive Church; they looked for Him constantly as long as they lived. The Post-Millennialists are not looking for Him now and with this view cannot look for Him until the Millennium has come and run its happy thousand years and is numbered with the annals before the flood.

Our Lord commands us frequently over and over to be always ready and watching for Him, and pronounces a terrible woe on the people who are unwatchful, saying, *"My Lord delayeth His coming,"* Matt. 24:50. He actually pronounces such a man a wicked servant and says that his Lord will come in a day he does not look for Him, at an hour he does not expect Him, and will cut him off and appoint him his part with the unbelievers and hypocrites, and "there shall be weeping and wailing and gnashing of teeth." I know nothing except what the Lord tells me, therefore I would rather this moment seal my fate with my blood than to believe anything that would put me in an attitude of disobedience. The post-millennial view of the Lord's coming is absolutely incompatible with that constant outlook for His appearing which He has positively commanded, more frequently than anything else. O beloved, shall we not all take God at His word and look for Jesus every moment and, by His wonderful redeeming grace and sanctifying power, be constantly robed and ready to meet Him at His glorious coming?

(19.) "APOSTASY" is also another of the twenty-seven dime booklets. A subtle heresy has somewhat pervaded the ranks of the holiness people, assuming that the forfeiture of sanctification necessarily and invariably deprives you of your justification, bringing you under condemnation and relegating you back into the kingdom of Satan. This view really saps the very foundation of the Movement by actually nullifying the second work of grace, without which we certainly have no holiness people on the earth in contradistinction to the justified. A momentary analysis will enable you to see the possibility of this statement. If simultaneous forfeiture of justification and sanctification be true, then the Zinzendorfians are right in their hypothesis of simultaneous reception.

As Israel had two crossings in her journey from Egypt to Canaan, and we know that apostasy means retrogression over the ground we traverse in our escape from Satan's bondage, then there must be two crossings in the retrogression of Israel from Canaan back to Egypt. They assume that we cannot commit a sin without losing our sanctification, which we frankly admit. Then they go on and tell us that every known sin brings us under condemnation and forfeits our justification. Therefore they conclude that every sin committed by sanctified people forfeits not only sanctification, but justification, too; this we frankly admit. Their argument is true, but they have a false premise, which in every case must produce a false conclusion, even though the reasoning be correct. That false premise is the assumption that we lose sanctification by committing some known sin, which is not true at all. The fact is the sanctification must be lost before you ever get your consent to do wrong. If your sanctification were on hand, you would die in your tracks rather than do anything which your conscience condemns. Sanctification is not forfeited by a willing act of sin, but by the inadvertent leakage of love, and imbition of depravity, imparted by evil spirits around you, both excarnate and incarnate. In this way, and by unwatchfulness, the Holy Ghost is grieved away, as in the case of Sampson, who knew not that the Spirit of the Lord had departed from him till he found himself utterly incompetent to whip the Philistines. So in this way sanctified people grieve away the Holy Spirit, lose their power to resist temptation, and the moment they commit a known sin their justification is gone; whereas the Sanctifier had been grieved away sometime previously and consequently Satan, too strong for you, gains the victory over you and takes you captive. This is a great practical truth and ought to be understood by all the holiness people. For the want of special light and Biblical instruction at this point, the Holiness people are fast dropping down the standard to the normal level of regeneration.

(20.) "THE BIBLE." This booklet expounds the great work which the Holy Ghost does through the medium of His Bible. Paul says, *"All Scripture is God-breathed," i. e.*, it is the very breath of God, thus settling forever the controverted question of its plenary, verbal inspiration. It is of the greatest importance that we ascertain the interpolations which uninspired men have added to the Bible, and which really constitute no part of it whatever. You who do not read the Greek independently ought to have my translation, so as to see just what is Scripture and what is not. The dear people have importuned me with all their might to translate the Old Testament, but it is too late for me to undertake it, neither do I feel any leading in that direction. It is beautiful and true, but we are not living under the Old Testament dispensation, but the New, therefore the thing for us to do is to learn from the New Testament all the great vital truths constituting the redemption scheme. This we can do by the help of God, so that none of us need walk in darkness, nor the dim light of the moon and stars, but amid the glorious noonday, with which the Sun of Righteousness floods all duly appreciative Bible students who have given up all of their own wisdom, creeds and sectism, and content themselves to sit meek and lowly at the feet of Jesus, saying, like little Samuel, *"Speak, Lord, thy servant heareth."* Meanwhile the Holy Ghost is freely given to teach us the deep things of God and the wonderful truths of the Kingdom.

Infidelity in the form of higher criticism is Satan's latest investiture of his old infidelity of ages long ago, forged in the crucibles of Hell. So many of the higher clergy are getting tilted by this new fangled legerdemain that it is now incumbent on the rank and file of the holiness people to take the Bible into their own hands, repudiating the human *ipse dixit* forever and demanding a positive *"Thus saith the Lord"* for everything they accept.

You will find this booklet, which tells you what the Bible is and what it does, exceedingly helpful in your apprehension and comprehension of this invaluable Waybill from earth to Heaven. The Holy Ghost is the Guide, but He guides all true pilgrims through the Guide-book which He has given us. Therefore, we must not fold our arms and content ourselves with easy-chair piety while Satan rocks that arm-chair and sings lullabies over us till he can dump us into Hell. If we do not prove ourselves assiduous students in the school of Christ, always teachable by the blessed Holy Spirit lighting up His precious Word and using His faithful people to instruct the juveniles and humble catechumens of this blessed Guide-book, we need not be surprised to find our necks lassoed by Satan's crafty sophistries. In our study of the Bible, we must ask God to deliver us from our sectisms, creedisms, dogmatisms, and prejudices of every kind; not only giving us a clean heart under the cleansing blood, in which He will condescend to dwell, but a purified intellect from which all the debris of superstition and idolatry in all its forms and phases has been expurgated, so that it may be blank and clean and ready for the inscriptions with which the blessed Author of the precious Word in mercy may write the cordival, vocalized truths, constantly to serve as beacon lights along the heavenly highway.

(21.) "GOD'S ECCLESIA." This is the word translated "Church" throughout the Bible. It is a Greek compound from *ek,* out, and *kaleoo,* to call; therefore it means "the called out people," in all the earth. When Jesus was speaking of His sheep, in John 10, He said, "I have other sheep which are not of this fold. It behooveth me to bring them hither, that there may be one fold and one shepherd." Of course those sheep were among the Gentiles. When God put the spirit of prophecy on

Ananias, the wicked high priest who was thirsting for the blood of His Son, and he said that "it behooved that one man should die for the people and that the whole nation should not perish," he spoke this not of himself but, being high priest that year, he prophesied that Jesus was about to die for the nation, and not for the nation only, but that He might gather into one the children of God who had been dispersed abroad. These children of God are scattered through every nation under Heaven, having been born from above, regenerated by the Holy Ghost, and consequently become members of God's family, which is but another name for the Church. You see, then, that God's Ecclesia are scattered over every land between the cardinal points and it is the work of the Gospel ministers to gather them all into the New Testament organization in order to their edification by the graces of Christian fellowship and the mutual instruction and encouragement of each other.

Denominationalism has seriously confused the popular mind in reference to the character and constituency of God's Church. It has nothing to do with sectarianism in any form whatever, but includes all truly regenerated people in Heaven and in earth in its membership, and all of the sanctified people in the world constitute the official board and the ordained ministry. The fires of the Holy Ghost when Jesus baptizes us utterly consume all humanisms which divide God's people, *e. g.*, lodgery, creeds, dogmatisms and all of the appurtenances of sects and denominations. Nothing but the wonderful efficacy of the cleansing blood in entire sanctification, and the refining fires of the Holy Ghost constantly by the blessed indwelling Comforter can effectually fortify God's Ecclesia against the contaminations of heterogeneous human dogmatisms.

(22.) "CARNALITY." This word is synonymous with depravity and means the old man of sin; the Satanic nature in the heart transmitted from the fall. The same is Ishmael whom God commanded Abraham to take away that he might not be an heir with Isaac in the patriarchal patrimony. The same is also Agag, the king of the Amalekites, who fought against Israel forty years to keep them out of the Promised Land. When God commanded Saul, in his royal representation of all Israel, to go and exterminate them, and he spared Agag and the best of the sheep and cattle that he might offer fat sacrifices to God, then He utterly cast him away, no longer answering him either in dreams or visions, nor by Urim and Thummim. Saul there drifted away and turned spiritualist, finally winding up his miserable life by suicide. Thus appallingly is illustrated the sad fate of every Christian who does not have Agag slain, *i. e.,* old Adam crucified and the body of sin utterly exterminated. Compromise with sin anywhere means ultimate damnation.

Saul had had a bright conversion. The Word positively says that "when he met the Lord's prophets God gave him another heart." He reigned over Israel forty years, making them a good king, both wise in counsel and valiant on the battle-field. In his case carnality took the form of self-will and never would fully let up; you see his awful end, dying on Mount Gilboa amid terrible and signal defeat and going down to a backslider's Hell. Let every one take warning and adopt the maxim of Cato, the great Roman statesman, with which he wound up every powerful speech, delivered in the Senate Oral

Chamber, "*Carthago delenda est*," "Carthage must be destroyed." Let us make a slight change in the phraseology and ring out now, and never compromise, "Carnality must be destroyed." You will find this booklet a blessing to you as the Holy Spirit will use it as a heart-searcher.

(23.) "JOHN THE BAPTIST AND THE APOSTLE PAUL." These were the two greatest preachers the world ever saw, except the Conqueror of Mount Calvary. They tower in their intellectual majesty, the lights of both dispensations. Though John lived and died in the Old, he proleptically enjoyed the Pentecostal experience of the New, being filled with the Holy Ghost from the womb of his mother, *i. e.*, sanctified wholly. Paul unfortunately backslid from his infantile justification, Rom. 7:9, "*I was alive at one time without law, but the commandment having come, sin revived and I died, and the commandment which is unto me for life the same was unto death, for sin having taken occasion through the commandment deceived me and by it slew me.*" Here we see that Paul, like every other son and daughter of Adam's fallen race, enjoyed justification through the normal grace of Christ, till he got old enough to know right from wrong, then his hereditary depravity rising up antagonized the law, causing him to become a transgressor and fall under condemnation.

He was reared up in a godly home and with the greatest possible educational facilities in the world of his day, not only graduating in the Greek College of Tarsus, but in the Hebrew Academies of Jerusalem. He became a great theologian, his extraordinary intellect and transcendent culture giving him a place in the Sanhedrim and at the front of the theocracy. But evidently all this time he was under the condemnation which supervened upon the forfeiture of his infantile justification above mentioned and thus preaching ahead in a backslidden state, till the lightning flashing from the glorified person of Jesus sent thunderbolts of conviction to his guilty soul, and prostrated him an importunate mourner in the house of Judas, till gloriously converted under the ministry of Ananias.

While preaching with all his might he soon realized the need of the second work and, going away into Arabia, where Moses sought it forty years and received it at the burning bush, he agonized in the burning sand three years, trying to get it by the law, until, giving up in utter desperation, he turned the body of sin over to Christ and immediately shouted the victory, Rom. 7:24. Then and there he was transformed into a cyclone of fire, flashing and flaming over Asia and Europe, till he lost his head at Nero's block, sweeping up to Heaven in a chariot of fire.

Oh, what worlds of spiritual detriment supervened to that mighty man because he lost his infantile justification! How signally contrastive was the experience of John the Baptist, who, instead of backsliding from his infantile justification, added to it the glorious experience of proleptical sanctification, actually entering into the Pentecostal power in anticipation, thus the greatest preacher the world has ever seen, his thrilling eloquence, stentorian oratory and fiery pathos literally magnetizing all who came within the sound of his trumpet voice, till he actually emptied the cities and populated the wilderness with the thronging multitudes, the rich on their camels, the middle classes on their donkeys, and the poor trudging along the dusty way on foot, from dewy morn to dusky eve. All this that they might hang spell-bound upon the lips of the paradoxical prophet of the wilderness.

You find at least an approximate solution of the problem in the fact that when Herod sent the soldiers to murder the babes of Bethlehem, Zachariah and Elizabeth took their son and fled into the wilderness and never came back. They reared him up in rural simplicity among the Essenes, the poor holiness people who lived there for the sake of room, peace and solitary communion with God.

Oh, how all of our Sunday-school teachers need awakening to the blessed feasability of having their pupils converted before they forfeit their infantile justification and then sanctified before they backslide, and do you not know that this is the very way to bring in the Millennium? You need this booklet to give you light and help you to study these glorious realities so delectably revealed in the precious Word.

(24.) "THEOLOGY VERSUS CREEDOLOGY." Our lands abound in theological schools. They are all misnamed, unless it is some of the Bible Schools conducted by the holiness people. They should be called "Creedological Schools," from the simple fact that they study the Bible in view of bending it to their creed, which is an awful mistake; it should be the reverse, *i. e.*, bending their creed to the Bible. There never was a creed made on earth till after the conversion of the Emperor Constantine, when, A. D. 325, they called the Æcumenical Council to Nice in Bithynia, over which the Emperor presided, sitting in a golden chair. The sudden promotion of the

Christians from the lion's mouth and the burning stake to the royal palace and the first places in the empire, revived carnality and superinduced the desire for a human creed. So long as they burnt them at the stake, and used them to fatten their lions, tigers and bears, they never thought of any creed but the New Testament, nor any doctrine but "Holiness to the Lord." The Council at Nice proved to be the prolific mother of all the creeds of Christendom and is still used in the Roman Catholic Church, the Episcopal being a modification and the Methodist an abstraction from that. There is no reason why every church in the world should not drop her creed this day and adopt the New Testament; not that we have any criticism for the Old, but we are not under that dispensation.

Theology is from two Greek words, *Theos,* God, and *logue,* speech; therefore it simply means the word of God. The Bible Schools, in the literal sense, are the only theological institutions we have, as all of the so-called theological colleges of the denominations really conserve their creed to which they are committed, making it the end in view to bend the Bible to it in order to bolster it up and sustain it, instead of bending their creed to the Bible, the thing pre-eminently reasonable and proper. If all denominations would drop their creeds and make the Bible their text book, perfectly independent of their creed, you would soon see a felicitious approximation either to other. These creeds have done more to sunder and alienate the body of Christ than any other influence. In heathen lands we now see an auspicious trend on the part of all denominations either to other. In great India, where I preached three months, I everywhere found an earnest call and a hearty welcome. You need this booklet to edify and post you in this great and important truth, *i. e.*, the absolute supremacy and sovereign independency of God's Word.

(25.) "THE SEVEN CHURCHES." You find them catalogued and described in the first three chapters of Revelation. These Churches consecutively represent Christendom, down to the glorious coming of the Lord. The Church at Ephesus represents the backslidden Apostolic institution. A whole generation had passed away into eternity after it was established by the labors of Paul, as John did his writing sixty-five years after our Lord's ascension; consequently the Pauline converts had mostly exchanged the battle-field for the mount of victory, whereas the new membership perhaps had never been so spiritual and zealous as their predecessors, while doubtless some of them had never been converted and others, though saved, had never received the Holy Ghost. We here have the sad revelation that they had lost their first love; consequently the Holy Ghost commands them to repent and do their first work over lest He come and take away their candlestick, *i. e.*, lest they actually lose their organization. This has been signally verified and that great and magnificent city of Ephesus has long ago become a heap of ruins.

Smyrna represents the Martyr Church during the first three hundred years, when, it is estimated, one hundred millions sealed their faith with their blood. If you read this scripture you will find that there is not a solitary charge against Smyrna. History says that they actually carried the Gospel to all nations, pushing the battle so heroically that they even got the emperor gloriously converted and, through his influence, sent their flaming heralds to the ends of the earth. God warns them that they shall suffer persecution ten days; that means ten different great persecutionary epochs, which broke out afresh at the expiration of every thirty years in which the reigning emperor always did his best for their extermination. But the more they killed them the more rapidly they spread to the ends of the earth.

Pergamos represents the proud Imperial Church which followed the martyr age, which wound up with the conversion of the emperor. The normal effect of this wonderful promotion to the royal palace, which ruled the whole world, was to gradually bring the world into the Church; and meanwhile millions of pagans were only nominally converted, responsive to the imperial edict, their priests turning Gospel ministers.

The Church of Thyatira symbolizes Roman Catholicism which followed the Constantinian age, actually paganizing Christianity by bringing in the worship of angels, the Virgin Mary and the canonization of saints. We see her reprimanded for tolerating that woman Jezebel who taught the people to eat things offered to idols and commit fornication, which means spiritual deflection from God and departure from entire sanctification, which brings us into the Bridehood, eternally discarding all earthly lovers.

Then we have the Church of Sardis, to which the Apostle positively says, *"Thou hast a name to live but art dead"* This is the awful state of spiritual death in which Luther, Wycliffe, Zwingle, Melancthon and Erasmus found the Church. However, John says that there are a few in it who have not defiled their garments and they shall walk with Him in white.

The sixth is the Church of Philadelphia, which symbolizes the great Lutheran Reformation of the sixteenth century, which brought a glorious sunburst on the black darkness which had filled the world a thousand years. If you will examine the paragraph descriptive of this Church, you will find not a solitary allegation against her.

Last of all we have the Church of Laodicea, which symbolizes the fallen Protestant denominations of the present day. God says to her, *"Would that thou wast either cold or hot, but because thou art neither cold nor hot, but lukewarm, therefore I will spue thee out of my mouth."* Thus you see lukewarm indifference is worse than outbreaking wickedness, because it makes people harder to save and surer of Hell. That is the awful state of things in the great Protestant churches this day. They are lukewarm, neither cold nor hot, but indifferent; therefore vastly harder to save than the poor victims of slumdom whose wretched condition has already given them a prelude of Hell. Now where is the Holiness Movement? You find it in the words *"Behold, I stand at the door and knock . . . ,"* Rev. 3:20. God help us to knock our best.

(26.) "MIGHTY TO SAVE." Isa. 62:1. Man has been denominated by philosophers, "The religious animal." When I traveled around the world I was profoundly impressed with the significant fact that all the heathen are, if possible, more religious than the Christians and the same is true with the Mohammedans, (who are practically heathen). They pray five times a day, even whenever they happened to be on ships packed with people, till it seemed that they could not get room for genuflection, yet they always found room and time to pray, and were utterly dead to all criticism.

The poor Hindus worship three hundred and thirty millions of gods. I found their temples and shrines everywhere and saw them worshiping and plunging into the holy rivers and tanks to wash their sins away.

The heathen world is crowded with altars, shrines, temples and gods, but the trouble is that none of them can save. Many heathens seem actually to entertain a correct idea of the one omnipotent God who created the world, yet, amid all their superabounding religious ceremonies, shrines and temples, they have no god that actually takes their sins away and saves them, but always their crushnig burden of a guilty conscience haunts them night and day. The most efficient preaching we can do among the heathen is faithfully to tell them that Jesus has actually taken away our sins and we know it. We may tell them as much as we will about the Bible and our God and the great truths of our religion, but they, as in India, have their bible, the Shastras, and their books, the Vedas, but no realization that their burden of sin is taken away. They travel on long pilgrimages for the privilege of baptism in the holy rivers, the Ganges and Jumna, but still have no consciousness of the burden removed, of a new heart and actual salvation.

Of course Christendom is full of religious forms and ceremonies, rites and legalisms, yet it is only comparatively few who, in utter and eternal abandonment of everything out of harmony with God's will, pray through and meet the omnipotent God in Christ, revealed by the Holy Ghost, get under the blood and, through receptive and appropriative faith in the infallible promises, actually reach the consciousness of personal salvation. These witnesses to Him, "Who is mighty to save," are comparatively few in Christendom and utterly minus in Pagandom. Yet this is the crowning glory of the wonderful Christ revealed in the Bible, *i. e.*, this matter of fact, of experimental realization that He veritably is mighty to save.

King Manasseh reigned in Jerusalem fifty-three years from his coronation to his death, including a period of several years which he spent in Babylonion captivity. Although his father was the great leader of the holiness movement, even travelling all over the country destroying idolatry and bringing all Israel back to Jehovah, yet, when Manasseh succeeded him, he not only went back into idolatry, leading the nation with him, but polluted the house of the Lord with idols and worshipped them there, filling all the land with idolatry and wickedness—an enormously aggravated case, as he led the whole nation into most horrific idolatry and all forms of wickedness. Consequently God let the king of Babylon carry him off in chains and torment and punish him awfully. Amid his deep distress and tortures in his captivity, he repented in sackcloth and ashes, and greatly humbled himself in the dust before God, fasting and weeping days, months and years. Thus he cried unto the Lord of his fathers to have mercy on him and forgive his sins. God heard his prayers while enduring the awful tortures his tormentors inflicted on him in his captivity, delivered him, brought him back to Jerusalem and reinstated him on his throne. After this he did his best to bring all of his people back to God to purify the country from idolatry. I mention this as an illustration of our Christ's omnipotency to save.

When Jesus preached in Gadara, you remember He saved the legionaire, actually casting out ten thousand demons. You see it was a clear and glorious case of actual salvation from that demoniacal arm. The man turned preacher and wanted to go with Jesus, as an apostle, but he was a Gentile and our Lord's Apostles were all Jews, who, in the gracious economy, were the first to receive the Gospel. So Jesus sent him, as you remember, to his own people to tell them the mighty work which He had done for him. History says that he proved exceedingly efficient, preaching all over that country.

Pella was one of the ten cities in that country (Decapolis, *deca,* "ten," and *polis,* "city"), to which the Christian Jews fled when Jerusalem was destroyed and their nationality exterminated, and history says they found a joyous welcome by a great number of Gentile disciples who had been saved through the preaching of the legionaire. So you will find this booklet, "Mighty to Save," helpful to you, energizing your faith in Him, "who is mighty to save."

(27.) "GOD'S TRIPLE LEADERSHIP." Man is a trinity, consisting of spirit, soul and body. Harmonical with this trinity is the Divine leadership, His providence lealing the body, His Word the soul, and His Spirit the human spirit. Oh, the unutterable beauty and glory of the redemptive scheme! It is absolutely inscrutable and incomprehensible, verily passing all understanding. No soul can offer the slightest apology at the judgment bar, when turned away to the awful doom of endless woe, from the simple fact that the gracious economy is so transcendently complete and perfect in all its phases and ramifications, as forever to sweep from the field every vestige of apology. Our probation involves constant and awful temptation from the simple fact that we have a most formidable enemy who never sleeps. Besides, he is co-operated by countless millions of sleepless myrmidons. While our enemy is great, our Friend is infinitely and inconceivably greater. Therefore we have nothing to do but give Him a chance and be true. Victory comes along all the time as a normal sequence of our loyalty to the omnipotent Conqueror of Mt. Calvary.

God's providence faithfully manages my body, just where He wants me to be; just as safe on the other side of the world as in the dear "Old Kentucky Home." Neither barbarians, savages, wild beasts, railroad wrecks nor ocean storms, cholera nor small-pox, can destroy this body till its work is done, if I abide in the center of His sweet will, from which I would infinitely rather die than to deflect an iota.

God's precious and infallible Word leads my intellect. I must be studious and industrious as He has commanded me, 2. Tim. 2:15, *"Study to show thyself approved of God, a workman not to be ashamed, rightly dividing the Word of Truth."* Therefore I am to be an assiduous student, sitting at the feet of Jesus, meek, humble and lowly; pride, vanity, egotism and my own ways consumed by the fires of the Holy Ghost, meanwhile, like little Samuel, saying, *"Speak, Lord, for thy servant heareth."* Since old Adam has been crucified, I am dead to every voice but that which rings down from the effulgent throne. As the Bible is my only Guide, like John Wesley, I am truly *homo unius libri,* a man of one book; meanwhile I avail myself of the multitudinous human teachers He has given me expository of His precious Word.

The Holy Spirit is the only leader of my spirit. We are all in eminent danger of seduction and delusion by evil spirits, playing the Holy Ghost. They are more easily detected and exposed than we generally think. If you follow them, they will quickly lead you to do something out of God's Word and providence, which is a certain evidence of their Satanic identity. As God made my body, mind and spirit, His leadership will always be characteristic of this beautiful triple harmony. These evil spirits will lead you into fanaticism, where you will ignore God's Word and providence, which is a certain evidence that you are on your way to ruin. Satan is now stirring earth and Hell to ruin the holiness people by deflecting them from the straight and narrow way of "Holiness to the Lord." You need this booklet to instruct you in reference to this wonderful and glorious triple leadership, which is our only security from the side-tracking, derailing and ditching devices of the enemy, who is constantly hounding the track of every soul who has escaped out of his clutches. He will capture you soon or late, if you are not true to God's triple leadership.

These twenty-seven dime booklets, which you get for so little money that you cannot miss it, will furnish you a splendid library, not only posting you in the great Bible truths of full salvation, but fortifying you against the myriad Satanic devices which lurk around you, and hang upon your track like the lightning upon the skirts of the clouds, constantly ready to strike you dead with a thunderbolt forged in the arsenals of damnation. Besides, you ought to keep a supply of them to loan to your friends. That is the reason why they are made so cheap, that every friend of Jesus can financially well afford to keep a circulating library. Oh, what a light will you be in your neighborhood, always ready to put in the hand of your neighbor the very book he needs for conviction, conversion, sanctification, establishment, and fortification against this heresy or that. If you had a supply of these twenty-seven dime booklets for loan, having people return them after reading a few times, studying and understanding them, reading one and then another and so on until they had read them all, what good you might do. These booklets are much condensed, so that they contain as much truth as many of the dollar books now in circulation, meanwhile their brevity qualifies you to read them through in a little spare time, then to re-read and study till you actually appropriate the truth so that you can use it for the glory of God in preaching the everlasting Gospel.

SECTION NINE.

"Around the World, Garden of Eden, Latter-day Prophesies, and Missions."

It is not at all probable that you will ever travel round the world, as not more than one in a million is likely to make that greatly arduous and expensive tour. Therefore you cannot afford not to avail yourself of this journey by proxy. The Lord gave me an extraordinary memory and a splendid education, which I have industriously endeavored to use for His glory. Three times has He permitted me to travel in Europe, Asia and Africa and preach the Gospel, 1895, 1899 and 1905-6. In all of these tours I have availed myself of every possible opportunity to get acquainted with everything which will be a matter of interest to the reader. Therefore in this large volume you will find an epitome of universal history, from the days of the patriarchs down to the present. I became a good reader at the early age of six years and especially fond of history, which I read much and have remembered all my life. In this book you will find the most important historic epitome of all the prominent nations of the earth, as I purposely took them in my route, England, France, Italy, Greece, Turkey, Syria, the Holy Land, Egypt, Abyssinia, Abrabia, Persia, India, Oceania, China, Japan and the Hawaiian Islands. Therefore the historic phase of this book will absolutely prove to you invaluable, giving you most important facts appertaining to all of the nations, perhaps as much as you can remember. Therefore it ought to be in your home for your children to read and study. You need it also as a priceless auxiliary to Bible study. In this respect you will find it more helpful than you think. Among the forty-three chapters, constituting that large and elegantly cloth-bound book of about six hundred pages, you will find about a dozen chapters directly expository of Biblical history. You will find so vast an amount of information in it which you will not likely strike anywhere else that you cannot afford to forego the infinite benefit which you will see by a careful perusal and study of that variant and comprehensive history.

Besides, the book will give you an acquaintance with our mission fields, which will prove delightfully edifying and at the same time impart an inspiration which will profitably react in copious blessings on your soul and conduce to the enlargement of your philanthropy, broadening your spiritual horizon and bringing you into closer proximity and more immediate sympathy with our dear brothers and sisters toiling in the regions beyond, while God, in His condescending mercy, is using them to evangelize the millions sitting in darkness and in the shadow of death.

You will find in the book five large chapters on great India, which is now visited with the Pentecost for which the missionaries have been praying and toiling for a third of a century. As the Lord permitted me to travel six thousand miles in the great interior, visiting the mission fields and preaching for them, you will be much interested in the information you will there reach. You will also be much interested in the two chapters on China and the two on Japan, as well as those on Oceania and the Hawaiian Islands. I have all my life been studying and trying to locate the Garden of Eden. I realize that the Lord has revealed it to me. In this book you will find a chapter on that subject, expounding and locating it.

SECTION TEN.

My "Autobiography."

In this history of my life, you will find a variety of almost everything. Many questions which you would find it difficult to answer by reading any of my other books, you will see solved in this. My life has been quite stormy and eventful. My providential deliverance from the vices and follies so fatal to childhood and youth will prove helpful to parents in protecting their children from these terrible pitfalls of Satan. The prosecution of a thorough collegiate education, despite the greatest financial impediments, will prove an inspiration to the youth thirsting for the blessings of a classical education. The clear and definite spiritual experiences which God, in His mercy, gave me, regeneration at the age of sixteen and sanctification at thirty-five, will prove instructive, encouraging and inspiring to pilgrims beating their march to the Better Land, and especially to inquirers after the way of truth, peace and holiness.

My ten years' war with the Campbellites will be luminous to all the people who desire true light and available instruction on the controverted subject of baptism. Along these lines the multitudes stand in imperative need of solid and reliable information, helping them out of the difficulties in which Satan's sophistries and fallacies have entangled them.

My war with the Seventh Day Adventists, the Holy Spirit will use helpfully to people who are entangled with those heresies.

The many revivals rehearsed during the long years of incessant war with Satan, especially in the great South, will be used by the blessed Holy Spirit as an encouragement and inspiration to the young people now engaged in the same conflict.

While I have thus been briefly sketching over my books I remember one whose name I have not yet mentioned, *i. e.*, "JESUS IS COMING." It is a nice little cloth bound volume which sells for twenty-five cents. It has received quite an extensive circulation and has been a blessing to thousands. You will find it exceedingly helpful as an exposition of the prophecies, expounding the ages and epochs and periods, and showing conclusively that we are living in the time of the end, and that the prophecies have been so fulfilled that we have even reason to be on the constant outlook for our Lord's glorious appearing to take away His waiting Bride.

In this catalogue of my writings, it is pertinent to observe that my "BAPTISM," which has received a very extensive circulation and is still much in demand, is out of print because the publishers have lost the stereotypes. They are hunting for them diligently and say that if they do not find them soon, they will make more; therefore the people may rely on the circulation of the book as in former years.

These books and booklets, all told, number forty-eight, if we are not mistaken. Many of the dear saints are exceedingly anxious to have them all in their private library. This is certainly a very wise decision on their part, as in that way they will avail themselves of my whole life of constant toil, amid extraordinary opportunities. If we did not avail ourselves of the knowledge accumulated by our predecessors, we would make very slow progress and accumulate but little during this fleeting life. In that way the world is constantly growing wiser, every generation availing itself of the achievements wrought by its predecessors. My successors ought to transcend me in the accumulation of knowledge, because they have the benefit of my long life of constant labor, amid circumstances exceedingly favorable to the acquisition of knowledge. The rising generation has ample opportunities from my books, substantially to receive and appropriate and utilize everything that I have ever learned. This is God's method of transmitting the inspired oracles from generation to generation. 2 Tim. 2:1, *"Therefore, thou, my child, be filled with dynamite in the grace which is in Christ Jesus, and whatsoever thou hast learned with me through many witnesses, commit thou these things to faithful people, who shall be able also to teach others."* We thus learn God's truth and then teach others, and so it goes on from sire to son, indefinitely to the latest generation.

My books are plain and easily understood. Therefore with reasonable industry, the rising generation can substantially learn everything I know, thus availing themselves of my long life of constant toil, amid facilities and environments exceedingly favorable to the acquisition of knowledge. The books written in our day are easier for the present generation to understand than those of bygone ages, whose language has largely become obsolete. All living languages are constantly undergoing changes; therefore the writings of your contemporaries will be more easily understood than those who lived several generations ago. Besides, we have the benefit of the great and important discoveries which have been made in the realms of science, art, literature and also Biblical exegesis. The scholars of the present day know some things of great importance revealed in the Bible, which John Wesley and his contemporaries did not know, because important discoveries have been made since their day, correcting errors in the Scriptures which they knew nothing about. As my greatest desire is to transmit to my successors all of the knowledge I have accumulated in a long life of assiduous study, I am very anxious that they shall have the full benefit of my books. In one respect I feel, as many able preachers have told me, that my writings convey more truth in the same space than any they ever saw. My small books are especially distinguished for the characteristic, *multum in parvo, i. e.,* "much in little," conveying a heap of truth in a few words. My large books you will find cheaper in proportion to their contents than any others in circulation.

SECTION ELEVEN.

Divine Healing.

My experience along the line of bodily healing abundantly corroborates the great fact that God is the only Healer. He made the body as well as the soul, consequently He alone knows how to repair them both, when out of order. While He is the only Healer, it does not follow that physicians are not useful in their place. We need them for diagnosing, *i. e.,* to tell us what the disease is. As they have made the human body their lifelong study, of course they have knowledge appertaining to this mysterious organism which those who have not the benefit of a medical education do not possess.

When I was seventy years old, I fell and broke my arm till it just turned back like a broken stick. I immediately hastened to a physician who set it and braced it, putting no medicine on it whatever. Then, at my suggestion, he gladly knelt with me in prayer and we turned it over to the Great Physician to heal it. I went on preaching, carrying it in a sling. At the expiration of six weeks I returned to him. He took the bandage off, which he had put on it, removed the braces, and behold, it was well, and not a scar surviving. He was delighted to see that it had grown together precisely right, not leaving a ridge nor any other mark to survive as a memento of the former breakage. Without that medical attention, in view of my age, I would very likely have lost the use of it the balance of my life. Yet he applied no medicine to execute the healing, but left it with the Lord alone, therefore, you see I needed him to do a mechanical work, which my friends could not have done, as they would neither have known how to set it or brace it.

In 1901, while preaching in Fresno, California, I lost my life by the inhalation of illuminating gas escaping in my room and was found dead the next morning at ten o'clock. As I am not in the habit of taking breakfast, they did not look for me at the table, but as I did not come downstairs, the lady of the house, feeling a little uneasy, at ten o'clock went up and rapped at my door, but received no response. Then opening she looked in and saw my shoes and knew I was there, but instantly became affrighted because she could not make me speak. Felicitously I was enjoying the hospitality of Dr. Meux, a good holiness friend, who also believed in Divine Healing. Fortunately he was at home, when his good wife ran down the stairway and told him that I was speechless. He ran up instantly and meeting the gas suspected the trouble and upon examination found that all breathing had ceased and he had a dead man on his hands. Instantly he resorted to what physicians call artificial respiration, and after vigorous efforts within a very short time he saw me catch my breath, thus resuming the respiration.

I knew not my whereabouts till forty hours from the time of my retirement had elapsed. He said that without the mechanical operation, which he brought into availability, I certainly never would have breathed again. I am satisfied that I was out of my body.

My experience during the time reminds me of Paul in 2 Cor. 12, when at Lystra they stoned him to death, and God raised him up again to go on and finish his work. He said that he was caught up to the third heaven, (*i. e.*, the heaven of saints and angels, the atmosphere being the first heaven and the astronomical spheres the second) where he saw and heard things impossible to tell,—not unlawful, as the English Version has it, for there was no law against telling it. But it was impossible to tell, because we cannot reveal heavenly glories through the medium of mortal language. The most of our language here is metaphorical and symbolical, in order to reach us in these material tenements. Not so in Heaven, where there is no material body but all is spirituality. There the language is all lightning, without taking time to thunder. I verily believe that I was out of the body, as when I found myself in it and again in this world, I deeply realized a mysterious alienation from transitory things. I resorted at once to prayer, asking God to put His hand on me and re-adapt me to the work He still had for me to do in this world, as I felt that my congeniality for probationary life had been marred.

During the time of my alienation from the body, I heard and saw things which were utterly impossible for me to tell, *e. g.*, music most sweet and delicious, but I could tell nothing about it, and I especially had an unutterable sweetness in my own soul. I believe I was dead and God used that noble physician to raise me to life again. As a rule, the resurrections in the Bible took place very quickly after the expiration, the four days in the case of Lazarus being quite an exception.

God, in His wonderful mercy, has healed my body so frequently that time would fail me to tell you all about it. I will only give you a few salient, illustrative cases. His healing has been so prompt and speedy, that I have spent almost no time in my whole life on a sick bed.

Thirty-four years ago, two eminent physicians, graduates of Cincinnati Medical College, gave me up to die of serious lung trouble, which had developed into conjestion of the lungs by the inundation of the blood from the system, so flooding them as to stop respiration in the air cells, the breathing only continuing in the *trachea bronchia* and the larger air tubes. I was in a protracted meeting working hard and was suddenly attacked so severely that the friends called a physician and he became alarmed and sent for another to assist him in a case which he regarded as exceedingly critical. All pulsation had ceased in my members. They, assisted by a number of the brothers and sisters, labored six hours in the vain attempt by external friction and internal stimulants to stop the congestion, and restore the circulation. Then our family physician coming to me, notified me that I would be dead in two hours at most, and was liable to die at just any moment. Then both physicians and all the people quit their efforts to restore the circulation and just waited to see me die; meanwhile the papers reported that I was dead.

I had been in the sanctified experience four years, but my dear wife had not entered Beulah Land. Though naturally timid, and having no experience in leading meetings, she at once took command of the crowd and observed, "These doctors have given my husband up to die, but I am not willing to let him go, and believe the Lord has much work for him to do yet, so get on your knees all of you and join me in prayer for his healing, that we may prevail with the Great Physician to come and take the case in hand, as I know He can heal him." The dear woman had no light on Divine Healing except what the Holy Spirit gave her, as at that time there was nothing said about it. She kept them all on their knees, (and there was quite a crowd, as all of my members who had heard came at once,) exhorting them like a holiness evangelist conducting an altar service, to hold on, assuring them that the Lord would heal me. It is an obvious fact that the blessed Holy Spirit had imparted to her the gift of faith for my healing. The doctors said they knew no one to survive pulsation more than eight hours. Already when they ceased to minister for my healing and communicated to me the information of my speedy departure, six hours had elapsed since I had gone into the conjestion. Therefore all were watching the clock on the mantel which would soon tell the last moment the doctors said I could live. But when the two hours had flown, instantaneously the healing came. The conjestion gave away and the blood began to flow from my heart out through the arteries into my members and the veins resumed their office, carrying it back to the heart, and thus complete restoration of the circulatory organs at once supervened. I then spoke to our family physician, standing twenty feet away and looking on me, every moment expecting me to cease breathing, and said, "Doctor, I am healed." He instantly leaped to my bedside, snatched up my arm and examined my pulse, responding, "That's so, you're healed. Your pulse is going all right and healthy. You are a well man." In three days I mounted my horse and went away preaching and have been at it ever since. I have consulted physicians in reference to the conjestion of the lungs. They all tell me it is very difficult to cure and when relieved nearly certain to come back. The Great Physician certainly did give me a miraculous cure on that occasion, as I have never had any lung trouble of any kind since. I have been preaching constantly these thirty-four years, and frequently four to six times a day. I suppose I have done more speaking than any other man in the world in this time and never had any lung trouble.

It is pertinent here to say that when the doctor found I was healed, he fell on the floor and poured forth gushing tears of penitence, entreating the dear saints whose prayers had been answered in my healing at once to unite for his soul, that the Great Physician who had come and healed the body of his patient, should in condescending mercy save his soul. He was a church member, but, as he confessed, not saved.

There is no mistake about it, this wonderful Savior certainly healed my body.

As I was preaching in Texas twenty-two years ago, I was stricken down suddenly with an awful attack of rheumatism. In two minutes after it struck me I was utterly incompetent to stand on my feet or walk. I continued preaching, going on crutches. The Lord wonderfully healed me. Though I have never since enjoyed my full former activity, yet I have no rheumatic trouble and am considered an extraordinary example of pedestrian power and activity. After He healed me it was two or three years before the pain ceased to visit me ever and anon, apparently a mere souvenir of by-gone dominion. When it would strike me, whether in the night suddenly waking me or in the day time instantaneously halting me in a peregrination, I made it a rule at once to put my hand on the place and turn it over to the Great Physician, asking Him to speak to it and bid it depart. As a rule it would go at least in two or three minutes. It has been many years since I have been troubled with the unwelcome visitor.

About a dozen years ago, a troublesome sore, which had come on my body under my clothing continued to get worse and being denuded gave me much annoyance by the friction of my clothing. One day at the dinner table of Dr. Kelley, a cousin of mine, an eminent physician practicing in Portland, Oregon, I told him about it. He said, "Cousin Will, after dinner I will examine it." Upon examination he said, "Cousin, that is a cancer and the thing for you to do is to go at once to Cincinnati, and have it cut out. We could do it here, but you are too far from home for a surgical operation." Then he wrote me a letter to hand to the surgeons in Cincinnati (with whom he was well acquainted, as they had educated him) turning me over to them for the removal of the cancer. Then he proceeded to put a bandage on it for my comfort, preventing the friction of the clothing. Here you see how we still need physicians, mechanically as well as diagnostically and hygenically. He did not put any medicine on it nor insinuate that his treatment would cure it, but simply administered to my present comfort, by fortifying it against friction, which I had labored in vain to do. I had then a large round of appointments on the Pacific Coast, and through the great interior, which I had promised to serve before returning home. Therefore, instead of obeying the order of my dear cousin of the healing art, I went at once to the Great Physician, and turned over the cancer to Him. I realized my utter dependence on the Holy Ghost to inspire my faith for present healing, but He did it and I so realized. I went on preaching in Oregon and let the bandage stay till it wore off, which was about a month. Then I looked in vain for my cancer. It had disappeared, and left only the scar, which I carry to-day, the souvenir of my unwelcome visitor. I found quite a test of my faith in the healing of this cancer. I actually had to heroically face the music and take the bit in my teeth, soliloquizing, "Jesus, I believe you've healed this cancer," and there abide and refuse to doubt. Then I was enabled to appropriate His current axiom, during His ministry, Matt. 9:29, *"As your faith is, so be it unto you."*

There is no mistake as to the great Bible doctrine of bodily healing. You will find it in the commission which our Lord gave the twelve Apostles, and also in that of the seventy disciples. He commands them all to heal the sick, as well as to cast out demons.

When I was embarking from New York for my

around the world tour, I was advised to carry a little cholera medicine, as it is so common in the countries I contemplated visiting. The Lord had given me wonderful health till I reached Rangoon, Burmah, a country celebrated for the prevalence of that terrible destroyer. Two of my young men had suffered with it in India. Sure enough it struck me suddenly and unexpectedly. I at once took the medicine, but am satisfied it did not stay in my stomach a minute, as the eructation was such that it was utterly impossible to receive anything internally. I need not attempt to describe the sufferings characteristic of cholera. Therefore I will leave you to your own imagination, and advise you to ask the Lord to save you from an attack.

When it seemed to me that I was certainly face to face with the King of Terrors, (who had no terror for me), the Texas boys took hold of me and cried to God for my healing. As they held on, one of them spoke out and said that he had heard from Heaven that I was healed, and the other two soon joined him in their testimony. Cholera does its work quickly, and there was no time to hunt a physician. Eleven days subsequently, when I was convalescing quite slowly, much impeded by the climate, as I was not only in the torrid zone, but had by this time reached the Equator, where the heat was almost killing me in the terribly prostrate condition in which cholera had left me, God made Dr. West, presiding elder at Singapore, a great blessing to my feeble body. Well can I say, *"In Thee we live, and move, and have our being."* As I am now seventy-three years old, my bodily organs are failing, and if He did not keep His hand on this frail tenement night and day, I would break down and die. Oh, how wonderfully He keeps me, and enables me to do more work than almost any young man. I am a continual astonishment to myself; but it is all His keeping power.

During all of my ministry, especially since the Lord sanctified me thirty-eight years ago, I have constantly served Him in the ministry of bodily healing, as well as soul saving. Throughout the South I have preached much in the malarial regions, where distressing fevers of every kind abound. The Lord has everywhere used me in the ministry of healing. In countless instances I have prayed for the people burning with fever, and it abated at once, and they got up and came to meeting.

I was called to hold a protracted meeting in Central Georgia. When I began I found a goodly number beautifully clear in regeneration, but not sanctified. I began at once to preach that glorious doctrine, corroborating it by my testimony to the experience, when the pastor spoke out in the presence of all the people, boldly antagonizing me. Of course I did not strive with him a moment, as I had to respect his office and authority; but I inwardly turned him over to God and cried, though inaudibly, to God to put His hand on him and help me out of the difficulty. I realized my audience in Heaven and entered into inward rest, feeling assured that God would manage the man and conserve His own cause. In twenty-four hours we missed him out of the meetings, and the news came that he was sick. I went to see him. He saluted me kindly and said, "Bro. Godbey, I am attacked with this bad fever and will not likely be with you any more in the meetings." I said, "My dear brother, Jesus is here to-day and ready to rebuke your fever as He did that which burnt Peter's mother-in-law." I fell on my knees and putting my hand on him turned him over to the blessed Omnipotent Healer. While I was praying I felt the abatement of the fever, as his body began to cool off and the perspiration to come out.

I went away to the meeting and had only passed through the introductory songs and prayers when he arrived and took the meeting out of my hand, electrifying the congregation with his thrilling testimony to bodily healing, (which was little known in that country), telling them of how he was burning, as if in a furnace, and I had prayed for him and told him how to trust Jesus for healing, and his fever was gone, and the perspiration was on his body, which in that region is regarded as *prima facie* evidence that the fever is gone to stay. Then suddenly running to the altar he shouted as he went, "Now, Brother Godbey, I want that other thing you have been talking about." His congregation followed him as the flock follows the shepherd. He and many others got gloriously sanctified, and he is a leader in the Movement to-day.

You will always find bodily healing a powerful auxiliary of soul saving. In all of your peregrinations, never fail to visit the sick and pray for their healing. In that way you will reach many wicked people, otherwise utterly out of your reach.

When I was conducting the Free Methodist Campmeeting at Emporia, Kansas, among the people who received bodily healing was a dumb woman who had not spoken in two and a half years, dear Sister Jones, the wife of a Free Methodist preacher. While I was laboring with the seekers at the altar, who had come on the invitation for bodily healing, and they had all risen with bright faces and some of them even shouting testimonies, this one sister continued at the altar. I did not at that time identify her as the dumb one, but then the presiding elder in an undertone notified me, as I appealed to her and received no answer, that she was the dumb sister and he had never heard her voice, and she was seeking the healing of her dumbness. Then I appealed to her straight: "Believe, my sister, that Jesus now heals your dumbness and gives you back your speech which you lost two and a half years ago. John Wesley says, 'We are to believe that He doeth it.'" Then she became exceedingly energized, evidently exercising all her spiritual powers of abandonment, supplication and faith, at the same time falling back on the carpet and turning her face Heavenward, the movement of her mouth indicating the prayer of her heart. Then I saw a light flash over her face, and her eyes sparkle with preternatural brilliancy; when suddenly she leaped to her feet and shouted louder than I could and running up and down the aisle continued to shout aloud. All the people present knew her and were so excited that they shouted aloud with her.

When the noise somewhat abated, a fine looking man arose and asked permission to speak, which was freely granted. He proceeded to state that he was that woman's physician, and had done everything in his power to restore her voice, even taking her off to cities and having her treated by specialists, and he just wanted to testify that her healing was a miracle of the Lord. Oh, how that miraculous case of healing did stir the city and boom the camp-meeting! It is a great mistake of the Lord's people to neglect bodily healing.

Some of our beloved holiness people tell us that healing is not for sinners, but only for Christians. This is a mistake, as you see in the case of the ten lepers whom our Savior healed, only the one who turned back and shouted out his joyous testimony being saved. In case of sinners, we should always give the preference to the salvation of their souls, and never encourage them to seek healing and leave out the salvation, because it may be that God needs the temporal affliction to bring them to repentance, and save them from Hell. We should never fail to visit the sick and pray for their healing, but in case of the unconverted, we should show them the infinite value of their souls above their bodies, and exhort them to repent and seek the pardoning mercy of God and bodily healing, too, assuring them of His abounding love in using the disease to bring them to repentance and make it an auxilary to their salvation. If God did not heal the wicked, they would soon all be dead, because He is the only Healer, and all mortals are full of diseases, of which sickness is simply their development. Oh, how amiable the attitude of a Gospel preacher coming with the panacea of all human woe, healing not only the soul but the body. While Satan is the author of all physical ailments, of every form and phase, the transcendent victory of Christ is gloriously illustrated in the sanctification of all diseases and physical ailments and disabilities to our spiritual good. If everybody were to enjoy perfect health to the end of life and drop dead suddenly with no time to repent, very few would be saved. Such is the awful power of sin, the dominion of Satan and the alarming potency of temptation, that we need aches, pains, fevers, chills, wounds and bruises to keep us constantly reminded of our mortality, on the lookout for death and therefore robed and ready every minute to meet the Lord.

All of these sufferings, with the misfortunes and apparent calamities of this transitory life, are included in the "all things" that work together for good to them that love God with divine love. The same is true of Satan and all his myrmidons. Surely God makes them a blessing to His true people. This probation is full of mysteries, which we will never comprehend in this dark valley of sin and sorrow, but will perfectly understand when we reach the glorious Beyond.

I here give you the key to this great problem of Divine Healing. Rom. 8:11, *"And if the Spirit of Him who raised up Jesus from the dead dwell in you, He that raised up Jesus Christ from the dead will also create life in your mortal bodies through His Spirit who dwelleth in you."*

As above observed, this is the key that unlocks the mystery and solves the problem of Divine Healing. The normal attitude of bodily healing is with the sanctified who have the Holy Ghost dwelling in them. As the soul is the man proper, and the body only the tenement, therefore the normal economy of grace first administers full salvation to the soul and afterward heals the body so long as God willeth our abiding in it. The bodily healing of the unsanctified is His superabounding mercy. *"This is my will, even your sanctification."* 1 Thess. 4:3. Therefore the normal economy is to save and sanctify all who will humbly and appreciatively reciprocate the gracious interventions of the Holy Ghost, now, through the intercession of the glorified Christ, freely given to all as a Convictor of the wicked, Regenerator of the penitent and Sanctifier of the believer, and an indwelling Comforter of the sanctified; *e. g.*, you are living in a house in Cincinnati, a break appears in the roof, and you have it repaired, then you find another in the wall and calling in the mechanics you have it repaired at your own expense; the chimney falls down, and you have it rebuilt, and so you keep on repairing your house. But the time will come when your house is really out of kilter and every passer-by recognizes that is needs repairing again, and still you are not doing it, though the dilapidation is getting worse all the time. Then what do your neighbors think about it? Why, they have entirely quit talking about it, because they have all settled down in the conclusion that you are not going to repair it any more, but take it down and build a new one.

The application is easy. The Holy Ghost is dwelling with me in my tenement of clay. It has often been seriously out of kilter and He has repaired it. Thirty-four years ago physicians gave it up and took hands off, leaving it to die of lung trouble in its worst form. He repaired it so perfectly that I have never had a vestige of that ailment since. Sciatic rheumatism twenty-two years ago disqualified me to walk a step without a crutch. He, so far as I can tell, perfectly repaired my body, so I am entirely free from rheumatism. Twelve years ago the physicians pronounced a troublesome sore on my body a cancer, and told me I must have it cut out as quickly as possible. I turned it over to the Great Physician, who took it away, leaving only the scar as a souvenir of His mighty work. I have, in cases innumerable, been so afflicted that I was utterly disqualified for work, and He healed me suddenly. When conducting a Free Methodist Camp-meeting, ten years ago and surrounded by the presiding elder and all of his pastors, they had me teaching the Bible morning and afternoon, and preaching every night, leaving them for the street preaching and the altar work. I got up in the morning and found my body so violently attacked that it would have been impossible for me to have attended any of the meetings. I had a good old Free Methodist preacher get down by me, put his hands on me and pray for my healing; which came, so far as I could tell, at the very moment, at least the ailment left me and returned no more and I went along in the three meetings that day.

God has so wonderfully healed me and done it so quickly that I have lost less time from His work, perhaps, than any other person you can find. In the above instances of healing, I stopped longer in the case of that lung trouble than any other, and that was only five days. While my heart is full of praises for His miraculous healing, which is not speaking extravagantly, as He is a God of miracles, and they have not ceased, as some say, I am assured that if He does not soon appear and translate me, as I am constantly watching and waiting, the time will come when this body will be out of kilter in some way, and perhaps in many, and He will not heal it. Why? Because the house will be no longer worth repairing and my work will be done, the battle over and the victory won, then I will know Heaven is nigh and begin to shout the approaching triumph.

"Some morning fair I am going away,
And not get back till millennial day,"

For I know I have another building not made with hands.

You see the danger of running the doctrine of Divine Healing into fanaticism. I have known good holiness people to make this serious mistake. They pray for the sick, anointing them with oil, laying hands on them, and because they do not get well, they so vehemently labor to get them to believe for healing that they actually reflect on their faith to their spiritual detriment, and almost make them believe that they are backsliders, because they do not get healed.

N. B. We are saved and sanctified by the grace of faith, Eph. 2:8; Acts 26:8; but we are healed by the gift of faith, 1 Cor. 12:9. Now remember these extraordinary spiritual gifts, which you find in the Pauline catalogue, 1 Cor. 12:8-11, are not necessary to salvation, as we are saved by grace and not by gifts. The normal attitude of these gifts contemplates our efficiency in the salvation of others. Therefore when your work is done and God is going to take you to Heaven you will have no faith for your healing. The promise of your faith, "so be it unto you," Matt. 9:29, is just as true of the body as the soul. The grace by which we are saved is constant and abides forever; while the gifts are bestowed for the immediate emergency, pursuant to the sovereign discriminating grace of God. Hence you see the perfect harmony of Divine Healing with the fact that we do not always get healed, for if we did we would never get to Heaven. When God is ready for us to go to Heaven, the Holy Spirit, the Custodian of His own gifts, will no longer impart to us the gift of healing. Therefore we will have no faith for healing. When the Lord healed me of lung congestion, rheumatism, cancer, cholera and other incidental ailments too numerous to mention, I had faith for healing and He did it according to my faith. Matt. 9:29. But if He tarrieth the time is near when I will have physical trouble again and no faith for healing. Then I will begin to shout, because I will know Heaven is nigh and I am fast approaching the sacramental millions beyond.

"My latest sun is sinking fast,
My race is nearly run;
My strongest trials now are past;
My triumph is begun.

CHORUS.

"Oh, come, angel bands,
And bear me away
On your snowy wings
To my immortal home.

"I know I am nearing the holy ranks
Of friends and kindred dear,
I have brushed the dews of Jordan's banks,
The crossing must be near.

"Oh, bear my longing heart to Him,
Who bled and died for me,
Whose blood now cleanseth from all sin,
And gives me victory.

"I know I am nearing my Heavenly home;
My spirit loudly sings,
The holy ones, behold they come,
I hear the noise of wings.

When you find the saints are no longer competent to exercise faith for their healing, instead of discouraging them you ought to shout with them. They have no faith for healing because God is going to give them Heaven this time instead of health, which is infinitely better. Therefore, it is a time of rejoicing.

I saw this vividly illustrated about ten years ago, when arriving at Scottsville Camp-meeting, Texas, and finding Pastor Lively, who had been sanctified in my first meeting in the state in 1884, prostrate with that stubborn malarial fever. Gathering around him his wife and daughter and other saints, we prayed for his healing; myself and sister receiving faith for him and telling him so. He had settled down under the conclusion that he had to lie there and go through a routine of medicine, break down and go through disease, spending a month on his bed, as was usual. I exhorted him with all my might to exercise present faith for his healing, assuring him that it was his privilege to have it now. Then leaving him alone with the Lord and still holding on to God to inspire his faith and heal him, I ran away to the bedside of Father Scott, nearly eighty years old, and prayed for his healing, but received no faith. When I was about bidding him good-bye, he said to me, "Brother Godbey, tell the Camp-meeting people to pray for my soul, but not for my body; for my good wife died this year, and, if God will, I prefer not to be healed, but to go on and join her in the bright upper world where I will never suffer again."

I hastened back to the parsonage, as my faith for Brother Lively's healing was actually booming. On arrival I looked on the vacated bed. He had been healed and jumped off with a shout and ran out to the Campground, where, as usual, he stood in the front of the battle during the ensuing campaign. Of course Father

Scott went to Heaven and I never saw him afterward.

You cannot be too diligent and indefatigable in your visitation of the sick. That is God's auspicious time to make you a blessing both to their souls and their bodies. It is better to obey the Word in the use of the olive oil, anointing them, although the oil has nothing to do with healing them; it says *"the prayer of faith shall save the sick."* The utility of the oil is to symbolize the Holy Ghost, who imparts the gift of faith for healing. The oil in bodily healing is precisely what the water is in salvation. Both oil and water are symbols of the Holy Ghost, the former in bodily healing and the latter in the salvation of the soul. Thus you should invariably visit the sick and obey the Scriptures, putting hands on them, anointing them, and praying for their healing, assured that God will answer your prayer and give them either health or Heaven. Therefore do not think your prayer is in vain if they are not healed, for Heaven is infinitely more desirable than health. Of course when you do not happen to have the oil, never make an excuse for not helping the sick, as it has no more to do with the healing than water baptism has to do with salvation.

As Christian workers, you not only need the gift of healing for the sick, but all of the nine gifts, recorded in 1 Cor. 12:8-11, as the other eight all appertain to spiritual salvation. How can I procure these gifts? Get in position to receive them and then, in utter abandonment to God, all the time receive by faith the very one you need at that moment. Radical repentance and perfect consecration put you in position to receive all of these gifts, pursuant to the sovereign discriminating wisdom of the Holy Ghost. These nine gifts constitute the

Christian soldier's panoply. The Holy Ghost is our Omnipotent Armor-bearer. He goes with us to the battle-field every time and carries all of our arms, leaving us perfectly unincumbered and light as birds of paradise, just ready for Him to use us freely in the terrible battle with the world, the flesh and the devil. He imparts each gift the very moment you need it. V. 11, *"All these work in you one and the same Spirit, dispensing unto each one severally as He willeth."*

When you have performed the ministry of healing, by simple faith receive from Him the gift of bodily healing. At one moment you especially need the gift of wisdom so you may know how to proceed in the emergency. At another moment you especially need the gift of knowledge, which is insight into divine truth. While faith is the hand by which we receive everything from God, in that sense it is the grace of faith. You see it is also laid down in the catalogue of the gifts. In that sense it means the power to believe God's promises and to perfectly confide in Him. The fifth gift is the workings of dynamite. The Gospel is all dynamite. Rom. 1:16, *"The Gospel is the dynamite of God unto salvation to every one that believeth."* The Sinai Gospel is the dynamite of conviction, Calvary that of conversion, Pentecost that of sanctification, and the Transfiguration that of translation. The gift of prophecy is preaching in all its forms and phases, to an individual or a multitude. Discernment of spirits enables you to tell what Gospel to preach wherever you are, whether Sinai for conviction, Calvary for conversion, Pentecost for sanctification, the coming of the Lord to get the people ready for translation, or Divine Healing for the benefit of the sick.

The gift of tongues, *i. e.*, language, is simply the utterance of the Holy Spirit, keeping you always supplied with words so you do not run out. The gift of interpretation is the illumination of the Holy Ghost on the words you hear and read, giving you the understanding you need. Of course in the missionary fields where you have to learn a language and serve as interpreter, these gifts, *i. e.*, language and interpretation, have a broader and deeper signification and become very precious and exceedingly valuable. It is a common thing for the missionaries, to their own surprise, to find themselves preaching in the native tongue before they have given it much attention, thus magnifying the gift of the Holy Ghost. You should be perfectly familiar with my books, "Spiritual Gifts and Graces," "Works of the Holy Spirit" and "Incarnation of the Holy Ghost." These three directly devoted to the elucidation of His mighty works should be substantially committed to memory. You should add to these "Demonology," which will post you on the devil's side of the battle-field. A war history which does not describe both sides is radically deficient. You cannot successfully study the mighty works of the Holy Ghost and leave out those of Satan, His inveterate foe. As Christian soldiers, it is utterly impossible for you to prove a success without the grand panoply of these nine gifts, which the Holy Ghost freely bestows on every true warrior in Immanuel's army. While a classical education, when utilized by the Holy Ghost, is a powerful auxiliary, it is in no way essential to real efficiency. Regardless of the amount of learning possessed by any person, these gifts really solve the problem of soul saving efficiency. If the holiness people would duly appreciate and utilize these gifts, they would all be successful preachers of the glorious Gospel, for which the millions are perishing. Human learning has much to do with ecclesiastical position and when fully consecrated to God and used by the Holy Ghost it truly augments our efficiency for good. But from the simple fact that the people who have it are apt to depend on it, we often realize an actual detraction, rather than augmentation, of the normal efficiency. Before I received a collegiate education I do believe my preaching to the slaves was more evangelical than after I graduated in college, till God, in His great mercy, sanctified me and gave me the Holy Ghost, thirty-eight years ago. Before that notable epoch, in 1868, I preached by the power of my intellect and education, using them as vain substitutes for the Holy Ghost. Since that happy experience I have preached "with the Holy Ghost sent down from Heaven," 1 Peter 1:12, which, of course, I could not do before I received Him.

While we exhort you to avail yourselves of all the gifts of the Holy Ghost, pursuant to the positive mandate of God, Eph. 6:1, *"Put on the whole armour of God that you may be enabled to stand against the methods of the devil,"* we would not minify a single one of these immortal nine. As this section is on Divine Healing, I give you a few concluding remarks. Do not fight the doctors, as we need them in three ways, diagnostically, *i. e.*, to tell us what is the matter with the patient; mechanically, *i. e.*, to set and bandage broken limbs, and do other things which they alone understand,

and hygenically, *i. e.*, to tell us how to live conservatively of the laws appertaining to health. I have consulted the ablest physicians of the age in reference to their claim to heal the sick and they have uniformly told me they have made no such claim, but were only humble helpers of nature, recognizing with me that God alone can heal the sick.

Fighting the doctors instead of diseases is like fighting churches instead of devils. While we must be true to God and holiness, church or no church, we have no time to fight the churches, because we have all we can do to preach the Gospel and get souls saved. Satan is very anxious to get the holiness people to fight the churches so that he can effectually obstruct their access to those people, whereas God has sent us to all. Therefore we should be all things to all men, like Paul, that we may save some. If you will be content to do nothing but the work which God has given you, with a full heart flooded with divine love, preach the Gospel with the Holy Ghost sent down from Heaven, sparing sin nowhere, but thundering against it like a messenger from Heaven; having no time to fight anything but sin and devils; constantly discriminating widely between sin and sinners, doing your utmost to destroy the former and save the latter, I go your security that you will find more open doors in churches and elsewhere than you know what to do with. This war on churches is the trickery of Satan to turn your efforts away from him and to make you fire on something else. God has sent us to save the church people as well as outsiders. All the while you hate sin with all your power of soul, mind and spirit, so you will die in your tracks before you will make the slightest compromise with it, whether in church or out, you love sinners with the everlasting love which brought Jesus down from Heaven to die for them. Therefore you are constantly ready for martyrdom.

CHAPTER XII.

PERILS.

In my youth, a very vicious man drew a gun on me, pointing it so that if it fired it must hit me, as he was very near. He pulled the trigger and endeavored to shoot, but signally failed to do anything but to make it snap. To my knowledge the gun had fired all right but a few minutes previously. Of course I believe God put His hand on that dangerous fire-arm so my enemy could not kill me. As I was always an uncompromising whiskey fighter, running it out of the cricuit which the Conference gave me, saloon-keepers often threatened my life on different occasions, actually looking me in the face with terrible oaths and threatening to shoot me if I did not desist from my efforts to arouse all the people to destroy their business. I never in my life loaded a fire-arm nor carried one. When they threatened to kill me, I simply told them in kindness that, if they did, some one else would kill them. I have frequently had mobs arise against me. On one occasion I had scarcely pronounced the benediction when a dozen sanctified men rushed to me saying, "Get ready at once, we have sent to the livery for a conveyance to haul you away as there is no train till morning." The Holy Spirit, quick as lightning said to me, "I do not want you to go to-night, but abide in my will," consequently I said to the brethren,

"I can't go with you; send the conveyance back." But they said, "You *must* go, for there is a great mob, too many for us, now ready to take you, and we want to slip you away before they get their hands on you." I persisted in my refusal to go. They then lit on a plan to guard me through the night and for this purpose accompanied me to my lodging. Having arrived in my room, I called all to prayer, lifting my voice, "O Lord, these good brethren have come to guard me through the night. My body is weary of toil and needs rest. I fear that if they guard me I will not get my needed sleep. Now I beseech Thee, for Thy name's glory, dismiss their fears, send them home and refresh them with peaceful slumber. Amen." Then they looked at each other somewhat bewildered a minute or two. When the oldest in the group came to me and, reaching out his hand, said, "Brother Godbey, I do not know what better we can do than to answer your prayer. Good-night." They all did likewise and went away; I retired and slept.

I have been stoned a few times, and beaten with prairie dirt, when they could not find rocks, and with frozen potatoes, when there was a deep snow on the ground hiding all of the rocks, and often threatened with immediate death. It was a common thing for the brethren to walk on either side of me, especially in the night, to keep them from doing me violence, and many a time I have known that stepping aside alone after night-fall would cost me my life. Of course there is nothing of that now, because I no longer have the physical ability to preach the Sinai Gospel, which is the only kind that raises the devil. He knows that his exposition will cause his people to get dissatisfied and forsake him. He never gives them up without a fight. He retreats only from the point of the bayonet.

I have been in very dangerous railroad wrecks, but never seriously injured. When I crossed the Atlantic the second time, an awful storm struck us five hundred miles this side of Gibraltar and was on us for two thousand miles in midocean, lasting five days, during which we never saw a glimpse of sun, moon or stars, and could not discriminate between midnight and noonday. Mountain seas rolled over our ship, burying her in the ocean. She often climbed the mountain to its summit and then, with quivering shock, pitched down to the bottom of a deep valley, with awful crash like thunder peals, impressing us all that she was breaking in two in the middle. Every door was closed water tight and we could only look out through the port holes, which were all the time closed tight, and see the mighty mountains rolling, climbing the skies, and the billows leaping and, in the bold language of Homer, the grand old poet, "lashing the stars." As the mighty rolling seas on all sides were white with foam, this gave us the only light we had.

Our ship was German, consequently all the sailors spoke that language. As we had sailed from Italy, the most of the passengers were Italians, speaking that language. There were but few English speaking people on board whom I could understand. They were all crying to God, "O Lord, just let me put my foot on land once more and I'll never sail again." They asked me why I did not join them in that prayer. I told them because I did not know but He might want me to sail again, and if so I certainly would.

I was exceedingly happy during those memorable five

days. I never before nor since realized so profound an apprehension of the Divine presence, as when I looked through the port holes and saw the mountain billows white as snow chasing each other. It seemed the great ocean was plowed to the bottom, and that I could actually realize the presence of the Almighty on His chariot of foam, drawn by cyclone steeds, commanding the great ocean to rise and fall, roll, heave and swell at His bidding. The boundless ocean is to me the grandest symbol of His incomprehensible Divinity I have ever contemplated.

That ship was a great German Lloyd with thirty-six boilers. When I sailed again four and one-half years afterward, I found that she had been soon after that voyage condemned by the Board of Admiralty as unseaworthy and laid aside, and this was one of the last runs she ever made. When she cracked so frightfully, loud as thunder-claps, terrifying the people with the impression that she was breaking to pieces, if the sound had been verified by the fact, how quickly would we all have gone to the bottom of the great ocean, there to await the Judgment trump, "When the sea shall give up her dead," and the old ocean, responsive to the archangel's trump, will give one tremendous heave and from the deep recesses of his coraline beds, throw forth his clumbering millions. But I always had faith for God to put His omnipotent arm under the ship and keep her from going down.

Once in Georgia I was booked to go on a train, but something detained me till the next one. When I heard that the train was wrecked and a number of people killed and others wounded, I saw the hand of God in keeping me over. My whole life has been amid perils seen and unseen, but He has in mercy kept me till I can finish my work. Glory to His wondrous name!

Chapter XIII.

LIFE'S EVENING.

I am now in it and appropriating the quaint maxim, "Old men for counsel and young men for war." Preachers, as a rule, are superannuated and laid on the shelf before they reach my present age. If the Lord had not in mercy sanctified me in 1868, I would have been laid on the shelf in the Kentucky Conference ere this. But instead of superannuation, (which is only given when the preacher is so worn out that he is no more wanted by any of the people,) instead of that state of things in my own case, I have wide open doors enough for a thousand men,—splendid openings for ministerial usefulness which I would be much delighted to enter. Why do not all the preachers get sanctified, as a sure guaranty against superannuation, which they all dread worse than their coffins. Only get sanctified, and you will never be superannuated.

I am still as competent to preach the Calvary, Pentecost and Transfiguration Gospels as I ever was. I've only had to give up the Sinai Gospel, which requires thunder, in order to its real efficiency, as well as the lightning. We frankly admit that the thunder does not kill anything; all that is reserved for the lightning to do, but it is exceedingly useful to scare the devil, which is of great importance, if possible to precipitate him into a stampede. The Sinai Gospel actually needs a trumpet voice, which I have possessed in my youth and vigor, but it is worn out and gone. The Sinai Gospel, whose province is conviction, is the potent enginery to reach the impenitent, wicked people. The awful roar of Sinai's thunder peals, accompanied by the trembling, quaking earth and the rending rocks, is God's provision to wake up the souls, by millions, slumbering on the brink of Hell. This is the Lord's war against Satan, in which the young people with crocodile constitutions, alligator mouths and lion voices, find a boundless open door to walk in and enjoy the grandest privilege in the universe, *i. e.*, to spend and be spent for Him who gave His life for us all. I have toiled long and hard at the front of the battle, seeking the thickest of the fight, where the shot and shell rattled down like a hail storm, shouting the battle cry,

"Come one, come all,
This rock shall fly
From its firm base,
As soon as I."

"The glory summons to the martial plain,
The field of battle is the field for man;
Where heroes war, the foremost places claim,
The first in danger and the first in fame."

This was written by the melodious old Homer, three thousand years ago, who had in his mind the warrior's fame. Of course we now substitute for it the glory of God.

The little remaining remnant of my pilgrimage legitimately belongs to the didactic department of the Gospel. To preach means to proclaim, and realizes the value of a clear, stentorian voice. Teaching is another signification of Gospel preaching, which only requires vocal power enough to be heard and understood. The example of our Savior along this line gives us all a lesson of pre-eminent value and importance. Three days would have been sufficient for Him to come and lay down His life to redeem the world from sin, death and Hell; but we see He imperatively needed those three years that He might have time to teach His disciples so to qualify them to launch the Gospel Church. During this time He was a constant fugitive from His enemies who were after Him thirsting for His blood, having resolved to kill Him, and His friends who were on tiptoe to crown Him King, in which case the Romans would have put Him to death under charge of high treason. He often alluded to the fact that His time had not yet come. Hence we see how amid the great conceivable difficulties He prolonged His life those three years, in order to finish that curriculum of instruction, which was absolutely indispensable to qualify His apostles for the great and responsible work of launching the Gospel Church.

God says in the Old Testament, *"My people perish for the lack of knowledge,"* and in the New Testament, *"Study to show thyself approved of God, a workman that need not be ashamed, rightly dividing the Word of Truth."* 2 Tim. 2:15. While the world and the worldly churches need salvation, and consequently the Sinai Gospel, which is the grand *sine qua non* of conviction, without which there can be no conversion, and of course no sanctification, the Holiness people and all of the really sanctified in all the Churches need teaching most imperatively, not only to qualify them to preach the Gospel and save the Hellward bound millions, but to feed their souls so they will flourish like trees planted by the riverside, bringing forth fruit in their season and thus fortifying them against apostasy.

The good shepherd who understands his business, will make the care of his flock the great speciality. If he gives them plenty of wholesome food and pure water, and protects them from wild beasts and robbers, they will multiply till the lambs will skip over all the hills and race across the plains, like Texas ponies. The unwise shepherd goes for numbers, seeking quantity, rather than quality. God is our infallible exemplar, who always goes for quality instead of quantity. If we can take care of our Holiness people, teaching them the blessed Bible faithfully and heroically and diligently fortifying them against the dangerous heresies, in whose insidious manacles Satan keeps Hell constantly embargoed, we will soon have a panoplied army marching forth with banners flying, unfurled to the breezes of every land and clime, marching on to the conquest of the world for our glorious Christ, who has bought it with His own blood and now intercedes for it at God's right hand.

The Bible School phenomenon in the Holiness Movement is most encouraging. Such schools are springing up everywhere like mushrooms in the night, not only throughout this country from the Atlantic to the Pacific and from the Gulf to British America, but they are also dotting the dark pagan empires of the antipodian world. We have now twenty-five hundred Christian schools in heathen lands, attended by a million of heathen boys and girls. Do you not see how the salvation and sanctification of these heathen pupils constitute the golden key that unlocks the mystery and solves the problem which has puzzled Christendom from the Apostolic age, *i. e.*, the evangelization of the whole heathen world? We only have about a thousand millions in all heathendom. If we can only get these million students saved and sanctified, we will have a preacher for every thousand pagans in the whole world. We certainly have these million in our own hands and do enjoy the facilities, evolving the gracious possibility of saving and sanctifying them all.

I have already stated that I am bewildered with a thousand open doors, inviting me to enter and labor for the salvation of souls. All of the Bible Schools and Holiness Colleges in the whole world keep the doors wide open and the Macedonian cry ringing in my ears, "*Come over and help us.*" The last year I spent traveling around the world and preaching in all lands, therefore, I've done no work in America. Now, as I contemplate entering the field immediately, I am literally bewildered with calls. Not only the cities and large towns throughout the continent, inter-ocean, but these Bible Schools, which have sprung up everywhere and are multiplying so rapidly that it is difficult even to keep a list of them before me for prayer, which I so much desire to do, are calling me, and how to pass by any of them in my peregrinations across the continent breaks my heart to contemplate. Many of these Bible Schools and Holiness Colleges beg me hard to stay with them all the time. As I feel debtor to them all, realizing the endearing relationship of spiritual consanguinity, therefore, I cannot get my consent to give all of my time to any one of them, lest I might grieve the Holy Spirit who has established all of them, that He may teach the people

His own Word and qualify them to go and teach others, as this is His method of evangelical succession, 2 Tim. 2:2, *"The things which thou hast learned with me, commit thou to the faithful people, who shall be able to teach others."* I do very much need all of my time to spend teaching the Bible in these different schools, which the blessed Holy Spirit has founded since the Movement has rolled the revival wave over the world and brought full salvation within the reach of millions. But if I were to confine my labors to the schools, I would have to give up the churches, which the blessed Holy Spirit has organized throughout the Movement, which now girdles the world. Hence you see how multitudinous are the open doors on all sides, ringing out their Macedonian cry, *"Come over and help us."*

I would be most delighted to spend life's evening with my dear old companion, whom God has made an angel of mercy, shining along my pilgrimage these forty-four years; and meanwhile my preaching son and son-in-law do beg me hard to quit work and give them a chance to take care of me and their mother as long as we live. Here you see what sanctification does for us. If I did not have it, I would certainly accept that kind offer and superannuate, but it really makes us young forever, opening for me a thousand delectable doors, which I would be so delighted to enter, as I love the work so dearly that I surely will continue on the battle-field till the chariot descends and the angels bid me mount aboard. Therefore life's evening with the sanctified is infinitely better than the most successful blooming youth without it.

I remember when I was a student in college I read

in the Latin language in the course of study, "Cicero on Old Age." This prince of Roman orators and champion statesman with his trenchant pen undertakes to show up the possibilities of the bright, cheerful, contented, happy, sunshiny old age. His argument is really able for a heathen philosopher. He shows up the facilities of science, literature, philosophy, poetry, æsthetics and the pagan religions to fill old age with perennial flowers, ever ripening fruits, and glorious sunshine. However the end of his life by suicide casts a shadow over all of his eloquent and able writings on the serenity, tranquility, placidity, quietude and resignation which characterized the declining years of the philosopher. When the decisive battle of Actium sealed the doom of the Republic in which Cicero had spent his life, and he saw it go down in the gloom of an eternal night and the Monarchy superceded it, yielding to the temptation of a broken heart he committed suicide. If that great orator and statesman had only enjoyed the light of Christianity, he could have shouted victory for his own soul while the Republic went down. No tongue can tell the unutterable glories of the full salvation which sweetens declining years, and makes us bloom in immortal youth forever.

CHAPTER XIV.

THE EXODUS.

It is more suitable, as a rule, to write the life of a person after the journey is over, because we then have access to all of the facts. Now I have gone through mine from the cradle to the final exodus, *i. e.*, the departure out of this world, which someone else will have to write, after I shall have exchanged the battlefield for the Mount of Victory, labor for rest and earth for Heaven. Of course the writer of this last chapter, if it ever is written, must have an intimate acquaintance with the subject of the biography. Rev. H. C. Morrison, of the "Pentecostal Herald," has known me intimately all his life. I am twenty-four years his senior. I heard him say in a great sermon which he delivered to an immense camp-meeting audience, that I passed him while he was a little bare-foot boy, put my hand on his head, lifted up my voice and said, "O Lord, make a preacher of this boy." He says that moment he heard the call from Heaven, which never evanesced from his juvenile mind, but he held on and developed into the noble preacher of the Gospel we all so much appreciate. He is not only my Gospel son, but the consanguinity of my dear wife; she and his mother both being Durhams, members of the same good old English family, their grandfather, John Durham, the first Methodist class-leader in Kentucky, coming over the Cumberland Mountains from old Virginia, with Daniel Boone, the pioneer.

As life is uncertain, I will in this connection also give the name of my son-in-law, Rev. F. M. Hills, so he and Brother Morrison can mutually follow the leading of the Spirit in the matter, the one serving as the alternate of the other.

I will avail myself of this opportunity to write my last will and testament. In the providence of God all of our children have gone to Heaven but one, my son William H., who is a faithful preacher of the Gospel, and has faith in God to feed him like He feeds the birds and to clothe him like the lilies. Therefore I shall not will him nor any of my consanguinity one cent, but leave it all for the missionaries, when I am gone. I have no real estate, never did own but one hundred and seventy-three acres of land, and donated every inch of it to Kentucky Wesleyan College, many years ago, not reserving enough to bury me, and paying the lawyer five dollars to make a clear warranty-deed to the Board of Education, thus turning it over to them forever, to use in the interest of the college.

While I own nothing in the world but books, those of my writing all belong to the publishers. My books are made by four different publishing houses, the "Revivalist" Office in Cincinnati, the "Pentecostal Herald" in Louisville, "The Living Waters" Office in Nashville, and the "Pickett Publishing House" in Louisville. Pursuant to my own convenience, I purchase from the other three houses in large quantities and ship them to Cincinnati, where I keep them in a depository, subject to my call in my peregrinations, as otherwise I would have to order from four houses instead of one, which would be too much trouble. Consequently I constantly have several thousand copies from those houses on deposit, waiting my calls. Of course I expect to move along preaching, teaching the Bible and circulating the books of my own writing, till He takes me away. I do not feel that I am a book-agent, as I only circulate the books of my own writing for the solitary motive of preaching the Gospel by pen as well as speech. It has been many a day since I circulated any books except my own writing, from the simple fact that I have so many that I really have no time to devote to any others. Before I ever dreamed of writing a book, seeing how my converts backslid, or rather starved out for the want of soul pabulum, I proceeded to circulate John Wesley's "Plain Account of Christian Perfection," which I used to purchase by the thousand and carry with me in all of my peregrinations, finding it so helpful to the people whom the Lord had blessed in my meetings.

Dr. G. D. Watson wrote his "Holiness Manual" before I began to write books, or even thought of it. In my circuit I happened to run on a copy, stopped on the spot till I read it through and seeing that its plain teaching was the thing my people needed, I wrote him a postal card ordering a thousand copies. He answered me stating that he supposed I had made a mistake and meant one hundred. I responded to him, "No, I want one thousand." Then he wrote me that he did not have a thousand, but would send me all that he had and the balance as soon as he could have them made. I soon circulated the thousand copies and then ordered two thousand. Meanwhile the people to whom I was preaching begged me hard to write something, as they said that they understood my teaching better than any they had ever heard, and wanted it in print so that they could study it.

The first book I ever wrote was my "Baptism," which I designed for a pump, as Kentucky had been under swimming water a half century, (water salvation preached by the Campbellites,) so we just had to go to pumping to get it dry enough to kindle a fire, as all true religion is the blessed Holy Ghost and His fire, which burns up all sin, defeats Satan, bankrupts Hell and saves us forever. Oh, the blessedness of the "one baptism," (Eph. 4: 5) which Jesus gives with the Holy Ghost and fire, (Matt. 3: 4) by which He baptizes all of His true and faithful people into one body and makes us to drink in one Spirit, (1 Cor. 12: 13). Then I wrote my "Sanctification," which really proved the pioneer in the dear old Sunny South and the great West. This was followed by "Holiness or Hell," which awfully stirred Satan, and the Lord wonderfully used it, especially with the preachers. Soon I wrote "Victory" over the world, the flesh and the devil, whose circulation was really paradoxical for the rapidity and the extent.

As the Lord has led me hither and thither throughout this continent preaching the living Word, He has thus permitted me to use the two-edged sword, dispensing His precious truth both by speech and pen. It seems to me that I must be the happiest old man in the world, because He lets me preach so much. When I dictate a book I am preaching to an audience of fifty to a hundred thousand people, *i. e.*, all who, in the providence of God, will ever read the book. Besides I teach the Bible every day and preach every night, thus doing the double work of a teacher and a preacher *viva voca.* Preaching the Gospel is the sweetest and richest blessing this side of Heaven. I would rather preach the Gospel to the poor in the slums and sweep the streets for my living than to be a millionaire and not preach. I have but one motive in writing and circulating books and that is to preach this glorious everlasting Gospel that does not run a hoax on the people and deceive them, but saves them gloriously with an everlasting salvation. The reason why I circulate my books is because they clearly expound and lucidly teach the plain way of salvation and at the same time fortify the people against the multitudinous heresies which Satan, through his emissaries, is propagating both boldly and clandestinely. Through his false prophets and counterfeit preachers, scattered throughout the country, he is preaching "no-hellism," "water regeneration" and many other insidious forms of occult and seductive heresies and diversified *ad captandum* dogmatisms, hatched in the bottomless pit.

As I have several thousand copies of my books, which these other houses make and I have brought here (to Cincinnati) for my own convenience in circulating them, doubtless when I wind up there will be quite a lot of them on hand. All of these I here and now will to the missionaries in all heathen and Mohammedan lands, to be distributed by the Missionary Board of the "International Apostolic Holiness Union," according to their godly judgment. I also will to them all of the royalty, which shall accumulate on my books, indefinitely, after my exodus, also to be distributed by the I. A. H. U. through their Missionary Board, according to their godly judgment. This is certainly fair and impartial, because it is the privilege of all the holiness people throughout the world to be identified with this I. A. H. U. If you are not now a member of it, you have nothing to do but to address them at the "Revivalist Office," Cincinnati, Ohio, and they will give you a hearty welcome. Then you will have an èqual chance to participate in the benefits of my will in the interest of your missionaries, as in this matter there will be no discrimination whatever.

N. B. Membership in the I. A. H. U. will not conflict with your membership in your local Church or Holiness Association, or even our National Association, as this is International, in order to unite all the nations of the earth in the common cause of universal salvation. Therefore none of the holiness people in this country, or any other, have anything to lose by membership in this I. A. H. U., but everything to gain. It is in perfect harmony with the United States motto, *"E Pluribus Unum,"* "One out of many;" "United we stand, divided we fall;" "In union there is strength."

Holiness people should all go into this Association for the mutual encouragement of one another. Some of our holiness people who are good, true and all right are not members of any church organization. Therefore this universal Association will be helpful to them as well as to all others in the way of Christian fellowship, which is one of the beautiful graces of the Holy Spirit. This Association has no creed but the New Testament, no authority but the Word of the Lord. Our National Association is deficient in the fact that its name would restrict it to this great and mighty Yankee Nation. The "Holiness Movement" is now well represented in all heathen lands. It certainly will be well pleasing to the Lord and encouraging to the dear saints of all lands to enjoy mutual fraternity and fellowship in one great Association, including all other associations, churches and nations, with a single bond of union, *i. e.*, "Holiness to the Lord," as revealed in His own blessed Book, independently of all human creeds.

We must all learn the great lesson of harmony, fraternity, fellowship and union on the one great all-absorbing Bible doctrine of "Holiness unto the Lord," scriptural, experimental and practical; entire sanctification as the second work of grace, received and appropriated by faith in the cleansing blood administered by the Holy Ghost in the expurgation of inbred sin, after a clear experience of justification through the vicarious substitutionary atonement, received and appropriated by faith, and the happy experience of regeneration wrought by the Holy Ghost in the heart and clearly and indubitably witnessed by the same. Meanwhile we extend perfect liberty of conscience on all of the ecclesiastical phases of the kingdom, *i. e.*, the ordinances, and the different forms of church government. We have but one end in view and that is to save the lost world for whom Jesus died.

PERORATION.

"Brethren, all who disagree,
  That would have charity to please us,
Union there can never be,
  Unless that we're one in Jesus,
One as He is one in God,
  In spirit and in disposition;
This the Holy Scriptures teach,
  'Tis plain without an exposition."

Now, beloved, you have the book for which you long clamored, *i. e.,* my autobiography. It simply falls in line with its forty-seven predecessors, having but the one end in view and that is that, by the superabounding grace of God in Christ, freely dispensed by the omnipotent Holy Spirit, all of the dear Holiness people to whom the entire library of my writings is dedicated, regardless of nationality, race, sect, denomination or color, shall certainly enjoy the supereminent experience which is the crowning glory of New Testament saintship. That experience is the real Pentecostal experience, which means a heart cleansed by the precious blood through simple receptive and appropriate faith (Acts 15:9), and copiously filled with the Holy Ghost (Acts 2:3). While we have every reason to fear that the rank and file of nominal Christendom are actually below the salvation line, under condemnation and exposed to wrath and Hell, *horrible dictu,* "horrible to tell," there is no doubt but at least nine-tenths of the real citizens of God's kingdom on the earth are far back in the Old Testament dispensation, under legal bondage, and consequently almost utterly powerless as soul-savers, whereas it is the glorious privilege of all of God's children in the wonderful Pentecostal experience actually to be done with self, saved, sanctified, filled with the Holy Ghost and both efficiently and joyfully co-operating with Jesus in their intercessory prayers for this lost world, and successfully used by the Holy Ghost in the conviction of enemies, conversion of penitents, sanctification of believers and the conservation and edification of this "glorious Church without spot or wrinkle, washed in the blood of the Lamb."

This is really the normal attitude of New Testament saintship. Of course all of the Holiness people, without a single exception, hold up the standard to that identical supernal altitude, which means radically sanctified and copiously filled with the Holy Ghost. Rest assured that means an everlasting victory over the world, the flesh and the devil, experienced in the heart where Christ is enthroned and verified in the life in which He reigns without a rival.

When I was a little boy General Jackson was elected to the Presidency of the United States. He purchased from the French Government the territory bounded on the east by the Tennessee River, south by the State of Tennessee, north by the Ohio River, and west by the Mississippi River, and added it to Kentucky. It was a howling wilderness hitherto inhabited by wild beasts and savages. Of course the United States people at once poured into it. At that time the Methodist Church had no missionary society. Good old Bishop Seoul, as he rode around on his horse through the blue-grass region of Kentucky, which was then well populated, gathered up money in all of his meetings to establish missions in that country, known as "Jackson's Purchase." We had no way to send them the money as we do now, and consequently he had to carry it in his pocket. While riding along on his horse alone, through a great dense forest, suddenly a burly robber walked out of the thicket, took his horse by the bridle, looked him in the face and said, "Give up your money or you are a dead man in a minute." The venerable saint, looking the robber straight in the face and putting his hand on the money in his pocket, said, "I have got money, I do not deny it, but it is God's money and you cannot get it." He had not a solitary weapon, not so much as a pocket-knife. As he continued to look the robber in the face, he turned pale as a corpse, let go the bridle and disappeared in the forest. The man of God went on his way rejoicing and delivered the money to the missionaries. The solution of this was the simple fact that God was in the old bishop. Therefore utterly unarmed he was more than a match for the big robber with his implements of death.

The last time I ever saw Bishop Kavanaugh, we rode together on the train about fifty miles, spending the time in profitable conversation about the things of God. He much interested me telling about the pioneer preachers of Kentucky, among whom was a very angelic little man by the name of John Sinclair. He said that at one place on his pioneer circuit in the wild woods the people had built a rough, unhewn log meeting-house, whereas everywhere else he preached in their cabins or beneath the trees. One Sunday morning while preaching, some ruffians behaved so very rudely as to constrain him to rebuke them severely, upon which they all retired from the house. After the old Methodist style, he wound up with a class-meeting, in which they all told their experiences, and the Lord poured on them from Heaven a wonderful Pentecost, giving them a glorious shouting time. Then mounting his horse he proceeded on his journey through the dense forest, pursuing a blind bridle-path. After he had gotten clearly away from all the dispersing people, he recognized three men before him in the road, and as he drew nigh identified them with the ruffians whom he had rebuked. They all met him, took his horse by the bridle and told him that they were the young men whom he had insulted that morning, and they were going to whip him. Then they proceeded to tell him that they would not take advantage of him, as they had already cast lots and determined on the one who should give him the thrashing, while the other two stood by to see that he gave him fair play. Therefore they told him to dismount, to take off his coat and get ready. Sitting in his saddle, he looked into the face of the one selected to give him the whipping, and said, "Sir, I want to thank you twice before you begin; first, I thank you for the whipping, because they gave it to my Savior and His Apostles, and I am so glad to have the honor and the blessing of their succession; then I want to thank you again for giving it to me now, because I am in the best fix to take a whipping that I ever was in my life, as I am just out of a wonderful meeting in which God flooded my soul with Heaven." Thus looking them in the face, he was just unutterably happy. Then turning to his fellows, the ruffian said, "Boys, there is too much God Almighty in this man for me to attack him, and I am not going to do it; therefore if he gets a thrashing one of you will have to give it to him." But the other two came to the same conclusion that there was too much God in him for them to lay hands on him, therefore he got no thrashing, but preached to the young men and went on his way rejoicing.

When I was called, early in the "Holiness Movement," (as God used me as a pioneer from the Atlantic to Mexico), into Mississippi to conduct a camp-meeting, Satan had circulated so many awful lies on the Holiness people, reporting that we were Mormons and would separate husbands and wives and all kinds of falsifications throughout that country where they had never seen Holiness people, that the night before they were going to set up the tabernacle a great mob came to burn it. Among the few sanctified people in that country was a little woman of ninety pounds, whose Christian husband had received the tabernacle, shipped from St. Louis, and laid it on the veranda. At midnight there was a voice. He opened the door, and they told him to go back, as they had come to burn that tabernacle and they were going to do it. Then the little woman said, "Jim, stay with the children and I will meet the mob." Having plead with them not to burn the tabernacle, and prayed for them, but all apparently in vain, she climbed upon it, sat down and said, "This country has long needed a martyr, and will have one now, as I will surely burn with this tabernacle." In vain they strove to scarce her off. Finally, when they saw that she was going to burn with it, they gave up and went away. Before the meeting was over, I saw two hundred of those wicked people at one time stretched out on the ground, crying to God to save them. Among those who prayed through, quite a number testified that they were in the mob that came to burn the tabernacle. What was the solution? The little woman had God in her heart, and consequently was more than a match for the mob. So it will be with you, while He abides in your heart.

"My rest is in Heaven, my home is not here;
Then why should I murmur at trials severe?
Come trouble, come sorrow, the worst that can come
But shortens my journey and hastens me home."

THE END.

www.ingramcontent.com/pod-product-compliance
Lightning Source LLC
Chambersburg PA
CBHW031936080426
42735CB00007B/157
9781621717607